My
FAMILY
TIME WITH
GOD

MY
FAMILY TIME WITH GOD

Family Devotions for Every Day of the Year!

COMPILED BY
HAROLD VAUGHAN

Christ Life
PUBLICATIONS
P.O. Box 399
Vinton, VA 24179

All Scripture quotations are from the King James Version (KJV) of the Bible.

MY FAMILY TIME WITH GOD

ISBN: 0-942889-22-3
Printed in the United States of America
Copyright © 2013 by Harold D. Vaughan

Christ Life Publications
www.christlifemin.org

INTRODUCTION

Acquiring this book is a clear signal that you have a strong desire to shepherd the hearts of your children. From the beginning it was God's intention that parents be the primary communicators of truth to their offspring. "And these words, which I command thee this day, shall be in thine heart: And thou shalt teach them diligently unto thy children, and shalt talk of them when thou sittest in thine house, and when thou walkest by the way, and when thou liest down, and when thou risest up" (Deut. 6:6, 7). This responsibility and privilege of instructing children is as valid today as it was when these words were penned in Deuteronomy.

The practice of family devotions is rare among church-going people today. The main thing missing today in parenting is the parent. The main thing missing in child-training is the trainer. Sunday School, youth pastors, and targeted youth ministries are all relatively new in the spiritual economy. It is to be feared that what was initially designed to be supplemental in child-training has become central. The people and programs which were intended to "assist" parents have by-and-large replaced the parents.

The time has come for parents to take back the ownership, responsibility, and control of their homes. The place to start is a daily time of family devotions. All families must establish priorities, and worship in the home is essential.

My Family Time with God is a tool designed to assist you in this sacred duty of shepherding your household. It offers a concise, practical teaching for every day of the year. Any head of household can use this volume as a devotional and teaching aid to instruct his or her family in the things of God.

Bible reading and teaching, praying, and singing should be the norm in our Christian homes. I trust that *My Family Time with God* will be a tremendous asset to you as you lead your family.

Your Servant for Revival,

Harold D. Vaughan

Harold Vaughan

ACKNOWLEDGMENTS & AUTHORS

This project would not have been possible apart from the participation of many friends. I want to thank the following for partnering with us by contributing to this book:

Alton Beal

Alton Beal is an evangelist and the president of Ambassador Baptist College in Lattimore, N.C. He came to Christ at age seventeen. Alton and his wife Michelle have three children.

Jim Binney

Jim Binney is a fantastic preacher, author, and counselor. He has counseled ministry couples in crisis situations for decades.

Aaron Coffey

Aaron Coffey has been traveling in itinerant ministry since 2002, working in local churches and preaching the good news of Jesus Christ. His ministry focuses on helping churches be healthy, both in living out the truths of the Gospel and in sharing the Gospel within the context of their communities.

Sammy Frye

Sammy is an energetic speaker with a heart for God and a love for people. He is a gifted communicator of God's Word. He serves as a youth pastor in Whispering Pines, N.C.

Jim Van Gelderen

Jim Van Gelderen was raised in a pastor's home and attributes much of his spiritual training to his parents and grandmother, whose walks with the Lord were genuine and impacting. He surrendered to the call to preach in his teen years and soon after began to be burdened for young people. Thirty years later this burden is manifested in his traveling ministry to teenagers (Minutemen Ministries) and serving as Vice President of Baptist College of Ministry in Menomonee Falls, Wis.

Joe Henson

Joe and his wife, Garthea, are associates at Harvest Baptist in Guam. Joe has served the Lord as missionary and church planter. He is now involved in training men to serve God throughout the Pacific Islands.

ACKNOWLEDGMENTS & AUTHORS (CONTINUED)

Billy and Christy Ingram
The Ingrams travel in an evangelistic and revival ministry. They emphasize the victorious, Spirit-filled life.

Rick Johnson
Since 1986 Rick Johnson has served as pastor of Friendship Baptist Church in Huntsville, Ala. He and his wife, Paula, were married in 1979. God has blessed them with seven children.

Wayne King
Wayne King left a successful business to serve as a missionary pastor in Lander, Wyo. He and his wife Dawn have four children.

Stanley Long
Stanley Long serves as Director for Camp Eagle Ministries near Fincastle, Va. God has blessed him and his wife, Kelle, with nine children, and grandchildren.

Paul and Abigail Miller
Paul Miller was saved in 1986 at the age of 19. He, his wife Abigail, and their nine children travel America and Canada in full-time evangelism and music ministry. Abigail is a homeschool mother and is also an accomplished singer and songwriter.

Tom Palmer
In 1989, Tom Palmer founded Palmer Revival Ministries. Married since 1983, he and his wife, Patty, have three children. Through their revival ministry, they minister full-time in churches, Christian schools, and Christian camps.

Steve Rebert
Pastor Steve Rebert was saved in March of 1978. Upon his graduation from Bible college, the Lord opened the door to pastor Emmanuel Baptist Church in Winchester, Va. He has faithfully pastored Emmanuel for 27 years.

Jimmy Stallard
Jimmy Stallard is the Director of Treasures of Truth Ministries based in Atlanta, Ga. He has authored 15 books. His ministry focuses on revival and evangelism. He has been married to his wife, Eileen, for 37 years and has two grown children.

Rich Tozour
Rich Tozour has traveled in full-time evangelistic ministry. He is a powerful preacher and family man. He and his wife, Angela, have three daughters. They have traveled in evangelism for 20 years.

JANUARY 1
FAMILY WORSHIP STARTS TODAY!

Scripture Reading—Gen. 18:17–19

"And the LORD said, . . . Seeing that Abraham shall surely become a great and mighty nation, . . . For I know him, that he will command his children and his household after him, and they shall keep the way of the LORD, to do justice and judgment."

God had a very high estimate of Abraham. He confidently asserted that he, Abraham, would direct his family in the way of the LORD. Not only would Abraham pray with his family, he would also teach his family. But not only teach and pray—he would also use his authority to command those within his house. Abraham prayed, taught, and shepherded his children. All of this for the purpose that his family might live godly lives.

Fathers, as head of the home, you have a sacred privilege and responsibility to oversee those within your care. Remember, you are not raising children, but soon-to-be adults. During these formative years you have countless opportunities to influence your offspring in developing godly character.

My Family Time with God is a tool that will assist you in this blessed task and benefit your entire home. Every day is a new day with brand new prospects to instruct, inspire, and ignite a passion for our great God!

Children, you are very fortunate to have parents who love and care for you. They want to assist you in fulfilling God's plan for your life. You have a great advantage to have parents who will teach you about God and His ways. Every day when you sit down for family devotions, give your father and mother your full attention. Approach this time with eagerness and an open heart to learn something new.

Give your parents respect because God promises long and successful lives to children who honor their parents. If you sing songs, sing with all your heart. If you are praying, pray with all your heart. If you are listening, listen with all your heart. Every day you will draw closer to the Lord and one another.

ACTION POINT: This is the first day of a brand new year. Pause and thank the Lord for the chance to have family worship. Ask Him to direct your times together. Request His guiding presence each and every day in the coming year.

—Harold Vaughan

JANUARY 2
THIS IS THE WAY

Scripture Reading—Isa. 30:21
"This is the way, walk ye in it."

The Christian life can often be filled with the unknown. Sometimes we don't easily discern the presence of God, and it is during these times that God may be testing our faith and teaching us to trust him. I think of Job's exclamation when he was seeking God for an understanding of why he had seen his life crash down around him. Job 23:3 says, "Oh that I knew where I might find him!" It wasn't that God had left or forsaken Job, but sometimes it can seem to us like Heaven is silent to the cries of the heart. It is at those times God wants us to rest in him. The old hymn, *The Solid Rock*, says it well: "When darkness veils His lovely face, I rest on His unchanging grace."

There are other times when God's presence is real and his guiding hand is clearly evident. A person who has been a Christian any length of time can testify to this truth, and such divine guidance strengthens faith and brings encouragement. When the wise men traveled from the east to Jerusalem to worship the Christ Child, they were summoned before King Herod to detail the purpose of their visit. When they left that meeting they certainly were at a loss as to which direction to go next. It was nighttime, and they were in a strange city. Then they saw it! The star that they had followed to Jerusalem was once again directing them to their destination. Matthew 2:10 says, "When they saw the star, they rejoiced with exceeding great joy." Why? Because the presence of the star was proof to them that they were being guided by a Source outside of themselves, and that Source was God Almighty! Such a reality brought them "exceeding great joy."

DISCUSS: Discuss as a family the times that you sensed God was clearly leading and guiding you. Ask each family member to tell how God led them specifically. Such remembrances will strengthen faith and bring joy to the heart.

—Paul Miller

REFUSING TO CONFESS

Scripture Reading—Pro. 18:12
"Before honour is humility."

A person that cannot laugh at himself has a problem with pride. I agree with John Maxwell, who said, "We take ourselves too seriously and don't take God serious enough." Charles Swindoll tells a humorous story about how silly we are when we refuse to admit when we are wrong. Here's the story:

> A guy named Zeke Pike who lived in Muleshoe, Texas would not admit when he was wrong, no matter what. One day Zeke happened to shuffle into the blacksmith shop, sawdust all over the floor. What he didn't know was that just before he got there the blacksmith had been working with an uncooperative horseshoe and beat on it till it was black. It was still hot but wouldn't bend, so he tossed it into the sawdust.
>
> Unaware of it, Zeke walked in and saw that black horseshoe. He picked it up and naturally he dropped it very fast. The old blacksmith looked over his glasses and said, "Kinda hot, ain't it Zeke?"
>
> "Nope, just doesn't take me long to look at a horseshoe," Zeke replied.

The Bible tells us to acknowledge our sin (Ps. 32:5) and to confess our faults to one another (James 5:16). A Pharisee refuses to do either, but compares himself favorably to other people (Luke 18:11). Like Zeke, when we refuse to acknowledge our faults, we are far away from God.

A man who greatly influenced me through his books had a moral failure in his life. For several years he disappeared. He wrote no books but worked on his inner life and marriage. Years later he wrote a book on dealing with personal brokenness and failure. He stated that one of the keys to his being able to restore his heart to God was that he would never defend his sin.

Pride causes us to refuse to confess or admit what we have done. We are afraid we will lose face and others will pull away from us. The irony is that we deeply respect the person that is honest about his failures and sins.

MEMORIZE: Proverbs 18:12.

—Rick Johnson

JANUARY 4
ARE YOU THANKFUL?

Scripture Reading—1 Thess. 5:18
"In every thing give thanks: for this is the will of God
in Christ Jesus concerning you."

Lima beans. Rainy days. A hard test that you forgot to study for. Moving away. Little brothers and sisters. Not getting your way. There is always something for us to complain about. It could be something really big or really small. When we look around us and see things that we don't like or feel like things aren't going right, we are tempted to murmur and complain. Sometimes we don't think that God is doing what is best for our lives. Sometimes we think that we know what is best, so we complain when God doesn't do what we want.

1 Thessalonians 5:18 says, "In every thing give thanks: for this is the will of God in Christ Jesus concerning you." God commands us to be thankful in EVERYTHING. There's always something to be thankful for. Our family has started trying to think of things that we are thankful for before we go to bed at night. It helps us to see God's blessings in our lives. Sometimes when hard things happen to us—like our truck breaking down or having to leave a special place—we talk about what we are thankful for instead of finding the reasons to complain.

In that verse, it says that being thankful is "the will of God" for our lives. God wants us to be thankful. The only reason that we can really be thankful in EVERYTHING is because of what Jesus has done for us. I naturally find things that I don't like. But since Jesus lives in me, I can actually thank God for things that I would tend to complain about. We all deserve God's wrath because of our sin, so we can ALWAYS find something to be thankful for— like God's love and mercy! When we are thankful in all things, we start to see God's kindness to us in the midst of our day. So, what does God want you to be thankful for today?

ACTION POINT: Think of two or three things that you tend to complain about. Find some ways that you can be thankful instead of complaining.

—*Aaron Coffey*

JANUARY 5
AN ARGUMENTATIVE SPIRIT

Scripture Reading—Pro. 28:25
"He that is of a proud heart stirreth up strife."

Pride and division are associated in the Bible (Ps. 31:20; Pro. 28:25; 1 Tim. 6:4). How does pride stir up conflict in our relationships? Through our words, often arguing over silly and unnecessary issues.

Sometimes my wife Paula and I are with a couple that often disagrees over an issue, and the conversation gradually degenerates into an argument. We are always uncomfortable when this happens.

What is it that makes us so desperate to be right, even to the point of engaging in a heated argument? It is pride. When I have a tendency to dispute with others, something is very wrong in my heart.

Arguing only breaks the fellowship between two people. For husbands and wives, it gives our children bad memories of our home and creates insecurity in their hearts. They might wonder about our commitment to one another. Though unsaid, they might wonder if we will divorce one day.

One day I was thinking about how children perceive us as parents and if they ever wondered about the permanency of our marriage. I didn't want them to have that fear, so when I was alone with each of the kids, I would tell them that Paula and I were never going to leave each other or them.

I wasn't bashing the parents of their friends or our friends that had gone through a divorce. My heart's intent was to remove any fear they might have of that ever happening to us. How would they have felt if they heard me say that and later heard Paula and me fighting and arguing? Our example would destroy anything else I had said to the contrary.

Pride makes us defensive, and we argue to prove our point in order to protect our ego. The consequence is that we begin to grow apart from each other in our spirit. Pride will destroy our homes.

PONDER: Have you ever viewed your tendency to argue as a root of pride in your life?

—Rick Johnson

JANUARY 6
BITTER OR BETTER

Scripture Reading—Heb. 12:15
"Lest any root of bitterness springing up trouble you."

A family member once asked me this question: "What is the biggest problem you face in your counseling?" After 25 years of ministry to young people, my answer came quickly: bitterness! One definition I read of bitterness is, "a sin in my spirit resulting from a failure to thank God for every person and situation He has brought into my life." Bitterness can be our response when we want something and don't get it. It can also occur when something we had was taken away or when we get something we don't want. These seeds of hurt and disappointment can grow into a "root of bitterness" that will bring great heartache and grief into our lives and the lives of others.

In the third grade I was preparing to paint on one side of an easel while a little girl was painting on the other side of the easel. Suddenly, I was pushed out of the way, and I realized the one doing the pushing was the biggest bully in the class. He was bigger than me! In fact, everyone was bigger than me in the third grade! I was fuming, and in my anger I dipped my brush in my paint can and painted the back of his shirt as fast as I could. Then, I ran! The teacher caught me, and I got a paddling, which I might add, was well-deserved. Because something I had was taken away, I made a sinful decision and suffered the consequences for it. As we learned in our Scripture reading, bitterness troubled me and defiled and affected others.

What is the right reaction to the hurt and disappointment we all experience at some point in life? For the Christian, we certainly should be willing to forgive, since we ourselves have been forgiven (Eph. 4:32). Perhaps there is a need to confess our bitterness to the Lord and begin to pray for those who have hurt us. Becoming better, not bitter, will certainly please the Lord—while holding onto bitterness is like taking poison and waiting for the other person to die. Will you be "bitter or better"?

DISCUSS: Spend some time discussing the response of Jesus Christ to the hurt and suffering He experienced on The Cross.

—Sammy Frye

JANUARY 7
COUNT, DON'T COMPLAIN

Scripture Reading—James 1:2
"My brethren, count it all joy when ye fall into divers temptations."

Are you facing something in your family or personal life that makes no sense? Are you willing to trust God and "count it all joy"? To "count" means to stop and think, and to think rightly. Joy speaks of cheerfulness or gladness. God commands this response to difficulties as a faith response that demonstrates trust in His person, His plan, and His purposes for us.

One Saturday afternoon my grandson and I headed out for some fishing together. Our first cast was a success! As I reached to remove the rebel lure, the fish flopped, and I quickly realized I had a fishhook buried in my thumb. We hurried home and off I headed to the hospital. On the way, I had a good talk with the Lord and then with myself. I determined that I would trust and praise God in this "fishhook trial." So I began to thank Him and asked in prayer for the grace to please Him and that I would be open to the lessons He wanted to teach me. The emergency room was packed, and it looked as if I was in for a long night. So I decided to praise the Lord for the mission field before me. After passing out all my gospel tracts, talking to a few folks willing to listen, and then more prayer, I decided to call our family doctor. Fortunately, he was in his office doing paperwork and, thankfully, agreed to see me. His office was located a few blocks from the hospital. In a short time I was on my way home with a fishhook-free finger, still praising the Lord, and looking forward to some sweet fellowship with my grandson! There was triumph in the trial simply because by God's grace I was able to think rightly and count it all joy.

This influenced my attitude and helped me to remember that trials are God's way of teaching us to trust patiently in Him and in so doing to glorify Him. It is always best to "count, don't complain" as we trust in the Lord.

DISCUSS: Talk with family members about the right response to trials and share Scripture that will help us think rightly during difficult times.

—Sammy Frye

JANUARY 8
SOMETHING MUST BE DONE

Scripture Reading—1 Sam. 17:24
"And all the men of Israel, when they saw the man,
fled from him, and were sore afraid."

David knew that something had to be done immediately. David had come to the battlefield to deliver gifts from his father to his brothers who were fighting in Saul's army. Suddenly, Goliath came on the scene and once again issued his very intimidating threats. It was very obvious to David that this blasphemous giant was big, bold, and bad. However, as troubling as this Philistine giant was, there was something even worse. David was deeply troubled by the fact that each time the giant appeared, Saul and the men of Israel ran like scared rabbits. They were terrified by what they heard, and so they had done nothing to stop their enemy who was insulting their God.

David wasn't about to put up with this disgrace any longer. We might say that David was burdened by what he saw. When we speak of a burden, we are talking about an overwhelming sense of concern for a great need. David was burdened by the enemy's overwhelming attacks upon his God, but he was also burdened by the Israelites lack of confidence in their God.

Because most modern day Christians are so self-centered in their thinking, they rarely are burdened by anything other than their own problems. Christians rarely weep over the need of an unsaved person, a struggling nation, or a world without God. I have come to believe that typically the things that move us to tears are the things that really do move us. When you bear a burden, you carry the weight of someone else or something else that is suffering.

Those who make a difference are those who know how to see and sense the needs that exist around them. The burden provides incentive and motivation to do what can be and needs to be done to help. Without first having a burden, you will have little desire to make a difference for someone in need.

ACTION POINT: Think of someone you know who is having a difficult time right now. Remember him or her in prayer.

—*Tom Palmer*

8

JANUARY 9
THE FATE OF A NATION

Scripture Reading—Esther 4:14
"Who knoweth whether thou art come to the kingdom
for such a time as this?"

There was very little time for action. Yet, whatever was to be done needed to be handled with the greatest care. The fate of the nation Israel was in her hands. Queen Esther had been elevated to be Ahasuerus' queen, and she was the only one who could do it!

Notified by her uncle Mordecai of the wicked plot of Haman to destroy the Jewish people, she knew her task would not be easy. The words of Mordecai rang in her heart and mind—"And who knoweth whether thou art come to the kingdom for such a time as this?" (Esther 4:14).

The king did not know that she was Jewish (Esther 2:20), and it was against the law for the queen to come before the king without being summoned. But the queen was willing to die for her people. "And so will I go in unto the king, which is not according to the law: and if I perish, I perish" (Esther 4:16).

She left instructions to Mordecai to tell the people to fast three days, both night and day. They were going to cry out to God in the midst of their crisis. Did God answer? A few days later the enemy Haman was hanging from the gallows he had prepared for the Jews!

The story of Esther should encourage us because it reminds us that the key to any battle is seeking God's help in prayer! The people got serious about crying out to God! George Müller cried out to feed the hungry orphans in Bristol, England. D.L. Moody cried out to God to help him win the children of Chicago.

Arno C. Gaebelein cried out to God to help him reach the Jews of New York City. J.O. Frazier cried out to God to help him win the Chinese in western China. Great men and women of God throughout time have found God's help when the fate of nations or the work of God hung in the balance. Have faith that He will do the same for you and me.

MEMORIZE: Psalm 50:15.

—James Stallard

JANUARY 10
A JOYFUL MOTHER OF CHILDREN

Scripture Reading—Ps. 113:9
"He maketh the barren woman to keep house,
and to be a joyful mother of children. Praise ye the LORD."

It is natural for women to look at children differently than men. Just watch a group of young teenage girls see a baby in a mother's arm as they walk through a shopping mall. Their faces will light up. The reaction of young teenage boys just won't be the same.

For a married woman to be without children can be a great burden for her as it was for Hannah, who eventually delivered Samuel into the world (1 Sam. 1). Many godly women have lived their lives in great service to God as single women or married women, never having children. Still, it is natural for women to want to be mothers.

One pastor whose wife was childless heard a message preached on "How to Claim a Promise." This encouragement led him to Psalm 113:9, "He maketh the barren woman to keep house, and to be a joyful mother of children. Praise ye the LORD." He sensed in his heart that God was going to give him and his wife children. Within a month his wife was expecting their first child.

The highest calling of any woman is that of being a wife and a mother. "Keeping house" and being a "joyful mother of children" rates much higher in the mind of God than it does in our modern world. Yet, God uses mothers to teach their children, to make a home for their husbands, and to be powerful workers for the Lord in the church (Titus 2:5; Pro. 31:10–31).

The sweet spirit of a godly mother can bring a little piece of heaven on earth. When a woman is committed to God and His ways, she can find herself receiving from His hand the high calling of motherhood. There is a famous statement that says, "The hand that rocks the cradle rules the world." How many great men and women have there been throughout history that are known in the history books! But, how many of their mothers do we know? They are indeed known to God in Heaven.

DISCUSS: Discuss what the statement "the hand that rocks the cradle rules the world" means.

—*Tom Palmer*

JANUARY 11
THE JOY OF WINNING THE LOST

Scripture Reading—Ps. 126:6
"He that goeth forth and weepeth, bearing precious seed,
shall doubtless come rejoicing, bringing his sheaves with him."

Many days have been important in American history—the day President Kennedy was assassinated, the day Neil Armstrong set foot on the moon, the day the Space Shuttle Challenger exploded, or the day the Twin Towers fell after an attack by terrorists. These days were important because of the greatness of accomplishment or the horror of tragedy that occurred on them.

But there has never been a day like the day that Jesus Christ went to The Cross to die for the sins of the world. Only Resurrection Sunday could compare to the day Christ paid the penalty that each of us deserves. What Christ accomplished He accomplishes for everyone.

There can be no greater joy in life than to see someone receive Christ as his or her personal Lord and Savior. For a person to do this is to receive eternal life (John 3:36), to be translated out of the kingdom of darkness into the kingdom of light (Col. 1:12, 13), to have forgiveness of sins (Acts 10:43), and to have a home in Heaven (John 14:1–3).

If our friends, relatives, or neighbors are to experience salvation, we must work and pray for them to be saved. Our prayers will bring God's power to our witness and enable us to lead someone to salvation.

It is amazing that so many people can become emotionally involved with so many worldly things and be moved to tears, but not be burdened over the most important thing in life, the salvation of souls. So many shed tears when their favorite football team loses a big game, but do not lift a finger to reach the lost for Christ.

We should not despise the "weeping" part of Psalm 126:6. It is hard to imagine weeping without praying. These must go together. If we are burdened enough about the souls of our loved ones and friends, we will be burdened enough to pray consistently for them.

ACTION POINT: As a family, ask the Lord to give you a burden for an unsaved person or family member that you could pray for and witness to over the coming year.

—*Tom Palmer*

JANUARY 12
THE TRAGEDY AND TRIUMPH
OF THE CROSS

Scripture Reading—John 12:32
"And I, if I be lifted up from the earth, will draw all men unto me."

There have been many tragedies in the history of planet earth. Some have been natural events, such as avalanches, blizzards, diseases, droughts, earthquakes, fires, famines, floods, heat, hurricanes, landslides, sinkholes, storm surges, tornadoes, tsunamis, and volcanoes. Others have been man-made, like arsons, civil unrests, murders, nuclear blasts, power outages, radiation contamination, terrorism, and war.

One of the greatest tragedies in modern history was the sinking of the Titanic. On April 15, 1915 the cruise ship Titanic sank. 1,514 out of 2,224 people on board died when it sank. The ship had been considered unsinkable and had put to sea with only one-third of her lifeboats on board. The last survivor of the Titanic was a woman who gave her final interview in 2000. She was asked about the attitude on board the Titanic as it was sinking, and she used two words to describe it—*unbelief* and *arrogance*.

The most important tragedy in history was something far greater than the sinking of the Titanic. The Bible describes it this way: "But we speak the wisdom of God in a mystery, even the hidden wisdom, which God ordained before the world unto our glory: Which none of the princes of this world knew: *for had they known it, they would not have crucified the Lord of glory*" (1 Cor. 2:7, 8).

The tragedy was that the perfect man, the Lord Jesus Christ, who was God in human flesh (John 1:14), would have to be put to death for the sins of the world. In this great crime, the greatest triumph was accomplished. The Cross became the holiest symbol of all time as the human tragedy was turned into a triumph of God.

Jesus did all this just as He promised, "And I, if I be lifted up from the earth, will draw all men unto me" (John 12:32). With this kind of triumph, we can face any tragedy this world can give us, for "if God be for us, who can be against us?" (Rom. 8:31).

DISCUSS: Compare the tragedy of the Titanic with the triumph of The Cross.

—*James Stallard*

JANUARY 13
WORSHIPPING THE ONE
WHO IS WORTHY

Scripture Reading—Luke 2:47
"And all that heard him were astonished at his understanding and answers."

It was a sight to behold. This little boy, who was turning into a young man, had confounded the wisest and smartest of the doctors of the Law.

His parents, Joseph and Mary, had gone to Jerusalem for the feast of the Passover. As they were returning home, they discovered that Jesus was not with the group of folks who were traveling with them (Luke 2:40–45). It was in the temple that they found Him.

How many of the doctors of the law realized they were standing with the One who was worthy of worship? The Messiah had entered their midst, and they did not recognize it. They indeed had been amazed by His heart and mind. "And all that heard Him were astonished at His understanding and answers" (Luke 2:47).

How often do we, as Christians, lose sight of the One to worship? We go to our Bible studies, prayer meetings, church meetings, business meetings, and other activities—but how often do we go to genuine worship?

His earthly parents did not understand (Luke 2:48, 49). Just like them, many of us do not understand either. Apart from true worship we cannot experience our full potential in the Christian life.

It is significant that in Heaven, in the future, that there will be two great declarations about God:

1. **God as Creator**— "Thou art *worthy*, O Lord, to receive glory and honour and power: for thou hast created all things, and for thy pleasure they are and were created" (Rev. 4:11 emphasis added).

2. **God as Redeemer**— "And they sung a new song, saying, Thou art *worthy* to take the book, and to open the seals thereof: for thou wast slain, and hast *redeemed* us to God by thy blood out of every kindred, and tongue, and people, and nation" (Rev. 5:9 emphasis added).

The little boy in the temple was both Creator and Redeemer and worthy to be worshipped.

ACTION POINT: Try to have a family prayer time for just thirty minutes and not ask God for anything. Just praise Him for what He has done and for Who He is. How difficult is it to worship?

—*James Stallard*

13

How Can I Know That I Am Saved?

Scripture Reading—1 John 5:13
"These things have I written unto you that believe on the name of the Son of God; that ye may know that ye have eternal life."

How can I know if I am truly saved? Did I pray the right prayer? Did I mean it enough?

Salvation describes how to *get eternal life*. Assurance, tells us how to *know* that we have eternal life.

In our verse, John is writing to Christians in order that they would not doubt that they are saved. How then can one "know" that he or she has eternal life? How is assurance possible? The answer is found in focusing one's faith and dependence upon what the Savior says in His Word! "These things have I WRITTEN . . . that ye may know that ye have eternal life."

Some may think that a preacher knows that he is saved because of what he *does* or *how he lives*. But that's not true! The surest, simplest, and most scriptural way anyone can ever know that he or she is saved is by depending upon what God says we have!

If the requirements have been met for salvation, then you can thank God for the results of salvation! It really is an issue of believing God. What does God require for salvation? Dependence upon Jesus! Have you placed your dependence upon Christ to save you? If you have, God says you have eternal life (present tense). That's what God says! (John 6:47).

Having prayed a prayer or simply knowing the exact date of your salvation isn't what saves you. It is Jesus that saves you! Focus your attention on Jesus and His Word. Dependence upon Jesus for salvation results in eternal life and the forgiveness of sin. Dependence upon God's Word for assurance will result in you "knowing it!"

SONG: Find and sing "My Faith Has Found a Resting Place."

—*Billy Ingram*

JANUARY 15
GROUND ZERO—THE FAMILY

Scripture Reading—Gen. 18:19
"For I know him, that he will command his children and his household after him, and they shall keep the way of the LORD."

On September 11, 2001, airplanes flew into the Twin Towers in New York City and killed 3,000 people. That spot is now called Ground Zero, meaning it is the place where a great battle or attack took place.

Spiritually, Ground Zero is the family. Families everywhere are under attack. Everywhere we turn, the family is in trouble with divorce, adultery, rebellion, and dysfunction. Yet, this is nothing new. Since the dawn of time, Satan has waged all-out war against the family unit.

In the beginning, God created the institution of the family (Gen. 2:20–24). Within one generation Satan drove a wedge between the first siblings and inspired the first murder (Gen. 4:1–16). When Cain killed Abel, it was merely Satan's early shot in an age-long struggle to disrupt and destroy families.

Why does Satan hate the family so much? He probably hates it because it is God who ordained it as the foundation of society. To build healthy churches we must have healthy families. To have strong nations we must have strong families. Without Christian families showing Christ's grace and standing for Christ's truth, our culture will not be able to survive Satan's continuing attack.

Abraham is commended because he had a strong family and would teach the truth of God to the next generation (Gen. 18:19). Lot, Abraham's nephew, was down in Sodom and Gomorrah, and his family was virtually destroyed because of the evil of those cities (Gen. 19:5–8, 12-14, 26).

What makes a family strong in today's world? The family needs a father who is a loving leader for God and his family (Gen. 18:19; Eph. 5:25–27) and a mother who is a loyal follower of her husband (Eph. 5:22–24; Titus 2:3–5). Children should also be willing to follow their parents through obedience and honor, trusting God to protect them through their parents (Eph. 6:1–4).

Yes, the family is Ground Zero in the spiritual war going on in society. Only a godly family can win the battle.

DISCUSS: Discuss Genesis 19. How could Lot have saved his family from destruction?

—*James Stallard*

JANUARY 16
CALLED TO VIRTUE

Scripture Reading—2 Pet. 1:3
"Called . . . to glory and virtue."

Fulfillment is found in knowing and doing God's will for your life. It's a mistake to focus on a specific place as being God's will for you. It is more about what you are than where you are!

The moment you became a Christian, God called you to become a person of virtue (2 Pet. 1:3). This means that there is a spiritual awareness that you ought to be holy and desire to be clean and right with God.

No one is interested in empty religious activities that are unrelated to what's in the heart. This is one of the reasons why people stop attending church—they become weary of going through the motions and not finding fulfillment. When we pursue virtue we find the purpose for which we were made (Rom. 8:29).

Today we have a lot of Bible knowledge. Yet, there is an emptiness and a lack of reality. Even Satan believes in an orthodox doctrinal statement (James 2:19), but he does not have virtue. I am not saying that sound doctrine is unimportant; rather I am elevating the value of virtue. So does God (2 Pet. 1:5).

If you have no interest in virtue and your profession of faith hasn't affected your heart, then neither will it alter your eternal destination. We are called not to spout Bible facts, but to live a virtuous life (2 Cor. 5:17; Ezek. 36:25–27). The most miserable person is a lost person trying to live like a Christian.

God has called us to live a life of virtue and has enabled us to do so (2 Cor. 3:18). John MacArthur said, "The verity of your salvation is not proven by a past act, but by present fruitfulness."

A Christian is not only saved from the penalty of sin (hell), but also from the power of sin (the pull of the flesh toward wickedness). God has called us and enabled us to be virtuous and live a life pleasing to Him.

PONDER: When you were born again, how did your life change? Do you presently have a heart to be virtuous?

—*Rick Johnson*

THE PRIORITY OF VIRTUE

Scripture Reading—2 Pet. 1:5
"Add to your faith virtue."

Whatever God establishes as a priority ought to be important to us. After someone is saved, typically, the first thing we do is instruct him or her in Bible facts. This is not God's order; virtue comes before knowledge (2 Pet. 1:5).

This is missing in many lives, and it explains why some young people drop out of church after high school. They know a lot of Bible truths, but something is absent—virtue.

The word conveys the idea of "moral excellence" and is cultivated by a personal relationship with Christ. Moral impurity deadens our spiritual affection for Christ (Matt. 24:12). Many people attend every service at church and have a head crammed full of Bible knowledge, but have a heart of ice toward spiritual matters. Knowledge, yes; virtue, no.

Knowledge without virtue makes one proud (1 Cor. 8:1). I was at camp in a cabin late at night listening to a teenage boy criticize a godly musician because his music was conservative. The young man had grown up in church, was home-schooled, attended a Christian school, and had loads of knowledge, but no virtue.

He thought I was sleeping, and I corrected him in front of those that were listening. His problem was that he loved the garbage of the world and had no appetite for virtue. This is a frightening problem in our churches and youth ministries. God's order isn't *knowledge, virtue, and faith*, but *faith, virtue, and knowledge* (2 Pet. 1:5).

If you have virtue it is because you have been intentional about it. We have to "add" it (2 Pet. 1:5). The purpose of a time alone with God isn't to satisfy intellectual curiosity, but to get manna for your soul.

Does your iPod reflect virtue? Are your text messages virtuous? Is your entertainment virtuous? Is your head filled with spiritual knowledge, but your heart void of virtue?

As you disciple your children and new converts, don't neglect virtue. Knowledge alone will not keep them faithful to the Lord and His church, but virtue will.

PONDER: What is your game plan to cultivate virtue in your life?

—Rick Johnson

JANUARY 18
WHEN YOU ARE ANGRY

Scripture Reading—Pro. 14:17
"He that is soon angry dealeth foolishly."

When we speak when we are angry, it isn't worth it. Rather than offering words that are helpful and wise, we speak as fools. Susan Marcotte wrote, "Anger helps straighten out a problem as much as a fan helps straighten out a pile of papers."

For me when I want to use sarcasm, I need to be quiet because what I am about to say is not worthwhile. When I lecture rather than simply listen and reflect before speaking, I speak words that I later on regret. Angry words hurt people and destroy relationships.

Even Moses, the meekest man on the earth, struggled with anger as he led the nation of Israel through the wilderness. When he spoke in anger, he spoke foolishly. "They angered him also at the waters of strife, so that it went ill with Moses for their sakes: Because they provoked his spirit, so that he spake unadvisedly with his lips" (Ps. 106:32, 33).

When his spirit was provoked, he "spake unadvisedly." The word means to "babble in anger." It has the idea of uncontrolled speech. Anger will do that to us. And we will say foolish and hurtful things that we never would have said otherwise.

"Often the difference between a successful marriage and a mediocre one consists of leaving about three or four things a day unsaid," wrote Harlan Miller. Some of those "unsaid things" are times when we are angry and ought to be quiet.

Have you ever said to someone, "I want to take those words back," after you had ripped them? Of course, the problem is that you can't. They are engraved on the mind of your child, spouse, or sibling. We must be careful before we speak—especially when we are angry. The problem is that our anger makes us want to speak quickly.

ACTION POINT: Are there any foolish words you have spoken to someone for which you need to seek forgiveness? Purpose to do so as soon as possible.

—Rick Johnson

JANUARY 19
WHEN YOU WANT TO DISAGREE

Scripture Reading—Titus 3:9
"Avoid foolish questions, and genealogies, and contentions."

Disagreements are a normal part of life. They are necessary to help clarify a position and to challenge error. It is vital that we be open to disagreements and when disagreeing, to do so in a gracious manner.

However, there is a type of person that is disagreeable about most anything. These people enjoy controversy and stirring the pot. And they usually have "facts" to defend their position.

Leaders are typically prone to this because they, of necessity, must have strong opinions. Good leaders have taken time to think through positions and to articulate them clearly. This experience makes them quick to speak to an issue, even on unimportant matters.

Some have personalities that enjoy pursuing details. They simply enjoy learning. However, this smorgasbord of minutiae can make one intolerable as they spout ironclad opinions that are not that important.

Years ago I learned something that helped me in reducing conflicts with others. I realized I didn't have to offer my opinion on every subject. Opinionated people tend to talk too much and listen too little. I learned to love people more than my opinions, to watch myself in conversations, and not to throw my thoughts in on every subject.

Opinionated people are inclined to major on the minors and minor on the majors. They focus on the trivial and insignificant. Obviously this leads to unnecessary conflicts. And that results in strained relationships.

Of course, it's not wrong to be interested in trivia, details, and minutiae, but it is wrong to elevate them to a place of such strong opinion that we find ourselves in constant quarrels over silly matters.

The Bible chimes in on the issue frequently (Titus 3:9; 1 Tim. 1:4; 2 Tim. 2:14, 23). While we are to defend the cardinal doctrines of Christianity (Jude 3), we are not to be petty about inconsequential matters. God is not only concerned that we have the right position, but that our disposition be right too.

Someone wrote, "As a man grows older and wiser, he talks less and says more."

MEMORIZE: James 3:17.

—Rick Johnson

JANUARY 20
HEARING ON PURPOSE

Scripture Reading—Rev. 2:7
"He that hath an ear, let him hear
what the Spirit saith unto the churches."

You've experienced it I'm sure—that blank stare and moment of panic when you realize that you drifted off when someone was talking with you. Now you have absolutely no clue what was said! We all have the incredible ability to listen without actually hearing. That's why Jesus made the command for His people to hear on purpose the message of God's Spirit to them. In fact, God gave the command at least seven times in two chapters!

Advertisers have reported that if they want their message to reach the point where they are assured it has covered the vast majority of a TV audience, they must have their commercial played 17 times. Even advertisers recognize that while people may be listening, it does not guarantee that they are hearing.

Hearing takes practice. In Ephesians 6:1, built into the command that teaches children to obey their parents is the concept of hearing on purpose what the parents say. This then, does not allow for a child to say, "I didn't hear what you said," as a reason not to obey. It is the child's responsibility to learn to hear what parents say and mean in order to be able to do. How children respond to their parents will condition them as to how they will ultimately respond to God.

What is your response and attitude towards the Word of God? We are to hear on purpose what God says, either through the preached Word or in our private time with the Lord. God's idea of hearing Him on purpose is so that we might absorb what He desires and apply what He commands.

ACTION POINT: The last words of Jesus in Revelation 2 and 3 require the Christian to hear the message of the Holy Spirit concerning revival. Practice hearing God on purpose today. Read these chapters and locate each time the Lord says, "He that hath an ear, let him hear," and note the benefits of obeying this command as well as the detriments of disobeying this command.

—*Christy Ingram*

JANUARY 21
JOB DESCRIPTION

Scripture Reading—1 Cor. 15:58
"Therefore, my beloved brethren, be ye stedfast, unmoveable,
always abounding in the work of the Lord, forasmuch as ye know
that your labour is not in vain in the Lord."

In the early 1980s employees working for a South Carolina company that made power plant parts found themselves in unusual circumstances. The owner would never lay a person off even when the company had no orders for the product they sold. While we might chuckle at such a prospect, the employees found that weeks of having nothing to work on became very boring, and before long, morale began to drop.

It would be difficult to work any job if no one explained what we were supposed to do. Many jobs come with job descriptions. Have you ever considered what the Bible says is your job description? Ephesians 4:11, 12 tell us that God has given the teaching pastor for the equipping of the saints to make them completely operational. This equipping of the saints enables them to do "the work of the ministry." Mature people want to serve. Anyone who has a vibrant relationship with the Lord has a desire to do works of service for Him.

The job description for the New Testament believer is to do "the work of the ministry." Get involved using your God-given gifts and abilities in an area of your local church. Help build it through the teaching and ministering gifts given to you. Use the maturity you have gained to minister physically and spiritually in the lives of others. "Iron sharpeneth iron; so a man sharpeneth the countenance of his friend" (Pro. 27:17).

Enter into your church this coming Sunday and ask the following question: "God, show me where you can use me?" Look around for opportunities. Ask church leaders about places of service that you could possibly be used! Can you imagine the holes that would be filled in your local church if the people who were not serving began to serve with a rainbow collection of gifts and abilities?

PONDER: If your church were to place a "help wanted" advertisement—where could you serve?

—*Steve Rebert*

21

JANUARY 22
DID YOU FORGET ANYTHING?

Scripture Reading—Pro. 3:1
"My son, forget not my law; but let thine heart keep my commandments."

I still remember those early mornings when I would have to wake up, get ready, and head out the door to ride the bus to school. My usual routine was to get out of bed, get into the shower, get dressed, grab my backpack, and make the walk down my driveway to wait on the bus. Breakfast never even entered my mind.

Every morning, my faithful mother would catch me before I went out the door and ask me a simple question, "Did you forget anything?" Sometimes I hated it when she asked that question. The night before, I may have left my pencils and erasers on the table. As a result, I had to take off my backpack, take the time to load the missing items, and then head out the door. While I didn't like slowing down at the time, I was glad mom asked that question when I got to school later that morning!

Every day, many Christians walk out the door forgetting something far greater than pencils and erasers. We walk out of our homes and into a busy day forgetting the Word of God. Through the proverbs of Solomon, God pleads with us to not forget His law.

How important is God's Word? Hebrews calls it a "twoedged sword" (Heb. 4:12). God called it a fire and hammer in Jeremiah 23:29. Imagine a soldier without his weapon or a carpenter without his tools. Both of those men would be very limited without his sword or hammer. The same is true for the Christian who forgets God's precious Word. Don't limit yourself by neglecting the Bible.

Every day, we must be mindful of the Word of God and the importance of it in our lives. If your mother or spouse stopped you and asked if you forgot anything, what would you say? Could you say you have been in the Word?

PONDER:
- When do you spend time in the Bible?
- What book in the Bible are you reading now?
- What is a lesson you have recently learned from the Bible?

—Alton Beal

JANUARY 23
THE PRESENCE OF THE SPIRIT

Scripture Reading—John 14:16
"And I will pray the Father, and he shall give you another Comforter."

Jesus gave the name of "Comforter" to the Holy Spirit. The word "Comforter" refers to one who is called alongside of someone else to exhort and encourage him or her. It is the same word translated "advocate" in 1 John 2:2, referring to the Lord Jesus. According to Elmer Towns, this word was used in ancient times to refer to:

- A lawyer who pleaded someone's case.
- A tutor who instructed his pupils.
- A doctor who comes to the bedside of a sick person.
- A friend pleading the cause of another.
- One who comes to the aid of another to encourage and comfort.

The name "Comforter" is a good one. Every Christian has the Holy Spirit indwelling him (Rom. 8:9; 1 Cor. 6:19, 20). Jesus sent the Spirit to reveal truth about God (John 14:20).

It makes all the difference in the world to know that, when you face terrible fears, someone is always with you—for Jesus said that He will "abide with you for ever" (John 14:17). Also, when you struggle to understand the Bible, the Spirit guides you, for "he shall teach you all things" (John 14:26).

Imagine that you are going on a long journey in a ship from the 1800s. You will be traveling alone to a place you have never been. On the journey you will come across people you do not know. There are no friends who are close by or anyone who knows your needs.

You have no one you can talk to about your burdens or troubles. You have no one who understands the purpose of your journey. How alone would you feel? How fearful would this make you be? For the child of God, no journey is ever taken truly alone, and He will never forsake us (Heb. 13:5).

> **QUOTE:** "We are not alone, abandoned, helpless, and hopeless! Wherever we go, the Spirit is with us, so why should we feel like orphans? There is no need to have a troubled heart when you have the very Spirit of God dwelling within you!" —Warren Wiersbe

—James Stallard

PRAYERLESSNESS LEADS TO SPIRITUAL MEDIOCRITY

Scripture Reading—Neh. 2:4
"I prayed to the God of heaven."

When you work, you get what you can do. But when you pray, you get what God can do. God's greatest promises in the Bible concern our prayers (John 15:7).

God honored Nehemiah's prayer with provisions for his trip and resources to rebuild the wall around Jerusalem (Neh. 2:4). Elijah prayed, and God supernaturally answered concerning the weather (James 5:17, 18).

"All our failures are prayer failures," John R. Rice said. I believe that. No amount of work or human cleverness can compensate for a lack of God's power and blessing.

Jerry Falwell said, "Prayer can do anything God can do. Since God is omnipotent, prayer is omnipotent." What a great motivation to pray and to trust God for the impossible! Mediocre lives, families, and ministries are a reflection of our prayerlessness.

On many occasions I have prayed about a matter, and God didn't give me liberty to pursue it. In hindsight I have been able to see that it has kept me from a thousand sorrows. I won't know until eternity the goodness of God and how He protected me.

There have been other times after I prayed that God has given me His peace to go in a certain direction, and that decision has proven to have His blessing over and again many times.

For me, the will of God has never been a difficult matter. I have brought opportunities and promptings before the Lord and prayed and fasted over them. I have served in four churches through the years, and each one of them came to me as an open door that I did not seek.

In those times I clung to the promise in Genesis 24:27: "I being in the way, the LORD led me." Part of being in the way of blessing and guidance was praying—not about the opportunity. I didn't even know about it. I was simply communing and walking with God. He led me clearly, and my life has been incredibly enriched.

ACTION POINT: If your prayer life is mediocre, begin to seek the Lord this week and watch Him bless you.

—Rick Johnson

JANUARY 25
GOD DOES NOT ALWAYS DELIVER

Scripture Reading—Rev. 2:10
"Fear none of those things which thou shalt suffer . . .
be thou faithful unto death."

As Christians, we sometimes imagine that if we find ourselves in a great trial of faith that God will deliver us if we just ask. After all, the Bible says, "If we ask any thing according to his will, he heareth us" (1 John 5:14). So why does it seem that God doesn't deliver when we ask? Why does it sometimes seem that when we ask God for deliverance from trials, He seems disinterested, or as if He's not listening? Does He care?

Of course God cares! The Bible is full of promises that demonstrate this: "I will never leave thee" (Heb. 13:5); "Casting all your care upon him; for he careth for you" (1 Pet. 5:7); "Call unto me, and I will answer thee" (Jer. 33:3); and many more. The truth is that God always delivers His children, but on His time scale and in His way, not ours.

"But," you might say, "sometimes a person will die without being delivered from their trial. Did God fail them?" No! God is also interested in reaching those around us, and He will allow us to go through trials so that others will glorify Him, even if our deliverance is going to Heaven through death. Remember Lazarus in John 11? When Lazarus died, Jesus said the trial was "for the glory of God" (v. 4). Consider the blind man in John 9. It was assumed he was blind because of sin. Jesus refuted that claim and said the blindness was "that the works of God should be made manifest in him" (v. 3). That deliverance was for others to witness, as well as for him.

We are all in the "school of Christ," and God is trying to teach us valuable life lessons. Trials are like classrooms, and God allows them to do their work in our lives. Once the lesson is learned, He will remove the trial.

Someone once said, "Trust the Lord. Trust the process." There is rest for the weary believer in that statement.

DISCUSS: Read Daniel 3, and discuss how God delivered from the fire in His way and in His time.

—Paul Miller

JANUARY 26
STRANGE NOTIONS THAT PEOPLE HAVE

Scripture Reading—John 9:2
"Master, who did sin, this man, or his parents, that he was born blind?"

People sometimes have strange notions. Tragedy can strike another person's life, and immediately some people believe that this person's life must be under the judgment of God.

While God may certainly judge anyone for their actions and attitudes, it is not wise for us to become judges based on what we see happening to others. The disciples of Jesus were like many ordinary people of their day. They believed that people were suffering because God was judging them.

For example, they thought the man born blind was being judged for sins he perhaps committed in the womb (John 9:1–3). On another occasion, people asked Jesus about the Galilaeans who had gone into the Temple to hide from the authorities. These were criminals, and Pilate decided to violate the Temple, as a Gentile, and go in and take the criminals out. God allowed it to take place.

They also asked about a tower in Siloam that fell and killed eighteen people. Were those people being judged by God? Jesus gave some sobering comments to anyone who would listen:

"Suppose ye that these Galilaeans were sinners above all the Galilaeans, because they suffered such things? I tell you, Nay: but, except ye repent, ye shall all likewise perish. Or those eighteen, upon whom the tower in Siloam fell, and slew them, think ye that they were sinners above all men that dwelt in Jerusalem? I tell you, Nay: but except ye repent, ye shall all likewise perish" (Luke 13:2–5).

Think about some bad things you know that have happened to other people. Why do you think those bad things happened? Should we consider those people to be worse sinners than we are because those things happened to them? Do you think God knows more about what is happening in all of our lives than we do? It would be very wise for us to leave the judging to God, for we too will stand before Him one day!

ACTION POINT: Have dad and mom check out some news from the newspaper, Internet, or television. Discuss some of the bad things that have happened to others. Compare that to today's devotion.

—James Stallard

LIVING IN REBELLION AGAINST GOD

Scripture Reading—1 Sam. 15:22, 23
*"To obey is better than sacrifice . . . For rebellion is as the sin of
witchcraft, and stubbornness is as iniquity and idolatry."*

There are those who would falsely assume that disobedience is a respectable sin, if there even is such a thing. Somehow they assume that "not doing right" is better than doing wrong. Doing wrong includes things like lying, cheating, and stealing, and these prideful folks assume that disobedience is nothing like that.

Saul certainly underestimated the seriousness of his disobedience. In 1 Samuel 15:13 he even boasted, "I have performed the commandment of the LORD," knowing full well that he had not done exactly what God told him to do. Though Saul had not committed a crime or been immoral, he lost the kingdom because of the seriousness of his disobedience against God. Tragically, there are times when people live in passive rebellion against God, not because of the wrong they are doing, but because of the right they are not doing!

When our children were younger, we did a study on obedience as a family. One of the key principles we learned said: **"A proper attitude in obedience means that no opposition is shown, no opinion is expressed, and no options are suggested."** As a family we sought to understand that obedience is essential when God speaks to His children and when Mom and Dad speak to their children.

I remember as a child hearing my parents say, "Don't talk back," when as children, we occasionally tried to dispute or debate what we had been instructed to do. God expects implicit obedience, and parents need to do the same. Otherwise young people grow up assuming that there is always a "Plan B" if they are not interested in "Plan A." For Saul, the punishment was harsh (1 Sam. 15:23). I am certain that if Saul could have had a second chance, he would have been far more careful to do exactly what God had commanded him to do.

ACTION POINT: Compare what God said in 1 Samuel 15:2, 3 with what Saul did in 1 Samuel 15:7–9. Note Saul's explanation in verses 15, 20, and 21.

—Tom Palmer

JANUARY 28
BURDEN OF BEREAVEMENT

Scripture Reading—Job 2:13
"So they sat down with him upon the ground seven days
and seven nights, and none spake a word unto him:
for they saw that his grief was very great."

One of the heaviest burdens of all is the grief you experience when you lose a loved one or close friend. To say goodbye, even for a while, to someone you care deeply about is a great burden. God never required of us not to sorrow (1 Thess. 4:13), but in our grief we have hope because of the promise of Heaven.

Job's sorrow was so great that he didn't have words to express it (Job 6:2, 3). When Stephen was buried, his friends "made great lamentation over him" (Acts 8:2). Our Lord understood the emotional pain and sorrow of loss (John 11:33, 35). Grief is normal, but if it is not checked with God's promises, it can become a long-term burden.

One afternoon I received a call that a friend of my mom's had died, but this was not just any friend. They had known each other for more than 30 years, and it was her closest friend. Immediately I drove to Mom's house, and she was not there. This was before the age of cell phones, and I had no way to know where she was.

So, I sat there and waited. More than two hours later, she walked in the door and saw me seated in a chair. We didn't say much. I got up and embraced her and told her how sorry I was for her loss, and we wept together. What she needed then was someone to just care for her and be there.

Warren Wiersbe said, "We don't live on explanations; we live on promises." Understanding why doesn't remove the sting, but the promises of God give us hope and relieve our grief.

ACTION POINT: When someone is grieving over a loss, resist the desire to compare your own sorrow with his or hers or to attempt to explain why it might have happened. Just show up and be there for that person.

—*Rick Johnson*

JANUARY 29
STUDYING THE BIBLE

Scripture Reading—2 Tim. 2:15
"Study to shew thyself approved unto God."

Some mistakenly think that study is the responsibility of pastors, teachers, and those that communicate God's Word. Bible study is for every Christian (2 Tim. 2:15). The word "study" means "to be diligent in an effort." It has the idea of an earnest, laborious study. This person is called a "workman." This word means "one that toils and labors." It refers to a teacher that labors to help his students learn.

This is the primary reason people do not study the Bible; it is hard work. If you want to learn God's Word, you must put in time and effort. Failure to learn it not only stunts a person's spiritual growth but also is the source of division in a church (1 Cor. 3:1–3).

It isn't God's will that you always be spoon-fed from your pastor, but that you graduate from milk to the meat of the doctrine of the Bible (Heb. 5:12–14). This requires the discipline and work of study.

The author of the Bible, the Holy Spirit, will be your teacher (1 Cor. 2:14). This happens as you read, memorize, meditate upon, and study the Bible. Being a good Bible student isn't related to your intellect, but to your willingness to learn and obey (John 7:17).

God complimented the Bereans for their attitude in receiving God's Word and in studying it daily (Acts 17:11). This is our privilege and responsibility too (John 5:39).

When I was a teenager, I was watching television, and a religious program sponsored by a cult came on. I saw the teacher's Bible—it was well-worn and well-marked with notes in the margins and had verses highlighted. Almost everything he taught was wrong, but the Spirit of God convicted me as I watched the program. It wasn't from his message, but the way his Bible had been used. My Bible wasn't like that.

That night I promised the Lord that I was going to be the best Bible student I could be. It was a life-changing decision. Have you ever made that decision?

ACTION POINT: Ask your pastor for some good Bible study tools.

—Rick Johnson

JANUARY 30
WATCHING FOR THE LORD

Scripture Reading—Pro. 8:34
"Blessed is the man . . . watching daily at my gates."

One afternoon in our small town in Wyoming, I noticed a man being assisted by a companion as he walked down the sidewalk. He extended a long straight cane in front of him to warn him of hazards, so he could avoid tripping and falling. My thought at the time was that this man could not see. And then I began to think of the vast majority of us who have this marvelous gift of vision and how much we misuse it. Every day by choice or default, we "see" things God never desired or intended for His creation to witness—immodesty, vile bumper stickers, crude billboards, deceitful drug advertisements, along with the constant barrage of a fallen society that says, "Look at me!"

A blessing is promised to those who watch for God. In Scripture, watching is often described as the opposite of sleeping. Simply defined as being on guard, it denotes circumspection, diligence, and attention. The Levites "watched" at the gates of the temple. Watchmen were employed in towers and atop walls to keep guard against the enemy and protect the Lord's interests.

God employs his children to be watchmen, to be guardians over hearts and souls. A father is to be a watchman over his family, and believers in the church should be watching over each other's spiritual welfare.

Notice the word "daily." The enemy never rests or sleeps. Therefore, there must be a continual "watch" taking place at the Lord's gates. Before we assume that all this responsibly falls on us, let us remember the scriptural promise: "For he shall give his angels charge over thee, to keep thee in all thy ways" (Ps. 91:11). Thank the Lord we are not the only ones watching in these perilous days!

DISCUSS: As a family discuss three areas that must be watched to protect the Lord's gates in your home.

—*Wayne King*

JANUARY 31
HOLDING YOUR PEACE

Scripture Reading—Pro. 11:12
"A man of understanding holdeth his peace."

Years ago at a social setting, my wife Paula and I were seated at a table of ten, and we didn't know anyone at the table. We would be there for a while sharing a meal, and it was appropriate for us to get to know those immediately around us. However, we never got a chance to do so.

We were all held hostage by a man that talked the entire time—to all of us. I honestly don't think anyone else said more than three or four sentences. He pontificated on whatever came to his mind. We were his captive audience, and he relished it. The minutes torturously and slowly dragged by.

When we were finally away from the table, I told Paula, "Have you ever heard anyone that was so impressed with himself and dominated a conversation like that?" After I finally quit griping about it, I said, "You know, Paula, I feel most sorry for his wife and kids . . . and his church." Sadly, the man was a pastor. He should have known better.

"A wise man thinks without talking; a fool talks without thinking."

When I have a difficult conversation with someone, I try to make it a habit to think through precisely what I need to say, rather than just speak extemporaneously. To just speak is not only unwise, but it is unbiblical. Words mean things and arouse emotions in people. Wise people are not only careful with their words, but economical with them as well.

The Bible in seven words sums up the issue: "A fool also is full of words" (Eccl. 10:14). Notice that of the seven words six of them are monosyllables—simple, but profound. Even God is economical with His Words to us.

I like what one person wrote, "It would be better to leave people wondering why you didn't talk than why you did."

ACTION POINT: Look for an older person at church that usually doesn't talk much and ask them some questions about a problem you are facing. You might be surprised at their wisdom.

—Rick Johnson

FEBRUARY 1
WAITING ON THE LORD

Scripture Reading—Pro. 8:34
"Blessed is the man . . . waiting at the posts of my doors."

We all know the phrase, "Patience is a virtue." And we all know that patience—real patience—is a virtue that most of us lack. Today's proverb promises a blessing to those that will wait.

As Scripture tells us, we are a "kind of firstfruits," and if born again, we are charged with cultivating the character and nature of Jesus in our lives. Though the humanity of Christ is shown through His grief, care, hunger, righteous anger, and more, not once do we see an impatient, demanding, or self-willed Savior. Though disciples would try anyone's patience—as would hundreds of other people he encountered—He did not lack patience.

The discipline of waiting requires Christian discernment of and submission to the Divine will. We must *know* that God *is* in control, and His will is worth waiting on. Philippians 1:6 tells us, "Being confident of this very thing, that he which hath begun a good work in you *will perform it* until the day of Jesus Christ." Faith and confidence will help the believer to wait on the Lord.

Waiting has an expectation accompanying it. If we're waiting for a guest, some indication has been given that the guest will arrive at a certain place at a certain time. "The post of my doors" (wisdom, truth) is a great place to wait for the Guest we expect to arrive! Some scholars have suggested this passage is a metaphor for eager students "waiting" for the doors to open to let them enter into learning. Certainly, with Christ as our Teacher bringing the Word, we should wait with eager anticipation to learn at the feet of the Master.

Christian, what are you waiting for from the Lord? Deliverance? Healing? Wisdom? His soon return? Are we waiting at the right location or at a wrong address where the Lord will not reveal himself? May the Lord indeed find us hearing, watching, and *waiting* patiently for Him.

DISCUSS: Discuss what you are (or were, or will be) waiting on from the Lord.

—Wayne King

FEBRUARY 2
PURGING SIN FROM OUR FAMILY
Scripture Reading—Pro. 16:6
"By mercy and truth iniquity is purged."

Every individual Christian needs to deal with sin on a daily basis. That means he must confess it and turn from it in order to maintain fellowship with God. For this task the Lord has given us 1 John 1:9 to use every day of our lives—"If we confess our sins, he is faithful and just to forgive us our sins, and to cleanse us from all unrighteousness." We confess and God forgives and cleanses. This process of cleansing could be called a "purging."

That takes care of our own individual sins. But what about purging sin from other people around us? Proverbs 16:6 gives us the keys to helping others deal with sin in their lives when it says, "By mercy and truth iniquity is purged: and by the fear of the LORD men depart from evil." Those keys are found in two words: **mercy** and **truth**.

If a parent wants to deal with sin in a child, these two words will come in handy. For example, there will always be a need to apply **truth** to any situation. If a young girl has rebelled against her parents and faces the consequences of her actions, the truth of God's Word needs to be followed to help her. Honoring parents is still commanded by God (Exod. 20:12).

But, the second word is important as well. To purge sin from a life, there will also be the need to apply **mercy** in the situation. Truth forced on someone without mercy will never purge away sin. It is difficult for most parents to know how to balance these things. They must cry out for wisdom from God (James 1:5).

We see the great example in the teaching of the Prodigal Son (Luke 15:11–32). The Prodigal came to himself in the hog pen and went back to his father. The Father could have said, "I told you so," in a display of truth. Instead he showed mercy and love. Truth and mercy together should always be the ticket to purge sin successfully from any family.

ACTION POINT: Read aloud together Proverbs 16:6 three times.

—James Stallard

FEBRUARY 3
THE PROBLEM WITH ADVERTISEMENTS

Scripture Reading—Pro. 19:3
"The foolishness of man perverteth his way:
and his heart fretteth against the LORD."

Billboards, TV commercials, and magazine ads all have one thing in common. Each one is carefully designed to breed discontentment so that people will buy the product being sold. Let me show you some examples of what I mean.

Let's suppose I was a salesman for a bicycle company that had just created a new fifteen-speed tricycle. My sales pitch would go something like this: "You don't have to ride your old trike any more. It's rusty, squeaky, and hard to peddle, right? Our new Turbo Trike will change your cycling experience from despair to delight. You could be coasting both downhill and uphill on our new trike. Our new seat design is so comfortable that you can take a nap while you ride. You can turn on the heat when it's cold, and turn on the air conditioning when it's hot."

OK! Enough is enough! I am being ridiculous, but are you getting the point? I am trying to make you miserable by trying to convince you that what I have to sell you is much better than what you already have. Of course I am hoping that if you are miserable enough you will want to buy my product.

Do you see how advertising works? It doesn't matter if it is makeup to make you beautiful, a weight loss program to make you slim, or a new mattress to help you sleep better. In each case, discontentment sells! Discontented people spend lots of money trying to make things better when many times what they already have is not too bad.

Beware of subtle advertising and slick salesmen. If what you have is sufficient to meet your need, maybe it would be best to just stick with it for now—and be content!

ACTION POINT: Play a little game with a family member, trying to sell him or her a new car. Pay attention to how quickly your family could become unhappy with the car you already have.

—Tom Palmer

FEBRUARY 4
A TESTIMONY OF VIRTUE

Scripture Reading—Ruth 3:11
"All the city of my people doth know that thou art a virtuous woman."

Virtue is the basis of your testimony. Virtue isn't so much what you do, but who you are. If you want to make a difference, you have to be different. When a person is genuinely different in their spirit, people will notice.

A virtuous woman has influence (Pro. 31:10). The city of Bethlehem knew of Ruth's virtue; her testimony came from her virtue (Ruth 3:11). She was different in her spirit, and it was obvious to all around her.

Another way to express the idea of a personal testimony is to have a life message. Everyone has one, for good or for bad. Virtue has impact only if it is a consistent life message, not something that is sporadic.

How do people detect virtue in your life? Since virtue is a matter of the heart, one of the ways it is expressed is through your words (Matt. 12:34). Our speech is but an overflow of our heart, and we are to meditate on things that are virtuous (Phil. 4:8). It is impossible to live a virtuous life without a thought life that is virtuous.

So, if you want to "add virtue" to your faith (2 Pet. 1:5), ponder the Lord Jesus and His words. The Spirit of God takes the Word of God and changes you from being wicked to being virtuous (2 Cor. 3:18). It is a transformation that stands out in a dark world (Phil. 2:15).

Take time each day to fill your mind with God's Word, for it is pure (Ps. 12:6; 19:8; 119:140; Pro. 30:5). As His words come into your mind, they confront that which is unholy. When He changes our thinking, we begin to be virtuous and then we have a life message that is influential.

"When we pray, we talk to God, and when we read the bible, God talks to us; and we need to do most of the listening." —D.L. Moody

ACTION POINT: Don't just read the Bible, but meditate upon it today.

—Rick Johnson

35

FEBRUARY 5
THE HERITAGE OF A FAMILY

Scripture Reading—Ps. 16:6
"The lines are fallen unto me in pleasant places;
yea, I have a goodly heritage."

The verse before us speaks of family tradition, blessing, and heritage. The first section mentions "lines" and "pleasant places," which refer to surveyor's boundaries for property. Each family in Israel received a territory by line and lot when the nation went into the Promised Land. This inheritance stayed in the family through all generations.

The second part mentions a "goodly heritage." While we often think of inheritance in terms of money and possessions, it can also refer to the blessings that God has provided for us through family down through the years. Many years ago I wrote this prayer in the margin of my Bible next to Psalm 16:6:

Thank you, Lord, for my Mom and Dad, for my Grandparents, and my family history. Thank you for all the homes and friends you have provided through all the years. This verse is true of me.

It would be a good exercise for every family member to remember and recall the blessings that have come through his or her family. Can you say before the Lord that "the lines are fallen unto me in pleasant places?"

Perhaps someone you know was raised in a bad situation. You could not see how anything good could come out of that family. Maybe it was an abusive drunken father, a domineering mother, or maybe some strong-willed children that disrupted the home. How could that be called "pleasant"? How could anything associated with it be considered a "goodly heritage"?

Anyone who is a true believer can know that God has brought him or her to Himself for His glorious purpose (Rom. 8:28, 29). Whether or not you grew up in a believing home or not, you can rejoice in what God has done to bring you to this point in your life as part of His family.

We need to look at things the way God looks at them. The previous verse declares, "The LORD is the portion of mine inheritance" (Ps. 16:5). The Lord Himself is the center of our inheritance. Not only His blessings, but God Himself, is our portion.

ACTION POINT: Have each family member praise the Lord for their family.

—James Stallard

FEBRUARY 6
SLOW TO SPEAK

Scripture Reading—James 1:19
"Let every man be swift to hear, slow to speak, slow to wrath."

Most often the words I regret speaking are those spoken when I was angry. Sadly, the vast majority of these times have been with my family. Heated words hurt people and cause them to pull away from us emotionally.

Someone wisely noted, "Speak when you are angry and you will make the best speech you will ever regret." Even when our position is correct, if our disposition is wrong, the truth will not be received. People remember our attitude longer than our position on a subject.

The Bible relates being "slow to speak" and "slow to wrath." As the proverbial snowball going downhill gathers speed and grows bigger, so our words become more heated the more we become entangled in a contentious conversation. And the sure result soon after is regret over what should not have been said.

A soon-angry man "worketh not the righteousness of God" (James 1:20). That simply means he is not reflecting the heart of God and that he is not right with God. Some of the most damaging things ever done to a person have been when he or she was the recipient of words from an angry parent or an angry spouse. They remember them—every word—sometimes for a lifetime.

Anger causes us to lose our self-control, and we spout words that are designed to hurt. There are two words that are typically used that only raise the temperature of an already-heated environment: "always" and "never." "You always come home late. You never have supper ready on time. You always spend too much money." These words only cause the other person to become defensive and withdraw even more.

Later on, when we have had time to think about what we said, we wish we had kept our mouths shut. But it's too late. A heart has been wounded, and, too often, it belongs to someone we love dearly—a husband or wife, son or daughter, or parents.

ACTION POINT: Ask the Lord to help you to be swift to hear, slow to speak, slow to wrath.

—*Rick Johnson*

FEBRUARY 7
CONTENTMENT OR COVETOUSNESS?

Scripture Reading—Pro. 15:27
"He that is greedy of gain troubleth his own house."

The question was asked of a rich man: "So what does it take to satisfy you?" The rich man replied, "Just a little bit more." His response leads us to consider the subject of covetousness, which is basically an uncontrolled desire for more.

Jesus offered a warning regarding covetousness. In Luke 12:15 He said, "Take heed, and beware of covetousness: for a man's life consisteth not in the abundance of the things which he possesseth." There is certainly nothing wrong with having a possession, but when having more things becomes an obsession, we are in trouble. In 1 Timothy 6:9 Paul said, "They that will be rich (want to be rich) fall into temptation and a snare, and into many foolish and hurtful lusts." Paul was explaining that the desire for money will take you in, the deception of money will take you away, and the destruction of money will take you down. Money is an important thing to have as long as you control it, but you must never let it control you. Interestingly enough, "the love of money" spoken of in verse 10 can be a problem when you have $5 in your wallet or $5 million in the bank. It is not an issue of your bank balance, but your attitude.

Our modern society has come to believe that the more money you have, the more you can buy, and the more you can buy, the more you can have, and the more you can have, the more you can do, and the more you can do, the happier you will be.

For this reason there are many who are driven by an uncontrolled desire for more and more money. Sadly, they fail to realize that the greatest things in life are the things that money cannot buy. When it comes to money, never allow yourself to get caught in the trap of seeking "just a little bit more"—you may not get out.

ACTION POINT: Consider several things that you have as a child of God that cannot be bought with money. Consider why they are so valuable to you.

—*Tom Palmer*

FEBRUARY 8
A Prayer List: Specific Requests

Scripture Reading—James 4:2
"Ye have not, because ye ask not."

God doesn't answer generic prayers; He answers specific prayers. Aside from unbelief, the greatest hindrance to answered prayer is generality.

Paul prayed for churches he founded, and these prayers were very detailed and to the point. He prayed for their love to grow in discernment, for their priorities to be on things that are excellent, for their lives to be genuine, holy, and filled with God's righteousness and spiritual fruit (Phil. 1:9–11).

Here's another specific prayer list that he used. He prayed that they would know God's will and have wisdom, that they would walk pleasing to the Lord, that they would be fruitful in their ministry, that they might grow in their knowledge of God, and that they might be strengthened with spiritual might and have godly character (Col. 1:3, 9–11).

The greatest thing you can do for a person is to pray for him or her. But let's be honest, most of the prayers we pray and hear are "bless" the missionaries, "bless" the service, and "bless" my family. I have learned that the vast majority of people don't even know what it means for the Lord to "bless" someone.

Take these passages above and pray them for those you love—your spouse, children, parents, brothers and sisters, church members, friends, and pastors. When you pray specifically your prayer time will take on a new life, and God will honor your requests. He will be delighted that you care enough to pray specifically.

I pray every day for my children that they would be pure in heart and do God's will. I pray for our teenagers and college kids at church—for their moral purity while they are at school. Right now I'm praying for a specific amount of money for a personal need. I even mention the precise amount to God. He told us to do so.

Pray for your business needs in specific terms. Pray for people and personal needs in detailed ways.

ACTION POINT: Change your prayers from "bless" and "help" to very specific words. Write it down on your prayer list.

—Rick Johnson

FEBRUARY 9
LOVING GOD AND PEOPLE

Scripture Reading—1 John 4:7, 8
"Beloved, let us love one another: for love is of God;
and every one that loveth is born of God, and knoweth God.
He that loveth not knoweth not God; for God is love."

There is an emphasis today on developing "people skills" so that we might be successful. The deeper need is to develop a heart that loves the Lord. A person that genuinely loves God will love people too. Loving God is so intertwined with loving people that the Bible says, if you do not love people, you have never been born again and do not know the Lord (1 John 4:7, 8, 20; 5:1).

Our church has a Bible memory program for children. They learn the verses, the definition of key terms, and other facts about the Bible. While this has a place in developing a godly legacy, it is not enough. Facts and memorized words alone will not change a person. There must be a heart for God and His Word.

The first step to a heart for Christ is a personal understanding of the Gospel and then to begin a relationship with God. This comes through faith in the Person and work of Jesus Christ. This faith—and resulting change of life—is experienced in the heart (Rom. 10:9).

Parents, aim for the heart (Pro. 23:26)! Focus on the personal needs of your child, even their failures, and allow the power of the Gospel to change them internally that it might be genuine and lasting change.

I was spending some time alone with one of my sons when he was nine years old, and spontaneously he said, "Dad, I think you're the best dad in the world. When I get older I want to be a preacher too." My eyes filled with tears as I remembered that, not far from that very place, when I was a boy I told my father the very same thing.

Later on as I thought about it, both situations had a common thread—it wasn't a formal situation. We were just spending time together. I was giving my son my heart—and then he gave me his. I learned to do that from my father.

ACTION POINT: Have each member of the family share their personal testimony of salvation.

—Rick Johnson

FEBRUARY 10
HONESTY IS THE ONLY POLICY!

Scripture Reading—Eph. 4:25
"Wherefore putting away lying, speak every man truth with his neighbour: for we are members one of another."

Jim is a nice guy, and usually a happy young man. He likes people, and he likes to talk to people, especially to his family. Usually he's pretty honest, but sometimes he's tempted to tell people not what they need to hear, but what he thinks they want to hear. And that's not good!

Jim is learning the lesson of telling the truth. His dad taught him that "a lie is the intent to deceive," and that it's never right to lie. Jim has read in the Bible that as God's children we must "speak every man truth with his neighbour." God says that lying is out, and being honest all the time is what's important.

In order to stop being a liar, a person must do at least two things. First, he must stop telling lies. This means he must stop thinking and speaking deceitfully. But that's not enough! Secondly, he must always speak the truth. God's Word says, "As a man thinketh in his heart, so is he." My lies come from my lying heart. I must have God's help in order to change the way I think. Only then can I change the way I act. Being honest is not always easy, but it is what God always expects of us. Dishonesty is always wrong, and being honest is always right.

But what should we do when we know that "speaking the truth" may hurt someone? God's Word has an answer for that as well. Not only are we always to "speak the truth," but also we must speak the truth lovingly (Eph. 4:15). *How* we tell the truth is as important as the fact that we are telling the truth.

DISCUSS: Discuss Romans 12:17, "Recompense to no man evil for evil. Provide things honest in the sight of all men." Why do we need to tell the truth even when others do not? What are things that hinder us from telling the truth? How can we learn to tell the truth always? How can we get God's help to change our hearts?

—*Joe Henson*

FEBRUARY 11
THE MOST IMPORTANT PERSON IN YOUR HOME

Scripture Reading—Gal. 5:16
"This I say then, Walk in the Spirit."

Who is the most important person in your family? Dad is thrilled that finally someone is going to set things straight. Mom wants everybody to know that it really is her. Of course big sister and baby brother think that their moment has finally come. However, you would all be wrong.

The most important person in your home is none other than the Holy Spirit of God. In reality the person of the Holy Spirit is God Himself living in your home. He is the One Who must be in control of each person and each thing that takes place in your house. As each member of your family responds to the Gospel and receives the gift of salvation through Christ, the Spirit takes up residence, not just in the house, but also in the body of each individual. He then can begin to control each one.

In Luke 1, we have an example of a family where each member was filled and controlled by the Spirit of God. We have a father named Zacharias who is filled with the Spirit (v. 67). We also have a mother named Elisabeth who is filled with the Spirit (v. 41). Then we have a son named John who is filled with the Spirit (v. 15). No doubt their home was under the control of the Spirit of God because each member of the family was under the control of the Spirit of God.

The beautiful thing is that when families are controlled by the Spirit of God, the end result is that the fruit of the Spirit will become reality in their home. What a blessing to live in a home that is filled with love and joy and peace and so on down through the list (Gal. 5:22–24). Truly the Holy Spirit brings more to the atmosphere of the home than any person could ever hope for.

ACTION POINT: Read 1 Corinthians 3:16 and 6:19 together and then discuss what is the real house (dwelling place) of God.

—*Tom Palmer*

FEBRUARY 12
EYES FIXED ON NEED

Scripture Reading—Acts 3:6, 7
"Then Peter said, Silver and gold have I none; but such as I have
give I thee: In the name of Jesus Christ of Nazareth rise up and walk.
And he took him by the right hand, and lifted him up:
and immediately his feet and ankle bones received strength."

Acts 3 tells the amazing story of ministering to a man in tremendous need! As Peter and John went into the temple, Peter fixed his eyes upon a man with an insurmountable need. The Lord then used Peter to do a mighty miracle, which brought praise to God, met the physical need of the man, gave witness to all who saw, and opened an opportunity to share the Gospel with many other people.

One of the great benefits of knowing Jesus Christ as our Lord and Savior is the opportunity to serve Him by serving others. A key to accomplishing ministry is having eyes that notice the needs of the people around us. Every day we come into contact with people who are in need physically, emotionally, mentally, and spiritually. Do you notice them or are you just wrapped up in the routine and needs of your own life?

Noticing or not noticing the needs of others around you is a reflection of your walk with the Lord. Peter and John were living in such a way that as soon as they saw the lame man they immediately took notice of his need and they sought to meet it. Ministering to the man's physical need also opened the door to ministering to the spiritual needs of many others.

Our ministry to others first starts with eyes that see need. Do you notice the needs of others around you? Do you instantly act when you see those needs? As a family, look for opportunities to minister to the needs of others, and see the amazing ways God is glorified!

ACTION POINT: Think together as a family of someone who has a need. Then discuss ways in which you can meet this need.

—*Stanley Long*

FEBRUARY 13
WHEN YOU DON'T KNOW WHAT TO DO

Scripture Reading—James 1:5
*"If any of you lack wisdom, let him ask of God . . .
and it shall be given him."*

Have you ever had one of those times in your life when you knew that something just had to be done? You may have even known **who** had to do it and **when** it had to be done. Maybe you even knew **why** it had to be done. However, maybe you were in that situation where you just didn't know **what** had to be done. Unable to eat and unable to sleep, it seemed like you continually wrestled with your own thoughts as you sought to determine what to do. Unfortunately, with every passing day you only became more confused. That was when you needed this special prayer described in the New Testament.

Wisdom is the ability to see things in life the way God sees them. Of course we understand that God knows all things. Though we cannot be as God, wisdom does allow us to know what needs to be known so that we can do what needs to be done. This wisdom comes from God and is given when we are willing to simply ask for it.

This concept was clearly demonstrated in the life of King Solomon. In 1 Kings 3:7, 8, Solomon expressed his inability to know what he should do as king. In verse 9, Solomon prayed a prayer and made a request for wisdom. God chose to answer that request when He said, "I have given thee a wise and understanding heart" (v. 12). With the wisdom of God, Solomon became a wise king who knew what to do even when difficult situations and problems came his way.

So, you don't know what to do? In prayer let God know that you don't know what to do. Then ask Him to show you and allow Him to guide you. It is amazing how quickly those question marks can begin to disappear when we seek God's wisdom. Thankfully, God has promised that He will answer and give us wisdom.

ACTION POINT: Read 1 Kings 4:29–31 and pay attention to how God specifically answered the prayer of Solomon.

—Tom Palmer

REVIVAL AND CONFESSION OF SIN

Scripture Reading—Pro. 28:13
"He that covereth his sins shall not prosper: but whoso
confesseth and forsaketh them shall have mercy."

Genuine revival seems to be a rare event. It seems that throughout history there have been great departures from truth, but comparatively few revivals. But there have been some mighty moves of God throughout history. He moved in the Old Testament to deliver Israel out of Egypt and gave them His law.

In the New Testament, there was a great moving of God in the church at Jerusalem in the book of Acts. In history, we see God at work in the days of the Reformation through men like Martin Luther and John Calvin.

In early America we catch a glimpse of revival during the Great Awakening in the days of Jonathan Edwards and George Whitefield. The Welsh Revival at the turn of the 20th Century was another moving of God.

Yes, God has been at work. And everywhere He works there is **confession of sin**. It seems when men truly see themselves as God sees them and they see God for Who He is really is, the natural response is one of recognizing how sinful we really are.

Isaiah came to confession in the presence of God (Isaiah 6). Peter saw himself for what he was in the presence of the miracles of Jesus (Luke 5). In the days of Jonah, the entire city of Nineveh confessed sin and repented (Jonah 4). David gives us the very personal Psalm of revival in Psalm 51, which is mostly devoted to the confession of sin.

It would be a good practice for us to keep confession of sin on the front burner of our lives. We cannot control what everybody else does with their sins, but we can control what we do with ours. 1 John 1:9 declares, "If we confess our sins, he is faithful and just to forgive us our sins, and to cleanse us from all unrighteousness." If revival is to come to our lives, this verse must become one of the most-used verses in our Bibles.

ACTION POINT: Memorize Proverbs 28:13 as a family and try to apply its meaning into your lives immediately.

—*James Stallard*

FEBRUARY 15
DON'T MISS YOUR OPPORTUNITY

Scripture Reading—Eph. 5:16
"Redeeming the time, because the days are evil."

Redeeming the time is taking advantage of the opportunity when it comes since we might not have another. On a recent trip of ours, my wife and I had a chance to stop at several small towns and cities along the coast. The tour director shared a word of wisdom with us: "If you see something you like at the right price, buy it because you may not see it again."

I found a handmade knife with a handle made from bone or antler from the Alaskan permafrost. I decided to wait and not buy it. I never saw those knives offered again on that trip. When we have opportunities we better take them! More importantly, it is often the Lord who wants us to take them.

We are people of liberty, people of freedom—and yes—here in the USA, people of strength. Yet, place us up against the "tower of time" and we can only shrink away. We have no weapons against it, no knowledge to conquer it, or slow it down. "Turn back time" is only a phrase that exists in the miraculous and found only to be true with God.

If we are to accomplish anything of consequence in our life, it must be done in taking opportunities out of the time that we will never have again. We must march according to the beat of time's moments. We are challenged to make investments for the most valuable of assets. The Bible clearly teaches us that investments with the right motives reap Heaven's interest! I did not get the knife because I waited too long. Let's not do the same in our service for the Lord. We only have so much time in which to invest our talents and treasures because each day is lost to the "tower of time." I meet many people who consider doing something but end up doing little, and then the opportunity is gone!

QUOTE: "Much of life is lost in getting ready to live it." —Source Unknown

—Steve Rebert

BIG GIANT, BIGGER GOD

Scripture Reading—1 Sam. 17:37
"David said moreover, The LORD that delivered me out of the paw
of the lion, and out of the paw of the bear, he will deliver me
out of the hand of this Philistine."

Goliath was big! At somewhere between nine-and-a-half to ten feet tall, he made everyone around him look small. That is, everyone but David. Saul and the men of Israel could only see a human impossibility. Not David. He saw a divine opportunity because he had a big view of his God. That is what vision is all about. Vision can be defined as a God-sized view of what could be. In 1 Samuel 17:36, David told of killing the lion and the bear, and his statement was, "This uncircumcised Philistine shall be as one of them." Size was not an issue to David because size was not an issue to God.

Situations, problems, and needs have a way of overwhelming us any time we fail to keep God in the picture. Saul had become cowardly because he could only think about what he could do in the situation, and that wasn't much. David became courageous because he was focused on what God could do in the situation, and that was unlimited.

I am often aware of the fact that so much of what goes on in the work of the Lord has become very explainable. Even apparent successes are explained by borrowed money, modern technology, talented personnel, and excellent resources. Yet there is something special about the times when there is no explanation but God. Those who are difference-makers for God approach even the most overwhelming odds as a possibility, not because of who they are or what they can do, but because of Who God is and what He can do.

We can never allow impossibilities to limit our effectiveness for God. He is the God of the impossible. David saw the giant as being so small because he saw his God as being so big.

ACTION POINT: List several other individuals in Scripture who were used by God to do things that seemed humanly impossible.

—Tom Palmer

FEBRUARY 17
A TALEBEARER REVEALS SECRETS

Scripture Reading—Pro. 11:13
*"A talebearer revealeth secrets: but he that is of a
faithful spirit concealeth the matter."*

I am grateful that my parents didn't dump any church gossip on our kitchen table while we ate meals. Sometimes I did learn about negative issues, but not from my parents. It was from the "talebearers" in our church that spread the news. Such people are destructive to a fellowship.

I have a simple principle that I live by: I don't have to share all that I know, and I must not share anything that someone has entrusted me with.

Parents, be careful around your children with sensitive conversations. Even a casual talk between a husband and wife in the car or at the kitchen table can divulge private information that little ears pick up on.

A "talebearer" (Pro. 11:13) is one that bears or carries stories or information to others. The word "secrets" has the idea of sharing personal and private details to an intimate circle of friends. The word "conceal" has the idea of withholding information that is confidential or damaging. One that does not gossip is "faithful" and loyal with his words to his friends.

Even if someone has given me a green light to share with a few people, the strict guideline I must operate on is whether or not that person is part of the solution. If not, I need to be faithful to the person that gave me the information and be quiet. It's true, if someone will talk about others to me, they will talk about me to others.

As a pastor I am often in the middle of messy situations that involve very sensitive information. There are things that I will take to my grave that have been shared with me in confidence. Even in our families, we know things about our parents, children, or siblings that never needs to be repeated. These are important times to be quiet! May we not be talebearers but faithful to those that have confided in us.

ACTION POINT: Purpose to be loyal to the person that is absent in a conversation.

—*Rick Johnson*

TAP OUT!

Scripture Reading—Jude 9

*"Yet Michael the archangel, when contending with the devil
he disputed about the body of Moses, durst not bring against him
a railing accusation, but said, The Lord rebuke thee."*

Our family travels America in evangelism. As you would expect, we see a lot of different people, places, and things. We see a lot of "fads" when it comes to styles of clothing in different parts of the country. One very common piece of clothing we see is shirts containing the word "Tapout." What does that mean?

The term comes from combat sports. It's a term for yielding to the opponent, resulting in an immediate defeat. When a player "taps out" by tapping his hand on the floor or his opponent, he is admitting that he cannot continue to fight. It's an act of submission to a stronger opponent.

Christians can be good fighters. But there are times when they need to understand that they are "out of their league." They are no match for Satan, and when he is harassing them, God may be waiting for them to "tap out" and submit to Him before He steps in to deliver them. "Submit yourselves therefore to God. Resist the devil, and he will flee from you" (James 4:7).

When we humbly surrender ourselves to God, He gives us the strength and grace we need to resist. "But he giveth more grace. Wherefore he saith, God resisteth the proud, but giveth grace to the humble" (James 4:6).

Admitting defeat is humbling, but it can also save your life. "Let go, and let God," someone once said. Are you struggling with getting victory over the Devil? Maybe it's time for you to "tap out" and allow One that is mightier than you to deliver you.

ACTION POINT: Search the Scriptures to find characters that realized their enemy was too strong for them, and see how God delivered them when they yielded to Him.

—Paul Miller

FEBRUARY 19
How to Tell Who is Spiritual

Scripture Reading—Luke 18:14
"I tell you, this man went down to his house justified rather than the other: for every one that exalteth himself shall be abased; and he that humbleth himself shall be exalted."

How do you tell who is really spiritual and who is not? Many people do good things, such as helping their neighbors, giving to the poor, or providing for their families. Others will go to church, say their prayers, preach the Word, or try to get others to follow the Bible. However, a person can do all these things and still be totally unspiritual.

Jesus told the story, probably based on a real incident, of two men. One of those men looked spiritual on the outside. People would recognize his good deeds and religious activities. The other man would be despised and hated for who he was and what he had done. But something each of these two men did caught the eye and heart of Jesus. Notice these two men in Luke 18:9–14.

First, there was the Pharisee. In the Temple, he thanked God he was not like the other man. He boasted to God of how good he was based on the things that he had done. He was not an extortioner, unjust, or an adulterer. He reminded God that he fasted two days a week and that he gave tithes of his income and possessions (v. 11–12).

Second, there was a publican. This man stood a good distance away, not feeling worthy to be close to God in worship. He would not even lift up his head toward Heaven and smote his chest with his hand saying, "God be merciful to me a sinner" (v. 13).

The contrast could not be clearer. One was filled with pride. One was filled with humility, confessing his need for mercy and forgiveness. Jesus points out that the religious Pharisee did not get mercy, but the hated publican was justified before God because of his heart (v. 14). In the eyes of Jesus, who was the most spiritual?

PONDER: What does Jesus see when He looks at our hearts? Does he see people who brag about how good they are? Does He see people who think they are better than everybody else? Does He see a family that looks down their nose at another family in the church who does not measure up? What does Jesus see?

—James Stallard

FEBRUARY 20
IT'S GOING TO BE A GOOD DAY

Scripture Reading—Ps. 63:1
"Early will I seek thee."

What makes you think it's going to be a bad day? Well, you might think it's going to be a bad day:

• if you jump out of bed fifteen minutes before your alarm goes off only to realize that the electricity went out for two hours during the night.

• if you put a whole handful of vitamins in your mouth and then realize that you forgot to get a drink of water to wash them down.

• if you sprayed on what you thought was deodorant only to realize that you just used the hair spray.

• if you wake up and your braces are locked together.

• if you extend your arm to pull on your shirt over your head and your fingers get smacked by the ceiling fan spinning above your head.

OK, that's enough! Let's face it—sometimes it's tough to start the day off right. And yet the truth is that the way you start the day often determines not only how you will end the day, but also how the hours in between will go.

Unfortunately, bad things do happen on good days. You can't always eliminate bad things, or even control bad things, but you can be prepared when they come.

A good start is key to a good day. The Psalmist in our text was learning this great truth. That is why he used the word "early" to describe when he would seek the Lord. His personal meeting with God was something that occurred early every day.

George Müller wrote: "It has pleased the Lord to teach me a truth, the benefit of which I have not lost for more than fourteen years. The point is this: I saw more clearly than ever that the first, great, and primary business to which I ought to attend every day was to have my soul happy in the Lord."

ACTION POINT: Have each person tell what time he or she gets up in the morning. Who are the "morning people" in your house? List reasons why "getting up" can be hard.

—*Tom Palmer*

FEBRUARY 21
OUR KNOW-IT-ALL GOD

Scripture Reading—Ps. 139:3
"Thou compassest my path and my lying down,
and art acquainted with all my ways."

Ron Hamilton wrote a unique song with the strange title "They Got eyes," which says:

"They got their idols, Idols of silver, idols of gold. all them idols is lifeless and cold. They got hands, but they cannot feel; They got feet, but they cannot walk. They got ears, but they cannot hear. They got eyes, but they cannot see; They got mouths, but they cannot speak. They got noses, but they cannot smell; but my God do whatever He please."

Think of it! Idols have eyes, ears, and mouths, but they cannot see, hear, or speak! This analogy comes directly from Psalm 115:1–9. Contrast the God of Heaven with the idols of the heathen: "The eyes of the LORD are in every place, beholding the evil and the good" (Pro. 15:3). When Cain murdered Abel, he learned that nothing escapes the gaze of God or the ear of the Almighty. God confronted the murderer by asking, "Where is Abel thy brother? . . . What hast thou done? the voice of thy brother's blood crieth unto me from the ground" (Gen. 4:9, 10).

King David, trying to cover up his adultery, had come to the realization that God sees, hears, and knows all. In Psalm 139, he wrote, "Thou knowest my downsitting and mine uprising [when I sit down and get up], thou understandest my thought afar off. Thou compassest my path [to encircle, as you do with a compass in geometry class] and my lying down, and art acquainted with all my ways. For there is not a word in my tongue, but, lo, O LORD, thou knowest it altogether" (vv. 2–4).

The writer of Hebrews declared, "Neither is there any creature that is not manifest in his sight: but all things are naked and opened unto the eyes of him with whom we have to do" (4:13).

Your God **sees** what you do, **hears** what you say, and **knows** what you think. In light of that fact, how ought you to live? "For God shall bring every work into judgment, with every secret thing, whether it be good, or whether it be evil" (Eccl. 12:14).

PONDER: Nothing escapes the eyes and ears of God: Live life accordingly!

—Rich Tozour

FEBRUARY 22
THE FATHER'S HEART

Scripture Reading—Mal. 4:6
*"And he shall turn the heart of the fathers to the children,
and the heart of the children to their fathers."*

It doesn't snow much in Alabama, but if it does it is even less likely that we would get a measurable amount of snow. One winter we did have a large snowstorm for our area. My father and I went to the store and took along my two oldest sons, who were seven and nine years old at the time.

When we returned home, my father led the way up to our house and held the hands of my two boys, his grandsons. As I followed carrying the groceries, I noticed something and lagged behind them. Perhaps it was because I have always been sentimental, but what I saw spoke deeply to me. There in the snow were the big footprints of my father and on each side of him the small footprints of my sons.

I came alongside of where my boys had walked and placed my own footprint. I thought about how quickly life was passing by. Here I was with my two oldest children and my father, all of us spending time together doing something rather mundane. I paused there and asked the Lord to help me to be a godly dad and to have the same kind of influence on my children that Mom and Dad had on me.

A meaningful legacy is not haphazard, but very intentional. The Scripture above emphasizes that the heart of the father must turn to his children first. The good news is that the same verse says that it is God that turns the heart of the father. His grace not only gives us a desire to do right, but also enables us to do so.

Are you strategically engaged with your children and grandchildren in leaving a godly legacy? God puts the burden upon the father, not the children, to take the first step. Give them your heart, and they will give you theirs.

ACTION POINT: Parents, make a list of key areas you want to pass on to your children. Share with your children some ways your parents impacted your life.

—*Rick Johnson*

FEBRUARY 23
THE GLORY OF GOD IN THE HEAVENS

Scripture Reading—Ps. 19:1
"The heavens declare the glory of God."

If men want to know how great God is, all they have to do is look up. There is no such thing as "Mother Nature," but there is a "Father God." To look up is to see His greatness and glory of God, for "the heavens declare the glory of God; and the firmament sheweth his handywork" (Ps. 19:1).

The "heavens" and the "firmament" refer to what we see when we look up. God created the sun, moon, and stars on the fourth day of creation (Gen. 1:14–19). Ever since then, man has been looking up into the sky and seeing the wonders of the Creator.

God pointed out this glory to a man named Abram, who would later be called Abraham. The Bible says that God "brought him forth abroad, and said, Look now toward heaven, and tell the stars, if thou be able to number them: and he said unto him, So shall thy seed be" (Gen. 15:5). Abram believed what God said when He showed him the glory in the heavens. David, the human author of Psalm 19, certainly pondered these glories as he watched his father's sheep at night.

Many years ago while I was studying for the ministry I stayed at a farm with open fields. Getting out of my car one night after church, I saw an amazing sight. The entire field, as far as I could see, was filled with the light of thousands of lightning bugs! I was awestruck! Then I looked up into the night sky and became overcome with emotion at the sight I saw.

It was a clear night, and the stars of the Milky Way were out in all their fullness. I thought about how great a God I had and how he made all that was around me. Then I thought of His care for me, an undeserving sinner. The glory in the heavens added a little bit more surrender to my life that night. Perhaps it is what the Lord intended for both you and me.

ACTION POINT: Plan a night to go out and view the moon and stars through a telescope and consider the truths of Psalm 19.

—*James Stallard*

FEBRUARY 24
SPECTATOR OR PARTICIPATOR?

Scripture Reading—Rom. 12:2
"Present your bodies a living sacrifice, holy, acceptable unto God,
which is your reasonable service."

Having been in a football stadium before, I am well aware of the fact that there are many types of people who attend football games. For example, there are the spectators who simply come to watch what is happening on the field. Sitting in the announcers' booth are the commentators who talk about what is happening on the field. Near the stands are the cheerleaders who get excited about what is happening on the field. On the sidelines are the coaches who always know what should be happening on the field. And finally around the field are the referees who always know when something goes wrong on the field.

The interesting thing is that none of these people ever make a play on the field. Spectators never make a tackle, commentators never catch a pass, cheerleaders never recover a fumble, coaches never score a touchdown, and referees never make a first down. Though there may be 100,000 people attending the game, a very small group of individuals known as the players does all of these things. Players are unique in that they are there to do something to impact the game itself.

Having grown up and lived my life in the church, it seems to me that the Church is filled with a lot of people who just want to "be there." They like to see what God is doing, and they talk about it and even get excited about it. Of course they always know what should be happening, and they know when something happens that is not right. The problem, however, is that they never do anything. Those who really do make a difference for God are those who have decided that they will do something for God. Difference-makers are participators who impact the work of God by doing something for God.

ACTION POINT: Discuss one new thing that each member of your family could do at your church to make it a better place. Then determine to do it!

—*Tom Palmer*

THE CERTAINTY OF HIS COMING

Scripture Reading—John 14:3
"I will come again, and receive you unto myself."

From television, radio, newspapers, Internet, and even the church, we hear doomsday predictions and dire warnings. In this age of terrorism and nuclear weapons, we live on the cusp of a major catastrophe. To be afraid is practically our national pastime.

But the Bible declares there is hope that transcends all political chaos, economic troubles, marriage difficulties and family distress. Jesus did warn of a time when men's hearts would be failing them for fear (Luke 21:26), but God has promised that He will intervene in the affairs of this planet and will ultimately remove all fear.

In John 14:3 the Lord Jesus proclaimed, "And if I go to prepare a place for you, I will come again, and receive you unto myself; that where I am, there ye may be also." He is not referring to coming for the believer at the time of death, but rather to the time when He physically comes again at the end of the age.

During World War II, when he was forced to flee the Philippines because of the advancing Japanese armies, General Douglas MacArthur promised, "I will return." Three years later he fulfilled that promise as we see in the famous picture of him wading ashore. He came declaring, "I have returned."

A Bible teacher named Mark Cambron once stated that one out of every twenty-five verses in the New Testament refers to the Second Coming of Christ. With that much testimony, we can know that God means business. Jesus will return as He promised!

Perhaps we are on the verge of an age of trouble warned of in times past. But, for the believer, these troubled times should not be cause for alarm or fear. Our faith should be encouraged because we know that the "blessed hope" (Titus 2:13) of the soon return of Jesus for us is on the horizon.

Cannot the Lord Who will bring all this to pass also help you through any crisis you are facing today? Cannot the One Who will come again help you through your time of sadness or despair? Yes, walking in the light of this truth will give us faith for our fears!

SONG: Sing the chorus of "The King is Coming."

—*James Stallard*

FEBRUARY 26
THE BOUNDARY OF PRAYER

Scripture Reading—1 Sam. 1:11
"Then I will give him unto the LORD all the days of his life."

When our children were born, we gave them to the Lord. I remember dedicating them to Him the very moment I held them. Consecration is the idea of taking your hands off of something. It isn't a formal dedication of something as much as releasing that which has already been dedicated. It is the recognition that something belongs to God in a peculiar way.

For example, the tithe is holy unto the Lord (Lev. 27:30). We take our hands off of it as it is consecrated unto the Lord. We don't give our tithe as much as we return it. It all belongs to God, but the tithe belongs to God in a peculiar, special sense. God has set a boundary around it.

Children are God's gifts to us (Ps. 127:3). Before our children were even born, and to this day as they are adults, we are mindful that we as parents are but stewards of God's gifts. One of the best examples of this is when Hannah dedicated Samuel to the Lord. I believe Samuel served the Lord because of what his mother did.

Here is an important principle: parents cannot establish every boundary for their children. This is one reason why we commit our children to the Lord—that they might serve Him the rest of their days. One of the saddest things to see is a teenager that has been consecrated to God and, yet, lives without regard to the boundaries in which he or she was trained.

My parents loved me, sacrificed for me, and taught me God's Word. How dare I walk away from their investment! A Chinese Proverb says, "A child's life is like a piece of paper on which every person makes a mark." As parents we had better make sure that we are making the right marks and the most marks on our children's lives!

ACTION POINT: Parents, tell your children or grandchildren how you have dedicated them to the Lord. If you have not dedicated them to Him, do so now.

—*Rick Johnson*

FEBRUARY 27
THE BOUNDARY OF GOD'S WORD
Scripture Reading—2 Tim. 3:14, 15
"But continue thou in the things which thou hast learned and hast been assured of, knowing of whom thou hast learned them; and that from a child thou hast known the holy scriptures, which are able to make thee wise unto salvation through faith which is in Christ Jesus."

Boundaries are convictions we set up to help us stay true to our Lord. It is vital that the source of these convictions be God's Word. If not, we will waver from them.

It was Timothy's mother and grandmother that taught him the Bible, and the result was that he developed some basic operating values for his life. Jack Hudson said, "Courage comes from convictions, and convictions come from the Word of God."

We don't hear the word "conviction" much anymore. Though it is not a biblical term, the concept certainly is (Pro. 22:28; 2 Tim. 3:14). It is important to have convictions that are biblical. One of the key characteristics of a conviction is that it is consistent in your life. If it is not practiced faithfully, it is not a personal conviction, but a preference.

Someone said, "A conviction is not just an idea that you possess; it is an idea that possesses you." It seems that each generation has fewer and fewer convictions about right and wrong.

John Phillips accurately describes the process: "The first generation has the conviction; the second generation has the belief and doesn't have to pay the price of the first generation; the third generation only has an opinion."

Timothy's convictions began to be developed as a child (2 Tim. 3:15). This shows the importance of beginning at an early age to establish boundaries and convictions for our children.

Are you moving the biblical landmarks your parents have established? I have noted the most common areas where the boundaries are compromised are in the areas of entertainment, dress, and music. The boundary of convictions in each of these is given in the Word of God. We should note them and purpose to follow them with the Lord's help. The better you know the Word of God, the more solid your convictions will be.

ACTION POINT: Read Proverbs 6 and take note of the landmarks God gives in this chapter.

—Rick Johnson

FEBRUARY 28
TIME ALONE WITH GOD
AND DISCIPLINE

Scripture Reading—Matt. 6:6
"Pray to thy Father which is in secret."

A great pianist was asked about his practice routine. He said, "If I miss one day, only I know; if I miss two days, my friends and family know; but if I miss three days, the world will know." The same is true of our time alone with the Lord. When neglected it begins to tell on us in our actions and attitude.

Discipline is required for our time with God. Jesus was intentional about it; it was crucial to Him (Luke 5:16). It was something that no one else could do for Him. He had to do it for Himself. The same is true for us.

Even a casual reading of the Gospels shows the pattern of Christ was to pull away from the crowds to a quiet place to spend time with His Father (Matt. 14:13; Mark 1:35; Mark 6:31, 32; Luke 4:42; Luke 9:10, 18; John 6:15).

God's plan is that you have a private place dedicated to seeking Him (Matt. 6:5, 6). Our Lord favored the mountains to be alone (Matt. 14:23; Mark 6:46; Luke 6:12). The place is not as important as the consistency of doing so. Jesus' disciples were aware of Christ's secret places to pray (Luke 11:1; Luke 22:41; John 18:2).

Do you have a time alone with the Lord? A place where you meet Him? What are the things you do in that time? Here are some suggestions to get you started: time in God's Word (reading, memorizing, meditating), confession of sins, worship (contemplate the attributes of God), thanksgiving, and prayer. This is a simple list, but it will provide reality and power to your walk with the Lord.

A missionary taught his converts the value of time alone with God. Soon there were worn trails from their huts going to places in the jungle to pray and seek God's face. Whenever one began to neglect their time with God, a friend would approach them and say, "Brother, grass is growing on your path."

ACTION POINT: Purpose to daily withdraw to a quiet place and have a meaningful time alone with the Lord.

—Rick Johnson

FEBRUARY 29
WHEN YOU WANT TO CRITICIZE

Scripture Reading—James 3:8
"The tongue . . . is an unruly evil, full of deadly poison."

There is a need in all of us for constructive criticism. Without it athletes would not improve, students would be mediocre, and artists and musicians would not reach their potential. But there is a destructive criticism designed to express displeasure rather than to build and help.

Someone wrote, "The unfortunate thing about constructive criticism is that nobody really appreciates it as much as the one who's giving it." One of my mentors in school, J.R. Faulkner, said about criticism, "If you want to say it, you probably ought not to do so; but if you don't want to say it, you probably ought to say it."

An environment of constant criticism is never a good place to be, especially when it is in the home. Fathers tend to be more critical of their children than mothers. It usually stems from a good motive, as they want them to be successful. So they push them hard. We must be cautious though, as a steady dose of criticism doesn't work over the long haul.

We pull away from those that criticize us over and again. Who enjoys being verbally punched, feeling beaten and bruised by the words of another person time and time again? When a child pulls away from his father or mother, he or she cannot be helped by their wisdom and insight.

To criticize is "to find fault, to judge unfavorably or harshly." The focus is on finding fault rather than seeing what is good and encouraging.

As a snake's venom can do great damage and even cause death, so critical words do great damage and kill the good reputation of other people (James 3:8). However, the fangs of a snake cannot inject poison when its mouth is shut. How much less destruction and hurt would we do if we just kept our mouths shut when we want to criticize?

PONDER: Do you excuse critical words in the guise of being helpful or that it is just part of your personality?

—Rick Johnson

MARCH 1
A DIFFERENT KIND OF REQUEST

Scripture Reading—Matt. 6:13
"And lead us not into temptation, but deliver us from evil."

I have been to many prayer meetings, and I have heard many prayer requests shared. Interestingly enough, most requests involve physical needs, such as illnesses or injuries or for those who are having medical tests or surgeries. Then there are those requests that involve jobs, travelling, vehicles, money, and other material needs that people have. As it ends up, most—if not all—of the requests focus on either physical or material needs.

It is only on rare occasions that you hear a request that involves the spiritual realm of life. Imagine someone raising their hand to ask for prayer because they were discouraged and needed encouragement, or they were defeated and needed victory. It might even seem more shocking if someone said, "I am having a real hard time with temptation and sin. Will each of you pray that I will not continue to live in my sin?" Though that may seem out of the ordinary, that is exactly what Jesus was teaching us to pray about. Though maybe more of a personal request than a public request, He was emphasizing the need to ask God for protection from sin. There is certainly nothing wrong with talking to God about our physical condition, but in the same way it is important to talk to God about our spiritual condition.

The Bible makes it clear that God will never tempt any man with evil (James 1:13). Rather, in answer to prayer, there are times when God can blind and deafen people that they might not see or hear that which is sinful. In Psalm 19:13 David prayed that God would keep him from presumptuous sins that they might not have dominion over him. You too can ask God to do the same thing for you. I am certain that God loves to hear and answer that kind of a prayer.

ACTION POINT: Read 1 Chronicles 4:9, 10 and take note of the fourth prayer request that Jabez offered. What did God do in response to this request?

—*Tom Palmer*

MARCH 2
MAKING A LASTING IMPRESSION

Scripture Reading—Deut. 4:5
"Behold, I have taught you statutes and judgments,
even as the LORD my God commanded me,
that ye should do so in the land whither ye go to possess it."

My parents taught me some valuable truths that I still remember. I am very grateful for their teaching. However, what changed my life weren't their words, but their actions. Howard Hendricks wrote, "You impress people at a distance, but you impact them up close."

As a young teenager I wasn't reading my Bible regularly. One night I walked down the hall to my room and saw my father lying in bed on his side reading the Bible with great attention. He faithfully did this, and it impacted my life.

I came under conviction because of my failure to read the Bible. It wasn't the result of a lecture from Dad, but his personal example. I saw that it was highly valued to him, and it should be to me also.

We do not reproduce what we want, but what we are. A legacy of children that walk with the Lord is not as much the result of what we say, but what we do.

Someone said, "Every father should remember that one day his son will follow his example instead of his advice." Are you expecting those under your authority to follow your advice instead of your example? They will not do so long-term. They will be influenced more by what you are and what you do than by what you say.

Francis Bacon said, "He that gives good advice builds with one hand; he that gives good counsel and example, builds with both; but he that gives good admonition and bad example, builds with one hand and pulls down with the other."

Applying what we hear taught not only changes our life but also affects those that watch us. Remember—what parents do in moderation, children will excuse in excess. The best teaching is not our words, but our actions.

ACTION POINT: Read Deuteronomy 4:5–8 and list the benefits of the person that obeys God's Word. What area in your life needs strengthening or changing through heartfelt repentance?

—Rick Johnson

MARCH 3
THE MOST IMPORTANT RESOURCE IN YOUR HOME

Scripture Reading—Ps. 90:12
"So teach us to number our days,
that we may apply our hearts unto wisdom."

I was talking to a pastor who wanted to ask me a question. He asked me how my father, who was also a pastor, found time for his family while we were growing up. I knew this was important to him because this man was pastoring his first church and had two teenage sons. In all sincerity I never hesitated, but simply said, "My father never did find time—he made time."

I have come to believe that we will always have time for what is important in our lives. It is amazing that we live in the 21st century when we have more time-saving devices, and yet the one thing that nobody seems to have is time. Our culture has been handicapped by busyness. When people become too busy, relationships are the first things to suffer, and there is nowhere where this is more evident than in the family.

Then of course there is always the common explanation: "Well, we don't get a quantity of time, but the time we do get is quality." That sounds fine, but in reality both kinds of time are desperately needed if we are going to build relationships that are meaningful.

Many of the things that consume our time are good things, but even good things can keep us from the best things. I have talked to dads, including pastors, who have told me that they live with great regrets. They regret that when their children were growing up, they were always too busy with jobs, and even ministries, to truly give of themselves to their families. While you still have time, make it count. There will always be just 24 hours in a day, so make sure that you are using those hours wisely. I have never met a dad who regretted that he gave too much time to his family.

ACTION POINT: Couples, plan a date—just you two. Families, plan a family night—just you and yours. Play, talk, laugh. Enjoy being together.

—*Tom Palmer*

MARCH 4
WHO'S THE REAL ENEMY HERE?

Scripture Reading—Eph. 4:29
"Let no corrupt communication proceed out of your mouth,
but that which is good to the use of edifying, that it may
minister grace unto the hearers."

"Ready, aim, FIRE!" How many battles in history have been started with those words? We may never know. As hard as it must be to go and fight a war, just think about how dangerous it would be if you didn't know who your enemy was! Who do you shoot at? And even more importantly, who will be shooting at you? One thing is for sure, we need to know who our enemy is. Paul said, "For we wrestle not against flesh and blood, but against principalities, against powers, against the rulers of the darkness of this world, against spiritual wickedness in high places" (Eph. 6:12). With these words he makes it clear that our enemy isn't a person (flesh and blood), and our battle isn't physical, but spiritual.

In our verse for today, there are two kinds of "communication" mentioned—one kind that I should never use when talking to people, and another kind that I need to use every time I open my mouth.

Corrupt communication is when I use words that tear down a person's character (like name-calling, Matt. 5:21, 22), or words that tear them down and even hinder their growth (James 3:5–12). These are words that go around the real issues and muddy the water. These are the kinds of words that grieve the Holy Spirit. God doesn't want me to use any of these kinds of words to hurt others.

But on the other hand I should use the kind of words that are both edifying and encouraging (Eph. 4:15, 29). I want to build up my family and friends with my words. One way I can do this is by really watching what I say to them. Another way is to use my words to solve problems, not to cause them.

I need to ask the Lord to help me to always use *gracious words*.

DISCUSS: What kinds of words cause problems, and what kind of words help heal problems?

—*Joe Henson*

MARCH 5
FOCUS MAKES A DIFFERENCE

Scripture Reading—Matt. 22:37, 38
"Thou shalt love the Lord thy God with all thy heart, and with all thy soul, and with all thy mind. This is the first and great commandment."

What is the focus that will result in influencing our children to live godly lives? The word "focus" means the central point of an activity that is given careful attention.

This is crucial because God gives us the focus for our own heart and our legacy. It is not optional. The ultimate goal of our example and teaching is to see those that follow us have a heart that loves God. This means more than having them regurgitate details and facts. The focus is on loving and knowing God personally, not just knowing about God.

Believers in the Lord Jesus Christ must take heed of the tendency to embrace a doctrinal truth without applying and obeying it. The application must not stop with giving mental assent to our beliefs, but must be allowed to touch our hearts.

God's concern is that we not only know about Him factually but also that we love Him deeply and personally. This is the ultimate end of our obedience. "Now the end of the commandment is charity out of a pure heart, and of a good conscience, and of faith unfeigned" (1 Tim. 1:5).

When my children were very young, a faithful and dear man in our church would occasionally approach me and encourage me in my parenting. His words were always the same, "Rick, keep doing what you are doing with your children; teach them to love God. I lost my children to the world even though they grew up in church. They knew about God, but they didn't love Him. If I had it to do over again, I would focus on their hearts."

It is not enough to be a good example and to teach our children. We must also have the correct focus on their hearts that they might love the Lord.

ACTION POINT: What are some things we focus on that are good but can substitute for the best (loving God)? Why is it easy to do this sometimes?

—*Rick Johnson*

MARCH 6
MIRRORS DON'T LIE

Scripture Reading—James 1:23, 24
"For if any be a hearer of the word, and not a doer, he is like unto a man beholding his natural face in a glass: For he beholdeth himself, and goeth his way, and straightway forgetteth what manner of man he was."

I can't say that I really love mirrors. I suppose that is because I don't always like what I see in the mirror. When I see the dribble of spaghetti sauce on my white shirt or the wrinkles in the skin on my face, I don't really like what I see, but it is the truth. Mirrors have a way of "telling it like it is" so that necessary changes can be made for good.

A mirror can help us learn a great lesson about obedience. In our verse for today, James is talking about "hearers" and "doers" of the Word of God. A "hearer" is the person who "looks into the perfect law of liberty" (James 1:25) and sees himself as he really is. However, simply looking really does not change anything. At this point it is necessary to be "not a forgetful hearer, but a doer" who acts upon what he has seen.

I like to have jelly on my toast for breakfast. Suppose I have just finished my breakfast, and I take a look in the mirror only to find that grape jelly is smeared all over my face. It would be utterly foolish to head out the door singing "Heigh ho! Heigh ho! It's off to work I go" while having done nothing to address my disgusting appearance. As James says, to do so would be "deceiving your own self" (James 1:22).

There are times when God's Word shows us things about ourselves that must be changed. It may be an attitude, our language, or maybe even a specific area of sin. "Hearers" only hear, but "doers" actually do something about what God says, and their lives are much better because of their obedience.

ACTION POINT: Using Ephesians 4:25–31 as a mirror, do you see anything that needs to be changed in your life? If so—do it!

—Tom Palmer

MARCH 7
WHAT DO YOU WANT?

Scripture Reading—2 Kings 2:9
"Elijah said unto Elisha, Ask what I shall do for thee,
before I be taken away from thee. And Elisha said, I pray thee,
let a double portion of thy spirit be upon me."

What is your heart's desire? What do you really want? If Elijah asked what he could do for you, what would you say? Would your answer be to have a better-paying job? To live closer to family? To have a new video game?

While there is nothing wrong with these particular desires or wants, a spiritual person's greatest desire will involve his or her relationship with the Lord. Elisha was a spiritual person and evidenced this by his spiritual desire.

Elisha wanted what the man of God, Elijah, had—and even more! Elisha wanted the spiritual blessings of God upon His life. What are some spiritual blessings that God wants you to have and know?

- **Peace** that exists beyond the comprehension of present circumstances.
- **Love** for the lost world and those that we find to be unlovely.
- **Joy** given by the Lord and unexplainable.
- **Power** to live victoriously over sin and defeat.

A benefit of living life on the spiritual plane is that you can live without regret! I have met Christians who on occasions expressed regret for wrong or sinful choices they've made. I've heard many remorsefully say, "I wish I never would have snuck behind my parents' back." Or, "I wish I never would have taken that first drink of alcohol." Another would say, "I wish I never would have watched that bedroom scene on TV." Sin brings deep regret. A spiritual person will never regret being sold out to God.

PONDER: "Spirituality is not something that can be compared but something that is absolute." This means, that one is either a spiritual person and spiritually minded right now or is in need of getting right with the Lord and being filled with the Holy Spirit. What is your condition right now?

—*Billy Ingram*

MARCH 8
THE KEY TO FUTURE SUCCESS

Scripture Reading—Josh. 1:8
"This book of the law . . . thou shalt meditate therein day and night . . .
and then thou shalt have good success."

What makes a person successful? In the business world, a man can make a ton of money and be seen as successful. In the education world, a person can earn the highest degree in his or her field and be viewed as a success. In the sports world, someone can become an elite athlete, meaning a success in his or her sport.

But what makes a person successful spiritually? The text of Joshua 1:8 give us a direct statement about success in the spiritual realm. Joshua tells us: "This book of the law shall not depart out of thy mouth; but thou shalt *meditate* therein day and night, that thou mayest observe *to do* according to all that is written therein: for then thou shalt make thy way *prosperous*, and then thou shalt have *good success*" (emphasis added).

The key words have been put in italics and give us the right understanding. If we are to be successful, we must (1) meditate on the law of God, (2) obey what we observe through our meditation, and (3) the result will be spiritual prosperity and success.

To meditate upon God's Word includes the idea of thinking it over. This requires study (2 Tim. 2:15) and applying what we learn from our study (2 Tim. 3:16, 17). Memorizing Scripture is a great step to take as we study. But we must go beyond just reciting verses. We must ponder what God is saying in them. God can then give us wisdom on how to apply it to our lives.

Do you have temptations that haunt you continually? Then meditate upon God's Word (1 Cor. 10:13). Do you have a desire to lead someone to Jesus? Then meditate on scriptures that deal with prayer and witnessing (John 4:35–38; 15:16). Do you struggle with assurance of salvation? Then memorize and study passages of the Bible that deal with that topic (Rom. 8:35–39).

Our success may come in direct proportion to how much or how well we meditate upon God's Word. Let's commit ourselves to keep this as a priority in our lives each and every day.

ACTION POINT: Meditate upon Psalm 119 for future success.

—James Stallard

MARCH 9
ALL GIVE SOME, SOME GIVE ALL

Scripture Reading—2 Cor. 12:15
"I will very gladly spend and be spent for you."

I recently found this quote by George Bernard Shaw, which has been a great challenge to my life as a servant of God:

"This is the true joy in life—being used for a purpose recognized by yourself as a mighty one; being thoroughly worn out before you are thrown on the scrap heap; being a force of nature instead of a feverish selfish little clod of ailments and grievances complaining that the world will not devote itself to making you happy."

I love this challenge because it reminds me of what is really worth living for. Living for self does not bring joy, satisfaction, and fulfillment. These can only be experienced by living the invested life, which involves living for a cause greater than myself.

Jim Elliot only lived to be 29 years of age. In 1956, he and four other missionary men were martyred on a sandy beach in South America. Yet eight years before in 1948, Jim had written these words, "God I pray Thee, light these idle sticks of my life, and may I burn out for Thee. Consume my life, my God, for it is Thine. I seek not a long life, but a full one, like you Lord Jesus." Some might assume that Jim wasted his life, and yet only eternity will reveal the results and rewards of these invested lives. As reports came back of the deaths of the five men, more than 400 young people in Christian colleges surrendered to missions and went around the world with the Gospel. No doubt there will be multitudes of people in Heaven because of the efforts of these missionaries and the investment of the five men who gave their lives in 1956. Jim Elliot always said, "He is no fool who gives what he cannot keep to gain what he cannot lose."

ACTION POINT: Take a few minutes and pray for a missionary you know who is somewhere in the world sharing the Gospel. Write them a note and let them know they are appreciated and that you are praying for them.

—Tom Palmer

MARCH 10
LAZINESS AND SPIRITUAL MEDIOCRITY

Scripture Reading—Pro. 22:29
"A man diligent in his business . . . shall stand before kings."

God will not do for you what you can do for yourself, and natural gifts and opportunities alone will only get you so far. You must give your best. Dr. Bob Jones, Sr. said, "To do less than your best is sin."

A lazy person doesn't value preparation. Caring for the little things pays off in big ways later. This is especially difficult for a talented person. They are able to do the job, but do not reach their potential because of laziness. Part of being diligent is doing the work behind the scenes that no one sees. Some attribute to connections and talent what is really a matter of preparing when no one is looking (Pro. 6:6–8).

Here's the principle: failing to be diligent at a task will result in mediocrity. This is one of the common themes in the book of Proverbs (10:4; 12:24; 13:4; 20:4). The principle of promoting those that are diligent is mentioned throughout the Bible (1 Kings 11:28; Eccl. 9:10; Matt. 25:21). Laziness results in mediocrity; work results in God's blessing.

Consistently delivering the goods with your best effort and excellence is a hallmark of diligence. God directs, promotes, and uses busy, hard-working people. Lazy people languish in mediocrity.

One of the key influences in my life has been a Bible teacher from my college days named Dr. Wymal Porter. He is gifted, interesting, practical, and a blessing to hear as he preaches and teaches. I'm sure people listen to him and want the same knowledge he has. He paid a steep price for it—hours reading, digging, researching, and writing. It is no accident that he has made an impact on thousands. There was nothing mediocre about his unnoticed preparation.

Just as interest compounds, so does giving your best over time. One day you wake up and are surprised at the blessings of God.

A great piano player was approached by a fan, "I'd give my life to be able to play like you do." The pianist said, "That's what it will cost you."

PONDER: Are you lazy in spiritual disciplines?

—Rick Johnson

MARCH 11
A TIME FOR GOD

Scripture Reading—Eccl. 3:1
*"To everything there is a season, and a time
to every purpose under the heaven."*

What is time for God? Amidst all the other good things we can make time for, this is a great one to challenge the believer. What does it mean to set a time for God?

It means taking a piece of my time and purposefully placing God and me in it. A time for God and me is when my mind dwells only on Him, His Word, and His works. Loving Him, following Him, seeking Him! A time for God then is not simply doing what we know is required, but willingly giving of our time that is not required. A time for God is a gift for Him that is thought through, planned, and presented just as we set aside time for vacation or work. It is presenting to God, as a New Year's plan, a part of you that exceeds all other plans for the year. That's right—purpose to know your God and His Word better.

A time for God is one that cannot be rivaled by the best of your other joys. It is a time He can say of your heart, "Have you considered my servant _____?" Such a time He will accept and Satan will envy. Time for God must be cultivated like raising a tender plant from seed in early spring. Time for God must be sought out and fought over.

We could describe it as a fasting from all things temporal for a time alone with the eternal—a time to drain away carnal fear and gain a fearful reverence of omnipotence.

So among our church attendance, service, offerings, and sharing with others, let us set time for Him. It is a present worthy of a King that you can unwrap in His presence. It is worth more than all the other gifts we give this year. A time for God is a time to get serious. You cannot purchase this gift but will find it on the shelf of your own heart.

PONDER: Time for God is time for you!

—Steve Rebert

MARCH 12
THE MOST IMPORTANT WORDS IN YOUR HOME

Scripture Reading—1 John 4:7
"Beloved, let us love one another: for love is of God;
and every one that loveth is born of God, and knoweth God."

I still remember well the framed plaque that hung on the kitchen wall in my grandparents' home when I was a boy. It simply said:

"Houses are made of brick and stone,
Homes are made of love alone."

Pity the family that lives in a $500,000 home that is beautifully furnished and incredibly landscaped, but doesn't have the one thing that makes a house a home.

The three simple words, "I love you" are priceless when it comes to creating the atmosphere of a home. If it be true—and it is—that "love is of God" (1 John 4:7) and that "God is love" (1 John 4:8, 16), then the communication of love creates a godly atmosphere in the home.

There is nothing quite like hearing a little child at bedtime whisper, "I wuv you." There is nothing quite like hearing a teenager end a phone call by saying, "Love ya, Dad." There is nothing like hearing your spouse say, "Sweetheart, I really do love you." Statements of love communicate worth and value, care and concern, and above all, a demonstration of Who and what God is all about.

The most deprived child in the world is the child who has never heard a parent say, "I love you." New clothes, new bikes, and new ball gloves can never be equal in value to the reassurance of being loved. When a child or spouse knows that he or she is loved, it builds great security into their lives. Never allow yourself to become too grown up to say, "I love you." These words will ultimately become the glue that will hold your family together for time and eternity. Get in the habit of verbally expressing your love. There will be no spoken words more valuable in your home.

ACTION POINT: Determine that you will express love directly to each member of your family today either in spoken word or in a note.

—Tom Palmer

MARCH 13
DETECTING BURDENS

Scripture Reading—Neh. 4:10
"The strength of the bearers of burdens is decayed."

Some burdens are obvious, and some are not. Though you may not know the details or cause of a burden, you can detect the symptom. It is discouragement.

Discouragement is "being deprived of hope, courage, or confidence." When Nehemiah oversaw the rebuilding of the wall around Jerusalem, it was a massive effort. Thousands of people were involved, and they soon became tired and discouraged.

The Bible says their strength was "decayed." The word means to "waver or stumble because of weak legs." They were fatigued and had become unproductive.

If not dealt with, discouragement can become its own burden. It can lead to depression and cripple your life and ability to be effective for Christ.

Even the best of us get discouraged at times. C.H. Spurgeon, the great English preacher, was prone to depression because of severe physical problems. John Piper writes of Spurgeon, "Approximately one-third of the last twenty-two years of his ministry was spent out of the Tabernacle pulpit, either suffering, or convalescing, or taking precautions against the return of the illness . . . .. For over half his ministry, Spurgeon dealt with ever increasingly recurrent pain in his joints that cut him down from the pulpit and from his labors again and again. The diseases finally took his life at age 57 while he was convalescing in Mentone, France."

One night I called my daughter when she was in college, and she began to weep. She was heavily discouraged. I was 600 miles away but did my best to carry her burden. It was a sweet time of simply sharing the weight of a heavy burden.

When you minister to a discouraged person, you are not only investing in his or her life, but also developing a friendship. If you are lonely, stop complaining that you have no friends and start encouraging those closest to you. We grow close to the people whose burdens we help to carry.

Someone said, "Fellowship is two people on the same side of a burden."

ACTION POINT: Rather than seek someone to carry your burden, find someone with a burden and help to carry it.

—Rick Johnson

MARCH 14
ARE YOU A REBEL IN GOD'S EYES?

Scripture Reading—1 Sam. 15:23
"For rebellion is as the sin of witchcraft,
and stubbornness is as iniquity and idolatry."

Saul was the king over the people of God, and Agag was the king over the enemies of God. Saul was given explicit orders to destroy all of the Amalekites and not to leave any alive, not even their animals. King Saul set out to obey God but only did so partially. He kept the parts of the command that he thought were useful and important. This rationalization of Saul, to be "mostly right with God," is why God classified him as a rebel!

1 Samuel 15:3 tells us what God expected of Saul—to *"utterly destroy all that they have."* God expects absolute surrender and complete obedience. Verse 9, however, tells us that Saul "would *not utterly destroy* them."

God's perspective is that obeying His commands in only a partial way is rebellion. Saul was not a rebel because of what he did, but rather, what he did not do! Saul's reason for not obeying God was fear of what others thought, rather than fearing what God had said (1 Sam. 15:24). Then, when the man of God approached Saul with an opportunity to get right, he only agreed that he had sinned, rather than repenting of his sin.

What might there be in your life that has not been completed? Is there any command of God that has been neglected? Has the prompting of God's Spirit been ignored in any way in your life recently?

Is baptism still being pushed aside? Has church membership been ignored? Are tithes and offerings being withheld? Have you failed to respond in an invitation when the Lord prompted you? Have you ignored the Spirit's leadership to hand out a gospel tract to someone?

Don't look around and wonder where the rebel might be in the room, but ask yourself, "Is there a King Agag in my own life that needs to be utterly destroyed?" If so, deal with the sin and obey God! Don't settle for rebellion when you can have revival!

PONDER: We see Rebellion described as:
• Partial obedience
• Fear of what others think rather than God's Word
• A refusal to get right with God when confronted

—*Billy Ingram*

MARCH 15
WE DON'T KNOW WHAT
WE THINK WE KNOW

Scripture Reading—Pro. 3:5
"And lean not unto thine own understanding."

It is never pleasant to run into a "know-it-all." This kind of person thinks that he knows everything better than anyone else, and he tends to push his opinions on everybody. But this person shows a prideful attitude and needs to consider what God has said to all of us.

Our text for today tells us: "trust in the Lord with all thine heart, and lean not unto thine own understanding." A battle rages within each of our hearts to either trust God or trust our own understanding. The Bible warns us not to trust ourselves but to acknowledge the Lord in everything we do (Pro. 3:5, 6).

There is a natural tendency for each of us to become self-reliant instead of being God-reliant. We see things from our point of view without evaluating whether God's Word agrees with that point of view. This could lead us to make mistakes in our judgment and decide contrary to what God wants.

Sometimes young people do not like to follow their parents' wishes and try to follow their own hearts' desires. The end result can be disastrous. What protection is ignored by following selfish desires? What wisdom will be discarded by claiming selfish wishes for oneself!

History reveals what can happen. Karl Marx wrote the *Communist Manifesto* and established an atheistic philosophy that destroyed the lives of millions of people. Yet, he grew up in a Christian home and rebelled against his parents' teachings.

Charles Darwin was also raised in a strict Christian home, but grew up doubting the faith of his parents and leaned to his own understanding. When his daughter Annie passed away at ten years of age, that was the last straw for his accepting God's Word. He followed his own heart and developed the Theory of Evolution that has been used to deceive and destroy many people's lives for more than 150 years.

The safest and best course of action will always be to trust God instead of ourselves. Remember this truth—we really don't know what we think we know.

PRAYER: Lord, I surrender to your ways instead of my own understanding.

—James Stallard

MARCH 16
ONE DRINK FOR A THIRSTY SOUL

Scripture Reading—John 4:14
"But whosoever drinketh of the water
that I shall give him shall never thirst."

There was nothing about Jesus that was ordinary. Though He was a man, He was also God (John 1:1, 14). He decided to go through Samaria when other Jews would not, for He had an appointment with a woman there. "He must needs go through Samaria" (John 4:4).

John 4 tells of the woman at the well who encountered Jesus. Jesus instructed her that a one-time drink of living water was hers for the taking if she asked (John 4:10). But she was a needy and sinful woman who had to recognize her sin (John 4:11, 12, 16–19). She could drink continually of the physical water from the well and would still leave thirsty (John 4:13). But, she could find what she needed with just one drink of His living water: "But whosoever drinketh [one time] of the water that I shall give him shall never thirst; but the water that I shall give him shall be in him a well of water springing up into everlasting life." (John 4:14 emphasis added).

Later at the Feast of Tabernacles in the Temple, Jesus declared again, "If any man thirst, let him come unto me, and drink. He that believeth on me, as the scripture hath said, out of his belly shall flow rivers of living water" (John 7:37, 38). Yes, Jesus was talking about a drink that would last forever. This should encourage any believer to know that the moment he received Jesus Christ as his Lord and Savior he received eternal life. It lasts forever and can never be lost, diminished, or stolen.

Do you worry about your future? A true believer will never perish (John 10:28). Does God seem far and distant from you? You will never be separated from the love of God (Rom. 8:35–39). Do you feel the world, the flesh, and the Devil pulling at your soul? Remember, every child of God will be kept by the power of God (1 Pet. 1:5). All because of one drink of living water!

PRAYER: Thank you, Father, for allowing me to take that one drink that saves my soul forever.

—James Stallard

Promises Were Designed by God

Scripture Reading—Isa. 7:11
"Ask thee a sign of the LORD thy God."

One of the most remarkable blank check opportunities was issued in the Old Testament to a king named Ahaz: "Ask thee a sign of the LORD thy God; ask it either in the depth, or in the height above" (Isa. 7:11). Even though Ahaz was a wicked king, the Lord offers him a chance for his enemies to be defeated and for Judah to have help from God in their present circumstance. To convince the king, God offers a blank check through the prophet Isaiah. He says, "Ask it as high as you wish; I have signed the check." The sad reality is that the king trusted his own self-made alliances to defeat the enemy, and not God.

I wonder what it would be like to receive a blank check for a great need. Here is the check, fill in the amount, and use it as you will! It has been signed and funds set aside by the issuer. Such a transaction would have a purpose and goal in mind.

An old story shares the simple truth about two men in battle. The one lost track of his friend and later was surprised to see him walking into camp with a prisoner. When he asked his friend where he found his prisoner, the answer came, "The woods are full of them." Similarly we are surrounded with a wood full of the promises of God. We will find no greater offer for present need than the promises of God.

What a realization it is to know God's promises are just—that His promises are backed by the omnipotence of the mighty God we know. Let us go forward with boldness, finding the promise of God that holds blank-check opportunities as we ask for His glory and purpose.

What a promise is to the Bible, a handle is to a suitcase. The handle gives us the point of access. God gave us promises on purpose. Promises access the resources of God's Word! But a check unused is a promise dismissed.

PONDER: What is the last promise you claimed and stood by in believing faith until God answered?

—Steve Rebert

TOUCHED BY THE GLORY OF THE SON

Scripture Reading—Col. 1:27
"Christ in you, the hope of glory."

Bzzzzzzzz. I shut off my alarm and sprang out of bed. I wanted to watch the sunrise on our last day in this mountain home that a generous pastor and his wife had lent us for a week. We had enjoyed the comforts of this spacious house, but one of the biggest blessings was the gorgeous view. It looked out over several mountain ranges—a breathtaking sight!

I arrived by the window a little ahead of the sun. The sky was softly aglow. In the center of my view hung a lone, dark cloud just above the tops of the mountains, shapeless, and gray.

Waiting there, I knew that soon it would all drastically change. I meditated on God's greatness as I looked over this expanse of His creation. Gentle touches of pink lit tiny streaks of cloud. The cloud in the center remained stubbornly gray. Rather ugly, I thought. Then, seconds later, brilliant rosy light washed over it entirely, transforming it from an apparent blemish in the view into a splendid part of a glorious mountain sunrise. As I took in the beauty of this quiet miracle, I felt the Lord's quiet voice saying, "This is what I want to do with you."

That cloud had no light of its own, no inward radiance to share. But when touched by the glory of the sun, it was completely transformed by the power of reflection.

I am often disturbed at the ugliness I find inside myself. It can be discouraging to see what a "low-lying cloud" I am. My ability to be Christlike is limited by my humanity. But God knows what I am. This is why it must be Christ who lives in me. When the love of Christ is shed abroad in my heart, the God-given power of reflection comes into full play. God has not asked me to do the impossible—to be "glorious" on my own. He only asks that I be a reflection of Him, as Christ's life in me transforms me from a sinful human being into an instrument for God's glory.

ACTION POINT: Look up scriptures about the transforming power of "Christ in you."

—Abigail Miller

MARCH 19
No Sleep!

Scripture Reading—Ps. 121:3, 4
"He will not suffer thy foot to be moved: he that keepeth thee will not slumber. Behold, he that keepeth Israel shall neither slumber nor sleep."

Have you ever gone to a birthday party where your friends decided that they were going to stay up all night? Eventually, everyone got tired, and probably most of them fell asleep. God made our bodies in such a way that we have to have sleep in order to function properly. There's no one who can go night after night without sleep.

God never sleeps. He doesn't need to. He is unlike us in that He never grows weary or tired. He is God and doesn't need anything to help Him rule the universe. Sometimes we wonder if God sees things that happen to us or if He cares about the things that are bothering us. In the middle of the night, you may wake up with a bad dream or lay in bed wondering how something is going to turn out.

Did you know that God is working even when you're sleeping? Colossians 1:16, 17 says, "All things were created by him, and for him: And he is before all things, and by him all things consist." In other words, God keeps everything running. He is so powerful that He can still run the universe, keep your heart beating, make the earth rotate, cause the grass to grow, make your body heal itself of a scratch, and blow wind across a lake—all at the same time!

Not only is He working, but also He is watching over you while you sleep. God protects and keeps His children. His eye is always upon you, and He never goes away. David even said in Psalm 139:17, 18 that the number of God's thoughts about us are as many as the sands on the seashore. That's a lot of thoughts. What a comfort when we're scared or afraid of something—God is always thinking about us! He doesn't have to put off your problems until He has more time or energy to help you. He's always ready to help and listen.

ACTION POINT: Since God is holding all things together, think through your day today and talk about how you saw God's presence and protection.

—Aaron Coffey

MARCH 20
NEVER COMPARE YOURSELF
TO THE TASK

Scripture Reading—Num. 13:33
"And there we saw the giants . . .
and we were in our own sight as grasshoppers."

Sometimes what we face will cause us to back away from what we should be doing. The task, the opposition, the enemies seem too large and insurmountable. If we are not careful, what we see will cause us to stop dead in our tracks, and we will refuse to move forward.

The Israelites came to such a place at Kadesh-Barnea where they were just one step away from going into the Promised Land to possess it. The twelve spies came back with a report that frightened them. Joshua and Caleb clung to the promise of God and urged them to continue. But the other ten saw things differently.

To them the people in the Promised Land were strong and lived in walled cities (Num. 13:28). The ten spread their fear to the people by declaring it "a land that eateth up the inhabitants thereof; and all the people that we saw in it are men of a great stature" (Num. 13:32). They viewed them as "giants" and themselves as "grasshoppers" (Num. 13:33).

It is always a mistake to compare ourselves to the task or the enemy that stands in our way. The Apostle Paul reminded the Corinthian Church, "For we dare not make ourselves of the number, or compare ourselves with some that commend themselves: but they, measuring themselves by themselves, and comparing themselves among themselves, are not wise (2 Cor. 10:12).

On April 13, 1970, the Apollo 13 spacecraft was on its way toward the moon for a lunar landing with three American astronauts. But an explosion caused by a faulty fuel cell crippled the ship, and the world feared they would not make it safely back to earth. Thousands of people worked on the problem, and many more prayed. A few days later they landed safely. The task to get them home seemed overwhelming, but everyone did what had to be done.

So, too, the believer who has God on his or her side can overcome any burden, task, opposition, or enemy. Whatever we face will end up looking very small when compared to our God.

DISCUSS: Discuss some obstacles the family is facing right now.

—James Stallard

MARCH 21
UNBELIEF LEADS TO MEDIOCRITY

Scripture Reading—Matt. 13:58
"And he did not many mighty works there because of their unbelief."

We experience God and please Him through faith (Heb. 11:6). Failure to trust Him keeps us from seeing Him do mighty things. Unbelief will keep us in a life of spiritual mediocrity.

Most people have seen God work, but few have seen Him do extraordinary things. It isn't because we don't love Him, but rather that we do not trust Him.

Consider that Israel waited forty years for the Promised Land because of unbelief (Heb. 3:19). On the contrary, God blessed Abraham's faith with a miracle (Rom. 4:19, 20). If your heart is unbelieving, ask God to help your faith (Mark 9:24). He will.

The faith chapter, Hebrews 11, is filled with common people that did great exploits for God. It wasn't because of their talents or connections, but their faith in God's promises. He uses ordinary people in extraordinary ways when they trust Him. What are you asking God for today (Ps. 81:10)?

There are degrees of faith: no faith (Mark 4:40), little faith (Matt. 6:30), great faith (Matt. 8:10), full faith (Acts 11:24). It is our senses that limit our faith (2 Cor. 5:7). Faith rests in God's Word in spite of visible evidence (Heb. 11:1).

When was the last time you had a prayer answered? Are you content to live a mediocre, average life? Is your life mundane? We miss so much because of our unwillingness to take God at His Word.

Remember that the quality of your life is in direct proportion to your faith (Matt. 9:29). Ask the Lord to increase your faith (Luke 17:5), and act upon it by your actions.

One year when our church was working on our upcoming budget, one of our deacons challenged the leaders to establish a faith budget that would allow God to show Himself strong. To be honest I wanted to play it safe. However, I knew he was right and that my unbelief was displeasing to God. We did so, and God has honored it as we have increased it every year—by faith.

MEMORIZE: Psalm 81:10.

—Rick Johnson

MARCH 22
TAKE HEED HOW YOU HEAR

Scripture Reading—Luke 8:18
"Take heed therefore how ye hear."

We often believe that certain things are key for people to hear the message of Bible truth. The temperature in the building needs to be comfortable. The preacher needs to be exciting. The surroundings need to be just right.

In all of this we forget that the early church had no church buildings, thermostats, or even necessarily exciting preaching. There is nothing wrong with any of these things, but the statement by Jesus in Luke 8:18 tells us that the Lord focuses more attention on the hearer's response to the truth.

The key to receive the truth resides in us who listen. "Take heed therefore how ye hear: for whosoever hath, to him shall be given; and whosoever hath not, from him shall be taken even that which he seemeth to have." There are many kinds of hearers, and we should consider what kind we have become.

In the parable of the sower, Jesus gave four kinds of soil that the seed of the Word of God would fall upon—the wayside, stony ground, thorny ground, and good ground (Matt. 13:3–9). They represent the responses of the hearers (Matt. 13:18–23).

In any service at a Bible-preaching church, each person will hear the same preacher, the same message, in the power of the same Spirit. But, what kind of response will we see? Some may go home glad, others mad, while others will think about what they have heard or neglect what they have heard. The response of the hearer is the key.

Once, a pastor preached a message on a difficult topic. Two men met him at the front door. One was trembling with anger at what he had heard. The conviction was strong upon him, and he was furious. The other man told the pastor how much he appreciated the message on such a delicate topic. Two men. Two responses. Two fates sealed by hearing.

Jesus' words are so important—"take heed how ye hear."

QUOTE: "Life, death, hell, and worlds unknown may hang on the preaching and hearing of a sermon." —Charles H. Spurgeon.

—James Stallard

MARCH 23
ENTRUSTED WITH STEWARDSHIP

Scripture Reading—Luke 19:13
"And he called his ten servants, and delivered them ten pounds,
and said unto them, Occupy till I come."

The steward in New Testament times had a piece of property, usually with a small business, to oversee for his master. He was called to manage that trust. Likewise, God asks us to offer the stewardship of our lives to Him. In Luke 19, we are told to occupy till He comes. The idea is to stay busy and to occupy ourselves by using the things that have been entrusted to each one of us. The challenge is to put our talents, treasures, and time to use for the Lord. We must remember that what we value dictates our choices and sets the priority of service to God.

For a Christian the stewardship God has given us is vital. That's why it pays to be careful about where we invest our lives. A man in China learned this lesson recently when he spent $30,000 dollars on his new apartment. After renovating the new living quarters, he discovered that he had been shown the wrong apartment before the door numbers were up, and he had actually just spent $30,000 renovating and furnishing his neighbors' apartment. After the mistake was discovered, the request to change flats was rejected by its rightful owner. The investment was lost because it was invested in the wrong place. He had no claim to the contents and all was lost!

1 Cor. 3:14, 15 tell us, "If any man's work abide which he hath built thereupon, he shall receive a reward. If any man's work shall be burned, he shall suffer loss." To suffer loss before the Lord and have our stewardship judged as unworthy would be heartbreaking. Therefore, we must judge our own lives now. This requires us to think honestly about who we are, what we are, and where we are before God. Change is not easy, but a faithful steward is willing to take an honest look at his own work and implement the needed changes.

PONDER: What is the most important thing you have ever been entrusted with?

—*Steve Rebert*

MARCH 24
HAS GOD FORGOTTEN ME?

Scripture Reading—Heb. 6:10
"For God is not unrighteous to forget your work and labour of love."

It can be easy to think that God has forgotten us. Whether it is difficult trials, misfortune, or lack of desires being fulfilled, we sometimes wonder: Where is God? What happened to Him? Why will He not answer?

Mordecai was a "little" person who might have been tempted to think God had forgotten. He had saved the king's life by revealing a plot to kill him (Esther 2:21–23). Yet, Mordecai was not remembered and had to endure the plotting of another wicked man named Haman.

But God had not forgotten. He intervened by giving the king a sleepless night, and Mordecai was remembered for what he had done. The Bible is full of accounts of people who were seemingly forgotten, but then remembered. People like Daniel (Dan. 6) and Joseph (Gen. 40, 41) come to mind.

If we are waiting for God to deliver us and place us in a position of blessing, we might consider that God knows exactly where we are. Then, in His perfect timing, He will ease the hurt, relieve the suffering, and give grace to see us through. The Bible tells us, "For God is not unrighteous to forget your work and labour of love, which ye have shewed toward his name, in that ye have ministered to the saints, and do minister" (Heb. 6:10).

A young Christian soldier was the first soldier from the state of Florida to die in the Vietnam War in the 1960s. He bravely stood by his machine gun giving the company he commanded time to escape. His position was overrun, and he was killed. But all of his men escaped. It was an act that was largely overlooked. One day his mother, who was a member of the church where I served as pastor, got word that her son would be honored in the community where he was raised. More than 25 years after the fact, he was remembered for his gallant bravery.

Others may easily forget what we have done, but we can know that God will never forget our service for Him and others.

THANKSGIVING: Thank you, Lord, for never forgetting me as I faithfully serve you.

—James Stallard

MARCH 25
WHY WE WON'T FORGIVE

Scripture Reading—Matt. 6:15
"But if ye forgive not men their trespasses,
neither will your Father forgive your trespasses."

A man named John Oglethorpe made the following comment to John Wesley: "I never forgive." Mr. Wesley wisely replied, "Then sir, I hope that you never sin." It is a dangerous thing to say that you will never forgive.

Jesus makes it clear that the one who forgives will be forgiven (Matt. 6:14), but the one who refuses to forgive will not be forgiven by God (Matt. 6:15). Jesus is not talking about *eternal forgiveness* for sin's penalty (Acts 10:43), but to *fellowship forgiveness*, which maintains fellowship with God in our daily walk.

Some people refuse to speak to certain people. Some verbally attack others. Other people roll their eyes and show disgust for certain people. Still others slam doors and storm out of rooms. Many attempt vengeance—"I won't get mad; I'll just get even." Some people are unwilling to forgive someone who has hurt them. When we think about the greatness of God's forgiveness toward us, why would any of us not want to forgive those who have wronged us? Why won't we forgive? (Eph. 4:30–32).

In Luke 17, Jesus warned the disciples about this. He warned about offences (v. 1) and commanded total forgiveness (v. 3, 4). The response of the disciples was significant: "Lord, increase our faith" (v. 5). Here we find a major reason people do not forgive—they simply don't trust God!

Once at a funeral a grown son was heard to say, "I am so bitter at my father. He never came to a single one of my ball games when I was growing up." That's a sad testimony for a father. But it is also a sad testimony for a bitter son. If there is no forgiveness, there are no excuses. Forgiveness is God's plan, and trusting Him with our hurts is the only way to go.

> **QUOTE:** "We are not to respond to the issues of offenses we face on the basis of right or wrong, but rather on the basis of the principles of The Cross."
> —Watchman Nee

—James Stallard

OBEY AND HONOR

Scripture Reading—Eph. 6:1, 2
"Children, obey your parents in the Lord: for this is right.
Honour thy father and mother."

Here we have clear teaching regarding the will of God for children in their relationship with their parents. In an article about a young man who was in prison, I read these words, "I have to get up at 5 and go to bed at 8:45 at night. I can't eat what I want. I got to take a shower with four other guys. I got to get permission to get a drink of water." He goes on to say, "I didn't listen to my parents; I wanted to hang with an older crowd, build myself up with them. It all started with disrespect towards my parents." Here is a young man who chose not to obey and honor his parents, and sadly he lost his freedom.

God's word is clear—children are to "obey" and "honour" their parents. The right action is obedience. Rand Hummel states that children should "obey" quickly, sweetly, and completely. Obedience is doing what one is told to do without challenge, without excuse, and without delay. In our Lord's relationship with His parents, we read in Luke 2:51 that He was "subject unto them."

The right attitude is honor. Children should honor their parents and respond to them quietly, sincerely, and courteously. The word "honour" means "to reverence, hold in awe, to prize, fix a valuation upon." This means to show respect and love, to care for them as long as they live, and to bless them by the way we live. Ephesians 6:3 lets us know that this attitude of honor will be a blessing to the child who chooses to follow God's instruction.

Dad, when you love your wife, even as Christ loved the Church (Eph. 5:25), you are modeling honor before your children. Mom, when you "submit yourself unto your own husband" (Eph. 5:22), you are modeling obedience before your children.

God has given us clear teaching regarding our responsibilities in the family and the resources necessary to obey His will. May we please Him by right actions and right attitudes!

ACTION POINT: Take a moment with the Lord in personal prayer to confess any sin you are aware of in your family relationships. Do you need to seek forgiveness from a family member for wrong actions and attitudes?

—*Sammy Frye*

MARCH 27
WHEN YOU WANT TO RETALIATE
Scripture Reading—Pro. 15:1
"A soft answer turneth away wrath: but grievous words stir up anger."

How do we answer someone that is speaking to us with great anger and passion? We are not to retaliate in like kind, but with a "soft answer." The word "soft" means gentle.

God's wisdom is that we respond in the exact opposite way of how we are being treated. Sometimes we ought to be quiet and not say a word; sometimes we ought to answer "quietly," but never are we to respond in anger.

If we answer with angry words or tones, it only makes the situation worse. It is like pouring gasoline on a fire. The Bible says, "Grievous words stir up anger." The word "grievous" means harsh. These are words given with a stern tone of voice.

One night after coaching a baseball game, I had loaded the equipment in the trunk of the car and was about to get into the driver's seat. I was hurrying because I had to make a pastoral visit.

Before I had even gotten into the car, a very angry parent of one of the players whom I was coaching accosted me. He was ranting about why his son had not been able to play the entire game.

I was frustrated because I had to tolerate his temper, and I had an important visit to make. To be honest, I wanted to lash out at him. But, thankfully, that is not what I did. When he finished his tirade, I quietly asked him a question: "Did you see who was sitting by your son on the bench? It was my son. He wasn't playing either." He didn't say anything for about five seconds and just said, "Oh," and walked off to his car.

Twelve years later I stand up to preach, and there in one of our pews sat this same man. He was interested in our church and had been listening to my sermons on the Internet. He would not have been there if I would have retaliated. My response that night was a witness to the reality of God's grace.

MEMORIZE: Proverbs 15:1.

—*Rick Johnson*

MARCH 28
BOUNDARIES

Scripture Reading—Pro. 22:28
"Remove not the ancient landmark, which thy fathers have set."

In Bible times stones marked property boundaries. They were clearly identified and served as a public testimony that prevented lawsuits among neighbors. Under cover of night, a neighbor might gradually move the stone landmarks in such small increments that he stole his neighbor's property without him even knowing.

The same principle can be applied to our personal convictions. Far more important than land are the lives of our children. They need to know biblical boundaries if they are to live a life pleasing to the Lord.

Parents have a God-given responsibility to establish boundaries for children. Property landmarks were not haphazardly set up, but with great care and accuracy. Because of the value of our children, we must model and help them to establish boundaries for their lives (Eph. 6:4; Gen. 18:19; Pro. 4:1–4).

God has deputized the father to be the leader in the family, and one of his responsibilities is to set scriptural landmarks. When they are violated he is to "correct" his child (Pro. 29:17), else he be "left to himself" and bring shame to his parents and God (Pro. 29:15).

A child without boundaries is confused, insecure, and will end up with unnecessary regrets and sorrows in his or her life. If your parents provide you with direction and expectations, realize the treasure you have in them.

Children have a responsibility to respect and honor the boundaries that are taught and modeled. There are blessings of guidance, protection, wisdom, insight, and a meaningful life for those that honor them (Pro. 6:20–23).

God has given high regard to landmarks to protect one's property rights. He does the same with the boundaries parents give their children. As a pastor I have witnessed children reject boundaries that have been established by humble, godly parents and are based on God's Word. The result is not only broken-hearted parents, but children that experience destructive consequences.

DISCUSS: Discuss a boundary that has been established in your family and why it is in place.

—Rick Johnson

MARCH 29
REJECTING GOD'S COUNSEL
LEADS TO MEDIOCRITY

Scripture Reading—Ps. 81:13
"Oh that my people had hearkened unto me,
and Israel had walked in my ways!"

The Designer of life knows how life works. How foolish to reject the wisdom of God and expect a better result by following our desires! You never know where obedience to a command of God will lead. Also, failure to obey the Lord in the smallest of areas may cost you the rest of your life, and you may never know what you have missed!

We see this clearly laid out in the history of Israel (Ps. 81:8–16). To me this is the best example in the Bible of experiencing mediocrity because of rejecting God's ways and counsel. There are painful consequences for doing so.

When I was an older teenager, I sensed God leading me to preach, but I was afraid of the will of God. My hesitancy wasn't as much from a rebellious heart, but I feared I couldn't do it. If I had settled into my comfort zone, I would have missed God's best. I'm glad I surrendered to Him.

I still have struggles when God stretches me outside of my comfort zone. It never gets easy. Self-will will cause us to reject God's counsel. You will never discover God's will until you lose your own. Your decision on the matter will determine the quality of your life.

Self-will brings a loss of opportunity that is gone forever (1 Sam. 15:22, 23). Obedience to God brings opportunities you never dreamed could come. What is God asking you to do right now? Are you reluctant to obey Him?

In college I went to a tiny church in an unattractive building to serve with a pastor. I didn't know it, but in that place was my future wife. Initially I didn't want to go to that church, but I'm glad that I did. My life has been immeasurably blessed because of following God's direction. May you know that joy today!

ACTION POINT: Put the following statement in a well-traveled place in your home—"God always gives His best to those who leave the choice to Him."

—Rick Johnson

MARCH 30
KEEPING IT SIMPLE

Scripture Reading—2 Cor. 11:3
*"But I fear, lest by any means, as the serpent beguiled Eve
through his subtilty, so your minds should be corrupted
from the simplicity that is in Christ."*

The Apostle Paul warned the Corinthian church not to get sidetracked from "the simplicity that is in Christ." He wanted to present them to God in sincerity and pure simplicity (2 Cor. 11:2). Satan (the serpent) could beguile them like he did Eve in the Garden of Eden, so they had to be alert. Otherwise, they might be deceived by a false Jesus or a false gospel (2 Cor. 11:4).

Satan always tries to complicate things. God's simple command in the Garden was not to eat of the tree of the knowledge of good and evil. Satan, coming as the serpent, tempted Eve by complicating the command. He got Eve to question God's truthfulness, God's love, and His sincerity (Gen. 3:3–5).

Our world seems to make everything so complicated. Note the following:

• You go to a lawyer, and he draws up some legal papers with complicated language that hardly anyone understands.

• You go to a doctor, and you get a prescription with a complicated name you can't pronounce.

• You try to buy a car, and it seems you have to jump through all kinds of hoops at the car dealership in order to buy the car you want.

• You need help with your computer, so you call technical support and get someone halfway around the world. What they say is too complicated and always seems to take too much time, and your computer is still not fixed.

Life can be complicated, and spiritual truths can seem to be that way too. But the Bible tells us that our focus should be simple—keep looking to Jesus. Do not allow the Devil to complicate your life. Focus on "the simplicity that is in Christ." Paul also said it this way, "For I determined not to know any thing among you, save Jesus Christ, and him crucified" (1 Cor. 2:2). A simple focus for a simple life!

PRAYER: Lord, forgive me for allowing Satan to complicate my life. Help me to focus on You in all of my life.

—*James Stallard*

MARCH 31
DAILY DOSES OF COMFORT

Scripture Reading—Heb. 3:13
"Exhort one another daily."

All of us at times come home from work and school wearied and even discouraged. The place of our greatest comfort ought to be from our family members.

Some are better at encouragement than others. There is a spiritual gift of exhortation that some have (Rom. 12:8), such as Tychicus (Eph. 6:21, 22; Col. 4:7, 8). This gift is the desire and ability to minister encouragement to hurting people. Broken people are drawn to them. Others are better equipped at comforting because they have grown up in a more affirming environment. They heard positive words of blessing from their parents.

One of the purposes of a church service is to encourage (1 Cor. 14:31; Heb. 10:25). Part of a pastor's preaching ministry is to include encouragement (2 Tim. 4:2).

Children bring encouragement to their parents when they are obedient to them (Pro. 10:1), and a father ought to excel in being an encourager to his children (1 Thess. 2:11).

Here is the bottom line: God has called all of us to be encouragers, especially to those in our family. Ultimately it is God that brings comfort to a person, and He delights in doing so. One of His titles is the "God of all comfort" (2 Cor. 1:3). When we are grieving He offers us His comfort (Matt. 5:4). Thus, one that comforts others is being godly and Christlike.

One of the benefits we have in receiving encouragement is that it prevents us from developing a hard heart (Heb. 3:12, 13). During times of doubt and persecution, we need the comfort of others. This should be most and best given within the family. The verse at the masthead gives an incredible insight: encouragement is to be given daily. Every day someone in your family needs encouragement. Will you be the one that gives it to him or her?

Children, your parents especially need encouragement in their roles of leadership (Deut. 1:38; 3:28). Be intentional about blessing them by your encouraging words and actions.

ACTION POINT: Who excels in encouragement in your family? Give some examples. Look for ways to encourage your family this week on a daily basis.

—Rick Johnson

APRIL 1
FACING LONELY TIMES

Scripture Reading—2 Tim. 4:11
"Only Luke is with me."

It was no doubt one of the loneliest moments in his life. While the Lord was with him, Paul still needed the comfort and presence of human friends. We would certainly need such friends if we were in his place.

In the coldness of a damp dungeon prison cell, Paul faced his last moments on earth. He probably did not know how much time he had left. He would be executed in just a few hours, days, or weeks. That much he knew.

He had told Timothy, "Do thy diligence to come shortly (quickly) unto me" (2 Tim. 4:9 emphasis added). Paul knew he was ready for eternity:

"For I am now ready to be offered, and the time of my departure is at hand. I have fought a good fight, I have finished my course, I have kept the faith: Henceforth there is laid up for me a crown of righteousness, which the Lord, the righteous judge, shall give me at that day: and not to me only, but unto all them that love his appearing" (2 Tim. 4:6–8).

There was also a reason given for his urgency to have Timothy come to him. Someone else had left him—a man named Demas (2 Tim. 4:10). He left Paul when he needed him most. Paul says, "Only Luke is with me" (2 Tim. 4:11).

Loneliness can be an incredible burden for someone to bear. To be abandoned while facing execution was cruel, but Paul knew the Lord was with him and had even provided others to be with him as he faced the final hour.

God provides for His children whatever they need in life. The Psalmist declares, "For this God is our God for ever and ever: he will be our guide even unto death" (Ps. 48:14). We are never alone in the midst of our most difficult trials. The New Testament confirms this as well when it states, "For he hath said, I will never leave thee, nor forsake thee" (Heb. 13:5). Child of God, know that the Lord will always be with you in your loneliest moments of life.

SONG: Sing the chorus "I Will Sing of the Mercies of the Lord."

—*James Stallard*

APRIL 2
WHAT MAKES YOU BLESSED?

Scripture Reading—Ps. 1:1

"Blessed is the man that walketh not in the counsel of the ungodly, nor standeth in the way of sinners, nor sitteth in the seat of the scornful."

The first word of the Book of Psalms is a word that every person wants to be—"blessed." The word "blessed" could mean "happy" or an even better definition would be "satisfied." Every person who has ever lived wants to be satisfied—it's why we do what we do!

The "blessed" man in verse 1 knows that true satisfaction is not found by listening to the sales pitch of the world. This world (the ungodly, the sinners, and the scornful) is constantly telling us that true blessing can be found in this temporal world. In 1 John 2 the Bible tells us that all that is in the world—the lust of the eyes (possessions), the lust of the flesh (pleasures), and the pride of life (positions)—is not of God but is temporal and passing away.

My daughter Ella loves cotton candy! Personally, I am not a big fan. I think that cotton candy is the perfect picture of "vanity fair." It's just so big and fluffy in that bag, and little eyes just stare at how fun and yummy it will be. But as soon as it's in your mouth, what happens? It's gone! So you eat a little more and a little more till you start feeling yuck!

We have wrongly defined worldliness as a list of external "no no's"—don't wear this, don't go there, don't look like that, don't watch those. But true worldliness is internal, not external. It's about your heart and what you love! The result of getting this wrong is devastating. Since a movie is rated "G" doesn't mean we can watch it for hours and hours, or since it's rated "E" for everybody, then we can play it for 5 hours a day. When our affections are inordinately set on what will pass away, we are worldly!

Are you looking for "satisfaction" in this world? What are some specific areas where you are being "worldly" in your heart?

CONSIDER: Here are some areas to consider:
- Possessions: toys, clothes
- Pleasures: entertainment (TV, internet, video games), hobbies
- Positions: work, status

—Aaron Coffey

APRIL 3
CLIMB INTO THE WHEELBARROW

Scripture Reading—Rom. 10:10
"For with the heart man believeth unto righteousness."

Many people claim that they are going to Heaven because they have believed in Christ. But just what does that mean? Mark Twain said, "The difference in the right word and the wrong word is the difference between lightning and the lightning bug." We need some lightning around the word "believe."

A daredevil once walked across a tightrope above Niagara Falls with nothing but a balance pole and a wheelbarrow. A huge crowd watched in hushed silence as he made this death-defying journey. Slowly he placed one foot in front of another as he steadily crept across the slippery, narrow path of rope. When he finally reached the other side, the crowd burst into loud cheering. One overly vocal man disturbed the true hero, so he approached the loud voiced man and said, "Sir, do you believe I can do that again?"

"Of course I do," he loudly replied. "I believe it more than anything!" Whereupon the daredevil balanced himself and his wheelbarrow upon the rope, turned to the man and said, "Well then, climb into the wheelbarrow!" The outspoken man stood embarrassed and chagrined when he realized the difference between belief and trust. That is the difference between one who is truly saved and one who is lost; the saved have climbed into the wheelbarrow.

It is possible to believe something as a fact without trust. For example the Bible records a shocking fact about the devils: "Thou believest that there is one God . . . the devils also believe, and tremble" (James 2:19). They believed but were not saved.

But the Apostle Paul tells us that true salvation is a belief that includes trust. "In whom ye also trusted . . . after that ye believed" (Eph. 1:13). The devils certainly have not trusted. To confuse belief with trust is very dangerous. It is not enough to believe the fact that the tightrope walker can do it; it is also necessary to trust him to do it for you.

Paul warns us, "Examine yourselves, whether ye be in the faith" (2 Cor. 13:5). Do you trust the finished work of Christ as your only hope of salvation, or are you merely believing that He died on The Cross for sins. The difference is that of lightning and the lightning bug.

MEMORIZE: Romans 10:10.

—Jim Binney

TAMING THE TIGER OF ANGER

Scripture Reading—Gen. 4:7
"Sin lieth at the door."

Most of us would never think it possible for us to commit murder. The cold-blooded taking of innocent life is something that only wicked, violent people would do. But never us.

Scripture informs us, however, that anyone who develops an angry spirit of hate or bitterness is a murderer (1 John 3:12–15). The person who illustrates this the best (or worst) is Cain, the brother of Abel. While even children may be familiar with the story of Cain killing Abel, few are taught how to control the anger that leads to such a tragedy.

When God accepted the sacrifice of Abel (a blood sacrifice) and rejected that of Cain (a works sacrifice), "Cain was very wroth (angry), and his countenance fell" (Gen. 4:5 emphasis added). God confronted Cain about his heart's attitude by asking two questions and giving a warning:

• He convicted his conscience by asking the question: "Why art thou wroth?" (Gen. 4:6).

• He confirmed a second chance for Cain to bring the right offering and submit himself to God, "If thou doest well, shalt thou not be accepted?" (Gen. 4:7).

• He confronted him with a warning about the power of his sinful anger and its ability to dominate him, "Sin lieth at the door. And unto thee shall be his desire." Said another way: sin desires to rule Cain. But "thou shalt rule over him" (Gen. 4:7).

God's dealings with Cain tell us that we are not to allow anger to get the best of us. If any of us does not control his or her anger, sin will pounce like a tiger in our hearts, and our anger will stir up greater evil. Cain let his anger vent itself in violence. Our anger can do the same. This is why the Apostle Paul instructs us, "Be ye angry, and sin not: let not the sun go down upon your wrath" (Eph. 4:26).

DISCUSS: Have the family discuss the importance of not going to bed at night with anger in our hearts. Discover ways to check this each day to obey the teaching of the Bible. Ask whether anger in our hearts is ever right.

—James Stallard

APRIL 5
REMEMBER YOUR CREATOR
WHEN YOU'RE YOUNG

Scripture Reading—Eccl. 12:1
"Remember now thy Creator in the days of thy youth."

It is a great thing to come to know God when you are young. Trusting Jesus Christ as Savior as a child brings salvation just as certainly as trusting Jesus as an adult. There are many folks who were saved when they were older who wished they had trusted Christ when they were younger. It would have saved them many heartaches along the way.

Most pastors will baptize a few older folks in their 60s or 70s, but for the most part, people who come to Christ do so while they are young. One source declared that if you had 1,000 Christians sitting in front of you, here is what you would find:

- 1 would have been saved between 60–70 years of age.
- 3 would have been saved between 50–60 years of age.
- 15 would have been saved between 40–50 years of age.
- 96 would have been saved between 30–40 years of age.
- 337 would have been saved between 20–30 years of age.
- 548 would have been saved under the age of 20.

Seeing these statistics, it is easy to understand why God declares, "Remember now thy Creator in the days of thy youth, while the evil days come not, nor the years draw nigh when thou shalt say, I have no pleasure in them" (Eccl. 12:1). The older we get the more difficult it is to come to Christ because we become set in our ways. God warns that He "resisteth the proud, but giveth grace unto the humble" (James 4:6).

Even for those who have been saved, it is always wise to respond to God while young. It is amazing how often the Bible tells us to make spiritual decisions right away! The Bible says, "Behold, now is the accepted time; behold, now is the day of salvation" (2 Cor. 6:2 emphasis added). In a message for God's people, the prophet Isaiah declared, "Come now, and let us reason together, saith the LORD" (Isa. 1:18 emphasis added).

It is dangerous to put off your decision for another day. Now is always the best time.

PRAYER: Lord, I now surrender to you my life completely.

—James Stallard

APRIL 6
ALMOST HOME

Scripture Reading—Mark 12:34
"Thou art not far from the kingdom of God."

It is tragic to be so close to home and yet, so far away. Mark 12:34 records the statement of Jesus to a young scribe who seemed to have some understanding of the kingdom of God (Mark 12:32, 33). Then, Jesus told him that he was not far from God's kingdom (Mark 12:34). He did not tell him that he was *in* God's kingdom, but that he was *close* to God's kingdom.

One thief who hung on a cross next to Jesus continued to reject the message of hope from Christ—*so close, yet so far* (Luke 23:39). The Rich Young Ruler came to the right Person with the right question, but left without salvation (Luke 18:22, 23)—*so close, yet so far*.

Imagine two men who lived in Noah's day. One man lived far away from the Ark. He had heard about it, but chose not to investigate. The other man lived close to the Ark. He heard about it and was close enough to investigate, but chose not to believe what Noah preached. But the rains came and the earth was covered with water. The door of the Ark was shut, and there was no possibility of rescue—*so close, yet so far*.

On February 1, 2003, the Space Shuttle Columbia, a 178,000-pound spacecraft, exploded 39 miles above Texas as it tried to re-enter the earth's atmosphere. It was a great loss for the families of the seven crew members, for the space program, and for the nation. But perhaps the greatest tragedy was that they were so close to home.

Communication ended at 9 a.m. that Saturday. Their scheduled landing at Cape Kennedy in Florida was 9:16 a.m. They were sixteen minutes from home! *Almost home*—but now the farthest away from their earthly homes that they could possibly be. *Almost home was to be not home at all.*

When it comes to thinking about eternity, it is best that we make sure that we have truly entered the door. We need to be in the kingdom and not just near the kingdom, so we are ready for our heavenly home.

ACTION POINT: Read John 5:24 three times out loud as a family.

—James Stallard

APRIL 7
WALKING THROUGH THE OPEN DOOR

Scripture Reading—Rev. 3:8
"I have set before thee an open door, and no man can shut it."

A closed door can sometimes be a big help. If locked, a closed door can keep burglars from stealing our stuff. It can also keep the stormy winds outside from coming inside the house. While closed doors are sometimes helpful, it is better to have open doors.

An open door can be viewed as a gateway into a new beginning. When Jesus told the church at Philadelphia about an open door that no man could shut, He was speaking about an open door to advance the work of the Church.

We find this idea in the Bible when it talks about salvation. Jesus said, "I am the door: by me if any man enter in, he shall be saved" (John 10:9). Jesus provides an open door through Him for anyone who will put his or her faith in Him.

When Noah built the Ark, the day came when he, his family, and the animals all entered the Ark. Then God shut the door, and there was no more hope for those who refused to listen to Noah's warning (Gen. 7:16).

An open door also speaks of opportunities to serve God. Paul said, "For a great door and effectual is opened unto me, and there are many adversaries" (1 Cor. 16:9). It was an open door of ministry for Paul, and he knew it would be effective.

When I was eight years old, my parents took me to see a Detroit Tigers baseball game at old Tiger Stadium. I was a big fan but had never seen a stadium or a major league baseball field before. We went through the gate (door) and walked up the ramp into our seating area. My little heart was amazed at the new world that was now open to me.

God opens and closes doors of opportunity for us to guide us through life. If He gives you an open door, it is time to walk through it. The amazing result will be better than anything the world has to offer.

PRAYER: Ask God for an open door of ministry to another family.

—*James Stallard*

APRIL 8
OBEYING THE BIBLE

Scripture Reading—James 1:22
"But be ye doers of the word, and not hearers only,
deceiving your own selves."

There is a danger in becoming so familiar with Bible content that we equate the learning of truth with the application of truth. "God didn't give us the Bible to inform us, but to transform us," D.L. Moody said. Knowledge alone isn't transformation. With God's help, you must intentionally transition the Bible from your mind to your will.

Many are deceived, not from the orthodoxy of doctrine, but by thinking that knowing God's truth is the same as doing it (James 1:22). Those that are self-deceived cannot be taught. Pride of knowledge keeps us from receiving the Bible with meekness (James 1:21), which is necessary for our sanctification. Remember, Satan knows the Bible; he quoted it to Jesus.

Some people read the Bible and are confronted by its demands but never change anything in their thinking or behavior. They are content with what they know about it (James 1:23, 24). Sure, we will learn truths as we read and study the Bible, but we are to be looking for things to apply (James 1:25). Knowing the truth should lead us to do a "work" and "deed" that we have not been doing previously, or to stop doing something that we shouldn't be doing (James 1:25).

When we keep God's Word, He rewards us greatly (Ps. 19:11). Change comes by applying it (Ps. 19:7–10), not just by knowing it (Luke 8:15).

Obedience to the Bible brings purity (Ps. 119:9), wisdom (Ps. 119:24), success (Josh. 1:7, 8), understanding (Ps. 111:10; Deut. 4:6), and God's blessing (Ps. 112:1).

The goal of Bible study isn't to satisfy intellectual curiosity, but to accomplish life change (2 Tim. 3:16, 17). We are already educated beyond our obedience. If we obeyed the truth, our lives would be dramatically different, and we would experience personal revival. Do you need to repent of being deceived into thinking that knowing and doing the Word of God is the same thing?

ACTION POINT: In every lesson, sermon, or Bible reading you have, find something to do and begin to apply it immediately.

—Rick Johnson

APRIL 9
BALANCING CORRECTION
WITH ENCOURAGEMENT

Scripture Reading—Eph. 6:4
"Provoke not your children to wrath: but bring them up in the nurture and admonition of the Lord."

The "sandwich approach" is often used when criticizing. First, praise is given, then the criticism is addressed, and then another praise is given. Thus, the sandwich—*praise, criticism, praise.*

Imagine that you hear this method used frequently. Whenever you hear positive words, inwardly you are bracing for the negative words to follow. The encouragement means nothing.

Parents must correct, but we must also praise (Eph. 6:4). If both are not given, there will be no improvement in behavior, but only distance in our relationships as our children pull away from us.

I am so grateful my father let me enjoy sports as a boy and didn't continually correct me. It would have pushed me away from the sport and from him. Perhaps constant correction is why some children that grow up in Christian homes reject both their parents and their faith.

When I was in college, two students were at the sinks in the bathroom brushing their teeth before they went to bed. One of the men finished brushing and bent over with his mouth close to the faucet to drink some water to rinse off the toothpaste.

The student beside him was appalled and immediately rebuked him, "I can't believe you're doing that—drinking directly from the faucet! Didn't your mother teach you any better?" The fellow gradually stood up straight, wiped his mouth, and looked directly at the critic and said softly, "My mother died when I was five years old." And he walked out of the bathroom.

The critic stood there for awhile, stunned and embarrassed at his outburst and then quietly left. I think he went to his room and wished a thousand times over that he had kept his mouth shut.

PONDER: Do you tend to be more of a critic or an encourager?

—*Rick Johnson*

APRIL 10
SPARE THE PLACE

Scripture Reading—Gen. 18:22
"But Abraham stood yet before the LORD."

In Scripture, Abraham was called "the Friend of God" (James 2:23) because he knew God well. However, Abraham had also learned well how to communicate with God. That is why his prayer for Sodom in Genesis 18 is certainly one of the great prayers of the Old Testament.

Sodom was a wicked city filled with sinful men (Gen. 13:13). For this reason God was planning to destroy the city and its inhabitants. Knowing that Lot's family was living in the city, Abraham began to pray that God would spare the city from the judgment it rightfully deserved. He first asked God to spare the city if there were fifty people in the city who were living right. God's response was, "If I find in Sodom fifty righteous within the city, then I will spare all the place for their sakes" (Gen. 18:26). God's response to Abraham's request was certainly favorable. Abraham then offered the same request, if there were forty-five, and then forty, and then thirty, and then twenty, and finally ten. Each time God responded favorably, saying that the city would not be destroyed.

Tragically we know that Lot's family was not living right, and so even ten righteous people could not be found. Ultimately, God did destroy the city, but it was not because of the failure of Abraham's prayer, but rather the failure of Lot's family.

Abraham teaches us a great lesson about prayer. As an intercessor, he took hold of the need, and got hold of God and brought them together in prayer. God responds favorably to this kind of praying. Driven by urgency and desperation, Abraham was willing to do his part to prevent the coming destruction of Sodom. Right praying and right living have the potential to make a big difference in a culture and society that deserve God's judgment. If judgment comes, it will be the fault of those who do wrong—as well as those who knew to do right and didn't!

ACTION POINT: Spend some time praying that our nation will turn to God, seeking forgiveness for her sins.

—Tom Palmer

APRIL 11
THANKFUL FOR EVERYTHING

Scripture Reading—Eph. 5:20
"Giving thanks always for all things."

The Scripture above is a tough thing to do if all you see is the present. If you only have a part of the picture, it is impossible to be thankful, but if you had the entire picture, you would be thankful. Therein is the rub. We do not have the entire picture and have to trust God that it is for our good.

Gratitude is not something you do just when you are enjoying comfortable circumstances. We are to be ever grateful (Ps. 34:1). How can we do this? The secret is to combine the "all things" in Ephesians 5:20 with the "all things" in Romans 8:28.

Since "all things work together for good," that means that even the bad things will bring about an ultimate good. Only God can do this. This way of thinking allows us not to become bitter. We are thankful, not for the rigors of the trial, but for its result.

We see this in Joseph's attitude toward his brothers after terrible trials (Gen. 50:19–21). Without a trust in God's sovereign purpose, we will become angry rather than grateful in our adversity. This means we must see from an eternal perspective (2 Cor. 4:16–18).

The Bible says, "We know that all things work together for good" (Rom. 8:28), not "we see all things work together for good." Though I do not presently understand what God is doing, I know based on His Word and His character that it is for my good and His glory.

It is possible to be thankful to God in the most miserable of circumstances. The only alternative is to be filled with anger and bitterness. It's up to you.

There is a plant in Africa called the "tasteberry." No matter how bitter the taste in your mouth, when you eat the tasteberry, it turns your taste from sour to sweet. The "tasteberry" for the believer is Romans 8:28. If you are resting in the sovereignty of God, you can be grateful every day.

ACTION POINT: What is your biggest struggle? Take the time to thank God for the good He is going to work for you through it.

—Rick Johnson

APRIL 12
A SHELTER IN THE TIME OF STORM

Scripture Reading—Ezek. 11:16
*"Yet will I be to them as a little sanctuary
in the countries where they shall come."*

The old hymn refrain says, "Oh, Jesus is a Rock in a weary land, A Shelter in the time of storm."

The ancient Israelites had sinned terribly against God. They had committed every kind of wickedness that the nations around them had committed, and yet it was worse in God's eyes because God was their God. They should have known better.

The things that the Jews would suffer because of their bad choices were astonishing. Pestilence, famine, and the sword would kill them. Those who survived those things would be taken into captivity to a "weary land" where they would be oppressed strangers and slaves. Sin has a high price tag. But even in the midst of God's judgment, even when their own actions caused them great distress, God desired to show them mercy.

In our verse today, God tells His people that even after they suffer much and are taken into captivity, He will be their "little sanctuary." He would be the place where they could go to find a little relief from their trials. What blessedness!

God is great, and He desires to show mercy to His suffering children (Isa. 49:13). Sometimes we suffer the consequences of our own choices. But don't ever think that making bad choices means that God doesn't love you. His love for you never changes. If you have done wrong, simply seek forgiveness and move on. A Christian should never remain downcast once God has forgiven.

Satan tries to keep past failures ever present in order to keep us from accomplishing God's will. Don't allow him to do that. Get up and keep going for God (Pro. 24:16), and remember that, even in the most difficult times, God Himself is a "little sanctuary" for you.

ACTION POINT: Have each family member reflect on a time in the past when God was a "little sanctuary" during a difficult time.

—Paul Miller

APRIL 13
FAILING GRACE

Scripture Reading—Heb. 12:15
"Looking diligently lest any man fail of the grace of God;
lest any root of bitterness springing up trouble you."

Have you ever had someone wrong you? Maybe you felt betrayed? Or perhaps something was said that was hurtful?

Has life ever hit you with a difficult circumstance? At that moment you were at a crisis. Are you going to believe God, or are you going to doubt Him? When you believe God you access grace. When you say, "Lord this hurt, but I know you are going to work it together for good," you unwrap the gift of grace—God's supernatural involvement in your life.

When you doubt God, you fail grace. When you say, "That rots. Why did that have to happen? It makes me so mad," you have no grace. That is when bitterness springs up and defiles you.

Can you imagine walking out of church one day, and the pastor hands you a thousand-dollar check? (Now I know we are really imagining!) The rest of the day you find yourself complaining. "Man, that pastor, messed things up. He gave me $1,000. It makes me so mad. He ruined my life!" Not only would that be strange, it would not happen.

Yet that is what we do to God. Someone wrongs us. Things go haywire. We begin to complain. In a sense, we are griping about a spiritual "$1,000" that God is giving us.

Our complaining indicates that we really do not believe that God is going to take that person's wrong or that difficult circumstance and work it together for good. As a result, we fail grace. God's grace will never fail you, but you can fail the grace of God.

PONDER: Joseph faced some unbelievable wrongs. Yet at the end of his life, he was able to look the ones who had wronged him in the eye and say, "But as for you, ye thought evil against me; but God meant it unto good." How are you responding to people that hurt you?

—Jim Van Geldren

APRIL 14
ROUGH WORDS

Scripture Reading—Pro. 18:23
"The rich answereth roughly."

The Bible speaks about those that "answer roughly." This response is fierce, intense, and severe—words spoken with great force and power.

Authorities especially tend to do this because it gains quick results. It does, for the short-term. However, in the process of doing so, we lose far more than we gain.

We lose respect and the opportunity to have a close relationship with those we lead. People pull away from those that bully them verbally. Parents have the greatest loss—our rough words cause us to lose the hearts of our children.

Someone said, "God resists pride . . . and so do people." It is difficult to endure rough words from anyone, but especially from a family member. After a while we pull away from them because of the pain their words inflict.

A true story. A pastor stopped at a gas station for some fuel. He was in a hurry. Attendants used to come out to the car and pump the gas for you. The attendant was slow and puttered back to take the gas cap off. The pastor impatiently said, "Would you please hurry? I'm late for a meeting." The worker never said a word.

As the pastor waited, God began to speak to Him about his rudeness and abruptness. He knew that he was wrong and should make it right with the man. The attendant came to the car window to get the money, and the pastor said, "Sir, I want to apologize to you for the way I spoke to you. It was very wrong of me, and I shouldn't have done it. I'm very sorry."

The man said quietly, "That's alright, Mister. People always talk to me like that."

I wonder if our families have grown accustomed to our rudeness, our quickness to speak, our abruptness. Have we become accustomed to being rough in our speech?

I used to have a radio program and always closed it with the same refrain, "Remember, be kind to everybody you meet because everyone is having a tough time." Good words for us to remember every day.

ACTION POINT: Ask your family if you speak roughly?

—*Rick Johnson*

APRIL 15
DAILY DINING ON
THE MASTER'S MANNA

Scripture Reading—Exod. 16:4
"Behold, I will rain bread from heaven for you; and the people shall go out and gather a certain rate every day."

The manna from Heaven was food to sustain the children of Israel during their wilderness wanderings. It is a fitting picture of daily personal devotions from which God feeds the souls of His children.

Notice the lessons from the manna:

• It had **to be gathered** (Exod. 16:16).

One is not nourished from God's Word if he doesn't dig into it himself.

• It had **to be gathered early** before the heat of the day (Exod. 16:21).

Personal quiet time is best had early in the day before the heat of daily pressures comes upon us.

• It was **enough for daily sustenance** (Exod. 16:19, 20; Matt. 4:4; Job 23:12).

One day of devotions does not suffice for a week of activities—any more than a delicious Sunday meal does not give you enough energy for a week of work or school. Dine daily!

• It **ceased** the day they entered the **Promised Land** (Exod. 16:35).

In Canaan, they began to feed on the milk and honey of the Promised Land. When we enter into the victorious Christian life (abiding in Christ, being filled with God's Spirit), we shall pass from mundane manna meals to a biblical buffet.

The routine of personal devotions will pay dividends if you just stick with it! Daily dining in Scripture makes for godly growth in the life of the maturing believer. Start with a simple habit and grow it into a life of daily feeding on food for the soul.

PONDER: A daily diet in the Word of God makes for a healthy habit of growing in grace.

—*Rich Tozour*

APRIL 16
FRIENDS LISTEN

Scripture Reading—Exod. 33:11
*"And the LORD spake unto Moses . . . as a
man speaketh unto his friend."*

King Solomon had a friend named Zabud (1 Kings 4:5). The word "friend" means a companion and confidant. This was someone to whom the king was able to pour out his heart.

A component of a close friendship is that each person listens to the other. Listening is more than gaining information. It includes understanding and empathy. Some refer to it as "active listening." When Job was suffering he pled for his friends to listen to his feelings (Job 19:21).

Communication is always two-way. It is listening and talking. Without listening there cannot be a friendship. Both are part of our relationship with God (Exod. 33:11).

One of the outstanding friendships in the Bible is that of Jonathan and David. Jonathan's willingness to listen enabled him to encourage David at a low time in his life (1 Sam. 19:2; 23:16). He was able to strengthen David because he was aware of his discouragement. He knew what to say to him because he was a good listener.

We are the Lord's friends when we listen to Him (John 15:15). There are times when, of necessity, one friend has to listen more because of the burdens of the other. I'm so grateful for people that have caught my tears and fears when I wasn't able to speak about them publicly. I think Zabud met this need in Solomon's life.

Friendship is a give-and-take relationship. Sometimes you are on the giving end and sometimes on the receiving end. Sometimes you are talking, sharing your heart, and sometimes you are listening while the other shares his or her heart.

As foundational as listening is to communication, few do it well. Our focus is on being understood rather than understanding. It is one-way. Sometimes, we need to focus on understanding rather than on being understood.

How grateful I am my wife has listened to my heart and withheld judgment at times when I was hurting. How grateful I am for friends that listen well. May I do the same for them!

ACTION POINT: Which of your friends is a good listener?

—Rick Johnson

APRIL 17
MAKING MORNING
A TIME FOR GOD

Scripture Reading—Ps. 62:1
"Truly my soul waiteth upon God."

Let's face it—getting up in the morning is not easy! Dad hits the snooze button three times. Mom waits till the baby cries or somebody needs breakfast. Teenagers wait till the hundred-pound family dog named "Tiny" pounces on them and licks their faces. The younger kids wait until somebody pulls all their blankets off or drags them out of bed. Finally, one by one, each grumpy family member tumbles out of bed, moaning and groaning about needing more sleep and wishing they never had to get up.

Is this the way it is at your house? If you are like most families, morning may not be your favorite time of the day, but like it or not, it is an important time of the day.

Have you ever wondered why so many people, including Christians, are not so-called "morning people"? One answer might be that so many people are so-called "night owls." It is hard to get up early because we go to bed so late. Now don't get mad at me, but I am going to tell you why so many people, and sadly even many Christian people, go to bed late. Most of these "night owls" sit on their perch late in the evening in front of a television. "But I have to see the 11 o'clock news," they say, "And *Sports Center* doesn't come on until after the news."

Men, I want to challenge you. Turn that TV off one hour earlier, go to bed one hour earlier, get up one hour earlier, and give the first hour of the day to God. You will be a new man. That hour a day with God will transform your life. Your wife and children will know, but best of all, God will know it. Yes, it will take some effort and discipline, but it will be worth it. Let a seeking heart for God control your morning, rather than a sleepy head in bed.

ACTION POINT: Try it—set the alarm clock fifteen minutes earlier and start tomorrow morning in the presence of your God.

—Tom Palmer

APRIL 18
UNKEPT PROMISES

Scripture Reading—Eccl. 5:4
"When thou vowest a vow unto God, defer not to pay it."

God is very serious when He makes promises. The Bible says that He "cannot lie" (Titus 1:2) and that He is faithful to keep His Word (Phil. 1:6; 1 Thess. 5:24).

He is just as serious about the promises we make to Him. The Old Testament equivalent of the word promise is "vow." When one makes a vow to God, God expects it to be kept (Eccl. 5:1–6). Because God takes our promises to Him so seriously, He warns us to be careful with our words and to let them "be few." In other words, be quiet if you have no intention of keeping your promise.

I don't think any decent parents deceive their children. Parents want to do what is good for their children (and for each other), but life gets busy and commitments that were made in sincerity are tested. We shouldn't commit to something we cannot keep. This is true for God and people. Not keeping commitments happens frequently between parents and children, especially when they are young.

One reason we make rash promises is that we haven't counted the cost. Jesus warns against the failure to pause first and evaluate whether we have sufficient resources (time, money, energy) to finish what we begin (Luke 14:28–30).

We need to learn to say, "No" more often, or at least, "Let me consider it, and I'll get back with you." Good business practice includes under-promising and over-delivering on products and services; this would be an excellent way to build trust and good will with others.

Some make promises they cannot keep because they do not want to disappoint others. The result is making too many commitments and then getting angry about having to keep them! When this is done on a consistent basis, it destroys trust that is essential to any relationship.

One way godly character is expressed is through being faithful to our promises. Ask God to help you to be faithful to your word.

ACTION POINT: Do you say, "Yes" too quickly to requests without considering the cost?

—Rick Johnson

APRIL 19
DAILY PRAYER FOR DAILY BREAD

Scripture Reading—Matt. 6:11
"Give us this day our daily bread."

In most modern homes, there is hardly a shortage of food to eat. The kitchen cabinets are full, the pantry is overloaded, and the refrigerator and freezer are jammed. In the typical home it could hardly be said that there is nothing left to eat for the next meal. For that reason it might seem like there is really never a need to pray, "Give us this day our daily bread," because there is probably enough food to eat for the next month. With modern technology, it is possible to preserve food for longer periods of time than ever before, allowing most families to stock up with a ton of food.

In the day when Jesus lived, food preservation was very limited. There was no way for food to be canned, frozen, or vacuum-packed. Even refrigeration was nonexistent, allowing food to spoil very quickly. Vegetables and fruits were harvested, prepared, and eaten right away. When an animal was butchered, it was cooked and eaten immediately. For this reason the provision of food became a matter of daily concern.

In this prayer, Jesus was teaching about the need to depend upon God for the provision of physical and material needs. He also was teaching about the need for daily dependence upon God. You will remember that in Matthew 6, Jesus repeatedly said, "Take no thought for tomorrow" (v. 25, 31, 34), emphasizing the need to live for the present day. Through daily dependence upon God, there would be the evidence of God's goodness, which would be manifested and could be appreciated, thus making God more real to His people.

Once again it is obvious that prayer is to be so much more than just a way to get things—but rather it is a way to get to know God so much better. First, daily dependence upon God means the blessing of daily provision from God, but it ultimately means daily appreciation for God's goodness and blessing.

ACTION POINT: According to Exodus 16:4, 5, how much manna were the Israelites to gather? According to verses 17–20, what happened if they gathered too much?

—*Tom Palmer*

APRIL 20
BENEFITS OF BEING QUIET

Scripture Reading—Pro. 10:19
"In the multitude of words there wanteth not sin."

It is sad how careless we are with our words—even to those we love the most. Words are not neutral. Remember the little rhyme we learned in our childhood? "Sticks and stones may break my bones, but words will never hurt me."

That isn't true, is it? Sometimes words that break one's heart are remembered for a lifetime, but broken bones are easily forgotten. And it is the words that are said, not unsaid, that bring us the most pain.

All of us are guilty of saying too much or saying something with a wrong spirit. I have regretted saying things to my family. I wish I could have a do-over where I kept my mouth shut, but it's too late. The damage was done. If only I had been quiet!

There is a benefit in being careful with our words—it keeps us from sinning. The Bible teaches that the more you say, the more likely you are to sin (Pro. 10:19). This Scripture is a warning against verbosity. Those that speak their mind quickly often have great regrets later because of what they said.

I had a dear friend who is now in Heaven that was witty. His mind quickly associated different meanings to what was being said, and he was very creative in bringing humor into the conversation. It was unrehearsed and spontaneous, and I loved spending time with him.

One day after he had said something that made me laugh, I said, "I wish I had your wit! You are so funny and creative with what you say." Without hesitation, and very seriously, he replied, "Oh, no. You don't want that, Rick. I have gotten into a lot of trouble because I speak so quickly and without thinking." I never forgot that.

It's a good reminder: sometimes we speak spontaneously when it would have been better if we had been quiet.

ACTION POINT: Memorize Proverbs 10:19 and meditate upon it for a week.

—Rick Johnson

APRIL 21
WHAT DO YOU DO WITH A TROPHY?

Scripture Reading—Matt. 6:20
"But lay up for yourselves treasures in heaven, where neither moth nor rust doth corrupt, and where thieves do not break through nor steal."

Basketball was my game when I was in high school! Though I played for a small school, I gave it everything I had. I finally won a conference championship my senior year. During my junior year, I averaged 26.3 points per game, and during my senior year I averaged 23.7 points per game. On my shelf sat the three MVP trophies I earned tenth, eleventh, and twelfth grade. For a number of years those trophies were my pride and joy.

I must say, however, that over time things changed. I remember one day getting out my trophies to show to my children. I put them back together and lined them up for my kids to admire. I even took the opportunity to tell them what a great basketball player their Dad had been. And then—I know it's hard to believe—the children helped me carry my trophies to the trash can on the back porch.

Though a trophy may come as the reward for a job well done on the court or on the field, the ultimate reward is not the trophy. Let's face it, trophies will eventually get "rusted and busted," and many will finally end up in the landfill where they will rest in pieces. I have always believed that in athletics the eternal lessons that are learned will always be more valuable than the temporary rewards that are earned. Even when a team lifts a national championship trophy, they will still only be national champs for one year.

There is nothing wrong with winning a trophy or a championship. There is something even greater to play for though, and that is based not on what you do, but on what you become.

ACTION POINT: Ask if anyone in your family has ever won a trophy in sports. Talk about what it meant to them then. Talk about what it means now.

—Tom Palmer

APRIL 22
FOLLOWING THE ANCIENT PATH

Scripture Reading—Jer. 6:16
"Ask for the old paths, where is the good way, and walk therein."

God looks at matters much differently than His people often do. By the time of Jeremiah's day, Israel was facing the judgment of God by being sent into captivity. The Lord reminds Israel to "ask for the old paths, where is the good way, and walk therein, and ye shall find rest for your souls."

The "old paths" refers to an ancient path—the path that God gave to Israel in the beginning. He had given them His law and His ways which they were to follow. Every generation of Christians faces a choice to follow the ancient path of the Bible or to chart their own course. It seems that every generation desires to "reinvent the wheel" for themselves, making their own ideas supreme without regard to what God gave in the "old paths."

Think about what you have taught in your family. What truths or warnings did your parents teach you? What standards of holiness did they communicate while you were growing up? What commandments did they try to instill in your heart and mind to follow?

Every generation will face new challenges and conflicts over its faith. Many in each generation try to develop their own doctrines, standards, and ways of living. The past is viewed as unnecessary. The ancient path is seldom considered as valid.

Many in today's younger generation have evaluated the old paths of holiness and found them displeasing. Many today are reevaluating whether there really is a hell (Matt. 10:28), whether it really is okay to drink alcohol or do drugs (Pro. 20:1), or whether husbands and fathers should really be the leaders in their homes (Eph. 5:25–27).

God is much more concerned with our asking for the old paths than our finding new ways. He is concerned with passing along His truth from generation to generation. For God, there is no need to reinvent the wheel. The old paths will do just fine.

PRAYER: Lord, I commit myself to following the "old paths" of your Word.

—*James Stallard*

APRIL 23
TO THE UNKNOWN GOD

Scripture Reading—Acts 17:23
"TO THE UNKNOWN GOD . . . him declare I unto you."

The city of Athens was known as the philosophical capital of the Roman Empire. The Athenians worshipped various gods and debated all kinds of ideas. While preaching about Jesus, Paul was brought to Mars Hill where those debates took place (Acts 17:17–19). It was at this famous spot that Paul declared what are now famous words: "TO THE UNKNOWN GOD."

He had seen this on one of the monuments they had built and used it to talk about God. To a group of men who did not know anything about God, Paul talked about the basic themes of the Bible:

1. **God is the Creator of the Universe**—"God that made the world and all things therein" (Acts 17:24).

2. **God is the Redeemer of All Mankind**—"That they should seek the Lord, if haply they might feel after him, and find him, though he be not far from every one of us" (Acts 17:27).

3. **God is the Judge of All the Earth**—"But now commandeth all men every where to repent: Because he hath appointed a day, in the which he will judge the world in righteousness by that man whom he hath ordained; whereof he hath given assurance unto all men, in that he hath raised him from the dead" (Acts 17:30, 31).

What a simple and yet powerful testimony Paul gave! Here are three major themes—Creator, Redeemer, Judge—that run throughout the entire Bible. These are three truths that must be believed or a man will never come to know this UNKNOWN GOD. Have you come to know the UNKNOWN GOD? Have you accepted Him as the one who created you and gave you life?

Have you trusted what Christ did for you on the Cross? He died for your sins, paying the price you deserved to pay. It is by The Cross that He is not far from any of us. Do you understand that He is the coming Judge before whom you will stand? What an amazing thing it is that this UNKNOWN GOD desires to be known and found by each of us!

DISCUSS: Discuss the three main themes of the Bible and whether each family member knows this UNKNOWN GOD.

—James Stallard

APRIL 24
TRAINING WHEELS OR NOT

Scripture Reading—1 Pet. 1:7

"That the trial of your faith, being much more precious than of gold that perisheth, though it be tried with fire, might be found unto praise and honour and glory at the appearing of Jesus Christ."

Asa was filled with great expectation and excitement! His fifth birthday was coming up, and his parents had promised to buy him a bicycle. Running late as usual, his parents were at the store looking at the large selection of shiny bikes. After looking and debating, they settled on one that they knew Asa would like. Asa's mom insisted that they buy the training wheels for it. Asa's father insisted that he didn't need them. After some discussion, Asa's mother finally asked, "Why don't you think Asa needs these? Without them, he will never learn to ride this bike." Asa's father calmly answered, "I'll teach him to ride by running beside him. This way Asa will learn that I will be right beside him to catch him when he thinks he is going to fall."

Does it ever seem to you that God is willing to let you fall under the circumstances and trials of life? As hard as some things seem, our Lord is always there for us. He has promised to "never leave us nor forsake us."

Why do we experience trials then? God has told us in His Word that trials are opportunities for our faith to grow, which ultimately brings Him glory. When we, as His children, live by faith even in the midst of difficult times, He is glorified!

Are there trials and apparent hardships in your life? Will you trust your loving, heavenly Father to purify your faith through them? Will you trust that your God will NOT let you fall?

ACTION POINT: Think of a time in your life when you felt like you were all alone in the midst of a difficult time. Thinking back, can you see now how God was by your side through the trial? Discuss it together as a family.

—*Stanley Long*

APRIL 25
THE IMPORTANCE OF LISTENING

Scripture Reading—Pro. 10:19
"He that refraineth his lips is wise."

My temperament is that of an introvert, and so it is easy for me to listen. In fact, sometimes my reticence to speak has nothing to do with me being spiritual, but just because I am wired that way. However, with my family it is easier for me to talk more because we know each other so well. Sometimes it is not a blessing to them.

It is easy for me to fall into "lecture mode" at home when I should be listening. One reason is that I am a pastor, and leaders of necessity are opinionated. Much of my life is centered around talking—in the pulpit, in counseling sessions, in meetings, on visitation, on the phone.

I have had to learn to take off my "preacher hat" when I am at home and listen. I'm in my mid-50s and am still having to learn this. If I neglect to be a focused listener and lapse into talking, I can become an arrogant prattler and not impart wisdom, but become an aggravation.

Perhaps it might be wise to ask (privately) each member of the family a question: "Do you feel like I listen to you? Do you feel that I lecture when I talk to you?" The answers may be surprising, but very instructive and helpful—and life-changing for your family.

When my children were young, occasionally I would ask them a question, "Is there anything about Dad that you would like for me to change—something that bothers you that you wish I wouldn't do?"

Once I asked this and there was a hesitant reply, "No, Dad, there is nothing I can think of that bothers me." After some gentle encouragement they said, "Well, sometimes you don't listen."

What a bummer to have a father that was better at lecturing than listening to the most important people in his life!

It's true: "A wise man has something to say; a fool has to say something."

ACTION POINT: Ask your family members if you are a good listener.

—Rick Johnson

FRIENDS ARE LOYAL
Scripture Reading—Pro. 17:17
"A friend loveth at all times, and a brother is born for adversity."

The word "loyal" means that which is true, constant, and faithful. True friends are loyal even when it may cost them. Loyalty is not known until it is tested.

This happened in King David's life. In a difficult time David's heart was breaking, and he didn't know whom he could trust. His friend, Hushai, was loyal to him in a time of insurrection (2 Sam. 15:30–32). His friendship was proven through his loyalty.

This was not the first time Hushai had done so. He had risked his life for David (2 Sam. 16:15–19; 17:5–15). Loyalty is costly and will be tested. Sometimes you will be in the minority, and it will be difficult to stand by your friend.

Some do not pass the test. Aaron bailed out on Moses and failed to be loyal (Exod. 32:1–6). Ultimately our loyalty is not to any person, but to Jesus Christ. Nor is loyalty given to institutions, but to God, His Word, and His principles. As long as a leader is acting within the confines of God's will, we ought to be loyal to him.

The opposite of loyalty is betrayal. This brings deep hurt (Job 19:14, 19; Ps. 38:11; 41:9; 55:12-14; Zech. 13:6). Children hurt parents through their disloyalty (Pro. 10:1; 17:21).

A friend of mine asked Dr. J. Harold Smith what the greatest challenge in his ministry had been. He replied, "Being betrayed by a close friend."

God takes seriously the issue of our being loyal to friends (Job 42:7; Pro. 17:17; 27:10). At some point your loyalty will require sacrifice (John 15:13; 1 Sam. 18:1–4; 19:4). This is why it is such a rare quality. It is costly.

Both Jesus, a perfect man, and Paul, a godly man, experienced betrayal by those that professed to be their friends (Mark 3:21; 14:50; John 16:32; 2 Tim. 4:9–11, 16, 17).

"In prosperity our friends know us; in adversity we know our friends," said John Churton Collins.

ACTION POINT: Do you have any friends going through tough times? Let them know of your love for them.

—Rick Johnson

APRIL 27
FRIENDS ARE ATTENTIVE

Scripture Reading—Job 2:11
*"Job's three friends . . . came . . . to mourn with him
and to comfort him."*

"Fair weather" friends are present when the sun is shining, but cannot be found when things are tough. True friends help no matter the cost, time, or energy required. They don't turn away when the price tag is revealed; they are eager to help and serve.

John showed up at the time of Christ's greatest need (John 19:26). While Job's friends could have done better when they talked with him, initially their intentions were pure (Job 2:11).

Zabud was Solomon's friend. He was the son of Nathan (1 Kings 4:5), the prophet that had confronted David about his sin. Humanly speaking, he was the reason David got things right with the Lord. There was a unique connection between the sons of these two men. David even named one of his sons Nathan; that was Solomon's brother (1 Chron. 3:5).

"Nathan" means "to give." He fulfilled the meaning of his name by giving to Solomon a friend, his son, Zabud, to minister to him in times of great sorrow. It's important to note that it doesn't say that Solomon was looking for a friend, but that he had a friend. While I'm sure that Zabud felt close to Solomon, too, that wasn't his focus. His focus was to be his friend.

Zabud was Solomon's friend because he was looking out for his welfare when others were not. I have a dear missionary friend that was thousands of miles from America and in great despair. One of his friends flew at his own expense to minister to him. It was a turning point in my friend's life.

We miss opportunities to minister to our friends because we assume others are taking care of them. This is especially true when a person is in authority or well-known. God blessed Solomon greatly by giving him a friend in Zabud. Too often we long to have a friend like Zabud when God wants us to be a Zabud to someone else.

ACTION POINT: Invite your pastor and his family to a meal, and bless them with your friendship.

—*Rick Johnson*

APRIL 28
IT IS ALWAYS BETTER TO OBEY

Scripture Reading—Deut. 12:28
"Observe and hear all these words which I command thee,
that it may go well with thee."

Tucker was a dog that came to live with us when he was less than one year old. Raised to work cattle, Blue Heelers like Tucker are very valuable on ranches where cattle and horses are raised. Tucker loved to go for walks with me early in the morning. When we didn't go walking, he was always disappointed, even chewing the laces off my walking shoes one morning when we didn't walk.

Not long after Tucker and I started our daily walks, I taught him to lay down whenever a car would come by. As a vehicle would approach, I would say the word "down," and Tuck would immediately lay down and put his head on his front paws until the vehicle would pass. Eventually it got to the point where I never needed to say anything because Tuck would just automatically lay down when he heard a vehicle. One time he even lay down though there was not a car in sight. I finally realized that he had heard an airplane overhead. He learned his lesson well, and it was a good thing he did.

Cattle dogs must be very obedient dogs that learn how to respond to every command from their masters. I knew that Tucker would eventually be going with my son to live and work on a horse ranch with a large herd of horses. Tucker was going to take the place of another Blue Heeler named Crawford who had been trampled by a herd of horses. Crawford had been told to stay, but he ran in front of the horses leaving the corral and was seriously and permanently injured. I knew that if Tucker did not learn to obey properly, he too might face serious consequences. If obedience is important for dogs, it certainly must be important for children and adults too. Truly, things go better when we obey.

ACTION POINT: List several names of people in the Bible who suffered severe consequences for disobedience.

—*Tom Palmer*

APRIL 29
TOGETHER EVERYBODY
ACHIEVES MORE

Scripture Reading—Ps. 133:1
*"Behold how good and how pleasant it is for the brethren
to dwell together in unity!"*

I want to tell you about one of my favorite parts of the game of basketball. No, it is not the spectacular dunk, or the perfect three-point shot. It is actually a part of the game that usually gets forgotten because everybody remembers the dunk or the shot. I love assists. An assist takes place when a player gives up the ball and passes it to another player so that player can score. Rarely does a player ever get applauded for a great assist because assists seem like such a small part of the game. However, without assists, there would be no dunks or three-pointers to dazzle the crowd.

I love assists because assists are a great demonstration of teamwork. When a team plays like a team, every players seeks to do his or her part for the good of the team. Teamwork teaches unselfishness. Teamwork teaches cooperation. When I see the word T-E-A-M, I always think of this phrase: **T**ogether **E**verybody **A**chieves **M**ore. So much more is accomplished when every player does his or her part.

This is one of the reasons why I like athletics. Sports provide a great opportunity to learn what I call life lessons. After all, isn't life all about learning to work with other people? Teamwork is essential in marriage, family, work, and church. There is no such thing as "a one-man show" in any of these places. Whether there are lots of players or lots of people, what really matters is that each one works for the good of the team.

When team members can't or won't work together, the team usually is defeated. On the other hand, I have seen teams that were not as fast, talented, or experienced as their opponents, but when they played like a team, they were tough to beat. In reality, when the team wins, everybody wins. When the team loses, everybody loses.

ACTION POINT: What is a ball hog? Discuss how a ball hog will either help or hurt the team.

—*Tom Palmer*

APRIL 30
VANITY OR VICTORY?

Scripture Reading—Eccl. 12:13

"Let us hear the conclusion of the whole matter: Fear God, and keep his commandments: for this is the whole duty of man."

The word "vanity" means "emptiness," or we could say, "a wasting of time." God wants us to live a life of "victory" and not "vanity." But how? Let's learn from someone else's experience.

Solomon was a king who started out great. He was humble, and when God encouraged him to ask for anything he wanted, Solomon said, "I am but a little child." Solomon then asked for wisdom to lead the people. God was so pleased with his humble request that He gave Solomon both wisdom and wealth. But later in life Solomon disobeyed God's clear teaching, and his heart was turned away from God. The Book of Ecclesiastes is his search for meaning "under the sun." That means he tried to find meaning in life in pleasure, possessions, projects, and the pursuit of learning—all apart from God. The result for him was emptiness. He even got to the place where he said he "hated life." Solomon had forgotten God. In the last chapter he comes to his senses and declares, "Fear God, and keep his commandments: for this is the whole duty of man."

Do you ever forget God? People can be so forgetful. Have you ever seen people in the parking lot at the mall looking for their cars because they forgot where they parked them? It's one thing to forget where we parked, but it's really sad when we forget God. Ecclesiastes 12:1 says, "Remember now thy Creator in the days of thy youth." We remember God when we pray before a meal and when we look at the beauty of His creation. We remember God when we worship in church and spend time in His Word. There are many ways to remember God. Solomon also reminds us that life is short. He talks about getting old in Ecclesiastes 12 and lets us know what is ahead for us all. Then he encourages us to receive the words of truth, and lastly, to reverence the Lord by fearing and following Him! We can live in victory and not vanity!

DISCUSS: Discuss as a family the ways we can remember God. Why not take turns and have each person remember God in prayer right now.

—Sammy Frye

MAY 1
A WOMAN FOR THE AGES

Scripture Reading—1 Pet. 3:4
". . . even the ornament of a meek and quiet spirit,
which is in the sight of God of great price."

Who can women look to as an example? Today's world portrays women as superheroes who are able to perform great feats of physical strength. At the same time the world portrays these heroines as immodest and immoral.

A Christian woman who centers her life in her home and who shuns these worldly notions about her feminine role might be tempted to feel "left out." But God has not left women without a witness. When the Scripture looks to a woman to serve as an example to all women, it speaks of the godly woman known as Sarah, Abraham's wife.

Sarah was the mother of the Jewish nation, and though she was not perfect, she had the qualities that gave her the attention of Heaven. Note what the Scripture says about wives who have the right attitude toward their husbands. They are to have "the ornament of a meek and quiet spirit, which is in the sight of God of great price" (1 Pet. 3:4). Sarah is mentioned in the next two verses as someone who illustrates this meek and quiet spirit, and Christian women are called the daughters of Sarah as they follow her example.

To be meek is not to be a doormat with no ability. A meek person must be strong to surrender her rights to the needs of those she is serving. A successful wife and mother will desire to serve her family. A quiet person is one who is not controlled by fear, but instead exercises faith in God in the midst of her family situations.

Such a woman will find herself being praised by her family: "Her children arise up, and call her blessed; her husband also, and he praiseth her" (Pro. 31:28). She will surely be seen as a positive force in the Church as well as an example to other wives and mothers. May every Christian woman become a woman for the ages.

FAMILY PRAYER: Have each family member pray a prayer of thanksgiving for the wife and mother of the house.

—*James Stallard*

MAY 2
WHAT IS THE BIG DEAL ABOUT SPORTS?

Scripture Reading—1 Tim. 4:8
"For bodily exercise profiteth little:
but godliness is profitable unto all things."

A $100 pair of running shoes, 100,000 people crammed into a football stadium, or 100 million people in front of the TV watching the Olympics, it's all the same—sports are a big deal! When you consider the money that is spent, the crowds that gather, and the time that is involved, it becomes obvious that there are very few things more important in our modern culture than sports. There are those, however, who are quick to condemn anything involving athletics, assuming that God and the Bible have little or nothing to say about the subject. It seems to me that the key is understanding the proper place that athletics should have in the life of a person or family.

Yes, Paul did say that "bodily exercise profiteth little," but he did say that it profits. Bodily exercise becomes profitable when it helps us attain the ultimate goal of godliness, which is always profitable. As a player and a coach, I have always believed that being an athlete should make me a better Christian. You see, many of the personal qualities and disciplines that make a great athlete are necessary in the development of a godly person. Some of the greatest life lessons I have learned were on the court or on the field. Though many of the benefits of sports are temporal in nature, the benefits of godliness are eternal in nature.

If the ultimate goal of athletics is a trophy or a championship, then truly there is minimal profit for a Christian in sports. However, if the ultimate goal is to use the arena of sports as a training ground for life, then the maximum benefit will be attained. Whether in the gym, at the track, or on the field, a person must never neglect the ultimate spiritual goal. Even a world championship is only good for one year, but godliness will be eternally valuable.

ACTION POINT: Allow each family member to name their favorite sport and tell why he or she enjoys it.

—Tom Palmer

MAY 3
A SPLINTER OR A 4X4

Scripture Reading—Matt. 7:3–5

"And why beholdest thou the mote that is in thy brother's eye,
but considerest not the beam that is in thine own eye? Or how wilt
thou say to thy brother, Let me pull out the mote out of thine eye;
and, behold, a beam is in thine own eye? Thou hypocrite, first cast out
the beam out of thine own eye; and then shalt thou see clearly
to cast out the mote out of thy brother's eye."

Isn't it easy to find fault in the people around you? You see one of your siblings doing something wrong, so you hurry to make sure someone knows. Of course, you would maybe say that you don't want them to get in trouble, but there's something in you that finds joy in seeing someone else's sin. It's easy for us to be self-righteous and think that we are better than someone else when we see their sin. There's something that makes us feel good when we notice a sinful problem in someone else's life.

Jesus told a story about a man who noticed that his friend had a little something in his eye. He was quite concerned about the little splinter (mote), but he failed to notice that he had a big log (beam) stuck in his eye. Isn't that a funny picture? The man was so concerned about the tiny little splinter that he missed the obvious log sticking out of his own eye. Jesus was trying to show us that we are often in tune with the little things that other people do that are sinful but we often miss the obvious sins that are in our own lives. If we started to recognize our own sins, we wouldn't be so quick to find fault in others' lives.

Jesus says to take care of our own sin first and then try to help someone who we notice is struggling with sin. Before you go to someone in regards to something that they're doing wrong, look at your own life and examine whether your heart is right.

ACTION POINT: Do you find fault in others' lives? Do you struggle with the same problem?

—Aaron Coffey

DO YOU DELIGHT IN GOD'S WORD?

Scripture Reading—Ps. 1:2
"But his delight is in the law of the LORD;
and in his law doth he meditate day and night."

Psalm 1:1 tells us that the man who is truly going to be blessed in this life, first of all, understands that true satisfaction cannot be found by listening to the counsel of this world. In Psalm 1:2 we are told that true blessing and satisfaction are found by delighting in and meditating on the "law of the LORD." When the psalm speaks of the law of the Lord, it is talking about the Word of God itself—the Bible. The person who "delights" in the Word of God will find true blessing.

The word "delight" is a great word. It refers to what you get excited about, or what you get emotionally "pumped up" about. What do you delight in? We understand this word because we all have little things that we delight in. We delight in sports teams, in hobbies, in relationships, etc. We even delight in silly things like our favorite foods! Psalm 1 is telling us that the way to true satisfaction is through delighting in the Word of God.

I have a question for us to consider. Is there a difference between duty and delight? Yes there is. Duty is noble, but there is a difference in doing something out of duty and doing something out of delight. My brother-in-law served 3 deployments in the U.S. Army, faced much combat, and was decorated because of his heroism. But was that duty or delight? He served his country and his fellow soldiers out of duty—noble duty. But delight was back at home with his wife.

What is your attitude toward the Word? Are you stuck in duty? Why do you read your Bible? Why do you go to church? Is it just what you've always done?

This is not to diminish the importance of duty. There are times when we don't feel like doing what is right, and it is vital that duty kicks in and pushes us through. But by God's grace may we be people who get past duty-driven Christianity, and may we be people who truly delight in the Word!

PONDER: Take a moment to examine your attitude toward the Word of God. Are you driven by duty or delight? Why don't you take a few minutes and talk about it with your family?

—Aaron Coffey

MAY 5
YES, SPORTS ARE IN THE BIBLE

Scripture Reading—1 John 5:4

"For whatsoever is born of God overcometh the world: and this is the victory that overcometh the world, even our faith."

Let's begin with a simple biblical word study. Do you see the word "overcometh" in our key verse? In the Greek language, in which the New Testament was originally written, the word is spelled "nikao," which comes from the root word spelled "nike." Wow, that word sure sounds familiar, especially if you have ever been in a sportswear or athletic equipment store. It means "to subdue or conquer, to prevail or overcome, and to ultimately get the victory."

When an athlete or an athletic team enters competition, they seek to gain the victory over their opponent by conquering that opponent. Though there may be struggles and setbacks, defeat is not considered to be an option. A game plan is developed that will ultimately bring victory over the opponent. In this passage, John speaks of gaining victory over the world, which would seek to bring defeat in the life of a believer. An athlete understands that victory doesn't come automatically by simply showing up at game time. Rather victory is the result of dedication and devotion that involves a lot of hard work.

I remember a famous one-liner that said, "No pain—no gain." My players would say it when they were sweating and hurting during preseason soccer camp. This simple statement was a reminder of the commitment it would take to bring victory to our team. As a coach, that statement also gave me the opportunity to help my players understand the commitment it would take to be victorious in their lives as Christians. There is no victory by accident or coincidence!

Many times I sat with the teams I coached, and we prayed together that God would make us winners, not just on the field but in our lives for Christ. With that desire, you will not be a loser, regardless of the final score.

ACTION POINT: Find the athletic terms in the following passages: Heb. 12:1; 1 Cor. 9:26; Eph. 6:12.

—*Tom Palmer*

MAY 6
GOD CAN SAVE ANYONE
Scripture Reading—Matt. 19:26
"With men this is impossible; but with God all things are possible."

Some people seem so far away from God that we might think that they will never get saved. We pray for them for years and think, "It would be a miracle for them to be saved!" The truth is, it is a miracle that anyone is saved!

Jesus said that the new birth couldn't be fully comprehended by us (John 3:7, 8). Concerning salvation, our Lord said, "With men this is impossible" (Matt. 19:26). Keeping the law of God cannot save us, only resting in Christ's payment for our sin can (Rom. 8:3).

Perhaps you have witnessed to a loved one or friend, and they have rejected Christ again and again. It is easy to settle into a wrong pattern of thinking: "They are never going to be saved." Maybe it is someone that has done things that are so wicked and perverse that you cannot ever imagine them coming to salvation.

Remember, God saves sinners. Not "good sinners," just sinners (Rom. 4:5). We all have the same need: spiritual life. The Bible teaches that a person without Christ is spiritually dead (Eph. 2:1). There aren't classes of death—dead, deader, and deadest. The Gospel has power to penetrate the most hardened heart and give spiritual life to a lost person.

Have you succumbed to thinking your friend or loved one will never be saved? Don't give up. Keep on praying, believing God, and loving them. Salvation is a work of God, but He will honor your prayers and testimony before them (Matt. 5:16).

A friend at church had an unsaved brother for whom he was greatly burdened. He had witnessed to him for years, and there was no response at all. Though discouraged, my friend kept praying, trusting, and loving. His brother became very ill, and God began to speak to him. In the ICU ward my friend had the privilege to win his brother to Jesus. I know him, and he is a changed man. It's a miracle!

ACTION POINT: Have you stopped praying for someone because you have given up on him or her?

—*Rick Johnson*

THE GREATEST SPOIL

Scripture Reading—Ps. 119:162
"I rejoice at thy word, as one that findeth great spoil."

In 2 Kings 7, we have the amazing account of four lepers who were the first to discover the spoils left behind by the Syrian army, whom God had put to flight.

The sun was setting one evening in Samaria, and sitting at the gate were four lepers. They were outcasts, but they had one thing in common with the rest of Israel—they were being starved to death by the king of Syria and his army. It was just a matter of time before all Israel would die of hunger. The lepers recognized the hopelessness of the situation and resolved to seek mercy from the enemy with the hopes of getting food. They reasoned that if the Syrians killed them, they were going to die of starvation anyway, so it didn't matter. Little did they know that God had other plans for them!

As the sun was setting, the four lepers left for the Syrian camp. Upon arrival, they noticed that the camp was strangely quiet. They immediately realized that they were all alone. The entire army was gone! The soldiers had left in such haste that they didn't take any of their personal belongings, including their money, horses, and food. The lepers wasted no time in satisfying their hunger with the spoils of the Syrians. Soon they carried the news back to Israel, and the entire nation was delivered from starvation.

In Psalm 119:162, King David likened his attitude towards God's word to the feelings those lepers had that evening when they first saw the Syrian spoil. What joy! What relief! What provision from the Lord! What deliverance from oppression! This is what God's Word was to King David. It was to him the satisfaction of all needs in his life. Shouldn't it be the same for us?

Do you see God's Word the way David did? Imagine if we opened the Bible every day expecting "great spoil" from the Lord as we read. How our lives would change! We would bless His name for meeting our needs every day.

ACTION POINT: Attempt each day to come to personal and family devotions with a sense of excitement and expectation from the Lord.

—Paul Miller

GEORGE MÜLLER AND A GOOD CONSCIENCE

Scripture Reading—1 Tim. 1:19

"Holding faith, and a good conscience; which some having put away concerning faith have made shipwreck."

George Müller was a man known for his great praying and his great faith. In answer to Müller's prayers, God provided the needs of multitudes of orphans who were under his care. It is also noteworthy that at age 70 he began his worldwide evangelistic tours along with caring for the orphanages. Over the next seventeen years, Müller made a total of eight trips around the world. This is remarkable considering the fact that Müller was known as a man of weak physical constitution. As a young man, Müller had been disqualified from military service because of poor health.

It was late in his life, at age 92, that Müller wrote these words about the secret of his strength: "I have been able, every day, and all the day, to work, and with that ease as seventy years ago."

In explanation of this marvelous preservation, he listed three causes: "1) To the exercising himself to have always a conscience void of offense, both toward God and man; 2) To the love he felt for the Scriptures and the constant recuperative power they exercised upon his whole being; 3) To the happiness he felt in God and his work, which relieved him of all anxiety and needless wear and tear in his labors." In summary it might be safely said that when a man stays true to the Word of God and keeps his conscience clear, he will live a pleasant and enjoyable life. It is the consequences of sin that make a man's life miserable and unbearable.

Here is a great secret for "adding years to your life and life to your years." A man or woman with a clear conscience will be free of the burden of guilt and regret that comes from wrong choices. When your conscience has been fine-tuned by the Word of God, it becomes a reliable guide that you can safely follow.

ACTION POINT: Read this quote by Benjamin Franklin: "A good conscience is a continual Christmas." What do you think he meant?

—Tom Palmer

MAY 9
A PARENT'S FAVORITE VERSE

Scripture Reading—Eph. 6:1
"Children, obey your parents in the Lord: for this is right."

When children are old enough to memorize Scripture, it usually doesn't take long to introduce them to Ephesians 6:1. The smiles on mommy's and daddy's faces gets real big the first time they hear, "Child-wen obey yow pawents in da Lowd fow dis is wight." However, for most children learning obedience involves much more than just memorizing the verse. There must also be an understanding of why obedience is important.

Take for example the typical toddler who is fast approaching the "terrific two's." Lunch is finished, and the peanut butter and jelly has been scrubbed off the face and hands. After a short playtime, Mommy announces that it is naptime. Junior is laid in the crib and tucked in with his favorite blanket. As the light is turned off and Mommy walks out the door, Junior must determine what he will do. He can either obey Mommy by lying still until he falls asleep, or he can disobey Mommy by standing up, and jumping around using the crib mattress as a trampoline. Obedience will make his mother very glad, but disobedience will make his mother very sad. Disobedience may also make Junior very sad because it is likely that Mommy will need to remind him that she meant what she said.

Junior may not yet be two years old, but obedience is already a concept that he must learn. You see, as he learns to obey his parents, he is also learning how to obey God, even though at this point he does not even know who God is. God put parents into children's lives to teach them to obey, so that they ultimately would learn to obey Him. Obedience will also make God very glad, and disobedience will make God very sad. Whether a toddler or a teenager, obedience is the key in responding to parents, and to God. It is a lesson that must be learned by each and every child.

ACTION POINT: Look up Ephesians 6:2, 3 and note the promises made to children who learn to obey and honor their parents.

—Tom Palmer

A Priority Focus in Our Daily Lives

Scripture Reading—Pro. 4:23

"Keep thy heart with all diligence; for out of it are the issues of life."

We become what we focus on, and we produce what we focus on. Parents, what are you focusing on as you train your children—their behavior or their heart? Young person, is your focus on what you do or what you are?

Certainly, behavior is an indicator of the heart, but it is the heart that is the source of our behavior. The word "heart" in the Bible primarily deals with our thoughts and affections, rather than our emotions. Emotions follow our thinking and affections.

Parents must be careful about focusing on the ideal in the life of a child to the exclusion of the heart. As sinners we have a bent towards evil that we will struggle with until we go home to Heaven. That means there is a difference in the ideal and reality many times. Continually pointing to the desired standard will not change the heart.

Emphasizing behavior over the heart will not only fail to work long-term, but it is discouraging in the short-term. Worse, it teaches the child that the most important thing is to maintain a good performance at the expense of the heart. The result is a child that ignores the condition of his or her heart and focuses on externals alone.

Focusing on behavior alone and neglecting the heart will produce a Pharisee who is judgmental, angry, and self-righteous. It is possible for the outside to be in good order, but the heart be full of sin (Matt. 23:25–28; Luke 16:15).

As our children become teenagers, if they neglect their hearts, they will become self-righteous, rather than broken over their sin (Luke 18:9–13). When David committed adultery and murder, he pretended that things were right in the sight of others, but God wanted his heart to be right (Ps. 51:6).

Failure to guard and protect our hearts will have ungodly consequences in the end. The same is true if we focus on our children's behavior and ignore the state of their hearts.

ACTION: Write 1 Samuel 16:7 on a card and put it in a visible place to memorize it and meditate upon it.

—Rick Johnson

MAY 11
A FATHER'S PROTECTION

Scripture Reading—Job 1:5
"Job . . . offered burnt offerings according to the number of them all:
for Job said, It may be that my sons have sinned,
and cursed God in their hearts. Thus did Job continually."

Fathers, if an enemy were invading our home, we would want to do all we could to save the lives of our wife and children. This is even more necessary in the spiritual realm.

Today there are enemies of our souls everywhere trying to devour the Christian faith and destroy our families. Violence, drugs, pornography, abortion, teenage pregnancy, rejection of God and the Bible, immoral lifestyles, and many more horrors await families who go unprotected.

From a father's point of view, it is difficult to know how to protect his family. This is especially true in this day and time. Today the role of the father as a leader and protector has been challenged by the culture.

Many fathers know they should protect their families spiritually but are confused over what they should be and do. The Bible gives an account of a godly father who knew how to protect his family. This man's name was Job. We remember him for his endurance in the midst of suffering. However, the Word of God reveals the spiritual way in which he dealt with his family.

- Job lived a godly example in front of his family (Job 1:1).
- Job did not allow wealth and riches to turn him away from God (Job 1:3).
- Job was burdened and cared so much about the spiritual condition of his grown children that he sacrificed to God on their behalf (Job 1:4, 5).
- Job enjoyed a hedge of protection around him and his family (Job 1:10).
- Job remained spiritual in spite of an uncooperative wife (Job 2:9, 10).

What a testimony he had! Only God's purpose allowed the tragedy that took place in Job's life. We can rest assured that if we have the character of Job and pray a hedge of protection around our families that we can protect our wives and children the way God intends.

Family members should let the father know what makes them feel protected. A father does not always know automatically what is needed. Communication will be an open door to security in any home.

DISCUSS: Have each family member share ideas on how the father and husband can protect the family spiritually.

—James Stallard   132

MAY 12
THE VALUE OF VIRTUE

Scripture Reading—2 Pet. 1:5
"Add to your faith virtue."

Many young people that have grown up in Christian homes stop attending church after high school. Have you ever wondered why?

If we do not understand the cause of this problem and correct it, we will lose the generation that follows after us. I believe one of the reasons for this attrition is found in a vital ingredient that is neglected in our walk with the Lord. To miss this quality will result in the Christian life becoming an empty memorized routine.

Salvation is more than a fire escape from hell. It is an internal transformation that produces "life and godliness" (2 Pet. 1:3). The Spirit of God indwells every believer the very moment they are saved (Rom. 8:9), so that they might live holy lives (2 Pet. 1:4). This is not optional, but part of what it means to be a child of God.

The new birth is the beginning, but not the end, of being a Christian. We are to "add" to our faith (2 Pet. 1:5). With our faith in Christ as the foundation, we are to build on that faith. It is something that we are to do with "all diligence" (2 Pet. 1:5).

God gives a list of seven qualities that we are diligently to be adding to the foundation of our faith: virtue, knowledge, temperance, patience, godliness, brotherly kindness, and charity (2 Pet. 1:5–7).

The first quality, virtue, is the most important to cultivate after salvation. I believe a lack of virtue is the reason for the dropout rate among young people. We focus more on the second quality, knowledge, and ignore the first one: virtue.

The word "virtue" means "moral excellence." It is a quality of the heart and is the byproduct of a relationship with Jesus Christ. We must rediscover virtue and help instill it in our children if we would see them become godly disciples and not just Bible students whose minds are full, but whose hearts are empty.

PONDER: What is your plan to instill virtue into your life?

—Rick Johnson

DAILY EXHORTATION

Scripture Reading—Heb. 3:13
"But exhort one another daily, while it is called To day;
lest any of you be hardened through the deceitfulness of sin."

In these end days when Christians are running to and fro spending *precious* hours on iPads, iPhones, and i-this or i-that, we must be mindful of the writer of Hebrews' exhortation to "exhort one another."

Webster defined exhort as, "To incite by words or advice; to animate or urge by arguments to a good deed or to any laudable conduct or course of action."

Roget's Thesaurus lists these synonyms: "urge, press, push, encourage, insist, pressure."

Not only is there a great need to be exhorted but also to be an exhorter.

Frequency To Exhort

Our verse says daily, which goes beyond a friendly greeting once a week on Sunday morning at church. A study of both New Testament Christians and the early churches reveals that they had intimate acquaintance one with another on a daily basis. The body of Christ was a family and treated each other as such. They were mindful of one another's physical and spiritual needs. In other words there was no vacation from exhortation.

Reason For Exhortation

"Lest any of you be hardened through the deceitfulness of sin." Repeatedly in the Psalms, David describes the enemies of his soul, those that gaped upon him, attempted to destroy, wound, devour, and thwart his God-given purpose in life. The deceitfulness of sin comes in a multitude of forms, which every Christian is subject to. *Deceit can succeed only as long as it goes unrecognized.* God commands us to be our brother's keeper and to exhort and keep the spiritual enemies from gaining victory over us. Just as a soldier is responsible for his fellow soldiers in combat, the believer has a duty to exhort fellow believers to prevent the awful process of hardening from taking place. An exhorter is a watchman.

ACTION POINT: Write down a name (or names) of another believer to exhort. For one week exhort him or her on a daily basis with a Bible verse, conversation, email, or text message.

—Wayne King

MAY 14
RING, ROBE, REEBOKS, AND A RIBEYE

Scripture Reading—Luke 15:22, 23
*"But the father said to his servants, Bring forth the best robe, and put it
on him; and put a ring on his hand, and shoes on his feet:
And bring hither the fatted calf, and kill it; and let us eat, and be merry."*

We are looking today at one of the most beloved stories in Scripture—
the story of the prodigal son. "Prodigal" means "a waster, one given to
extravagant expenditures." This story was one of three given to confront the
Pharisees and scribes with their incorrect view of God (Luke 15:1–3).

In this parable the younger son said to his father, "**Give me** the portion of
goods that falleth to me." He later said **goodbye** and "took his journey into a
far country." While there, he ended up in the **gutter** (the pig pen) because he
"wasted his substance with riotous living," Fortunately, this young man "came
to himself" and made a decision to return to his father. He realized his father
was a good father and that he had sinned against Heaven and his father. He
decided to go home and offer himself as a hired servant in his father's house.
How would he be received?

When he returned, the Bible tells us his father showered him with kisses,
then presented him with a robe, a ring, shoes on his feet, and a feast. The robe
covered the rags and filthy clothing the young son wore and are a picture of the
righteousness Jesus Christ offers to guilty but repentant sinners (Rom. 3:24). The
father extended forgiveness to the son and dealt with the guilt and shame he most
surely felt. The ring represented "sonship" and the fact that the son would now
be able to transact business in the father's name. This meant the son was now
"accepted" back into the family and had regained full rights. The shoes on his feet
(Reeboks in my mind) represented a change in direction. The son is not walking
away from the father but is now walking with the father. The "fatted calf" (ribeye)
speaks of the satisfaction the son now enjoyed. Forgiveness, acceptance, change,
and satisfaction! All of this was the result of the love of the father for a wayward
son who returned having wasted his substance with riotous living.

DISCUSS: How do we treat sinners? Do we care enough to befriend them,
to pray for them, to show them the love of Christ, and to share the precious
Gospel with them?

—*Sammy Frye*

135

MAY 15
IMPATIENCE LEADS TO
SPIRITUAL MEDIOCRITY

Scripture Reading—Ps. 37:7
"Rest in the LORD, and wait patiently for him."

God is patient. He is never in a hurry, nor is He ever late. Over and again in the Scriptures, we learn of the necessity for patience (Ps. 27:14; Luke 21:19; Rom. 12:12; Heb. 10:36; Heb. 12:1).

The most difficult thing for me is to wait on God, but when I see the rich reward from it, I know it was worthwhile. Likewise, failing to wait on God will cause us to miss God's best for our lives.

Esau's impatience, the need to have a meal right now, cost him the rest of his life (Gen. 25:29–34). He was reminded every day of his failure to wait, and he regretted it.

Waiting time is not wasted time. God is building character in your heart to help you succeed in God's will. Without trials you'll never learn patience (Rom. 5:3, 4). And without patience you will make decisions that will keep you living a mediocre life.

When we tire of waiting, we become discouraged and quit. When we quit we miss God's best. Allowing a trial to have its full course in your life builds character (James 1:3, 4). Rejecting pressure is a sure recipe for a mediocre life.

Patience is required to discern God's direction (Ps. 106:12, 13). Patience is required for the Word of God to bear fruit in our lives and the lives of other people (Luke 8:15). Patience is required for future blessings and is a sign of spiritual maturity.

Teenagers need to learn the value of deferred gratification in areas such as marriage and physical intimacy. God's time is the best time.

Young couples need patience in making purchases early in their marriages that will bring difficulty in future years. Mediocre marriages are the result of an accumulation of decisions made without patience and a big-picture perspective.

Parents need patience as they guide and direct their children. A mediocre relationship with their children is the result of acting without waiting.

Remember that God will give His grace to help you wait (Isa. 40:31). "Let patience have her perfect work" today (James 1:4).

MEMORIZE: James 1:2–4.

—Rick Johnson

MAY 16
SCATTER THE GOSPEL

Scripture Reading—Mark 4:14
"The sower soweth the word."

God often compares His Word to seed (1 Pet. 1:23). As believers we are to scatter His Word, particularly the Gospel, all over the world (Mark 4:14; 16:15).

We are to scatter it at home, work, school, the mall—everywhere we go. The Bible is called "precious seed," and when we both sow and participate in the harvest, it brings great joy to us (Ps. 126:6).

The sowing is to be done with tears of compassion and concern (Ps. 126:5). It has well been said, "People don't care how much you know until they know how much you care." Scatter the Gospel with a broken heart. It will soften the hard ground.

A lady came to her pastor asking him to pray for her unsaved husband. He replied, "I will pray for your husband, but I know what the problem is with your own prayers." She was stunned and asked the pastor to explain, and he said, "It's your dry eyes."

It took persecution in the early church before believers scattered from Jerusalem and began to sow the seed wherever they went (Acts 8:4). Curtis Hutson said, "The only alternative to witnessing is disobedience." We must scatter the Gospel.

I try to carry gospel tracts with me everywhere I go. Sometimes I give them to people and ask them to read them, and other times I leave them in open areas where people can see them and read them. You never know when or where the seed you have sown will bear fruit. Remember that before the reaping is the sowing and scattering (John 4:36, 37).

My mother inserts a tract into every bill envelope she mails. One Christmas time she stuffed seasonal tracts into her payment envelopes. At a doctor's office as she was leaving, she noticed a tract just like hers that was on a small bulletin board by the receptionist.

She inquired about it and was told a patient had sent it in a bill, and she had read it often. It's our privilege and joy to scatter the seed.

ACTION POINT: Scatter the Gospel every day this week.

—Rick Johnson

137

MAY 17
OUR FINAL APPOINTMENT

Scripture Reading—Ps. 90:12
"So teach us to number our days,
that we may apply our hearts unto wisdom."

Having to face a deadline often helps focus our minds on the task before us. If we have a test coming up, how we plan time for study becomes important. If a project needs to be finished at the office, it forces us to plan our work better.

The Bible tells us that we all have a deadline that we will definitely come up against. It declares, "And as it is appointed unto men once to die, but after this the judgment" (Heb. 9:27). All men will face death unless the Lord Jesus Christ returns before that happens. It is an appointment that will not be missed.

But rather than living in fear, the believer is to use this knowledge to gain wisdom. Our text above says, "So teach us to number our days, that we may apply our hearts unto wisdom" (Ps. 90:12). To "number" our days means to "count" the days. The days of our lives on earth are limited, so counting them makes good sense.

An example of numbering our days can be found in the life of an Old Testament scholar named Robert Dick Wilson. Born in 1856 he studied at Princeton and Humboldt University of Berlin. He became a great teacher, scholar, and defender of the Christian faith.

Early in his Christian life, he understood that God wanted Him to defend the Bible against its critics. He asked the Lord to give him three segments of time for his life. First, he needed time to study languages that impacted on the Old Testament. Second, he needed time to do research on the issues of the day. Finally, he needed time to write to defend his findings. God fulfilled the request of Robert Dick Wilson who became a great professor, teacher, and writer defending the Old Testament from its critics until he died in 1930.

Whatever calling God may place upon our lives, it would be a good thing to number our days and wisely fulfill His plan for our lives.

PRAYER: Thank you, Lord, for the time you have given me to make a difference.

—James Stallard

MAY 18
A HARVEST OF PROVISION

Scripture Reading—Luke 6:38
"Give, and it shall be given unto you."

Whatever you scatter will come back to you. The absence of a harvest indicates an absence of sowing. Wherever there is a harvest, be assured that someone has sown some seed before you. The "Lord of the Harvest" observes how we give (Mark 12:41, 42). He will not be a debtor to anyone!

During your time of need, God activates a process of provision based on what you have sown in the past. Don Sisk said, "Tithing is a debt I owe; giving is a seed I sow." He is right.

Though we cannot predict the size or the time of the harvest, we know It is coming because God has promised (Luke 6:38). Your giving is like a trigger that activates provision for your needs. Like a seed that is planted—hidden away in the ground, out of sight, appearing to be wasted—your giving will one day come back to you.

When you sow a seed of corn, you don't just get one seed in return, nor do you get just one ear of corn. You get many ears on which are many seeds to sow more corn. Don't underestimate the importance of your sowing.

I spoke for 35 minutes at a church I had served at in the past, and they took up an offering for us. It was more than $2,500. A man in that church sent my daughter $1,000 for her missions trip. A short while later I came home from work, and there was a letter with a check for $1,200 from someone in that church. At that time we had some pressing needs in our family.

When we were in that church, we were faithful in our giving and sowed without an awareness of what or when the return would be. More than 20 years later when we had a need, God gave us a harvest to provide for us.

What you sow today is an investment in your provision in the future. It is your task to sow and God's to bring the harvest.

PONDER: Do you faithfully tithe and give generously to missions?

—Rick Johnson

Prayers Packaged in Praise

Scripture Reading—Matt. 6:13
"For thine is the kingdom, and the power, and the glory, for ever. Amen."

In this model prayer in Matthew 6, Jesus certainly did teach about asking for the right things in prayer. However, it is also worth noting that He began and concluded the prayer with praise and adoration of God the Father. When a person approaches the Heavenly Father in a spirit of worship, he is allowing his perspective of God to impact his petitions to God.

There are three things that are emphasized in this closing statement of praise. First, there is a reference to God's kingdom. It is noted that **God is the One Who is eternally sovereign in His position**. As David said, "Among the gods there is none like unto thee, O Lord; neither are there any works like unto thy works" (Ps. 86:8).

Secondly, there is a reference to God's power. We see that **God is the One Who is eternally supernatural in His power**. Once again referencing David we read, "For thou art great, and doest wondrous things: thou art God alone" (Ps. 86:10).

Finally, there is reference to God's glory. It is mentioned that **God is the One Who is eternally supreme in His preeminence**. David again says, "All nations whom thou hast made shall come and worship before thee, O Lord; and shall glorify thy name" (Ps. 86:9).

Whether we are beginning or ending a prayer, it is good to spend some time "bragging on God." Praise becomes like the envelope in which our prayer request card is placed before it is presented to God. When we package our petitions in praise, we will find that we will have an enhanced view of the God we are praying to. You will find that when you include praise in your communication with God, you will have a greater appreciation for Who God is and for what God can do. Praise will change the way that you pray.

ACTION POINT: Allow each family member to choose one thing about God that he or she is thankful for. Have a time of "bragging on God," and tell Him the things you chose.

—Tom Palmer

PRAYER IS NOT FOR EVERYBODY

Scripture Reading—Matt. 6:9
"After this manner therefore pray ye: Our Father which art in heaven,
Hallowed be Thy name."

In Matthew 6, Jesus taught what is often referred to as "The Lord's Prayer." Though only 66 words, this model prayer was given as a pattern for effective praying. Each section of this prayer includes another of the key elements of proper communication with God.

You will notice that this prayer begins with a personal address of God as "Our Father." This is a term that demonstrates relationship and is a title that can only be used by a child of God who is addressing his Heavenly Father. Sadly, there are those who are not children of God who assume that when they "say their prayers" they are talking to God. It must clearly be understood that it is not the privilege of any old kid on the block to jump up in the Heavenly Father's lap to ask for any old thing that he wants! Prayer is the privilege only of a born-again child of God. There is only one prayer of a lost sinner that God responds to and that is the sinner's prayer for salvation.

It is also important to note that the Father is addressed as being "in heaven" and having a name that is "hallowed." These thoughts speak of the position and the perfection of God. God is the great God of the universe, and we must acknowledge His supremacy. God is also a holy God, and we must recognize His purity. When these attributes of God are identified, we will have a better understanding of who we are talking to in prayer.

In the Hebrew culture names were often descriptive of the person to whom they had been given. When the name "Father" is used, it speaks much of the character of God. There is nothing more beautiful than the picture of a child and his father sharing close communication. This is the specialness of prayer for a child of God.

ACTION POINT: Look up Psalm 9:10 and 29:2 and make note of the significance of the name of God.

—*Tom Palmer*

INCONSIDERATE WORDS

Scripture Reading— **Pro. 14:3**
"In the mouth of the foolish is a rod of pride."

Words can wound people deeply. Especially damaging are those words that leave a deep hurt, and yet we are unaware of what we have done. The problem is a lack of consideration and sensitivity. We have grown accustomed to saying whatever comes to mind without considering how it might be received.

The Bible compares our words to a wooden stick that pummels someone and leaves bruises (Pro. 14:3). But the bruises are not on the body; they are on the heart.

A proud person fails to consider others when he speaks and foolishly believes his words are received no matter how they are delivered. We always ought to speak the truth, but we are to be gracious in how we say it. God instructs us to speak "the truth in love" (Eph. 4:15). Warren Wiersbe wrote, "Love without truth is hypocrisy, but truth without love is brutality."

I have known people that think it is a virtue to speak quickly, freely, and even brutally. Those on the receiving end perceive them to be harsh, rough, and rude. In their wake are people who have been deeply hurt—even the people they love the most. Pride blinds us to our lack of sensitivity and kindness.

Those that have grown up in a home where parents said the first thing that came to mind often struggle to be considerate in their words. No godly parent would ever hurt their children physically, but have hurt them emotionally with words spoken as a "rod of pride." The result is a bruised young heart that remembers what was said for a lifetime. God wants us to learn to be gentle in our words, rather than abrasive and inconsiderate.

Be considerate with your words, and you will build and edify people. Inconsiderate words create distance between people. We must remember that words communicate precise meaning, and we must be careful how we use them.

ACTION POINT: Ask God if you are prone to being inconsiderate with your words. Today, pause before speaking and filter your response through whether your words are kind.

—Rick Johnson

LAZINESS: THE SURE WAY TO GO HUNGRY

Scripture Reading—Pro. 19:15
"Slothfulness casteth into a deep sleep;
and an idle soul shall suffer hunger."

Nothing is more frustrating or annoying than having to put up with a friend or family member who is lazy. The Bible uses the "sloth" as a picture of the lazy person. In modern times sloths live in rainforests and secondary forests in Central and South America from Nicaragua through Venezuela, Brazil to Peru, Columbia, and in the Amazon Basin. But, they were known in biblical times and were used as a symbol of laziness.

Sloths basically hang in trees hardly ever moving while appearing to just eat and sleep. The Bible uses the sloth as a picture of a lazy person and then teaches the consequences of being slothful:

- Laziness can lead us to be controlled by other people (Pro. 12:24).
- A lazy person will find the path of his life difficult (Pro. 15:19).
- Laziness can lead a person to waste time and resources (Pro. 18:9).
- Laziness can lead a person to great hunger (Pro. 19:15, 24).
- Laziness causes a person to give excuses for being lazy (Pro. 22:13).
- The field or the house reveals laziness (Pro. 24:30, 31; Eccl. 10:18).

This idea of slothfulness applies to the physical *and* the spiritual life. Every member of the family should check up on themselves. Does the father or husband have hobbies that take him away from major responsibilities with his family? Does the wife or mother spend too much time on Facebook or watching television? Is the teenager slow to do chores around the house, but quick to help his or her friends? Do the younger children quickly complain when their parents ask them to do something like wash the dishes or help take out the garbage? Is anyone in the family lazy about reading the Bible every day?

Yes, a lazy person can go hungry, but "the hand of the diligent shall bear rule" (Pro.12:24). Which would you rather do: Go hungry or be a ruler of men? The choice is yours.

ACTION POINT: Make a list of chores for the week and make sure they get done on time. Have parents or siblings evaluate how you do.

—*James Stallard*

A DIVINE BENEFIT PACKAGE
Scripture Reading—Ps. 68:19
"Blessed be the Lord, who daily loadeth us with benefits,
even the God of our salvation."

I found a great thought that says, "As long as I am thankful, I will always be content, and when I am no longer thankful, I will no longer be content." You can count on the fact that those who demonstrate an attitude of gratitude are people who know what it means to be content. Here is a great poem written by an unknown author:

Thank You Lord…

Even though I clutch my blanket and growl when the alarm rings each morning,

Thank You Lord that I can hear. There are those who are deaf.

Even though I keep my eyes tightly closed against the morning light as long as possible,

Thank You Lord that I can see. There are those who are blind.

Even though I huddle in my bed and put off the physical effort of rising,

Thank You Lord that I have strength to rise, there are many who are bedfast.

Even though the first hour of the day is hectic, when socks are lost, toast is burned, tempers are short,

Thank You Lord for my family. There are many who are lonely.

Even though our breakfast table never looks like the pictures in the ladies' magazines, and the menu is sometimes unbalanced,

Thank You Lord for the food we have. There are many who are hungry.

Even though the routine of my job is often monotonous,

Thank You Lord for the chance to work. There are many who have no work.

Even though I grumble and bemoan my fate from day to day, and wish my modest circumstances were not quite so modest,

Thank You Lord for the gift of life.

ACTION POINT: Go back through the poem and thank God for each of the things mentioned. Focus on the ways God has been good to you and your family.

—Tom Palmer

MAY 24
ARE WE LISTENING?

Scripture Reading—Pro. 8:34
"Blessed is the man that heareth me."

Hearing is one of the most necessary human senses. Every day we hear the noise of man-made things, like cars and planes. We also hear the sounds of Creation—maybe we hear the song of a meadowlark, the whisper of a breeze, the bark of a dog, or the words of a loved one. In our verse today, blessing is promised to those who hear God. This takes spiritual hearing, which is only possible if the Holy Ghost is within us. This hearing is filled with worship, obedience, and faith and comes from listening to the voice of the Lord.

Consider the differences in hearing seen in a few Bible characters:

Adam, guilty and ashamed, sought to hide from the audible voice of His Creator. God confronted him with "Where art thou?" Adam **heard**, but he did not willingly "listen." And he certainly was not interested in a two-way conversation!

In the book of Samuel, we learn of a young boy named **Samuel** whom God spoke to the multiple times in one night: "And the Lord came, and stood, and called . . . Samuel, Samuel. Then Samuel answered, Speak; for thy servant heareth." A proper response to a Holy God! Samuel was on full alert and **hearing**, waiting for the next word from the Lord. 1 Samuel 3:19 states, "And Samuel grew, and the LORD was with him, and did let none of his words fall to the ground." Samuel from an early age valued the precious words of God, and what he heard he obeyed and acted on. These words took a rightful place in his heart, and Samuel did not trample under foot God's words that he heard.

Consider **Elijah**. After witnessing (and hearing) wind, fire, and an earthquake, he heard God speak with "a still small voice." Then God spoke to Elijah and asked him, "What doest thou here?" Elijah's next orders (and blessing) were given conditionally after **hearing** God's still small voice.

PONDER: We live in a noisy world with many things vying for our attention. Are we blocking out the world so we can hear God? When He speaks, are we listening with spiritually tuned ears, or are our ears dull of hearing?

—Wayne King

GUARDING A PRECIOUS TREASURE
Scripture Reading—Deut. 4:9
"Only take heed to thyself, and keep thy soul diligently, lest thou forget the things which thine eyes have seen, and lest they depart from thy heart all the days of thy life: but teach them thy sons, and thy sons' sons."

Leaving a godly legacy requires that parents be examples of what they want to see in their children's lives. An example is "a pattern or model that others can imitate and follow."

A simple principle of leadership is that people do what people see. Someone said, "A good example has twice the value of good advice." This is especially true in the home.

The Scripture above states that you are to "take heed to thyself" and to "keep thy soul diligently" (Deut. 4:9). Before we are to attempt to influence others, we must first be influenced by the truth.

The words "take heed" have the idea of securing or protecting a treasure. The word "diligently" means we are to do this with great effort. It is a focused and intentional effort to guard what is highly valued.

God wants us to value and protect our own spiritual condition. This example of devotion will be the foundation of your future legacy to those that will follow you.

The secret to personal integrity is guarding your soul. When the focus is on the heart, Christlike behavior will follow, and a consistent example will result. A predictable example is crucial if you would make an impact on those around you.

Bill Gothard said, "If you will take care of the depth of your life, God will take care of the breadth of your ministry." I believe this is true of your legacy as well. Who you are and what you do affects your children more than anything else you do. A godly legacy will not occur without a godly life and example.

ACTION POINT: Name someone that has influenced your life in a specific way because of his or her example. Take the time to communicate that to them through a note or an email, and let them know how they have challenged you in that area.

—Rick Johnson

WATCH YOUR WORDS
Scripture Reading—Ps. 139:4
"For there is not a word in my tongue, but, lo, O LORD,
thou knowest it altogether."

Many years ago a youth pastor was teaching a Sunday School class full of teenage boys. Wanting to teach them the lesson from our verse, he came up with a special plan. Before the boys arrived for class, he placed a tape recorder in a trashcan in the corner, and turned it on. After the boys were all seated, he said he needed to step out a moment. He went out in the hallway and just stood for a minute or two. When he returned to the room, he took the tape recorder from the trashcan, rewound the tape, and pressed PLAY. He said that the boys were nearly in a state of shock. Suddenly, they realized that the teacher was going to hear everything they had said while he had been gone. They were going to be held accountable for their words even though they assumed the teacher would never hear them.

It has been said that our tongue is in a wet place and so it is easy for it to slip. On the other hand there are words that are spoken that are not a slip of the tongue, but rather are intentionally unkind, untruthful, or uncontrolled. Even when spoken in a whisper, they are still heard by God.

Can you think of a time when you told a lie? Can you think of a time when you gossiped about someone quietly hoping that they would not hear you? Can you think of a time when you repeated a distasteful joke or story, making sure that your parents didn't hear what you were saying? Whether you realized it or not, God was listening.

The Bible says that it will be necessary to give an account to God for every idle word (Matt. 12:36). If you are going to say something that you don't want God or others to hear—then just don't say it at all.

ACTION POINT: Read the instruction regarding our words found in Psalm 19:14. Discuss how God knowing every word we speak should affect what we say.

—*Tom Palmer*

God Wipes Away Your Tears

Scripture Reading—Isa. 25:8
"The Lord GOD will wipe away tears from off all faces."

Wiping away tears is an expression of love and compassion. One night at dusk my son, Jeremiah, was at baseball practice playing catcher. He was warming up a pitcher without his mask on. He lost the ball in the twilight, and it hit him hard in the head.

He fell to the ground and began to weep as he called out to me, "Daddy, daddy, help me." I ran to him, knelt by him, and took my handkerchief and began to dab the tears away. It was easy to do because I loved him deeply and he was my son.

There is coming a time when all of our brokenness and tears will be healed and dried by the Son of God, and we shall "weep no more" (Isa. 30:19), and the "days of our mourning shall be ended" (Isa. 60:20)! Truly, the songwriter was right when he wrote, "What a day that will be!"

It is one thing for our tear ducts to lose their ability to function, but it is something far greater in Heaven. It is God Himself who will wipe our tears from our eyes (Rev. 7:17; 21:4). This is so tender and kind that it is like we are walking on holy ground to even ponder such a thought.

There are times when I remember those that are precious to me who have already gone to Heaven. In the wee hours of the morning while everyone is sleeping, I will weep. It isn't for their sorrow, but for my own. Though I know I shall see them again one day, for now I miss and love them very much.

What a blessed thought to know that there is not only coming a day when there will be no cause for tears but also that the living God will Himself comfort us as He wipes away our tears.

For now, we weep, but joy comes in the morning (Ps. 30:5)! Friend, if you don't know Christ personally, trust Him today and let Him heal your broken heart.

ACTION POINT: Rejoice, for that day when your tears will be no more.

—Rick Johnson

MEDITATING ON GOD'S WORD

Scripture Reading—Ps. 1:2
"In his law doth he meditate day and night."

The Bible will become rich to you and begin to transform your life when you begin to meditate on it. However, first you must memorize it, and before that you must read it. Bible meditation is a discipline that is greatly rewarded and much easier than most people think. If you know how to worry, you know how to meditate.

The word "success" is only used once in the Bible, and it is in association with meditating on God's truth (Josh. 1:8). Joshua was a busy man as the leader of the nation. He had decisions to make, people to meet, and plans to execute. Yet, he had time to read and meditate upon the Bible both in the morning and the evening.

The word "meditate" means "to murmur, ponder, mutter." It has the idea of studying a subject with your mind and then talking it through as you think about it. One reason the enemy keeps us from this discipline is because he knows the rewards of it.

Meditation brings wisdom (Ps. 119:97–100), joy (Ps. 104:34), and spiritual strength in one's soul (1 John 2:2–14). Meditation will change your life and character.

When we memorize and meditate on the Bible, it becomes "the engrafted word, which is able to save your souls" (James 1:21). That means it becomes a part of you, and the result is that your soul (thoughts, feelings, and choices) are aligned with God's ways.

The way we know we delight in the Bible is when we meditate upon it (Ps. 1:2). A convenient time to meditate is as we go to sleep at night (Ps. 63:6; 119:148). God promises to prosper us when we meditate on His Word "day and night" (Ps. 1:2; Josh. 1:8).

When I was thirty our ministry had severe financial problems. I thought I was having heart problems, but it was my fretting that was affecting my body. I purposed to memorize Psalm 37 and meditate upon it as an antidote to my fears—and it worked!

ACTION POINT: Select a Scripture that deals with a problem you are having. Memorize it and meditate on it.

—Rick Johnson

CONSEQUENCES OF MOVING THE BOUNDARIES

Scripture Reading—Jer. 6:16

"Thus saith the LORD, Stand ye in the ways, and see, and ask for the old paths, where is the good way, and walk therein, and ye shall find rest for your souls. But they said, We will not walk therein."

There are two consequences when we move our biblical convictions. First, we dishonor those that have established them. Godly parents pass along boundaries for a reason.

Oftentimes teenagers and young couples wrongly react to their parents' positions. When a pendulum is released, it doesn't stop in the middle—it keeps going to the opposite side.

The younger generation is rejoicing in some things that the older generation is weeping over (Ezra 3:12). It might do well to discover why the older generation is weeping. Perhaps it is because what is new isn't better.

Sadly, many young people treat the older generation as if they have nothing to offer. Rather than giving them respect and deference, we treat them like they are out of touch, maybe even stupid (Lev. 19:32). Churches that were built on biblical landmarks are now running senior adults off as the churches move the boundaries.

Before I bought my first car, I sought the advice of my father. When I considered coming to the church where I serve now, I sought the advice of my parents. How foolish it is to ignore their wisdom and fail to honor their contribution to my life.

A second consequence of moving the boundaries is that we miss God's wisdom. Rebellion blinds a person and causes him or her to miss the wisdom behind why a boundary was established in the first place. The Bible says, "With the ancient is wisdom" (Job 12:12). One of the ways God judges a culture is by removing the wisdom of the older people (Isa. 3:1–5).

Moving and disrespecting boundaries may give a temporary sense of freedom, but there is a great loss of wisdom. It is not done without consequence.

Basically there are two groups of people reading this: those setting up landmarks and those tempted to move them. Parents, keep on setting up biblical landmarks. Children, listen to those that have established them.

DISCUSS: Discuss what happens to a person when he or she ignores the boundaries of parents.

—Rick Johnson

MAY 30
THE MOST IMPORTANT BOOK
IN YOUR HOME

Scripture Reading—Ps. 119:105
"Thy word is a lamp unto my feet, and a light unto my path."

Having spent much time studying the history of the Oregon Trail, I know that families who headed west back in the 1800s had lots of questions. Each family needed to have a sturdy covered wagon and a strong team of animals to pull it. They needed bedding and cooking utensils and of course several firearms. They may have had a washtub and a plow, and some seed for planting. Obviously adequate food supplies claimed a large space in the wagon as well. There was, however, another thing that was absolutely priceless, and that was a book known as a trail guide. There were a variety of trail guides available, all written by men who had previously made this 2,000-mile journey to Oregon.

Families on the trail had questions, the answers to which were vital to their success. They needed to know how to cross a river, what route to take, and even what to do if attacked by Indians. The trail guides had the answers. Without a trail guide, the family was left to figure it out on their own, which made them very vulnerable in a wilderness that could be so unforgiving.

Families in our generation don't have covered wagons or flintlock rifles, but they do have lots of questions. Once again they need a book that has all the answers, and that book is the Bible. Only when families get back to Bible basics and are willing to live biblically can they properly deal with the many concerns they face. In Deuteronomy 6, the Israelites were instructed to get the Word of God into their hearts (v. 6). The key, however, is found in verse 7 where they are commanded to get the Word of God into their homes. Only a home full of the Word of God can produce a generation that is faithful to the Word of God. The trail is long and hard—make sure you take the Book.

DISCUSS: Discuss the four things for which the Word of God is profitable as from 2 Timothy 3:16.

—*Tom Palmer*

all scripture is given by inspiration
of God.
1. is profitable for doctrine
2. for reproof
3. for correction
4. for instruction in righteousness

151

MAY 31
BELIEVING THE CERTAINTY
OF GOD'S WORD

Scripture Reading—Pro. 22:21
"That I might make thee know the certainty of the words of truth."

When coming to the Bible, many people throw up their hands and say, "I just don't know what to believe!" They question whether it is possible to even know the truth. How can we be sure that it is true?

It is amazing: people will rarely doubt the existence of Julius Caesar from more than 2,000 years ago. Yet, they will stumble over the biblical record of Christ, even when the amount of material we have about Christ is thousands of times greater than what we have concerning Julius Caesar.

God has revealed Himself to mankind in two major ways. There is general revelation, where God has made Himself known through His creation (Rom. 1:19, 20) and in the consciences of men (Romans 2:14, 15). But there is also special revelation, where God speaks through His Word.

The Bible tells us that God wants us to trust Him (Pro. 22:19), that He has written down truth for us (Pro. 22:20), that we can know how certain and true these words are and that we can communicate them to others (Pro. 22:21).

Years ago I witnessed to a man who had doubted the truthfulness of the Bible because no one had answered a question for him. He told me if I could answer it he would trust Jesus as His Savior. I said, "Okay, I'll do my best to answer it." The question was simply this, "Where did Cain get his wife?" Satan had lodged that doubt in his mind for years.

I explained that if we take the Bible as it is, God created Adam and Eve as the first parents. Then their offspring would have to marry each other (brothers marrying sisters), and I showed him that Adam and Eve had many sons and daughters (Gen. 5:4).

When he saw the simplicity of the answer, he realized how horribly wrong he was to think the Bible could not be trusted. Within a few minutes he was in the Kingdom of God having received Christ as His Savior. Yes, we can know how certain and true God is when He speaks.

MEMORIZE: 1 Peter 3:15.

—James Stallard

JUNE 1
HAVE YOU LOST YOUR MIND?

Scripture Reading—2 Cor. 10:5
"And bringing into captivity every thought to the obedience of Christ."

In the early 1990s, retired President Ronald Reagan announced to the world that he had been diagnosed with Alzheimer's disease. This disease shuts down the memory of a person, and eventually they forget who they are and what they have done. He wrote a message to the people of America showing his courage and compassion for his wife, Nancy. He died from the disease in 2004.

There is probably not a family that has not been affected by this disease in some way. It is a horrible experience. But, there is something far worse than the physical form of Alzheimer's. We might call it "spiritual Alzheimer's." This is when a person has lost his mind when it comes to spiritual truth.

He cannot think right about God. He easily forgets what he has learned from any teaching and preaching he has heard. Are you like this? In spiritual matters, have you "lost your mind" by ignoring God's truth?

The Bible tells believers to be "casting down imaginations, and every high thing that exalteth against the knowledge of God, and bringing into captivity every thought to the obedience of Christ" (2 Cor. 10:5). Every part of our thinking should be brought under obedience to Christ.

This is a difficult principle. How easy it is for our minds to wander to think about things we should not think about. How easy it is for us to waste time thinking about things of no value. Many people become obsessed and can think of nothing else but entertainment, sports, fashion, or politics. Many of these things may have a legitimate place, but as Christians nothing should control our minds except God's Word.

The Bible warns us of the danger of not heeding what we have heard and the importance of not letting these things slip away from our minds (Heb. 2:1). We must evaluate every part of our thinking by the Bible, lest we forget what we have read and heard. Just as in the physical realm, so it is in the spiritual realm. A mind is a terrible thing to waste or to lose.

ACTION POINT: Read out loud 2 Corinthians 10:3–5 three times and then discuss it.

—James Stallard

153

JUNE 2
BROKEN PROMISES

Scripture Reading—Heb. 12:15
"Lest any root of bitterness springing up trouble you,
and thereby many be defiled."

Failure to keep our word to our family has consequences. I had to learn to watch my vocabulary and intentions when my children were younger. My wife taught me that young children do not comprehend words like "one day," "maybe," "real soon," and other expressions that made perfect sense to me.

Tell a child that something is a promise and it means now or at very latest this afternoon! This helped me to reduce "promises" that I never considered to be immediate, but as possibilities or future events. Though most children would never call their Mom or Dad a liar, in their hearts they lose respect for them when promises fail. They feel disappointed, hurt, and become bitter.

When we fail to keep our promises to our children, the seeds of bitterness are sown, and we gradually lose closeness with them. Then one day we realize something is wrong, and we wonder: "What happened to my relationship with my child? We used to be very close." Perhaps it was the compounding effect of making promises that were never fulfilled. At some point they closed their spirit to us.

I have spoken with adults that remembered words from parents that were never fulfilled—the promise of a special day, a vacation, an opportunity to play a sport, or a gift. Perhaps the parents even prefaced it with: "We'll see about that" or "maybe." But the hurt was still there. If you are reading these words and have been disappointed in the unkept promise of an authority, God will give you the grace to forgive.

I read that the great Civil War general Stonewall Jackson signed off his correspondence with the words, "Yours to count on." Under that was his signature. That's a weighty promise, but one especially important that we take seriously with our children.

One of the preventatives to creating bitterness in the hearts of our family is to say what we mean and mean what we say.

ACTION POINT: Release any bitterness you have to someone that has disappointed you.

—Rick Johnson

JUNE 3
FAILURE LEADS TO SUCCESS

Scripture Reading—Rom. 5:20
"Where sin abounded, grace did much more abound."

It is not God's will that we should sin as believers, but He has made provision for when we do (1 John 2:1). While He works in us through His Spirit to mature and grow us, He also cleanses and restores us when we sin and fail Him.

If we would have a teachable spirit and learn from our failures, God can and will still use us. One of our problems is that we don't want to admit to failure. We justify it and blame others, but we know that we have failed and so does God. The greatest obstacle to spiritual success is pride.

When you sin, confess it, forsake it, and don't wallow in it. Failure can be part of our journey to experiencing God's blessing, if we are humble enough to learn from it, rather than allowing it to defeat us.

I remember as a little boy when I got my first bike. Dad put little training wheels on the back so that I could get a sense of balance as I rode. The day soon came when he took those wheels off. I didn't want him to take them off because they represented security to me.

It was utter failure—again and again I fell. At one point I believed I would never ride that bike, but I stuck with it. Then the failure rate decreased, I got the hang of it, and I rode that bike. Unless a person is willing to fail, he or she will never learn to ride a bike—or do much of anything else.

The same was true as I first learned how to preach. It takes more than one sermon to improve and get to the point where you know what you are doing. It is a process.

This is where God's grace makes the difference (Rom. 5:20). No matter how deep the failure, grace goes deeper.

The measure of success is not whether you have a tough problem, but whether it's the same problem you had last year.

PONDER: What are some ways God can use failure in our lives to help us and bless others?

—Rick Johnson

JUNE 4
LET, DON'T LEAVE

Scripture Reading—James 1:4
"But let patience have her perfect work,
that ye may be perfect and entire, wanting nothing."

"Let" is a big little word. It means "to permit, to allow, to suffer." The individual who will "let patience have her perfect work" is someone who will keep serving God even when it is hard. Someone has said that when God is not doing something *for you*, He is trying to do something *in you* so He might be able to do something *through you*.

Have you ever felt like giving up? I remember selling books door-to-door in Sweetwater, Texas as a young man. Working six days a week, ten to twelve hours a day was challenging. My first roommates went home the first week. Suddenly, I was in an apartment alone and had a decision to make. Would I go home too? I decided to stay. It was hard work, a long ways from family and friends, and later that summer I was really homesick. I remember calling home one day, and when I heard my mother's voice, I started crying. And when mom heard me crying she started crying. She couldn't talk so she handed the phone to my dad. My dad listened awhile and then said something to me I will never forget. He said, "Son, get the job done and come on home." Those words were just what I needed to hear. I went back to work and finished what turned out to be a prosperous summer, and then I headed home.

There are times in life when we will be tempted to give up or run away, rather than staying put and pressing on when times get tough. God wants us to be steadfast and unmovable, always abounding in the work of the Lord. We are all tempted to give up at times and, if we do, we are likely to miss some wonderful blessings from the Lord.

By the way, at the end of that summer of selling books, I trusted Jesus Christ as my personal Savior! Praise the Lord! Will you finish the job and "let, don't leave"? God is up to something good in your life.

DISCUSS: Share about the times when you felt like giving up and who the Lord used to encourage you to press on and not give up.

—Sammy Frye

JUNE 5
I KNOW WHAT YOU ARE THINKING

Scripture Reading—Ps. 139:2
"Thou understandest my thought afar off."

Have you ever told someone that you know exactly what he or she is thinking? I have. In fact I have done it many times, and I have usually been right. When teaching children or preaching to teenagers, I have occasionally asked a student to stand up. I then tell them in front of the whole audience that I will give them ten seconds to think about anything they want to think about, and then I will tell the audience exactly what they are thinking. Usually they laugh as if to say, "There is not a chance." With someone keeping track of seconds, I say, "Ready, go." We allow the seconds to pass, and the student to think. At the end of ten seconds, I say, "You were thinking—he will never know what I am thinking." I told you, I am usually right!

Now, what I have done was somewhat of a trick and really just a play on words. Why? Because I really cannot know what anybody is thinking. In reality there are secrets that are known by only three people: "Me, myself, and I." The mind is a very private place and therefore a place that we often assume cannot be known by anyone. However, our verse tells us that God knows every thought that passes through our minds. Though even our closest friends and family members cannot read our minds, God still knows what we are thinking.

I asked a group of teenagers one time if they would like to see a video of the thoughts of one person in the group. They all said it would be fine—as long as it wasn't a video recorded in their thought life. I then reminded them of the truth of our verse today, which is the fact that God knows exactly what we are thinking.

ACTION POINT: Allow a family member to give three clues that describe a place. Allow the rest of the family to see if they can guess where the place is. Discuss the difference between guessing and knowing. Choose which one God does.

—Tom Palmer

JUNE 6
A MOST UNDERSTATED QUALITY—
FAITHFULNESS

Scripture Reading—1 Cor. 4:2
"It is required in stewards, that a man be found faithful."

The strength of a church is not based on the most gifted people, but on the people who have been quietly faithful, serving without notice, loyal to their Lord and their tasks.

The dictionary defines faithfulness as "being steady in allegiance or affection, loyal, reliable." God expects this of His children (1 Cor. 4:2; 15:58). The will of God isn't complicated. It starts with being faithful to what God has given you to do.

God is looking for faithful people to use. God used Abraham because of his faithful heart (Neh. 9:7, 8). If you want to be used of God, stop looking for a visible position and be faithful to your current task.

Faithfulness is an important quality to God, but it is a rare quality to find in people (Ps. 12:1; Pro. 20:6). Most people want to be faithful, but they allow their emotions to determine their actions. Rather than being faithful, they are fickle.

God's will is compared to a race—not a sprint, but a marathon. A long-distance runner has a different mindset than a sprinter. Rather than a quick burst of energy for a short period of time, he must be patient over the course of the race (Heb. 12:1).

You will never finish God's will for your life if you are impatient. Paul was able to say at the end of his life, "I have finished my course" (2 Tim. 4:7). He was faithful to the mundane marathon of life.

My daughter runs marathons. A marathon is a 26.2-mile race. Marathoners speak of "hitting the wall" around the twenty mile mark. Extreme fatigue sets in at that point, and the mind begins to shout, "You're not going to be able to do this. Why are you taking such punishment. Stop. You have gone farther than most anyone else has." If they get past "the mental wall," a second burst of energy comes, and you can finish the race.

"A fight well-fought; a race well-run; a faith well-kept; a crown well-won," reads the grave marker of Dr. Bob Jones, Sr.

MEMORIZE: 2 Timothy 4:7.

—*Rick Johnson*

I have fought the good fight, I have finished the race, I have kept the faith

158

JUNE 7
DECISIONS THAT STICK

Scripture Reading—John 15:16
"That your fruit should remain."

I love camp ministry. One reason is that it is where God changed my life. As a youth pastor I've seen hundreds of lives changed during camp week.

Recently, I was at a camp in the off-season. As I walked around reminiscing, I saw a large tree by a dormitory and recalled a conversation I had with a young man whose heart was broken. After a service one night, we stood under that tree and had a serious talk. He said, "I'm going to live for God, and I'm not going back to the way I used to live."

I wandered to the tabernacle where we had our services. I stared at a long church pew on the porch and remembered a request of a fine young man. "Please keep me accountable in my moral life," he asked of me. Of course, I agreed, and we worked together on that issue.

Peeking in the glass doors, I saw the altar, a sacred place, where many genuine tears of repentance had been shed. I remembered places and faces all over that building where decisions had been made for Christ.

Sadly, the majority of those young people failed to keep those promises. My heart grieves for them. They heard some of the best preachers in the world, and yet their decisions didn't stick. Of course, there were many whose lives were permanently changed at camp. They never got over it.

Adults are no different. They make very sincere decisions and later are not any further along than they were before. Why does this happen?

I'm not a cynic, but I am concerned about a lack of lasting fruit. Two people hear the same sermon from the same preacher on the same night and make the same decision, but do they both experience lasting change? What is the difference?

Those that stay faithful read and apply the Word of God after their decision. We often overestimate an event or decision and underestimate the process to reinforce it.

ACTION POINT: Discuss and memorize Luke 8:15.

—*Rick Johnson*   *But the ones that fell on the good ground are those who, having heard the word with a noble and good heart, keep it and bear fruit with patience*

JUNE 8
DOES THE DEVIL KNOW YOUR NAME?

Scripture Reading—Acts 19:15
"Jesus I know, and Paul I know; but who are ye?"

Imagine a meeting of several demons to discuss their day. One demon after the other declares his success, but one has a different story. He says, "I ran across Joe today. He's a new Christian who is spiritually growing like crazy! I could not stop him from following Christ! He would not fall into sin. He would not stop reading his Bible, and he would not stop witnessing to his unsaved friends!"

What about you? What would Satan and His kingdom say about you? Would the report be the same as Joe's?

Christians do not live their lives to be known in Satan's kingdom, but when we serve God faithfully, we will be noticed by the enemy. Does the Devil know your name because you have made a difference for eternity? Or are you unknown to the Devil because you merely sit on the sidelines while the war of the ages goes on around you?

What will make us known to the Devil? The Devil knows those who go on the offensive against him to witness for Christ. He knows those who are faithful in prayer. As we pray we can cause Satan and his kingdom to tremble. It was Mary Queen of Scots who reportedly said, "I fear the prayers of John Knox more than all the assembled armies of Europe." John Knox was known by his enemies. Do you think his prayers went unnoticed by the Devil?

Every morning a threat assessment is provided to the President of the United States from America's intelligence agencies. This report tells him of the latest threats to the security of the nation. It contains no trivial or insignificant concerns. If you are a big enough threat, you can be sure the President would know your name.

In Acts 19:15, when the sons of Sceva tried to cast a demon out of a man, the demon said, "Jesus I know, Paul I know; but who are ye?"

He knew of Paul's ministry. Does he know about you? Is your life considered a threat to Satan's kingdom? That is something we ought to consider.

MEMORIZE: Ephesians 6:10–12.

—*James Stallard*

JUNE 9
ESCAPING MISERY ISLAND

Scripture Reading—Job 3:20
"Wherefore is light given to him that is in misery,
and life unto the bitter in soul?"

Many people in our world feel trapped with no escape. Life has dealt them a hard time. They have tried to steer against the winds of God and have found that their ship has been broken up on the shores of trouble. They have landed at a place that we will call "Misery Island." It is a place of misery, loneliness, and hurt that seems to have no purpose.

Job was a man sent to Misery Island, not for his own wrongdoing, but for the hidden purposes of God. He wondered why "light" would be given to someone who sits in this place of "bitterness" (Job 3:20). We must all be reminded that Job never received a clear answer from the Lord as to why he went through the misery that he did. We may not be told the reasons for our plight either. God expects us to lay aside the misery of our island and escape the bitterness that can trap us there.

After the Civil War, Robert E. Lee attended church in Lexington, Virginia. The Southern pastor preached a message against what the north had done during the war. It was full of hate and bitterness. After the message was over, Robert E. Lee met the pastor on the front steps of the church. With only a short time left to live, the Southern general asked a simple question, "Does not the Bible tell us we are to love our enemies?" While many others, including that preacher, chose to take up residence on Misery Island, Robert E. Lee chose not to go there.

Neither should we (Matt. 5:44). We must make a deliberate choice that we will not allow the bitterness of life to overtake us. Whether it is an overbearing relative that is hard to live with or perhaps a coworker who always gives you a hard time on the job, you must choose not to allow bitterness in your soul. God will help every believer to obey His Word if only we will allow Him to do so.

PRAYER: Lord, forgive me for any bitterness that has put me on Misery Island.

—James Stallard

161

THE EYES OF GOD

Scripture Reading—Pro. 15:3
"The eyes of the LORD are in every place,
beholding the evil and the good."

I can still see that great big eye, the biggest eye that I had ever seen. I saw it in a classroom when I was a student in junior high. For whatever reason, the teacher needed to step out of the room for a moment. Before she left the room, she went to the blackboard, took a piece of chalk and drew an eye as big as the chalkboard. As she left the room, she said, "Now remember that while I am gone, my eye will be on you." She closed the door and walked down the hallway.

Now let's face it, junior high boys are known to get into trouble rather quickly, especially when the teacher is not looking. I suppose this would have been a prime time for a silly stunt of some kind, but nobody did a thing. Of course we knew the teacher could not see us, but with that big eye staring at us, we sure felt like we were being watched.

Sometimes teachers, particularly junior high teachers, have been known to do unusual things, but I guess it works. No paper airplanes, spitballs, or rubber bands flew across the room this time—no way! In fact we were all very good boys while the teacher was out. We were good because we felt like we were being watched, and we were. No, the teacher couldn't see us, but God could.

Our verse tells us that His eyes are in every place regardless of whether we can be seen by a parent, a teacher, a police officer, or anyone else. Our teacher was helping us learn a great life lesson about God. Though she used a unique method to teach it, I think we still got the point. It was a lesson we needed to learn.

ACTION POINT: If you know the tune, sing the little chorus and add verses about eyes, feet, and tongues:
> *O be careful little hands what you do, (repeat)*
> *For the Father up above is looking down in love,*
> *So be careful little hands what you do.*

—Tom Palmer

JUNE 11
THE COMING STORM

Scripture Reading—Joel 1:15
"Alas for the day! for the day of the LORD is at hand."

There have always been doomsday predictors who have warned of the end of the world. Many people ignore them, while others worry about what they say. "End of the world" language can be seen and heard everywhere in the media. Words like "Armageddon" are used to describe everything from global warming to asteroids hitting the earth to terrorism in the Middle East.

Several years ago my family and I were traveling north on Interstate 75 in the middle of a storm. Up ahead, about a mile or so, a funnel cloud dipped down out of the sky and hit the ground. Then it snapped up into the clouds, only to come down again in a field to the east. It was a scary sight! However, the signs of a tornado were everywhere before it hit.

In the same way God has warned us of a coming storm in the future called the Day of the Lord (Joel 1:15). Jesus also declared, "For then shall be great tribulation, such as was not since the beginning of the world to this time, no, nor ever shall be" (Matt. 24:21).

The only escape from the storm is to put our faith and trust in Jesus Christ for salvation (John 3:16, 36). The Bible promises, "For God hath not appointed us to wrath, but to obtain salvation by our Lord Jesus Christ" (1 Thess. 5:9).

In colonial days Paul Revere rode everywhere crying, "The British are coming! The British are coming!" What the world needs today are modern-day Paul Reveres who will boldly proclaim to those who are lost, "The storm is coming! The storm is coming!"

For the believer the horizon will always be glorious with the hope of Christ's coming for us (1 Thess. 4:13-18). But for our family, friends, and neighbors who are left behind, the storm will be a great catastrophe. The hope of the world truly is found in the Lord Jesus Christ who died and rose again for all men of every time period (1 Cor. 15:1-4).

PRAYER: Help us to share Christ with those around us before it is too late.

—James Stallard

163

JUNE 12
THE STRATEGY OF SATAN

Scripture Reading—2 Cor. 2:11
"Lest Satan should get an advantage of us:
for we are not ignorant of his devices."

The Corinthian church was one messed-up church. No other church in the New Testament had problems like this church. Just a simple reading of Paul's two epistles to Corinth reveals that they were divided over preachers, doctrine, and practice. It is clear from Paul's admonition from 2 Corinthians 2:11 that Satan had been busy working on their minds and hearts to cause these divisions. In fact, Satan, the adversary, had a clear strategy or plan for how to attack them spiritually.

First, Satan tried to separate them from their spiritual authorities. He got them to turn away from Paul the Apostle, who often had to defend his authority (2 Cor. 1:1–24; 11:1–5). Satan will do that in our lives too. He will try to separate children from the authority of their parents so that they listen to friends more than their parents. Parents are designed to protect children, and it is always best to stay under that protection (Exod. 20:12).

Second, Satan tried to tempt them with that which appeared "good." Paul tells of "false apostles, deceitful workers" (2 Cor. 11:13) who seemed to appear as angels of light (2 Cor. 11:14). They looked good, but did not speak for God. There are many voices in the world that "look good" or "sound good." They may even "look Christian," but we must be careful. The simple saying is still true—*the Bible will keep you from sin, and sin will keep you from the Bible.*

Third, Satan tried to get them to serve the Lord without love. The Corinthians tried to serve the Lord without a spirit of love in dealing with a sinful member of their church (2 Cor. 2:5–13). This denies the basic message of the love of Jesus found in The Cross (John 13:35).

We must be on guard to keep Satan from working in our lives or in our church. Only this way will we have the blessings the Lord intends for us.

PRAYER PROJECT: Carefully read Ephesians 6:10–19. Discuss and have each family member pray a prayer for your family concerning one piece of the armor of God.

—James Stallard

JUNE 13
THE REQUISITE OF FAITHFULNESS

Scripture Reading—Neh. 7:2
"I gave my brother Hanani, and Hananiah . . . charge over Jerusalem: for he was a faithful man."

Faithfulness is a requisite to being placed in spiritual leadership. This principle is given over and over in God's Word (Neh. 7:2; 13:13). Eli was not faithful in his leadership to his family, and God removed him from being a spiritual leader (1 Sam. 3:13). Pastors are to have faithful children as long as they are under their authority (Titus 1:6).

In the New Testament a steward was responsible for the possessions of his master. He wasn't the owner, but the manager. God uses this same term to describe our role concerning what He has entrusted to us. We are stewards. The most important quality in a steward is that he is faithful (Matt. 24:45).

When Paul sent people to minister, the quality that is most mentioned of them having is that of being faithful (1 Cor. 4:17; Eph. 6:21; Col. 1:7; 4:7, 9). This is not a trivial matter to God.

Spiritual leaders are to have a track record of faithfulness (2 Tim. 2:2). The wives of spiritual leaders are to have a testimony of faithfulness (1 Tim. 3:11). God calls men to preach that have been faithful in other things (1 Tim. 1:12).

When I was a boy we always entered the church through the same door. There was a greeter there named Mr. Smith. He was there every Sunday from the time that I was a little boy until I graduated and went to college. When I came home to visit, he was still at his post. He never taught a class, but he was faithful to his job and will receive a reward in Heaven one day for it.

The longer I live the greater respect I have for those that have faithfully stayed the course. If you want God to use you, be faithful with what you have now. It is a nonnegotiable with God.

ACTION POINT: If you are not faithful to your tasks, confess it to the Lord, repent, and become trustworthy.

—Rick Johnson

JUNE 14
THE BASIS OF OUR ULTIMATE HOPE

Scripture Reading—John 14:19
"But ye see me: because I live, ye shall live also."

If you take away a man's hope, you will destroy him. Many men and women have sought for something that would give them hope. In their search for truth and happiness in life, many have turned away from the one source of genuine hope—the Gospel!

Jesus was going to be crucified and raised from the dead. Then, He was going away to Heaven, leaving the disciples without His presence. He tries to encourage them by saying, "Yet a little while, and the world seeth me no more; but ye see me: because I live, ye shall live also" (John 14:19). Their life was bound together with His life. They would live because He would be raised from the dead. This is the foundation of our ultimate hope—the resurrection of Jesus Christ from the dead.

About 700 years after Christ, Mohammed searched the deserts of Arabia trying to find the way. But Jesus said, "I am the way." On his death bed, Buddha said, "I still seek truth." But Jesus said, "I am the truth." Confucius taught the paths of life. But Jesus said, "I am the life" (John 14:6).

Jesus stands out as the only option open to those who want true hope. The reason He stands out is clear. Mohammed lived, died, and his bones are still in the ground. Buddha lived, died, and his bones are still in the ground. Confucius lived, died, and his bones are still in the ground. Jesus died on The Cross for our sins, He was buried, and UP HE AROSE! The angel declared, "He is not here: for he is risen, as he said. Come, see the place where the Lord lay" (Matt. 28:6).

Because of His resurrection, Jesus could offer Himself as the hope of the world and say to you and to me, "Because I live, ye shall live also" (John 14:19). If we remove the resurrection of Jesus Christ from the dead, we have nothing left worth living for. For only a world full of hope can leave people with a true reason to live.

SONG: Sing "Because He Lives."

—*James Stallard*

JUNE 15
"10-45"

Scripture Reading—Mark 10:45
"For even the Son of man came not to be ministered unto,
but to minister, and to give his life a ransom for many."

This verse describes the genuine humility and sacrifice that the Lord Jesus Christ intentionally chose while upon earth. There is and will always be great difficulty in comprehending the degree of sacrifice that Jesus made, as God, to serve and die for sinful man. This sacrificial life of Jesus did not simply "put Him out" or cause Him to give up some things. Rather, it was forfeiture of everything on His part, and it resulted in His voluntary death on The Cross—all for us!

In our early years in evangelism, this verse made an impression upon me and on the team. Occasionally, an unpleasant situation would arise where either a team member or I might be tempted to grumble or complain. It could be regarding undesired food, unappealing accommodations, or unwanted assignments. Because these circumstances sometimes came up in a public setting, a team member would simply utter the phrase, "**10-45**," while trying not to draw attention from those outside the team. The "10-45" code would immediately take us back to a very important truth and serve as a necessary reminder of the privilege we had as children of God to minister to others.

The "10-45" code simply stood for Mark 10:45 and was always a valuable reminder that Jesus Himself did not come as the Son of Man to be pampered, while seeking to be great and famous. Rather, He came to give of Himself and serve others. Jesus knew and demonstrated, as any great leader can attest, that effective leadership hinges upon effective serving of others.

Success in serving is not possible by your own strength. The Lord Jesus, however, was a success in everything because He operated in the power of the Holy Spirit. This same victorious Jesus lives in you, if you are saved, and His power is available to enable you to serve others and even love it!

Remember, "**10-45**"!

PRAYER: Others, Lord, yes others, Let this my motto be, Help me to live for others, That I may live like Thee.

—*Billy Ingram*

JUNE 16
THE LORD HATH NEED OF HIM

Scripture Reading—Mark 11:3
"And if any man say unto you, Why do ye this? say ye that the Lord hath need of him; and straightway he will send him hither."

As I read this, I wonder how often does the Lord have need of something. This real story has a lasting application for us today. Needs can be short-term, long-term, physical, or spiritual. Needs open a door for things we cannot fix or satisfy ourselves. With all our advances the simple word *need* reminds us how dependent we are. Needs are a part of life that come and go without discretion.

This need of the colt appeared only for a short time and never presented itself again. Whoever helped meet that need did so to their eternal reward and earthly satisfaction. What does God need today? In His heavenly person, He needs nothing. He is absolutely complete. Yet He allows needs on this earth and will at times use us to meet them. The Lord hath need of those who will obey. The disciples did not know the who, the why, or the how about the colt. Yet they went. How many times in life do we obey immediately? Usually it takes several promptings of the Lord to move us toward helping others.

The Lord hath need of those who give freely. Can God count on you to open your heart and give that which no man had ever ridden on before? Such an animal was a prize in that day, kept for holy occasions. Here is giving your best, your first to God—not what's left over.

Does the Lord have need of your gift? How bendable are you in God's hand? How much longer do we have to fill a need for God? The hourglass of our lives falls away; let's not wait until the last minute. The point of the passage challenges us about this basic truth: the Lord hath need. Don't underestimate how much your local church could use you.

ACTION POINT: Announce to your pastor this Sunday that you will serve wherever needed. Then watch for his response!

—*Steve Rebert*

TRUE DEPTH

Scripture Reading—Ps. 1:3
"And he shall be like a tree planted by the rivers of water,
that bringeth forth his fruit in his season; his leaf also shall not wither;
and whatsoever he doeth shall prosper."

Psalm 1:1, 2 tells us that the man who is truly going to be blessed doesn't look to the world for satisfaction, but instead he finds his delight in the Word of God. In Psalm 1:3 we see what it looks like to be have true blessing and satisfaction in this life. The person who rejects the input of the world and delights in the Word of God begins to take on the characteristics of a big healthy tree that is planted by a river and nourished.

I live in eastern North Carolina where we have hot dry summers that are followed by hurricane season in September. As the hurricane winds begin to blow, there can be some major devastation as the eye of the hurricane hits the coast. It's always amazing to see the trees that get blown over by the winds. Many times a tree may look big and healthy, but when it has been blown over you begin to see the truth of that tree's foundation. Because the ground is hard and water is sparse, even big trees may have root systems that are wide and far-reaching, but many times very shallow.

I find this to be true in the lives of many Christians. We are involved in this and that and can be very busy with very good things, but if we are not very careful, we will be a mile wide in good activity and be an inch deep in true Bible depth. And guess what reveals the true depth of our lives? Hurricane season! When the winds of trials start blowing and difficulties arise, we many times find that our roots are shallow, and we don't actually have as strong of a biblical foundation as we thought. But if we will be people who truly delight in the Word of God, then we will be able to stand and not wither and even bear fruit in the midst of hurricane season. This is what true happiness and satisfaction looks like.

ACTION POINT: Are you busy but shallow? Talk through some trials that have revealed the true depth of your foundation—whether deep or shallow.

—Aaron Coffey

JUNE 18
KEEPING A CONFIDENCE

Scripture Reading—Pro. 13:3
"He that openeth wide his lips shall have destruction."

All conversations are not equal. Some carry more weight than others and can even determine the direction of one's life—for good or bad. Because of this it is vital for us to learn to have discernment concerning when we ought to be quiet about certain matters.

This is not easy. Silence tends to make us uncomfortable, and so we say anything to fill it. It is easy to know after the fact that you should not have said anything than it is on the front end of the conversation. We must be alert to the temptation to speak when it is best not to say anything.

Someone said, "You'll never hate sin until you see its consequences." Our conversations are like that too. We won't realize the importance of being quiet until we see the consequences of talking when we shouldn't. Pain and regret are great teachers.

Learning to be a good conversationalist is a key skill to learn, but it is just as important that you learn to be quiet during certain times. "Learning to speak several languages is not really as valuable as learning to keep your mouth shut in one!"

We have a responsibility to be quiet when we have confidential information. This is information that is to be kept secret because the person that shared it with you has confidence in you that you will not tell anyone.

The Bible forbids one to pass on private disclosures others have trusted you with—"He that keepeth his mouth keepeth his life" (Pro.13:3). The word "keepeth" means "to guard, protect, or conceal." If someone has trusted us with information, we ought to "keep" it.

Even in cases where we discover private information second-hand, it still should not be passed on. Our family has a right to expect that what they share with us will be kept confidential. Since trust is the glue of relationships, failure to keep confidences will hinder closeness in a friendship or in a family.

ACTION POINT: Learn to treat confidences as a sacred trust.

—Rick Johnson

JUNE 19
NO BIBLE, NO BREAKFAST!

Scripture Reading—Ps. 119:147, 148

"I prevented the dawning of the morning, and cried: I hoped in thy word. Mine eyes prevent the night watches, that I might meditate in thy word."

Nutrition specialists tell us that breakfast is the most important meal of the day. Our bodies need that initial dose of nourishment first thing in the morning to provide the energy that is needed for the day ahead. To simply skip breakfast is detrimental to a person's health and will eventually harm his or her overall physical condition.

In the same way, not only must the body be nourished physically, but also the life must be nourished spiritually. In our text, the Psalmist spoke of his anticipation as he looked forward to the morning for a time in God's Word. A consistent spiritual diet is essential for spiritual health and growth. For this reason it is important to make sure that each member of your family is enjoying a time of "spiritual breakfast" each morning.

First of all, parents must be sure that they are consistently spending time in the Word of God. Bible reading, study, memorization, and meditation are essential for growth as a Christian. Then parents should assist their children in choosing a way to get into Scripture. Teenagers, and children who can read, will be able on their own to follow a Bible reading schedule, or to use a devotional guide. Children who are too young to read will benefit from the reading of stories from a Bible storybook. When my children were very young, I would read the Bible with them. As we each held an open Bible, I would read one phrase at a time and have the child repeat it back to me.

This endeavor will take some effort. Yet the benefits will be wonderful. Consider making it a goal to get every family member some scriptural breakfast every day. Take care of the physical needs after the spiritual needs have been cared for.

ACTION POINT: What does 1 Peter 2:2, 3 say that the "milk of the Word" will enable us to do?

—*Tom Palmer*

JUNE 20
DID YOU KNOW THAT YOUR HEART IS SHOWING?

Scripture Reading—Eph. 4:31, 32

"Let all bitterness, and wrath, and anger, and clamour, and evil speaking,
be put away from you, with all malice: And be ye kind
one to another, tenderhearted, forgiving one another,
even as God for Christ's sake hath forgiven you."

These two verses show us two ways that we can respond when something bad happens to us. One way is to get mad, get sad, get bitter, or even plan how to get revenge on the person who wronged me! Or I can decide that I will be kind, have compassion, and forgive that person. I have to choose which way I will respond.

If I react in anger and bitterness, I've decided to follow my Genesis 3 nature. We are all sinners and have sinful natures. This is why it is so easy to sin and handle my problems like a sinner.

On the other hand, since I know Jesus Christ as my personal Savior, I now have a new nature—one that genuinely loves God and His Word and humbly desires to obey my Lord. Not that I'm perfect—not yet, but someday when I see Jesus, I will be! So right now, with my Lord's help, I am able to choose not to sin, but to respond to people the way that Jesus wants me too.

When I'm concerned for those who would treat me badly, I'm responding like Jesus. Like Him, I will forgive people who wrong me. That means I give up my desire to get back at people or hold a grudge against them. I will be kind, not just to my family and friends. Rather, I'll try to treat everyone the same way—with kindness.

Our heart determines how we react or respond. Our actions come to the surface because of how we are thinking in our hearts. Why not ask the Lord to replace any anger or bitterness in your heart with kindness, sympathy, and a forgiving spirit?

DISCUSS: What is the difference between reacting and responding to people who treat you badly? Talk about different real-life examples of what your family faces.

—Joe Henson

JUNE 21
CHRISTLIKENESS AND
BURDEN-BEARING

Scripture Reading—Gal. 6:2
"Bear ye one another's burdens, and so fulfil the law of Christ."

Something special happens when we help others with their burdens: we "fulfill the law of Christ." When Jesus came He fulfilled the Old Testament law perfectly and established a new way of living, guided by the law (principle) of love that was to be the guide and rule of life.

Jesus told us to love people the same way He loved (John 15:12). One of those ways was to bear others' burdens. The word "bear" (Gal. 6:2) means "to lift, take up, or carry." It usually takes time. It always takes love.

We often talk about being like Jesus, and here is one evidence a person is Christlike—he lifts the loads of others. We tend to complain about our own burdens rather than looking around for burdens to carry. Jesus never griped, but He did focus on helping others with their needs.

Usually the people that are most alert to others' burdens are the people who are carrying heavy burdens themselves. They realize the value of bearing burdens as others have helped them in the past.

Looking for needs and becoming a burden-bearer can forever change the environment where you are. It ought to be done best and first within your family.

My wife is currently out of town for several days. I inquired of my son, Jake, about his schedule for the day, and he said, "I'm going to clean the whole house for Mom before she comes home." (The second law of thermodynamics takes place when a bunch of guys are by themselves for a few days!

Jake knew that it would mean a lot to my wife Paula to have the house looking nice, and he helped to carry her burden. This is how Jesus lived—helping others. A Christlike person is a burden-bearer.

ACTION POINT: Distribute a piece of paper to everyone. Write down the names of everyone in your immediate family, and then discuss a burden each person is carrying and how it might be lifted.

—*Rick Johnson*

173

JUNE 22
THE BLESSING OF FAITHFULNESS

Scripture Reading—Pro. 13:17
"A faithful ambassador is health."

A house key that only works some of the time is frustrating. A computer that works only part of the time is disappointing. At some point you will get a new key or a new computer because the old ones are being unreliable. Likewise, unfaithfulness diminishes the good qualities of a person.

Faithfulness is the test of genuine friendships. Faithful friends hold your confidences (Pro. 11:13). A faithful friend is loyal in times of trouble (Pro. 17:17). Faithful friends are a blessing to have!

A faithful person blesses and improves the morale and environment wherever he or she is (Pro. 13:17). Faithfulness is a desired quality in an employee and is a blessing to an employer (Pro. 25:13).

Unfaithful people bring pain to those that are relying upon them (Pro. 25:19). On the contrary, those that are faithful bring great blessing to their friends, bosses, coworkers, churches, and even to the Lord Jesus Christ.

One of my college professors who has had a great impact on my life will turn 90 years old this year. Almost forty years ago he began to teach me the Word of God. His ministry of teaching did more than inform me—it challenged me to want to learn the Bible as he did.

Early in my ministry as a pastor, I had him come and speak to our church dozens of times. Our church family loved to hear him teach and preach God's Word. I had a conversation with him a few months ago in which he told me he could no longer travel and speak because of his age and limitations.

When I reflect on this dear man of God, I realized that it was not his competence as a teacher that touched me the most, but his character of faithfulness. He is finishing strong and faithful and has been a blessing to all that know him.

ACTION POINT: Who has been an example of faithfulness to you? Take some time to call or write that person and let him or her know specifically the area in which they have blessed you.

—*Rick Johnson*

JUNE 23
SCATTER YOUR MONEY

Scripture Reading—Pro. 19:17
"That which he hath given will he pay him again."

Everyone has something in his or her hand to scatter (Pro. 11:24). Before you can scatter the seed with the expectation of a harvest, you must open your hand and let go of it.

God has given us money to scatter. Our faith in God's promise is tried when the money gets tight. We are tempted to close our hand and hold on to the seed, not realizing it is going to affect our future harvest.

Once we were eating out together as a family, and one of my sons had ordered fried mozzarella sticks. I said, "Hey, can I have one of those." The groaned reply came: "Come on, Dad, I only have eight of them!"

What he had forgotten is that I paid for them and could get him some more. If I wanted to I could buy so many cheese sticks that he would be sick of them. It is foolish to be selfish with your Savior that has bought you, provided for you, and is able to provide more.

Every believer ought to tithe to his or her local church, and it shouldn't end there. We need to give offerings to support missions and bless other people. It need not stop at church. Learn to scatter your money during the week. God will bless you for your generosity (Pro. 19:17).

At the grocery store as you are standing in line and the person in front of you lacks money for something, help out. We are to live open-handedly with our money.

Years ago our family was eating out, and we spotted some friends from our church there too. We greeted them and then enjoyed our meal. When we finished I asked the waitress for the check of our friends, but to please not tell them. She returned with one check, their check. I was confused, and she began to laugh. She said, "Mister, they asked their waitress for your check like you did for them." Open your hand and scatter some money; it will bring joy to your heart.

ACTION POINT: Scatter your money anonymously this week.

—Rick Johnson

JUNE 24
OUR POWERFUL, UNCHANGING GOD

Scripture Reading—James 5:17
"Elias was a man subject to like passions as we are."

Christians today often believe that the men and women in Bible days were "super humans." We think that great men and women such as Abraham, Sarah, Moses, David, Paul, and John the Baptist had some "extra" power that is not available to us today.

However, the Bible informs us that just the opposite is true. God will grant to us all the power we need for whatever He has called us to do. The Bible uses Elijah as an example of how to pray. Our text above points out that he was a man with the same emotions and desires ("like passions") as we all have. And, yet, he was used of God through prayer to keep famine on the land and then to restore rain (James 5:17, 18).

In that same passage of Scripture, we are challenged, "The effectual fervent prayer of a righteous man availeth much" (James 5:16). If our prayers are fervent (strong, intense, or serious) and we are living righteous (godly and holy) lives, we can make an impact with our faith just like the great giants of the faith recorded in the Bible.

Our God today is the same God they had in times past—"Jesus Christ the same yesterday, and to day, and forever" (Heb. 13:8). He is fully able to do great things through His people, if only they will believe Him and meet the conditions He requires.

What great things does God want to do through your life? What keeps you from believing that God could use you to do great things for Him? Why not believe Him for great things right now!

In the late 1800s, a man named George Müller founded an orphanage in London by faith. Through prayer all the needs were met and Müller became the modern-day example of what can happen as we pray to a powerful God. Could not you be a modern-day Elijah or a modern-day George Müller?

QUOTE: "I saw more clearly than ever that the first great and primary business to which I ought to attend every day was, to have my soul happy in the Lord" —George Müller

—James Stallard

JUNE 25
DANGEROUS DESTRUCTION

Scripture Reading—Gen. 9:21
"And he drank of the wine, and was drunken."

The truth is that a good man can fall a long way. One who has been right-eous and walking with God can find himself doing strange things. This was the sad plight of one of God's great men, Noah. He and his family had been the only righteous people on the earth and the only ones to enter the Ark that Noah had built (Gen. 7:7).

After getting off of the Ark, Noah and his family were still sinners saved by grace. But, Noah remembered some things from the old world, "and he planted a vineyard" (Gen. 9:20). From that vineyard he made some alcohol, and alcohol will cause people to do things they normally would not do. In Noah's situation his condition led his son to sin and resulted in a chilling prophecy about the descendants of Canaan, his grandson (Gen. 9:24–27).

Who was to blame? Noah and his vineyard! It is significant that Noah lived a total of 950 years, but 350 years were after the flood. Nothing is mentioned about his life in those latter years. The truly sad part is that the last thing we remember about Noah is the sin brought about by the deadly demon from his vineyard.

This is the dangerous destruction that comes with alcohol and drugs. They often do away with any desire to stop doing what is wrong. Millions upon millions of lives have been destroyed all over the world because of the introduction of these things. One small drink sends a person toward a life-time of drunkenness. One giving in to the temptation from a friend to use drugs can bring about a lifetime of bondage and slavery.

There are many people in prison and out of prison who live miserable lives haunted by the experiment they have made with destruction. However, whether we have used alcohol or drugs in the past or not, we can be free. There is cleans-ing and forgiveness through the blood of the Lord Jesus Christ (1 John 1:9).

There is also power available to overcome any temptation. "I will not be brought under the power of any" (1 Cor. 6:12).

MEMORIZE: 1 Corinthians 10:13.

—James Stallard

no temptation has over taken you ercept that is common to man, but God is faithful, who will not allow you to be tempted beyond what you are able, but with the temptation will also make the way of escape, that you will be able to bear it.

JUNE 26
FEAR KEEPS US FROM GOD'S BEST

Scripture Reading—Heb. 11:6
"Without faith it is impossible to please him."

Most Christians treat unbelief as something minor, but it is a serious offense to God. We cannot please God without faith (Heb. 11:6). To Him, it is a moral issue. The presence or lack of faith in your life tells what you really believe about Who God is.

Living in unbelief isn't merely living in neutral ground without having any effect upon your life. There are consequences. We miss God's best for our lives.

The natural tendency when facing a difficult or impossible situation is to be filled with fear rather than faith. But the truth is that unbelief and fear always go together. Everyone wants to experience a miracle, but no one wants to deal with impossibilities. But you can't have one without the other.

When facing the impossible, there is a tension of living without knowing how God is going to resolve the situation. There are only two responses—faith or fear. Fear cripples us and robs us of what God is seeking to accomplish in us through the impossible situation. Faith instead looks confidently to God to give us His very best—whatever that might be. Living an exciting life of faith may not be comfortable, but a life of faith is a life of joy and wonder.

God is able to take our insignificant and multiply it beyond our dreams (John 6:11–13). The result is a life worth living. Fear keeps us from enjoying God's blessing.

When I was a senior in high school, I knew that God wanted me in the ministry, but I was introverted and felt unqualified. I wasn't running from the will of God because of rebellion, but because of fear (unbelief).

ACTION POINT: Read Hebrews 11. Discuss what is the one thing each person mentioned had in common?

—Rick Johnson

JUNE 27
SCATTER YOUR MINISTRY

Scripture Reading—Pro. 11:18
"To him that soweth righteousness shall be a sure reward."

Every Christian has a spiritual gift by which he or she can make a unique contribution to God's work. God compares our serving to sowing seed in the lives of people (Pro. 11:18). These seeds include the investments of our energy and time to advance the kingdom of God.

Everyone ought to have a ministry in a local church. Your life context, gifts, and experiences enable you to make a difference. We are to be sowing seed through our work and service that will one day result in great blessing. We will reap what we sow, but without sowing there will be no harvest (Gal. 6:7).

Sometimes the work gets heavy and appears to go unrewarded. We become weary in serving and scattering the seeds of ministry, but we must pursue to see the harvest come to pass (Gal. 6:9). We are to take advantage of these opportunities to sow in the lives of people (Gal. 6:10) and to scatter freely and faithfully. My pastor said, "It's alright to get tired in the ministry, but it's not alright to get tired of the ministry."

All of us are called to minister and to scatter the seed of good deeds everywhere we go. One day the opportunity to do so will be gone forever (John 9:4). There's an old hymn that states the feeling many of us will have at the Judgment Seat of Christ, "I'll Wish I Had Given Him More."

Concerning service, do you live with an open hand or a closed hand (Pro. 11:24)? People are stressed out and exhausted from constant demands placed on them. If we are not careful, we can become consumers and takers in our churches rather than contributors and givers.

One day in Heaven I will share my rewards with those that sowed time and effort into my life rather than being selfish. I wonder how many people have been helped because of the seeds of ministry I have sown into their lives?

PONDER: What ministry did you do this week that added value to the lives of people and advanced God's kingdom?

—*Rick Johnson*

JUNE 28
PLAY TO A STANDARD

Scripture Reading—Phil. 4:13
"I can do all things through Christ which strengtheneth me."

On January 7, 2013, thousands of fans descended on Miami, Florida to watch the national championship between college football's two best teams, #1 ranked Notre Dame and #2 ranked Alabama.

The game ended up a sleeper. Notre Dame fell behind early and never recovered on its way to a 42-14 defeat. Late in the fourth quarter with victory assured, Alabama could have easily coasted to the final whistle and celebrated their second-straight national championship. Then something happened that gave a glimpse into why that team became a champion.

With seven minutes to play, Alabama got a "delay of game" penalty. Their quarterback was visibly upset and got in the face of his center, apparently passing blame. The center did not appreciate the gesture and shoved his quarterback away in front of thousands of fans and the watching world.

After the game the center downplayed the incident, but made a statement that caught my attention. When asked why such an incident would occur at that point in the game over a penalty that would have no real impact with the game essentially over, he replied, "We don't play to a score; we play to a standard." In other words, "The game situation doesn't matter. What matters is that we strive for excellence for the entire game. Every snap. Every play. Nothing else is acceptable for this team."

Christians can learn a lot from that statement. Daniel 6:3 says, "Daniel was preferred above the presidents and princes, because an excellent spirit was in him."

All Christians should desire to live an "excellent" life. The Hebrew word for "excellent" also means "extraordinary," or "above ordinary." 2 Timothy 2:5 mentions a man who "strives for masteries" and is crowned, if he plays by the rules. It's important for Christians to give their very best for God in every facet of their lives—to "play to a standard." Such a life can inspire others to live for God too.

ACTION POINT: Strive to live a life of excellence for the Lord in everything you do.

—Paul Miller

JUNE 29
GOD HONORS YOUR TEARS

Scripture Reading—2 Chron. 34:27
"Because . . . thou didst . . . weep before me;
I have even heard thee also, saith the LORD."

The Lord not only cares about your tears, but He will also honor them. He will bless them in this life and in eternity.

He honors our prayers when they are accompanied by genuine brokenness and tears. This is one of the marks of fervent prayer. Sometimes our hearts are so burdened that our tears flow unhindered, and we do not have the ability to give words to the way we feel (Rom. 8:26, 27). No words can express our heart's burden.

Spurgeon said, "Groanings which cannot be uttered are often prayers which cannot be refused." Another wrote, "The best prayers often have no words." A broken heart is a key to effective prayer (2 Chron. 34:27).

God honors our ministry of tears. Compassion, not knowledge, is the difference-maker (Jude 22). Though they make a difference, tears are in short supply in the pulpit, Sunday School classes, and in the instruction of parents to children.

The maxim is true, "People don't care how much you know until they know how much you care." It's easier to dispense facts than to show concern and compassion.

Jeremiah wept (Jer. 9:1; 13:17), Paul wept (Acts 20:19, 31), as did our Savior (Luke 19:41; John 11:35). Theirs was not a ministry of empty ritual. They cried because they cared. And they impacted other people.

A lady approached her pastor after a service and began to complain about her lost husband and why he would not listen to her when she witnessed to him. She asked him what he thought the problem was for her lack of effectiveness.

Her pastor, who knew her well, replied, "Ma'am, I can tell you your problem in two words: dry eyes." Too often that is our problem too. Our eyes are dry because our hearts are cold.

God will honor your tears. Remember that present tears are an investment in future blessings (Ps. 126:5, 6; Luke 6:21).

MEMORIZE: Psalm 126:5, 6.

—Rick Johnson

V 5 Those who sow in tears
Shall weep in joy.
V. 6 He who continueally goes forth weeping
Bearing seed for sowing Shall doubtless
come again with 181 rejoicing. Bring his
sheaves with him

JUNE 30
GIDEON: THE RELUCTANT RECRUIT

Scripture Reading—Judg. 6:12
"And the angel of the LORD appeared unto him, and said unto him,
The LORD is with thee, thou mighty man of valour."

When He appears to Gideon in Judges 6, God makes two very intriguing statements to the very reluctant recruit:

1. **"The LORD is with thee, thou mighty man of valour"** (Judg. 6:12).

Mighty man?! Gideon had no military experience whatsoever. You may recall that King David had some "mighty men." The term means "warriors" and refers to specialized combatants. They were the special forces of that day, similar to the Navy SEALs and Army Rangers of our day. How could God call an inexperienced man like Gideon a mighty man?

Man of valor? Gideon was hiding from the Midianites. For seven years these enemies had oppressed Israel, stealing every bit of food they attempted to grow or raise. Gideon was cowering in a corner, trying to hold his own. How could he be called courageous?

Evidently, God sees a man for what he can become and not merely for what he is. He looks at potential, not merely at the present, when He chooses a leader. According to **1 Corinthians 1:26–31**, God has chosen "the weak things of the world to confound the things which are mighty."

2. **"Go in this thy might, and thou shalt save Israel from the hand of the Midianites"** (Judg. 6:14).

Go in your might? What might? Gideon seemed anything but strong, persuasive, or powerful! Yet the Lord declares that His work is done "not by might, nor by power, but by my spirit, saith the LORD of hosts [*Jehovah-saboath*, Lord of armies]" (Zech. 4:6).

Gideon won a powerful victory with God's help. Never underestimate what you can do for God, when you let Him do His work through you (John 15:4, 5; Phil. 4:13).

PONDER: God sees me for what I can become (through His grace), not merely for what I am (in my flesh).

—Rich Tozour

JULY 1
SCATTER YOUR MINUTES

Scripture Reading—Eph. 5:16
"Redeeming the time, because the days are evil."

I believe in time management and being intentional about life, but it is possible to schedule God out of our lives. When He changes our plans, we often see His kind providence as a rude intrusion.

As seed that is sown brings a sure harvest, so are we to sow our time for God's purposes. The most precious thing you can give someone is not necessarily your money, but your time. God instructs us to "walk circumspectly" (Eph. 5:15). This means carefully and with great focus and intentionality. It is characteristic of a wise person.

We waste so much time, God's precious gift to us to accomplish His will. We ought to have a daily—even a moment-by-moment—awareness of sowing and scattering the seed of God's will into our days (Ps. 90:12).

One of the primary ways that God wants you to use your time is to invest It in people. I have learned that people who are strong in management skills tend to make their schedule "people-proof" in order to accomplish the task. While there is certainly a place for organization and management, we must never forget that ultimately the ministry is about helping people. Don't see people as interruptions to your work; they are your work.

I read about a very famous pastor that was busy and in great demand. One day he had a contest in his church to have lunch with the person that brought the most visitors. He was shocked when he discovered that it was his little nine-year-old daughter that had won the award. When he asked her about it, she said, "It was the only way I could get some of your time." We'll never regret spending time with people we love.

The people that have changed my life for good have been willing to scatter minutes and hours into my life. They never had any idea of how those seeds would culminate into a fruitful harvest.

ACTION POINT: Be alert to God's intervention into your schedule with the needs of people today.

—Rick Johnson

JULY 2
SHOULD WE LISTEN TO OUR PARENTS?

Scripture Reading—Judg. 14:3
"And Samson said unto his father, Get her for me."

The woman he saw was just too beautiful to ignore. Her attraction drove his desire to demand of his parents, "Now therefore get her for me to wife . . . for she pleaseth me well" (Judg. 14:2, 3).

This man named Samson has become almost legendary because of his strength. Because of his Nazarite vow, he could not drink of the vine, eat anything unclean, or cut his hair (Judg. 13:1–5). Because of this vow, God endued him with strength at various times. Note what Samson did:

- He killed a young lion with his bare hands (Judg. 14:5, 6).
- He killed thirty Philistines in Ashkelon for answering his riddle (Judg. 14:19).
- He killed a thousand Philistines at Lehi with a jawbone of a donkey (Judg. 15:14–17).

What strength, and yet what weakness! It is amazing that this strongest of men was totally dominated by his desires. He did not have the strength of character to refuse the temptations that were laid in his path. Note what happened:

- His parents complained about his desire to marry a Philistine (Judg. 14:3).
- He forced his parents to finally agree to take part in the wedding (Judg. 14:3).
- He visited a harlot (Judg. 16:1).
- He became ensnared by Delilah, not knowing that the power of God was no longer upon him (Judg. 16:4–21).
- His eyes were gouged out by the Philistines (Judg. 16:20, 21).

If only he had listened to his parents. They were in the right. The law of God had forbidden the Jews to marry the heathen (Exod. 34:10–16; Deut. 7:1–6). The New Testament confirms this notion for believers in today's world when it says, "Be not unequally yoked together with unbelievers: for what fellowship hath righteousness with unrighteousness? and what communion hath light with darkness? . . . Wherefore come out from among them, and be ye separate, saith the Lord" (2 Cor. 6:14-17).

Though God used the occasion with Samson for His glory (Judg. 14:4; 16:22–31), Samson could have avoided the unnecessary heartache—**if only he had listened to his parents!**

MEMORIZE: Exodus 20:12.

—James Stallard

JULY 3
IN IT TO WIN IT!

Scripture Reading—1 Cor. 9:24
"Know ye not that they which run in a race run all,
but one receiveth the prize? So run, that ye may obtain."

Running is a popular sport. On a regular basis, I see advertisements for 5K races where the participants run a course that is 3.1 miles in length. The field is usually divided into different age brackets, and the winners receive an award. Advanced runners choose to participate in half-marathons (13.1 miles) or marathons (26.2).

Several years ago, one of my friends was preparing to run in a marathon. While talking one day, I learned that he ran twenty miles earlier that morning. I then asked him questions about his training. For the next hour, he told me about the importance of having the right shoes, using a good training program, and eating the right food. When we finished our conversation, I knew that he was serious about running.

You may not want to run in a marathon, but did you know that you are in a race called Life? In 1 Corinthians 9, the Apostle Paul used the sport of running to illustrate the Christian life. The Christian must exercise spiritual discipline just like the runner must discipline his body by running and eating the right things.

Why do some runners do poorly in the race? If you are not serious about the race, you will not prepare for the race. The runner must have the proper attitude about running. If he always thinks about what he can't eat or complains about how much he has to run, he won't do well.

Some runners do poorly because they do not eat properly before the race. A diet of junk food will tear your body down instead of building it up. For the Christian, he must drink the milk and eat the meat of God's Word to do well in life.

In this race of the Christian life, you must be "in it to win it." Use the spiritual disciplines of prayer and Bible reading to prepare you for the race.

PONDER: What spiritual exercise have you been doing to help you in the race? Are you serious about the Christian life?

—Alton Beal

Are You Up-to-Date?

Scripture Reading—Eph. 4:26, 27
"Be ye angry, and sin not: let not the sun go down upon your wrath:
Neither give place to the devil."

At first glance these verses might seem a bit strange. After all, when was the last time you were told that it's ok to get angry? Don't our parents usually tell us, "Now don't you get mad!"—as they should tell us. But our Lord says that sometimes we need to get angry. In fact we should get really mad but not use our anger to sin!

The problem with our anger is that we like to use it for the wrong things. It's easy to get mad at that kid who always cheats. It's easy to get mad enough to want to punch his lights out! But wait a minute. Our verse says that we should be "angry, and sin not."

The first thing I need to know is that anger isn't always sinful, but my anger is sin most of the time. Jesus was often grieved when people attacked Him personally. But we see from His life that He was angered when evil people did wicked things to poor and helpless people or when they said evil things about His Father. When He drove the moneychangers out of the Temple, we see His anger by His actions. But Jesus never sinned when He was angry, and He was only angry at those things that made His Father angry.

My anger becomes sinful when I use it to attack other people. Solomon reminds us, "He that hath no rule over his own spirit is like a city that is broken down, and without walls." Anyone can come in and control an angry person! God says, don't be an angry person. We need to learn to let our anger go quickly, and not hang on to it. Anger has a short shelf life, and if you keep it too long, it turns into resentment (sin), bitterness (sin), hatred (sin), and if let go long enough it can turn into murder (sin)!

Are you up-to-date? Or are you holding on to anger that God says you should let go of?

ACTION POINT: Are you mad at someone? If so, you need to go to that person and ask him or her to forgive you.

—*Joe Henson*

JULY 5
PRAY AND KEEP ON WORKING

Scripture Reading—Neh. 4:4
"Hear, O our God; for we are despised."

What is your first response when somebody laughs at you or mocks you for your Christian faith? Sometimes the pain runs deep. Everyone wants to be liked by everyone else. No one wants to be despised. Yet, believers still may often face intense pressures from loved ones, friends, co-workers, or neighbors—all because they believe in Jesus Christ and are trying to accomplish something as a Christian.

How should we respond when these things happen? One account in Scripture gives an illuminating picture of how to deal with these kinds of pressures. Nehemiah had been led by God to pray and then ask the king for permission to go back to Jerusalem to rebuild the walls that had been broken down. The walls around the city were in ruins, and that special city was exposed to the surrounding enemies.

When Nehemiah pressed on to do the work of God, he soon discovered his opponents. The Bible says that their first opposition was ridicule of the work of God. "He (Sanballat) was wroth, and took great indignation, and mocked the Jews . . . What do these feeble Jews? . . . and he (Tobiah) said, Even that which they build, if a fox go up, he shall even break down their stone wall" (Neh. 4:1–3).

How did Nehemiah respond? The same way we ought to respond when we face ridicule and opposition. He did not react, fight back, or defend himself. HE PRAYED AND KEPT ON WORKING. Note his prayer in response:

"Hear, O our God; for we are despised: and turn their reproach upon their own head, and give them for a prey in the land of the captivity: And cover not their iniquity, and let not their sin be blotted out from before thee: for they have provoked thee to anger before the builders. So built we the wall" (Neh. 4:4–6).

What a testimony! Pray and keep on working! In fact, Nehemiah condemned his critics by finishing the task God had called him to do. Would you want such a man praying against you?

ACTION POINT: Have each family member pray a prayer for wisdom the next time he or she faces someone who mocks their being a Christian or their belief in the Bible.

—James Stallard

JULY 6
GET DRESSED!

Scripture Reading—Eph. 6:11
*"Put on the whole armour of God, that ye may be able
to stand against the wiles of the devil."*

People are individuals, and each of us does things every day completely different from what others do. But there is one thing that we do every day that is exactly like every other person on earth: we get dressed. And it is not something that most of us put much thought into. We simply rise up every morning, knowing that we must get dressed, and so we do.

The Apostle Paul uses this common human routine to illustrate a very important aspect of the Christian life that is necessary for victory over the Devil. He says that Christians need to "put on" the armor of God—in the same way we put our clothes on each day: one piece at a time, thoughtfully, and with purpose.

"Stand therefore, having your loins girt about with truth, and having on the breastplate of righteousness; And your feet shod with the preparation of the gospel of peace; Above all, taking the shield of faith, wherewith ye shall be able to quench all the fiery darts of the wicked. And take the helmet of salvation, and the sword of the Spirit, which is the word of God."(Eph. 6:14–17)

We are told to put on the "whole armour." Who would leave home partially dressed? No one *I* know! We dress *wholly*, or completely, before we set out each day.

For the Christian engaging in daily spiritual warfare, it won't do to wear only part of our armor. If we do, the enemy will attack the unprotected areas, and we will become a victim. No, the Christian must put on the *whole* suit of armor in order to keep from being injured in battle. Have you taken time today to make sure you're properly and wholly dressed as a soldier of Christ?

FAMILY ACTIVITY: Read Ephesians 6:14–17 and have each family member define each part of the armor of God and explain how to "put it on."

—Paul Miller

JULY 7
THE PRAYER OF A QUITTER

Scripture Reading—Jer. 20:9
"Then said I, I will not make mention of him,
nor speak any more in his name."

Jeremiah was a spokesman for God who delivered messages that were not always well received. As a result, Jeremiah ended up being put in prison and being placed in the stocks, which certainly created a miserable situation for the prophet. Overwhelmed with fear and frustration, Jeremiah did what would certainly seem like the natural thing for any human being to do—he decided to quit. Jeremiah even went so far as to complain to God about all that had taken place.

It hardly seems appropriate that prayer should be a complaint, and yet there is a real sense in which prayer is telling God what we are thinking. In Psalm 142 David said, "I cried unto the LORD with my voice . . . I poured out my complaint before Him; I shewed before him my trouble" (v. 1, 2). Being the God that He is, God cares about the things that we care about. Sometimes our prayer may seem like little more than a complaint, but God is listening.

Though Jeremiah did some complaining, it did not take long for him to find encouragement. Two things encouraged him. First, he states, "His word was in mine heart" (Jer. 20:9), and secondly he states, "The LORD is with me" (v. 11). Because of these two realities, Jeremiah quickly concluded that quitting was not an option. In fact what started out as a pity party ended up being a song service as Jeremiah declares, "Sing unto the LORD, praise ye the LORD, for he hath delivered the soul of the poor from the hand of the evildoers" (v. 13). As Jeremiah communicated with God, God ministered to his need, and he found encouragement to keep on keeping on.

Are you discouraged? Do you have a complaint against God? Tell Him what you are thinking, but then allow Him to encourage you with Who He is. Then praise Him for it.

ACTION POINT: Read the account of what happened to Paul and Silas in Acts 16:19–25. Discuss the response of these men.

—Tom Palmer

THE RECIPE FOR CONTENTMENT

Scripture Reading—Heb. 13:5
"Be content with such things as ye have."

The recipe for contentment is the blending together of thanksgiving and satisfaction.

However, there are two basic ingredients for contentment that are found in the lives of contented people. The first ingredient involves the blessing of God's provision. It is the realization that God's provision is adequate. In other words, it is the realization that God has given exactly what He knows I need at this time. In Matthew 6:25–32, Jesus is talking about the basic necessities of life, such as food and clothing. In verse 32 He says, "Your heavenly Father knoweth that ye have need of all these things." That's why we read in 1 Timothy 6:8: "And having food and raiment let us be therewith content." You will be contented when you learn to thank God for His provision of your basic needs.

The second ingredient involves the blessing of God's direction. Discontentment often develops when we refuse to thank God for the place where He has us in life. Your home, job, school, or neighborhood may not be the place of your choosing, and yet they may be precisely what God had planned for you. When you recognize that truth and thank God for it, you will become contented. "As for God, his way is perfect" (Ps. 18:30) is the testimony of David. You can let God place you where He chooses, knowing that He will not make a mistake.

Martin Luther said, "Next to faith, this is the highest art, to be content in the calling in which God has placed you." In reality, contentment is a choice. It is a choice to accept and appreciate the way God is taking care of our lives. Truly as Paul said to Timothy, "Godliness with contentment is great gain" (1 Tim. 6:6).

A contented family will be a happy family because they are happy in God.

ACTION POINT: Take time as a family to thank God for some of the specific places that are significant in your lives. Be specific in your thanksgiving.

—Tom Palmer

Gideon: "Do as I Do"

Scripture Reading—1 Tim. 4:12
"Let no man despise thy youth; but be thou an example of the believers, in word, in conversation, in charity, in spirit, in faith, in purity."

In Judges 7, God had trimmed Gideon's army down to the bare bones. Now the time had come to issue the artillery. Imagine the surprise of his men when the weapons were issued: trumpets, pitchers, and torches! How would anyone defend himself with these?

Scripture teaches that "the weapons of our warfare are not carnal, but mighty through God to the pulling down of strong holds" (2 Cor. 10:4). God says that His children are to fight their battles "not by might, nor by power, but by my spirit, saith the LORD of hosts" (Zech. 4:6). Gideon trusted not in the sword but in the LORD.

He also set the ideal model for men in leadership. He said, "Look on me, and do likewise . . . as I do, so shall ye do." (Judg. 7:17)

Why do you suppose God armed His people with trumpets, torches, and clay pots? I think we can find some insight in 2 Corinthians 4:3–7. Take a minute to read that passage. Notice that the testimony of a Christian is likened to light (Matt. 5:16). "God . . . hath shined in our hearts, to give **the light** of the knowledge of the glory of God in the face of Jesus Christ" (v. 6). Then Paul writes, "But we have this treasure in earthen vessels, that the excellency of the power may be of God, and not of us" (v. 7). Just as Gideon's torches did not shine forth until the clay vessels were broken, so our testimonies do not really shine forth until we are broken (John 12:24). Trials are used by God not to make us bitter but to make us better.

Incidentally, when 300 torches shone forth instantaneously, the Midianites thought they were surrounded! The leaders of a battalion of soldiers would normally lead the way on a night march with a lighted torch. God outsmarted His people's enemy and caused confusion that resulted in them killing off each other!

The believer's battles are better won by trusting God than by resting on logic (Pro. 3:5, 6). Leadership is developed in us when we learn to depend on Him.

PONDER: Real leadership says, "Do as I say, AND as I do."

—Rich Tozour

JULY 10
WHEN LIFE DOES NOT HAVE
THE ANSWER

Scripture Reading—2 Kings 2:16

"And they said unto him, Behold now, there be with thy servants fifty strong men; let them go, we pray thee, and seek thy master: lest peradventure the Spirit of the Lord hath taken him up, and cast him upon some mountain, or into some valley. And he said, Ye shall not send."

Elijah had just gone to Heaven in the presence of the school of the prophets, and Elisha takes up his mantle to carry on in his place. Even though the prophets had viewed his Home going from a distance, they insisted that Elijah be searched for in case God had dropped him on the side of the mountain. Against his better judgment Elisha finally gave way to their demands to put an end to lingering questions, lest it hinder his ministry.

In the end Elisha was right. He sets forth the following principle: don't spend your time looking for answers that cannot be found on this side of glory. Many of his friends insisted on looking for an answer that only prolonged the journey for them. Why we lose people and end up in certain situations in this life cannot always be answered. Our acceptance of what God has allowed to be veiled is not a measure of our lack of love or concern. It is a decision to carry on with the course that God has set before each of us.

When we face unanswered questions, here are some points from Elisha to take to heart:

• I know I need more than what I have! Elisha ultimately asked a double portion from God.

• I know I want to do more than what I am doing! Elisha immediately went to work as he crossed the river performing twice the miracles Elijah did.

• I know I want to finish stronger than when I started! Elisha did not look back. He went forward with resolve.

• I know I need to carry forth what was entrusted to me! Elisha went forth with his mantle. "Commit thou to faithful men." I have a responsibility to my heritage before God.

ACTION POINT: Follow a worthy example!

—*Steve Rebert*

FRETTING AGAINST THE LORD

Scripture Reading—Ps. 37:8
"Cease from anger, and forsake wrath:
fret not thyself in any wise to do evil."

It is difficult to yield to God, but it certainly is our best option. Even when we look at others and see their faults, how they have hurt us, and how they have not lived up to the standards of Christianity in their lives, we still should obey God. Others' shortcomings are not an excuse for us not to do the right thing.

We have enough problems dealing with our own faults to respond to life based on the faults of others. This makes what the Psalmist says in Psalm 37:8 vital to our responses. This struggle will only increase a fretful spirit, unless we follow the teaching of the Lord. And our tendency will be not to yield to God, but to focus on others and our own choices instead.

Make no mistake about it: a fretful spirit will bring us to do evil. How many times have you been so worried that it caused you to make a bad decision? A college student gets so bothered about his or her grades that he succumbs to the temptation to cheat on a test. A young Christian lady begins to fret that she will be an "old maid" and never get married. So, her fretting leads her down the path to be immodest in dress, and then date, court, and marry a non-Christian man.

All this fretting seems to be part of our times. But, God's people don't have to live according to the spirit of the age. We have God's Holy Spirit to prompt us (Eph. 5:18–21) and the Word of God to guide us (Col. 3:16). These two, the Spirit and the Word, will always work together and will never contradict each other. If you are a fretter, let God be God. Let Him calm and settle your heart.

DISCUSS: Ask each family member (don't be afraid) to share the things that cause him or her to fret. Then carefully read Psalm 37:1–8 and apply it to your family. Study the meaning of the words **trust** (v. 3), **delight** (v. 4), **commit** (v. 5), and **rest** (v. 7).

—James Stallard

WHAT ARE WE TO DO UNTIL JESUS COMES?

Scripture Reading—1 John 2:28

"And now, little children, abide in him; that, when he shall appear, we may have confidence, and not be ashamed before him at his coming."

During World War II, superior Japanese troops had been sweeping through East Asia and the Pacific with fierceness. General Douglas MacArthur, who was stationed with his troops in the Philippines, displayed great resistance against the Japanese forces. Meanwhile, the continent of Australia was threatened with invasion and needed bolstering. MacArthur did not want to leave the people of the Philippines, but he was ordered to depart for Australia. In February of 1942, as General MacArthur prepared to leave, he spoke these words of hope, saying, *"I shall return."* He fulfilled that promise in October of 1944.

As children of God, we too have been given a promise, not from a general, but from the King of Kings and the Lord of Lords. The Apostle John recorded those words from Jesus in John 14:3, "If I go and prepare a place for you, I will come again."

In light of Jesus' promise to return someday for His people, John mandates what is expected of us *until* Jesus actually comes again. He says in 1 John 2:28, "Abide in him (Jesus)." The word "abide" is the idea of remaining and staying in place. Christians understand that one must come to Jesus for salvation and forgiveness of sins by placing his or her dependence upon Him. As Christians, we are to stay in dependence upon the same One who saved us.

John also suggests a scriptural motivation for depending upon Jesus today. He refers to the Judgment Seat of Christ, where every Christian will be examined as to the object of their dependence in this life. If we've been serving God in our own strength and power, we will be "ashamed" or disappointed. If we've been living our lives in dependence upon the One that saved us, we will be confident—in Him!

PRAYER: Lord, today please teach me how I can stay in dependence upon You! Thank You for making my responsibility simply to just trust You.

—*Billy Ingram*

JULY 13
"THINK BEFORE YOU SPEAK"

Scripture Reading—James 1:19
"Be swift to hear, slow to speak, slow to wrath."

Most of us have no idea how much we talk. If every word you said in a day were typed into a manuscript, it would equate to a small book. This book that you produced in the past week—how much of it would you want others to read? If we were able to read every word we said in a day, how would it reflect upon the Lord? Would there be lines you would want to mark out so no one else could read?

What makes this even more difficult is that we forget much of what we say, but others do not. During the past 24 hours, how many of your words can you remember? For me, I can't even recall verbatim the words I used in a conversation ten minutes earlier!

Our words are potent—for good or for harm. God's wisdom is that we should be careful to speak and more quick to listen (James 1:19).

When people are able to control their speech, it has positive residual effects to other areas of their lives. It is an evidence of spiritual maturity (James 3:2). The way a person uses his words is an indicator of how disciplined he or she is in other areas of life.

Our words will not be tamed by self-determination alone: "The tongue can no man tame" (James 3:8). Only God can enable a person to control his or her speech. This is crucial because the tongue is naturally evil, able to kill reputations, and is compared to a serpent with deadly poison in its tongue. "It is an unruly evil, full of deadly poison" (James 3:8).

Most relationship problems would be greatly reduced if we talked less and used our words with care. Someone wrote, "It takes a child two years to learn to talk, but it takes a man all his life to learn how to keep his mouth shut."

ACTION POINT: Write James 1:19 on a small card and put it in a prominent place in your home.

—*Rick Johnson* So then, my beloved brethren, let every man be swift to hear, slow to speak, slow to wrath.

JULY 14
SIN IN THE CAMP

Scripture Reading—Josh. 7:20
"Indeed I have sinned against the LORD God of Israel."

The horror of that first moment must have startled the man and his family. Word had just come to their part of camp that a search was under way. The leaders of Israel were looking for the cause of their defeat at little Ai after a mighty victory at Jericho. The answer came quickly—sin in the camp!

Someone had disobeyed the command of the Lord. The people were not to take of the spoils of Jericho, "but the children of Israel committed a trespass in the accursed thing" (Josh. 7:1). The man Achan, the son of Carmi, along with his family's help went against the order.

As the leaders went from tent to tent, the fear became greater and greater for Achan's family. Would they be discovered? Would they escape? The Bible had warned, "Be sure your sin will find you out" (Num. 32:23). Joshua confronted Achan, and he finally confessed.

"When I saw among the spoils a goodly Babylonish garment, and two hundred shekels of silver, and a wedge of gold of fifty shekels weight, then I coveted them, and took them; and behold they are hid in the earth in the midst of my tent, and the silver under it" (Josh. 7:21).

Note the progression of the temptation to sin—I saw. I coveted. I took. I hid. Achan chose riches over God, and judgment came upon him and his family. This incident stands as a reminder to our present day of the dangers of riches.

One day, as a pastor, a young man was brought to me by his father. The father wanted to show me what his wonderful Christian son had done. He had been guilty of stealing something out of a store and was caught in the deed. The son was brought to repentance because the father did not hide the sin.

But the same progression took place in this young man's life—he saw, he coveted, he took, he hid. But, sin found him out. Take care in your life that you avoid this progression of sin.

SONG: Sing "My Jesus, I Love Thee" as a family prayer to God.

—James Stallard

SPEAK EVIL OF NO MAN

Scripture Reading—Titus 3:2
"To speak evil of no man."

Speaking evil of others seems to come naturally to all of us. It is easy to run somebody down with our tongue but often hard to give praise to someone else. But as with most spiritual matters, it is easier to do the wrong thing than to do the right thing.

The context of our text deals with civil leaders when it says, "Put them (believers) in mind to be subject to principalities and powers, to obey magistrates, to be ready to every good work" (Titus 3:1). Then the next verse begins with "To speak evil of no man."

To "speak evil" comes from the word that means "to blaspheme." It is often used of speaking evil about God, but it can also refer to vilifying or speaking evil about other men. Christians are being told to be careful about their speech toward the unsaved world. This includes political leaders and those in authority over us, recognizing that God has allowed them to have their positions (Rom. 13:1).

A Christian man worked in a large Christian ministry as a supervisor over a department. His immediate boss told him to lie to cover for him with the big boss who was over him. The Christian man refused to do that and was almost fired from his job. But the Christian man refused to speak evil of his boss, even though he ordered him to lie, and in just a few short weeks was promoted to more work and freedom in his position. His responses to these things were very noticeable to those who worked with him and over him.

It never pays to be known as an angry person who speaks evil of others. But, it might be a good thing to be known as someone who can be trusted to say the right thing. As the Apostle Paul declares, "Let your speech be always with grace, seasoned with salt, that ye may know how ye ought to answer every man" (Col. 4:6). These words should never be far from our own lips.

ACTION POINT: Use a concordance or Bible dictionary to find verses in Proverbs that deal with the tongue or speech.

—James Stallard

JULY 16
HOW CAN I PREDICT MY FAILURE?

Scripture Reading—Matt. 26:34
"Jesus said unto him, Verily I say unto thee, That this night, before the cock crow, thou shalt deny me thrice."

Weather forecasters, known as meteorologists, predict what the weather will be like at any given time. These specialists use high-tech equipment, science, and advanced math to make accurate weather forecasts.

In Matthew 26:34, we see Jesus making a prediction concerning Peter—not about the coming weather, but about his coming failure. Jesus confronted Peter about his personal ingredient for disaster and the certainty of this soon-to-be defeat in his life. How could Christ predict such an event? One might suggest that Jesus was able to make this prediction because He is God and knows all things, including Peter's future failure. While it is true that Jesus is God and knows all things, the failure that He predicted in Peter's life is a failure that we are prone to as well if we have the same ingredient for disaster in our lives. Jesus wants us to recognize our own potential for failure and confront it in our own lives.

One of the fatal ingredients that led to Peter's failure was Peter's self-confidence. Peter believed in his own ability and was sure of his future success. Peter's self-reliance is revealed when he says to the Lord: "If everyone else falls and betrays you Lord, I will never" (Matt. 26:34, my paraphrase). Proverbs 16:18 reminds us of the danger of such an attitude: "Pride goeth before destruction, and an haughty spirit before a fall." When Peter said, "I'll never leave you, or deny you," he meant this with all of his heart. Peter's problem was not his lack of sincerity, but his lack of dependence upon God.

Simply put, pride is independence of God. The reason you don't pray or read your Bible at times is that you do not think that you really need God. That is pride and being independent of God! If this describes you, take this as a serious warning that you are heading towards even greater defeat!

PONDER: Peter's greatest problem was Peter. Our greatest problem is our own selves. That is why God's formula for spiritual success and blessing is to live dependent on Him and not independent from Him (James 4:6–8).

—Billy Ingram

JULY 17
THE PERMANENCE OF MARRIAGE

Scripture Reading—Matt. 14:8
"Give me here John Baptist's head in a charger."

In Matthew 14 we find one of the tragedies of the Bible. One of the greatest men who had ever lived lost his life after being falsely imprisoned. As the forerunner of the Messiah, John the Baptist had lived a life of holiness, baptizing thousands of the children of Israel unto repentance. He also fearlessly proclaimed the truth, no matter whom it upset.

John had preached against King Herod's sin, for Herod had taken his brother Phillip's wife. John proclaimed, "It is not lawful for thee to have her" (Matt. 14:4). He was preaching against the adultery and his divorce (Herodias had divorced Phillip to marry Herod). Herodias burned in her hatred toward John the Baptist until Herod's birthday promise gave rise to her opportunity (Matt. 14:6, 7). She asked for John's head on a platter!

So, John was beheaded because of Herod's foolish, sinful indulgence and the influence of his wife. It is significant to realize that if John the Baptist had the convictions of modern-day preachers, he would not have lost his head. But Jesus said upon hearing of John's beheading, "For I say unto you, Among those that are born of women there is not a greater prophet than John the Baptist" (Luke 7:28).

The obvious view of the Lord and John the Baptist was that the declaration against Herod was accurate. Marriage is to be between one man and one woman until death (Matt 19:4–6).

At the core of the breakdown of the family in modern times is the breakdown of marriage itself. Many husbands and wives feel trapped in a relationship they wish they could end. But God's solution is never to destroy the very basis of stability for marriage and family.

No husband, no wife, and no children will be perfect. But, whenever someone in the family fails to do what they should do, the solution is to trust in the Lord and never give up on the relationships that have been established (Pro. 3:5, 6).

DISCUSS: Have each family member suggest an idea that would make the family stronger.

—James Stallard

DO NOT TOUCH!

Scripture Reading—James 4:17
"Therefore to him that knoweth to do good,
and doeth it not, to him it is sin."

It is hard to imagine that two perfect people in a perfect place could still get into trouble—but they did. There in the Garden of Eden, Adam and Eve chose to disobey God, and immediately they placed themselves and all of human nature under the curse of sin. God had told Adam and Eve that "the tree of the knowledge of good and evil" was off limits for them (Gen. 2:17). In spite of what they knew, Genesis 3:6 tells us that Eve "took of the fruit thereof, and did eat, and gave also unto her husband with her; and he did eat." In disobeying, they sinned against God by doing the very thing they were told not to do.

Early in life, young children begin hearing those words, "Do not touch." Toddlers are told not to touch the "pretties" on the coffee table or the expensive items displayed in the gift shop. Touching is just part of being a kid, but learning not to touch is part of growing up. If Adam and Eve had obeyed God and kept their hands off the tree they were not to eat of, they would not have been punished by being kicked out of the Garden of Eden.

When parents tell a toddler "do not touch," it can seem frustrating for that little person. However, Mom and Dad are not just trying to protect the flower display on the table or the crystal vase on the shelf, they are seeking to protect their child. The child who will learn to obey when he is a young, will be much more likely to obey when he is older. Obedience will protect that child from the consequences of disobedience. If a person lives to be 100 years old, there will still be commands they must obey. It is best to learn this truth sooner, rather than later.

ACTION POINT: As parents, be honest in sharing with your children an incident from your childhood when you wish you had obeyed. Allow your children to learn from your experience.

—*Tom Palmer*

JULY 19
EBENEZER IS NOT A SCROOGE

Scripture Reading—1 Sam. 7:5
"Gather all Israel to Mizpeh, and I will pray for you unto the LORD."

Imagine coming together for a prayer meeting and finding out that your enemy was preparing to attack the prayer meeting. That is exactly what happened in 1 Samuel 7. The Israelites had been lamenting after the Lord (v. 2), and Samuel had brought them together to fast and pray and to confess their sins. As they are meeting with God, word came that the lords of the Philistines were preparing for battle. Panic set in immediately. Verse 8 tells us that the children of Israel said, "Cease not to cry unto the LORD our God for us, that he will save us." According to verse 9, Samuel "cried unto the LORD for Israel," and "the Lord heard him." Sound simple? I suppose, but in reality there was no other option at that point. In reality, the Israelites needed no other option because at that point God moved into action.

God chose to use thunder. He did not use F-16 fighter jets, army tanks, or Blackhawk helicopters—he used thunder, which made total havoc of the Philistines soldiers. The Israelites chased them down and beat them up, delivering Israel from what seemed like an inevitable defeat.

Once the victory was secured, Samuel prepared a monument to remind the Israelites of the victory God had given them. It was a simple monument made of just one stone with just one word on it: "Ebenezer" (v. 12). "Ebenezer" is a word that means "Hitherto (right here) hath the LORD helped us." The monument was a reminder that, in answer to prayer, God had helped His people. When God helps His people, they must never forget what He did. An answer to prayer is a significant encouragement to keep on praying when we seem helpless. No, "Ebenezer" was not just the scrooge; it was a reminder of a helpful God.

ACTION POINT: Using a hymnal, look up the words to Isaac Watts' hymn, "O God Our Help in Ages Past." Read or sing the words together, praising God for His help.

—Tom Palmer

JULY 20
DO'S AND DON'TS

Scripture Reading—Titus 3:5
"Not by works of righteousness which we have done,
but according to his mercy he saved us,
by the washing of regeneration, and renewing of the Holy Ghost."

So many times in our Christian walk we view Christianity as a bunch of "do's and don'ts." You better DO this! You better NOT DO that! DO this, DON'T DO that! This often becomes the way we view our relationship with God.

Is that what a walk with God is like? Is God just sitting on His throne waiting for us to mess up, so He can judge us and bop us on the head? Not at all!

There are a lot of things that we should do and not do as Christians, but those things are motivated out of understanding, spiritual maturity, and—especially—love. In other words, I want to DO the things that please God, but I DON'T want to do the things that displease Him. But the amazing thing is that whether I DO or DON'T—it doesn't affect my righteousness before God.

Titus 3:3–8 discusses this truth. Works don't save us! It's God's abundant mercy (v. 5) and grace (v. 7) that bring us into the right relationship with the Lord and make us heirs. We can't do anything to earn God's favor.

Where do works come in then? According to these verses, works are after salvation! They are the evidence of a life right with God. They are the result of the Holy Spirit within. They bring God the glory because without Him we can do nothing (John 15:5). They are "good and profitable unto men" (Titus 3:8). Works don't bring favor with God; they are the result of understanding God's favor.

Are you basing your standing before God in a list of "do's and don'ts"? Determine to live in the victory of God's mercy and grace! Thank God! He loves us through mercy and grace! Otherwise, we can never measure up.

ACTION POINT: As a family, thank God for his mercy and grace, and then discuss ways you can express your thankfulness to Him in good works.

—*Stanley Long*

JULY 21
SPIRITUAL MEDIOCRITY

Scripture Reading—Ps. 81:10
"I am the LORD thy God, which brought thee out of the land of Egypt:
open thy mouth wide, and I will fill it."

Those who are saved will receive rewards in Heaven one day for their faithful service motivated by love. I believe we underestimate the seriousness of this time. On that day some will be ashamed (1 John 2:28). What a tragedy to arrive in glory and realize that you have settled for far less than you could have ever imagined. And this will happen for many Christians.

That which is mediocre is "ordinary, of low, or moderate, quality." Someone said, "Mediocrity is the worst of the best and the best of the worst. Either way you end up with the worst."

Mediocrity has no impact value. No one is interested in settling for a mediocre restaurant, sporting event, or salary, but we accept mediocrity in our spiritual lives and think it is acceptable with God.

Whatever is keeping you from God's best in your life is not worth it. He wants to do significant things in your life. He will not only meet your needs, but will show Himself strong on your behalf (2 Chron. 16:9).

While there are rewards in Heaven, God delights to bless you in this life. He didn't save us to make our lives miserable, but to give us abundant life (John 10:10). This is the very opposite of mediocrity.

Living a life of spiritual blessing is available to all who would delight in the Lord (Ps. 37:4), abide in Him and His words (John 15:7), and expect Him to honor His Word (Eph. 3:20). Those that do these three things daily will be blessed of God beyond comprehension in this life.

Are you mired in mediocrity and living beneath your spiritual privileges? There is no need to have regrets and be ashamed at the Judgment Seat of Christ. Confess your mediocrity and begin to seek the Lord that you might know His best, even today.

PONDER: Which one of the three things that brings spiritual blessing mentioned above do you need to start doing today?

—*Rick Johnson*

JULY 22
A PRAYER LIST: THINGS THAT CONCERN ME

Scripture Reading—Ps. 62:8
"Pour out your heart before him: God is a refuge for us. Selah."

A four-fold process to answered prayer is to desire, pray, believe, and receive (Mark 11:24). All of them are important and a part of praying. The word "desire" means "to beg, ask, or crave."

What are your concerns today? What are the things heavy on your heart and mind? What kind of needs do you have? God wants you to present your requests to Him. This should be a part of a written prayer list.

For some reason we feel that God isn't really interested in the details of our lives. We think that He is too busy to be interested in our needs. That is a lie of Satan.

Every day you ought to make a short list of the things that are heavy upon your heart and present them to your Heavenly Father. He not only can do something about them, but He desires to do so (Matt. 7:7–11; John 15:7; John 16:24; James 1:5; 1 John 5:14, 15; Phil. 4:6).

The Word of God is filled with exhortations to bring your requests and needs to God. The verses above are just a sampling. There are many others. Why then don't we do this?

One reason is that we just don't take the time to do it. We occasionally throw up a "flare prayer" when we hurt bad enough, but we don't have a daily appointment to bring our concerns and needs to the Lord. Set a time to pray, make a list of the things that are heavy upon your heart, and petition the Lord with those concerns.

God wants you to do so! Don't worry about needs; pray about them. Don't complain about them; pray about them. He instructs us to "cast" our concerns on Him (Ps. 55:22; 1 Pet. 5:7). Give them to Him.

What are your concerns today? Bring them to the Lord and receive encouragement and rest (1 Sam. 30:6; Matt. 11:28).

ACTION POINT: Write out your concerns and then pour out your heart to the Lord about them. "Jesus knows our ev'ry weakness, *Take it to the Lord in prayer.*"

—Rick Johnson

BE A FRIEND, GAIN A FRIEND

Scripture Reading—Pro. 18:24
*"A man that hath friends must shew himself friendly:
and there is a friend that sticketh closer than a brother."*

Years ago at a morning service my family was attending, I noticed a young couple about our age visiting the church. After a few services it seemed they wanted to come in, then get out immediately.

One morning, before their exit, I purposefully introduced myself and struck up a conversation with the man, Glen. Through this effort we discovered we had several mutual interests. We began to hunt together, labor for the Lord, and introduce each other to relatives and friends. Long story short, a close friendship was born during that time. Fifteen years later and 2,000 miles apart, we still stay in touch, exchange prayer needs, and update one another on our families and ministries.

The word "must" is a must if we are to have godly friendships. The simple practice of Christian friendliness in a fallen world bears much fruit in our lives and those we reach. It opens the door to ministering to others. It gives us the opportunity to bear one another's burdens, and so fulfil the law of Christ. It allows us to experience a host of spiritual blessings that we miss when we don't follow the Way.

Consider the Lord Jesus—described in this verse as the Ultimate Friend. He befriended us through the sacrifice of Calvary. Not only does He stick closer than a brother, He sticks as a friend forever! Those we befriend and win to Christ and those we develop friendships with who are or become believers will be friends forever.

We reap eternal *rewards* simply by following Christ's example and showing ourselves friendly.

ACTION POINT: Pray, "Lord, give me someone specifically to show myself friendly to." (This could be a spouse, child, coworker, neighbor, or someone new at church). Take the initiative—sacrifice, witness, do a good deed, and count on God's promise. You'll gain a friend!

—Wayne King

A Prayer List for Revival

Scripture Reading—Ps. 51:3
"For I acknowledge my transgressions: and my sin is ever before me."

There is a simple chorus that says: "It's me, it's me, O Lord, standing in the need of prayer, it's me, it's me, O Lord, standing in the need of prayer." Though many of us have sung this chorus, very few of us have prayed this prayer. However, the best revival prayers are for the person who needs revival the most—me! That is the kind of prayer David prayed in Psalm 51.

David had taken a man's wife, which was adultery. He had also taken a man's life, which was murder. 2 Samuel 11:27 says, "The thing that David had done displeased the LORD." Realizing that his fellowship with God was suffering greatly, David began to pray with the focus on his own need. In Psalm 51:7–12 we find that David used the pronoun "me" a total of nine times. Here are some of his prayer requests:

- "purge me . . . wash me"
- "make me to hear joy and gladness"
- "create in me a clean heart"
- "renew a right spirit within me"
- "restore unto me the joy of thy salvation"

This prayer of David was a very personal prayer that did not make excuses or offer blame. David truly took responsibility for his sin and failure. This is the only kind of praying that is acceptable when dealing with our sin.

When David said to Nathan, "I have sinned against the LORD," Nathan said to David, "The LORD also hath put away thy sin" (2 Sam. 12:13). Though David still had to live with the consequences of his sin, God granted forgiveness and cleansing. David came to God and stated how bad he had been—not how good he had been—and God mercifully cleansed his life.

When a child of God is living in sin, there is no greater prayer that can be prayed than a personal prayer of confession. This is truly a great revival prayer. It worked for David, and it will work for you.

ACTION POINT: Look up Proverbs 28:13 and discuss its significance in the light of David's prayer.

—Tom Palmer

JULY 25
WHEN HOPE DIES

Scripture Reading—Mark 5:35
"Thy daughter is dead: why troublest thou the Master any further?"

The desperate synagogue leader Jairus must have been in agony of soul when he came to Jesus beseeching Him to heal his ailing 12-year-old daughter. He knew her life was in the balance. Her situation was utterly desperate.

Imagine how Jairus must have felt when Jesus stopped to meet another need. The woman, who had had a bleeding problem for twelve years (the same amount of time Jairus' daughter had been alive), certainly had no lesser of a need than Jairus did. But the ruler must have wished that the woman had caught Jesus at another time. How hard it is to look on another's needs (Phil. 2:4) when one's own circumstances are insanely dire! Here the Lord demonstrates that He can minister to all concerned parties without jeopardizing any one individual.

Jairus' heart must have sunk when there came one from his household saying, "Thy daughter is dead: why troublest thou the Master any further?"—as if it were some kind of trouble for Jesus to help! The statement implied that the situation was now beyond even Jesus' control. Scripture makes clear that **NOTHING** is ever beyond His control—that includes YOUR most desperate circumstances.

Jesus replied, "Be not afraid, only believe." Fear flourishes in the absence of faith and flees when faith is fostered.

When Jesus arrived at Jairus' home, there was incredible wailing. He asked the mourners, "Why make ye this ado, and weep? the damsel is not dead, but sleepeth." It was a matter of perspective, of course. The girl was surely dead, in human eyes at least. Yet God's view is markedly different than ours!

The mourners' wailing turned to laughter: the laughter of scorners! Jesus disregarded the scoffing and privately raised the girl from the dead!

Our Lord never works to impress. He labors to bring glory to God the Father. There is a marvelous modesty in the Most High. Yet there is also an optimistic confidence in those who trust His power.

PONDER: Fear flourishes in the absence of faith and flees when faith Is fostered.

—Rich Tozour

JULY 26
SPIRITUAL WIPEOUT WILL
HAPPEN WHEN . . .

Scripture Reading—Pro. 29:23
"A man's pride shall bring him low."

Lindsey Jacobellis was representing America in the 2010 Winter Olympics, in a snowboarding competition, one of the newer events in the Olympics. Unlike some of the other contests that require judges to determine the outcome, this is purely a racing event that consists of athletes leaving a start gate simultaneously and careening down a winding, jump-laden, 1,500-meter course. The first to the bottom wins.

With an extremely comfortable lead over her second-place opponent, all Lindsey needed to do was simply finish. Nearing the last segment of the course, instead of sticking to the basics, Lindsey used the last jump to "show off" with a little wiggle, while suspended in the air. The result was that it threw off the balance of her landing, and she wiped out, handing the win and gold medal to another.

Proverbs 29:23 warns of spiritual wipeout that will accompany pride. Probably every Christian would agree that pride is a sin, yet few Christians fail to treat pride as sin due to a misunderstanding of what pride is. Pride is much more than arrogance and a "better than thou" attitude. The essence of pride is simply, independence of God.

Too often, one condemns and attempts to deal with the results of pride rather than aggressively attacking the existence of pride. Pride's independent nature of God is expressed by self-reliance and confidence in oneself over God. It is pride when we fail to spend time with God in prayer, neglect to read His Word, or yield to any sin— since these are mere expressions of a heart that assumes that it doesn't need God.

If you are not living in dependence upon the life of Christ and His power, then you are already in sin and heading towards destruction. The deception of pride is that if you are seemingly doing ok, then you must be ok. God's Word teaches the contrary. Pride is sin, and unless you deal with it thoroughly as sin, you will wipeout!

PRAYER: Dear Lord, I beg you to reveal any area where I am not depending upon You or Your power. Help me to recognize the marks of pride and deal with it as the wicked sin that You hate.

—*Billy Ingram*

JULY 27
GIDEON: MULTIPLYING EFFECTIVENESS BY SUBTRACTING MEN

Scripture Reading—1 Sam. 14:6
"It may be that the LORD will work for us:
for there is no restraint to the LORD to save by many or by few."

In Judges 7:1–8, God called Gideon to lead his people into battle against the army of the Midianites. Now the time had come to raise an army for Israel. The military draft had resulted in a band of 32,000 soldiers—not a very big army when compared to the 135,000 troops allied with Midian. But God said, "The people that are with thee are **too many** for me to give the Midianites into their hands, lest Israel vaunt themselves against me, saying, Mine own hand hath saved me . . .. Now therefore go to, proclaim in the ears of the people, saying, Whosoever is fearful and afraid, let him return and depart early from mount Gilead. And there returned of the people twenty and two thousand; and there remained ten thousand" (Judg. 7:2, 3).

That day 22,000 men left for home. The army that remained (10,000) was now made up of only willing recruits. But the Lord said, "The people are **yet too many**" (v. 4). He then appointed a test: whoever drank from the water by getting on his knees to suck up a quick quantity was put in one group. Those who lifted the water in their hands and lapped it like dogs (presumably watchful with their heads up, as dogs are when they drink) were set in another group. The watchful group, a mere 300 men, was chosen as Gideon's band!

Scripture declares, "There is that scattereth, and yet increaseth" (Pro. 11:24). Remove one kernel from a sack of corn, plant it in the ground, cultivate it, and wait to see what happens. It produces a stalk, which then produces ears, which in turn produce dozens—even hundreds—of kernels. Indeed, little is much when God is in it! You may not feel like you're much, but when God is in you, your little becomes much.

PONDER: Little is a relative term in the eyes of a mighty big God!

—Rich Tozour

WHAT DO YOU NEED?

Scripture Reading—Luke 18:41
"What wilt thou that I shall do unto thee?
And he said, Lord, that I may receive my sight."

There are very few problems that could seem more difficult to handle than blindness. Blindness can bring a person to an incredible level of helplessness and can create a sense of real desperation.

Jesus met a man like that in Luke 18. Because he was blind, this man was also begging, having no other means to take care of himself (v. 35). Having been told that Jesus was nearby, this blind man began to call for Jesus, eventually gaining His attention. Jesus approached and asked the question found in our verse for today. Note how personal and honest the response of the blind man was. Sometimes people struggle to "tell it like it is" in prayer. That was not a hindrance to this man. He knew what his problem was, and he knew that Jesus could take care of it.

At the end of the chapter, we find the specifics of how Jesus answered this prayer. First, his eyes were opened. Jesus said, "Receive thy sight." Next we find that his heart was opened. Again Jesus spoke and said, "Thy faith hath saved thee." Finally his mouth was opened. We read that the man followed Jesus, "glorifying God."

I was recently talking to a man about a need that affected his family. I told him that I would pray specifically for the situation. I explained to him that prayer is not the least thing we can do, but rather the greatest thing we can do. As he gave me a somewhat perplexed look, I said, "Prayer brings God in on the situation." His response was, "I will accept your prayer."

You may not be dealing with blindness, but your situation or problem may seem helpless to you. In prayer, tell God all about it. Remember his question to you is, "What do you need?" He is waiting for you to ask.

ACTION POINT: Take time to thank God that He is able to help even when we seem so helpless. Look up Matthew 7:7 and read it together.

—*Tom Palmer*

JULY 29
LIVING ABOVE THE "LAW OF DEPRAVITY"

Scripture Reading—Rom. 8:2
"For the law of the Spirit of life in Christ Jesus hath made me free from the law of sin and death."

"Augh! I did it again!" Try as I might, I had fallen back into the same sinful habit. I hated it. I had confessed it—repeatedly. But I continued to be ensnared by the same "sin which doth so easily beset." Such was the battle of my mid-teen years.

Have you ever felt frustrated by repeated fleshly failures? Our text for today gives a strategy for success over sin.

First, take note of "**the pull of two laws**" (Rom. 7:14–25). A law is a binding principle. The **Law of God** is referred to in Romans 7:1, 4, 6, 7, 8, 9, 12, 14, 16, 22 and 25. It is God's declaration of righteousness, commandments to govern the conduct of men. The problem is that man in his sinful state cannot keep God's commands perfectly. Paul expressed this frustration in verses 18–24. The battle is with the "law of sin" (7:21, 23, 25; also called "the law of sin and death" in 8:2). I call it the **law of depravity**. Like the law of gravity, it pulls men downward into the snare of sin.

Next, notice "**the power to live right**" (Rom. 8:1–13). This power is ours because of **the law of the Spirit of life in Christ Jesus** (7:24, 25; 8:2f). "They that are in the flesh cannot please God" (8:8). It is only as the Holy Spirit gives us His power to overcome that we can prevail over temptation. We must depend on this power or fall prey to sin.

Let me illustrate. If I drop my pen from eye level, which way will it go? Down. How many times will that happen? Every time. Why? The law of gravity. Yet I have some pens in my possession that have been up to 37,000 feet! How did they get up that high? Simple: the law of aerodynamics—they were on a plane.

Just as the law of aerodynamics overcomes the law of gravity, the law of the Spirit overcomes the law of depravity. We CAN conquer carnal desires through Christ our Deliverer!

PONDER: You must get saved **out of** sin the same way you got saved **from** sin: by grace through faith (Col. 2:6).

—*Rich Tozour*

JULY 30
TAKING CARE OF THE TEMPLE

Scripture Reading—1 Cor. 6:19

"What? know ye not that your body is the temple of the Holy Ghost which is in you, which ye have of God, and ye are not your own."

Question—so where is God? Yes, I know God is in Heaven, and yes, I know that Psalm 139 teaches that God is everywhere. But where else is God?

It seems to me that the typical Christian fails to consider that his or her physical body is also the dwelling place of God. God does not dwell in a tabernacle as He did in the days of Moses, or in a temple as He did in the days of King Solomon. Physical bodies are now what our verse calls, "the temple of the Holy Ghost" as God comes to live within the bodies of believers.

If that is the case—and it is—then our view of our physical bodies becomes very important. The body can be used to "glorify God" (1 Cor. 6:20); it can be used to serve God (Rom. 12:1); and it can be used to "magnify" Christ (Phil. 1:20). Physical exercise is a great way to keep the body "in shape," which is part of taking care of the temple of God. When a Christian does not take care of the temple of his body, it will break down more easily and wear out more quickly. A broken-down and worn-out body will be greatly limited when it comes to glorifying, serving, and magnifying the Lord.

Exercising the body is a significant part of body maintenance. Whether it is a casual walk or an intense ball game, the body needs exercise. Muscles need to be strengthened. Breathing and circulation need to be improved. Coordination and motor skills need to be developed. Energy and vitality need to be restored. When these things are done consistently, the physical body will not only become but also will remain more useful and usable to God.

Go ahead. Get up and get going!

ACTION POINT: As an individual or a family, plan a time of physical activity or recreation and then talk about caring for our physical bodies.

—*Tom Palmer*

JULY 31
DEVELOPING A STRONG FAITH

Scripture Reading—Rom. 4:20
"He staggered not at the promise of God through unbelief;
but was strong in faith."

To be told that you would be the father of many nations would be astounding. For it to occur would require a miracle of God. Though his body was old and weak, his faith was strong. The Scripture goes on to say, "And being fully persuaded that, what he had promised, he was able also to perform" (Rom. 4:21).

Faith is confidence that what God has said is true and accurate and then acting accordingly. Abraham did not shrink from the command to believe God, and it brought much blessing to his life (Gen. 15:6; Rom. 4:17–25). His faith was so strong that the Bible says of Abraham: "Who against hope believed in hope" (Rom. 4:18). He had hope when there was no hope. With his back up against the wall, he still believed God's promise.

Weak faith still has value, but believers need to develop a strong faith. Suppose two men are going to fly on an airplane to the same destination. One is completely confident in flying, finds his seat, and basically sleeps the whole flight without worry. The other gets on board afraid of flying. He stays awake and worries about every little motion of the airplane. Both got on. Both arrive at their destination. One had strong faith; the other had weak faith. The weak faith was enough for the man to get on the plane.

This is the way it is with our salvation. The key is to have the right object of faith, which is the Lord Jesus Christ. Faith in Him, no matter how weak, will bring salvation (John 3:18). But, we need to go beyond that faith in our Christian lives and develop a strong faith.

Over and over again Jesus rebuked the disciples for their "little faith" (Matt. 6:30; 8:26; 14:31; 16:8; Luke 12:28). Any muscle gets weak if it is not exercised. So it is with the muscle of faith. We must exercise it through God's Word, and then we will develop a strong faith like Abraham's.

MEMORIZE: Romans 10:17.

—*James Stallard*

213

AUGUST 1
NICE TO HEAR FROM YOU

Scripture Reading—Ps. 5:3
"My voice shalt thou hear in the morning, O LORD;
in the morning will I direct my prayer unto thee, and will look up."

The 21st century has become the age of communication. Modern technology has made it possible to talk to almost anybody from almost anywhere at almost anytime about almost anything. Yet in spite of all these technological advances, there is still no greater privilege than being able to talk to God from anywhere at anytime about anything.

Andrew Woolsey, in his biography of Duncan Campbell titled Channel of Revival, made an interesting note about Mr. Campbell. In the flyleaf of his Bible, Campbell had written this:

"Give the best hours of the day to God. I have never found anything to compare to the morning watch as a source of blessing, when one meets God before meeting the world. It is a good thing to speak to Him before we speak to other people, to listen to His Word before we listen to the voices of our fellow man."

There is nothing wrong with "saying your prayers every night," as so many folks do. However, a time of communicating with God in the morning is far more profitable for preparing the heart and planning the day ahead. Someone has said, "Get your soul in tune with God before the orchestra of the day begins." Don't wait to bring God into your day until the day is nearly over. Rather bring Him into your day during the first few minutes.

Frequently, we have allowed significant time to pass since the last time we talked to a friend or family member. When they heard our voice, their first response was, "Nice to hear from you. It sure has been a long time." As you begin your day tomorrow, be sure to have a talk with your God. Not only will your time in prayer be a blessing to your life, but I can assure you that it will be nice for Him to hear from you.

ACTION POINT: Note when, where, and how, Jesus started His day in Mark 1:35.

—Tom Palmer

AUGUST 2
BOTHERED BY THE BLESSING OF GOD

Scripture Reading—Jonah 4:1
"But it displeased Jonah exceedingly, and he was very angry."

This just didn't seem right. Here was a prophet of God mad at God for being merciful upon a great city. We remember the story of Jonah. He had been called of God to preach repentance to the people of Nineveh (Jonah 1:2). Instead of obeying God's command, he ran from God's will (Jonah 1:3–16) and the result was his being swallowed by the great fish or whale (Jonah 1:17).

In the end, he overlooks the city in anger asking God to kill him (Jonah 4:2, 3). He is angry that God would show mercy to these people who might have devastated his own family earlier (2 Kings 14:25). Whatever the case was, Jonah was someone who was bothered that God would bless the Ninevites.

Have you ever been bothered because God blessed someone else? This may be an all-too-common occurrence. One young adult may see other young adults finding their life partner, but not them. A preacher may find God blessing another preacher's ministry more than his own. One family may see God blessing another family financially when they have to struggle to get by. The testimony of an answered prayer comes to one believer, but not to you.

How do we react when God blesses someone else? Maybe you think God could not possibly bless that person. Your secret attitude is that God is blessing the wrong person. Why is that pastor's church growing and not mine? Why did that person find a nice job when all I get are nice rejection letters?

Jonah is not the only Bible character who struggled with this. After Jesus told Peter that he would die of crucifixion some day (John 21:18), Peter wanted to know if John would also face the same fate. Jesus' response to Peter is significant to anyone who is bothered by the blessing of God upon another "If I will that he tarry till I come, what is that to thee? follow thou me" (John 21:22). Our task is simply to follow the Lord the best we know how and leave the blessing to Him.

MEMORIZE: Psalm 86:17.

—James Stallard

AUGUST 3
THE DAY THE SON OF GOD CRIED

Scripture Reading—John 11:35
"Jesus wept."

The pain they felt must have been deep. Mary and Martha lost their brother in death. They no doubt had seen other friends and family members die before. But that did not ease the terrible ache they felt.

To make matters worse, they had sent for Jesus to come so that Lazarus might be saved from the sudden sickness that had overcome him. But Jesus had not come, at least not in time. So there they stood, next to the Son of God, before the tomb of their dead brother.

Then, the Bible records a remarkable thing. The Word of God simply says, "Jesus wept" (John 11:35). This shortest of verses in our English Bible contains a powerful message. Jesus certainly cared for Mary and Martha and what they were facing. He also was concerned for those around them, who were lost in sin and needed desperately to believe in Him.

These tears of Jesus were not momentary emotions caused by the moment. They ran deep into His spirit—"For we have not an high priest which cannot be touched with the feeling of our infirmities" (Heb. 4:15). He identifies with us in all of our trials and heartaches.

When Jesus raised Lazarus from the dead, Mary and Martha were certainly glad to have their brother back. It was good for them to have Jesus there with them at the tomb. The believer should remember that He stands by our side in the heartache we experience. He not only feels our hurts, but He also took them upon Himself when He went to The Cross to die for our sins so that we might have life. "Surely he hath borne our griefs, and carried our sorrows" (Isa. 53:4).

Try this. Write down a list of deep hurts you have experienced, making sure to keep them private. Then try to remember how the Lord helped you face them. If you think long enough, you will find that He remembers every hurt and understands what we have gone through. "Thou tellest my wanderings: put thou my tears into thy bottle: are they not in thy book?" (Ps. 56:8).

SONG: Sing "Turn Your Eyes Upon Jesus."

—*James Stallard*

AUGUST 4
MEANING WHAT YOU SAY AND SAYING WHAT YOU MEAN

Scripture Reading—Acts 5:3
"Why hath Satan filled thine heart to lie to the Holy Ghost."

The church was in the midst of great revival, and church members were selling what they owned and were giving the money they made to the church to take care of the needy (Acts 4:32–37).

Into the midst of this revival walked a man named Ananias. He and his wife, Sapphira, sold a possession as did other church members. But they claimed they were giving all of it, but they had kept back part of the sale for themselves. In the emotion of the revival, they wanted to look good in the eyes of the Apostles, so they lied.

The consequence of this sin was staggering—"And Ananias hearing these words [of Peter] fell down, and gave up the ghost: and great fear came on all them that heard these things" (Acts 5:5). Three hours later Sapphira, conspirator with her husband, walked right up to her own death sentence (Acts 5:7–10). The lie and the consequences were complete. They committed what the Bible calls the "sin unto death" (1 John 5:16). God took their lives because of their sinful lying.

Before we look upon Ananias and Sapphira too harshly, we might ask ourselves some honest questions. Have we ever lied? Have we ever pretended to be, do, or give something when that was not true? In light of what happened to this Christian couple in Acts 5, how carefully should we be in telling the truth?

The Lord Jesus Christ taught in the Sermon on the Mount, "But let your communication be, Yea, yea; Nay, nay: for whatsoever is more than these cometh of evil" (Matt. 5:37). In other words, say what you mean and mean what you say!

Without a decision to be a truth-teller our lives and our families will be filled with confusion. Parents, do your children know you will speak the truth at all times? Children and teenagers, do your parents know that you will speak the truth at all times? In other words, can you be trusted?

ACTION POINT: Claim Psalm 19:14 as a family in prayer before the Lord.

—James Stallard

Let the words of my mouth and the meditation of my heart be acceptable in Your sight, Oh Lord, my strength & my Redeemer.

217

AUGUST 5
SURVIVING SATAN'S SIFTER

Scripture Reading—Luke 22:31
"Satan hath desired to have you, that he may sift you as wheat."

Many soldiers have been caught by surprise in the midst of a battle. The danger was always there, but they did not see it coming. As He approached The Cross, Jesus wanted to teach Peter and the other disciples that they were in a battle with the enemy, and He did not want them to be caught by surprise. He warned Peter that Satan wanted to "sift" him.

This enemy was real. Satan is not some impersonal force or symbol of evil in the world—he is a spirit-being who opposes God and God's people (2 Thess. 2:8, 9). He tempted Jesus in the wilderness (Matt. 4:1–11). Jesus believed the Devil was real. He considered Him dangerous. So should we.

Notice that Jesus says Peter's name twice, "Simon, Simon." If Jesus says our name once, it should be enough to get our attention. If He says it twice, we ought to consider the matter to be urgent. The Lord wants us to know that we are dealing with a dangerous and deadly enemy who wants to destroy us (1 Pet. 5:8, 9).

When the "sifting" time comes, pressure increases on each of us to deny the Lord Jesus. Our life is shaken up and disturbed by what happens. Friends try to get us to go along with what is wrong. Circumstances become overwhelming at work, stirring up anger. Troubles also seem to come in bunches, pressuring us to say, "No!" to God and His way.

It is always encouraging to know that others are praying for us when this happens. But there is something better than that. Jesus promised to pray for Peter, "But I have prayed for thee, that thy faith fail not" (Luke 22:32). When I focus on the truth that Jesus Himself is praying for me, my faith can soar in the midst of any sifting. He is a High Priest who understands what I am going through (Heb. 4:16; 7:25). He defeated the enemy at The Cross, and I can rejoice in His victory for me.

QUOTE: "Satan is a decided fact, a destructive force, and a defeated foe."
—Adrian Rogers

—James Stallard

AUGUST 6
THE MOST IMPORTANT ATTITUDE IN YOUR HOME

Scripture Reading—1 Thess. 5:18
"In every thing give thanks: for this is the will of God in Christ Jesus concerning you."

There is no doubt about the fact that attitude really is everything. Attitudes are everything because the attitudes that are displayed will determine the atmosphere of your home. When family members portray a good attitude, it will automatically make the home a pleasant place to be. When family members display a bad attitude, it will automatically make the home a miserable place to be. So what is the greatest attitude that can be displayed in your home? I would like to suggest that it is thanksgiving.

Unfortunately, there are many who assume that Thanksgiving Day is just a holiday in November. In reality every day ought to be a day of thanksgiving. Thankful people constantly display an attitude of gratitude, regardless of what should be, or would be, or could be if they had it all their own way. Thankful people have learned to count their blessings, realizing that God has been so good to them in giving them so many good things. Thankful people communicate appreciation to others who have been good to them. Thankful people are quick to give a testimony of praise to God in front of others.

Think about this. Would you prefer to be around someone who is thankful or someone who is a complainer? Do you enjoy being around people who are grateful, or do you enjoy whiners more? Which do you like better—appreciation or murmuring? I think the point is clear. You know what you would choose, and really it is exactly what most other people would choose. So, why not be the kind of person you would want others to be when they are around you—just be thankful.

Maybe it is time for some attitude adjustment. Write a thank you note, make a list of things you are thankful for, or simply offer praise to God. In so doing your attitude will get adjusted very quickly.

ACTION POINT: Go around and allow each family member to tell something that he or she is thankful for about another member of the family.

—Tom Palmer

AUGUST 7
PRACTICING THE PRESENCE OF GOD

Scripture Reading—Pro. 16:6
"And by the fear of the LORD men depart from evil."

There are two specific ways that the presence of God should affect a child of God. First of all the presence of God should bring comfort. When you are going through a difficult time, you can remember that God is "a very present help in trouble" (Ps. 46:1). Secondly the presence of God should bring conviction. That is the truth of our verse for today. When we speak of "the fear of God," we are talking about a sense of God-consciousness or an awareness of God. Many Christians become unconscious of God—their lives are little impacted by the truth that God is everywhere and knows everything.

When I have preached on this subject, I like to ask my audience, "Do you believe God is everywhere and knows everything?" Of course most people will lift their hand to indicate their agreement. At that point I quickly say, "I don't think you do believe it because if what you believe does not change your life, you don't really believe it."

Why do people automatically slow down when they see a police officer? Why do children stop misbehaving when their parents enter the room? Why do students stop talking and sit up straight when the teacher approaches them? It is because each one is aware of the presence of someone to whom they are responsible, and that awareness changes how they live. In other words **what we believe should change the way we behave!**

In Romans 3, we are given a horrendous look at the sinfulness of mankind (v. 10–19). In verse 18 we read, "There is no fear of God before their eyes." When men lose their awareness of God, there is no telling the depths to which they will go in their sin. One of the best ways to gain victory over sin is to always remember that God "presently" (right now) is "present" (right here).

ACTION POINT: Have each family member thank God for His presence. Then pray that each one will become more aware of His presence in everyday life.

—Tom Palmer

AUGUST 8
CHILDREN SAY THE
STRANGEST THINGS

Scripture Reading—Ps. 8:2
"Out of the mouth of babes and sucklings hast thou ordained strength."

Listening to children can be very entertaining because they say some of the strangest things. One little girl, just a few years old, grabbed her father around the knees, looked up, and declared, "When I grow up and get as tall as you, I will fall down from there." Another little boy ran down the hallway of his church and grabbed the pastor by the leg and would not let go. Finally, he looked up at his preacher and said, "I'm glue." Children's imaginations can run wild.

Another little girl quoted John 3:16 this way, "For God so loved the world that he gave his only begotten Son, that whosoever believeth in him should not parachute but have everlasting life." Yes, it would be great if we could have a tape recorder with us at all times to capture these cherished moments of the strange sayings of children!

While they might say some crazy things from time to time, they also can speak some golden truths—like asking from the back seat of the car while going home from church, "What speed are you driving, Daddy? Mommy, why did you tell the pastor that? Aren't we supposed to tell the truth all the time?"

The Word of God tells us that these children of ours are "an heritage of the LORD; and the fruit of the womb is his reward . . . Happy is the man who hath his quiver full of them" (Ps. 127:3, 5). Maybe we should listen more to what they are saying.

The Bible uses the picture of children to explain God's speaking to the world. "Out of the mouth of babes and sucklings hast thou ordained strength because of thine enemies, that thou mightest still the enemy and the avenger" (Ps. 8:2). Jesus quoted this verse when the chief priest and scribes heard the children crying "Hosanna to the Son of David" to Jesus in the Temple.

We need to realize that, while children are not innocent (Rom. 3:23), they are trusting. We all must come to God like a child, or not come at all (Matt. 18:3).

SONG: Sing the chorus "Jesus Loves the Little Children."

—*James Stallard*

GOD WILL PROVIDE FOR YOUR NEEDS

Scripture Reading—Exod. 16:15
"It is manna: for they wist not [did not know] what it was."

They had never seen anything like it before. They had been murmuring and complaining against Moses and Aaron in the wilderness (Exod. 16:2). They thought they had it good down in Egypt with plenty to eat, but now Moses is leading them to die (Exod. 16:3).

In response to their complaining, God sent some quail for them to eat in the evening (Exod. 16:12, 13), and the next morning there it was! God had sent something else to satisfy their hunger and to give them what they needed in the wilderness. They were puzzled at it and wondered, "It is manna" (Exod. 16:15).

The word "manna" was not a name or a title or even a description. It actually is the translation of a question, "What is this?" In modern English we might say something like, "What is this stuff?" Whatever it was, it was food for the Israelites, and Jesus uses this account to teach that He is the true manna or bread sent from Heaven (John 6:32, 33).

God's picture is clear. He will provide for us not only physically, but also spiritually. He did not just come to feed bellies—He came to feed souls. While the first is helpful, the second is absolutely necessary. The Lord Jesus Himself is the One to satisfy the hunger within our hearts. As we trust Him for salvation, we are satisfied with eternal life (John 3:16). As we walk by faith, we enjoy the abundant life He provides, "I am come that they might have life, and that they might have it more abundantly" (John 10:10).

It is encouraging to know that God still provided for the Israelites while they murmured and complained. So too it is with each of us. We often complain and gripe about situations we face, but God still is faithful and feeds us—"He knoweth our frame; he remembereth that we are dust" (Ps. 103:14).

PRAYER: Lord, thank you for caring so much for us that you provide for us in every way. To You be all the glory!

—James Stallard

AUGUST 10
THE DANGER OF CASUAL PRAYING

Scripture Reading—Dan. 6:10
"He kneeled upon his knees three times a day, and prayed,
and gave thanks before his God, as he did aforetime."

Daniel was in a predicament. His enemies were trying to get him in trouble with the king by getting a law passed that made it illegal for him to pray to his God. The king had signed the decree, and those who disobeyed it were to be cast into the lion's den. Daniel knew that if he obeyed the king, he would displease his God. He also knew that if he obeyed his God, he would displease the king. Oh yes—he would end up in the lion's den also!

Our verse tells us exactly what Daniel decided to do. He went to his house, opened the windows, got on his knees and started praying. Simply put, nothing changed! Daniel did what he had always done, just as he had always done it. Yes, it might have been easier to keep the windows shut, or to refrain from kneeling, so as to be less conspicuous. However, Daniel 6:4 says that Daniel was a faithful man, and he was not about to fail his God by compromising his faithfulness.

When it comes to prayer, there is no place for a careless attitude or a casual approach. Genuine praying requires sincerity even to the point of sacrifice. It is not enough to just pray when it is easy. Sometimes we must be faithful in prayer when it is difficult.

Daniel did spend the night in the lion's den, but when it was all said and done, something incredible happened. The king who had signed the decree also made another royal decree. He said, "I make a decree, That in every dominion of my kingdom men tremble and fear before the God of Daniel: for he is the living God" (Dan. 6:26). Daniel's faithful praying certainly did please God, but it also impacted the king, giving testimony to the fact that God was alive.

ACTION POINT: Spend time in prayer, asking God to make each member of your family faithful in prayer.

—Tom Palmer

AUGUST 11
THE PRIVILEGE OF PRAYER

Scripture Reading—John 14:14
"If ye shall ask anything in my name, I will do it."

With trouble surrounding the disciples, Jesus invites them—and you and me—to pray "in his name" (John 14:13) with the promise that "I will do it." Have you ever received an answer to prayer and known beyond a shadow of a doubt that God did it? Clear answers to prayer that offer no explanation except that God did it are a powerful witness to the world of the reality of God. It is also a powerful witness to the troubled heart of any believer facing trials, tribulations, distresses, and adversities.

If you do not get your prayers answered, it is always good to ask "why"? In order to get our prayers answered, we must ask in the "name of the Lord," which implies that Jesus approves of our prayer. God delights to answer the prayers of His children. But He is not a Santa Claus sitting on a cloud in the sky and dishing out goodies for rebellious children.

Prayer is not twisting His arm to do what we want, but our getting in line with what He wants. As we faithfully read His Word and follow His ways, we can have a greater power to see our prayers answered (John 15:7). God wants to answer our prayers "that your joy may be full" (John 16:24).

While every Christian parent wants to see his or her child follow the Lord, they also desire for their child to be happy and full of joy. God has a lot invested in His children through the gifts of His Son, His Spirit, and His Word. Part of the privilege of prayer is the joy that comes when God answers.

Knowing that God is looking in on our lives brings joy to the heart of the child of God. When fear increases, so should prayer. As answers come, so will great joy. And when darkness surrenders to the light, our fear will diminish in the presence of joyful praise.

ACTION POINT: Pray that God will answer a family prayer so that you will know that God did it.

—*James Stallard*

AUGUST 12
THE EASE OF HAVING A CRITICAL SPIRIT

Scripture Reading—Heb. 3:13
"Exhort one another daily."

It is easy to criticize. It takes little intelligence to identify and point out a problem. It takes creativity and initiative to solve a problem. Someone said, "Nothing is easier than faultfinding; no talent, no self-denial, no brains, no character are required to set up in the grumbling business."

Encouragement is just as easy as criticism. The difference is that you are looking for something to praise rather than something to condemn and criticize. Kenneth Blanchard, in his classic book *The One Minute Manager*, gives three principles of managing people, and one of them is to be on the lookout for things to praise in their work. This would be a great plan for parents with their children.

Our best cheerleaders ought to be those in our family. One person wrote, "Any old donkey can kick a barn door down, but it takes a good carpenter to build one." Learn to pay attention to your words. Are you one that tears down or builds up?

Most of the time criticism is given with incomplete information. It is especially easy to hammer leaders over decisions, but if you had the same information they did on which the decision was based, you may have come to the same conclusion.

One of my favorite proverbs is that "idealism increases in direct proportion to your distance from the problem." Perhaps a corollary might be: "Criticism decreases in direct proportion to your closeness to the problem."

Getting correct information and, even better, going through the same experience as another person will greatly temper your quickness to criticize. "It is better to be quiet until one understands," wrote Laura Adams Armer.

It is so easy to forget what it was like to be a child or a teenager when we are years away from that era of our lives. Better that we pause and remember our own struggles and tendencies at that age so that we might have wisdom and compassion when we want to criticize.

ACTION POINT: Focus on looking for the good to praise in others today.

—Rick Johnson

AUGUST 13
BIBLE READING

Scripture Reading—Matt. 4:4
"Every word that proceedeth out of the mouth of God."

"The Bible is, to many people, God's unopened letter," wrote Charles Spurgeon. You will never know the mind of God until you know the words of God found in the Bible.

One metaphor of the Bible is food that nourishes the soul. It imparts strength and builds spiritual muscle. It is like water (Eph. 5:25–27), milk (1 Pet. 2:2), meat (Heb. 5:12–14), bread (Matt. 4:4), and honey (Ps. 19:10).

Reading the Word of God is partaking of spiritual food, which will produce a healthy, strong, and vibrant soul. We ought to read every word of it (Matt. 4:4), which requires a disciplined and systematic approach.

When I was a teenager, I attended a major conference of preachers and dedicated church leaders. One of the speakers asked the audience how many had read every word in the Bible, and he qualified it by saying, "I mean all of the genealogies, every word." I was stunned at the small percentage of hands raised. I couldn't raise my hand. Since then, I have made it a habit to read the Bible through on a regular basis.

Years ago I read that 75 percent of seminarians had never read the entire Bible. A majority of those who have been called to teach the Word of God have not even read all of its contents. Friend, Satan's primary goal is to keep you away from God's Word.

Watchman Nee had a motto that he lived by: "No Bible, no breakfast." He based this on Job 23:12, which values the spiritual over the physical. Daily Bible reading will keep you spiritually clean (John 15:3) and help you gain assurance of salvation (1 John 5:13).

One of the highest compliments you can give an author is to say, "I read your book." One day when you stand before the Lord Jesus, will you be able to say, "I read Your book." I hope that you will be able to tell Christ one day, "Lord, I read Your book—all of it."

ACTION POINT: Get a plan to help you read through every word in the Bible.

—*Rick Johnson*

AUGUST 14
MEASURING TRUE SUCCESS

Scripture Reading—Acts 9:6
"Lord, what wilt thou have me to do?"

Past failure marks us at a deeper level than success. If not dealt with properly, failure can come to define you and limit your future. It is like an anchor that weighs you down. Satan uses our failures to keep us from God's best.

From the Garden of Eden, the human race has known failure. God designed it that when a person breaks His law that there is guilt in his spirit. Only the new birth brings forgiveness and gives us a fresh start. The grace of God goes deeper than any sin or failure we have ever known (Rom. 5:20).

However, sometimes people think they have failed when they haven't. Their problem is that their definition of success is wrong. Failure assumes coming short of a standard. If the standard is wrong, then your perception of failure will be wrong too.

The dictionary defines success as the attainment of a predetermined goal. That is an inadequate definition for a believer. All goals are not worthy of a Christian.

George W. Truett gave my favorite definition of success: "Success is finding the will of God as early in life as possible and doing it." This means that success is inextricably related to obedience to God.

The word "success" is only used one time in the Bible (Josh. 1:8) and that in association with obeying the Word of God. Someone said, "Inside the will of God there is no failure, and outside the will of God there is no success."

This doesn't mean that an obedient Christian never has difficult times, nor does it mean that a person that is lost cannot enjoy earthly blessings. It does mean that those walking in obedience cannot miss God's full blessing, nor can a person in disobedience ever know God's best for his life.

The will of God is unique for every person; so don't measure how you are doing by comparing yourself with others. Focus on your own race; it is unique to you (Heb. 12:2; 2 Tim. 4:7).

ACTION POINT: Write Truett's definition for success on a card and memorize it.

—Rick Johnson

AUGUST 15
GOD CARES WHEN YOU HURT

Scripture Reading—Ps. 34:18
"The LORD is nigh unto them that are of a broken heart."

A Christian is not immune to sorrow and adversity. It is possible to be right with God and have a broken heart. Sadness is a common denominator of being human.

The pain of sorrow can break our hearts when we travel by a place where we have experienced deep sorrow. Jacob's wife, Rebekah, had a nurse named Deborah that died and was buried under an oak tree. They named the tree "Allonbachuth" (Gen. 35:8), which means "oak of weeping." It was a place where tears were poured out for someone that was well loved.

God told Israel that they would have continual problems with their neighbors because of their disobedience. They wept over this (Judg. 2:3–5). They called the place where this happened "Bochim," which means "weepers." Physical landmarks trigger both pleasant and difficult memories.

I have places like that in my life—hospital emergency rooms where I have sat with family members and friends to hear a doctor say, "I'm sorry, we did all that we could." There is an intersection I drive by almost every day where my best friend was killed in a car accident. I remember him and feel a sense of loss every time I travel there. I frequently drive by the place where my father passed away and went to be with the Lord. Though I know He is enjoying the bliss of Heaven, I miss him. These are all places where I have wept, and seeing them reminds me of those whom I have loved deeply. It brings to my mind a sense of loss.

Oh, but there is good news! God responds to our tears of sorrow. We need not grieve alone. Our Heavenly Father wants to bring us comfort through His presence. His promise is true: "He healeth the broken in heart" (Ps. 147:3).

ACTION POINT: Recount a place and time where your heart was broken, and share how the grace of God has brought comfort to you.

—*Rick Johnson*

AUGUST 16
ONLY ONE LIFE TO OFFER

Scripture Reading—2 Cor. 5:15
"And that he died for all, that they which live should not henceforth live unto themselves, but unto him which died for them, and rose again."

Bill Borden used to ask, "Are you steering or drifting?" He then would ask, "Where are you going and who's on board?" He believed that indecision led to shipwreck in a life.

Bill took his first missionary trip at age seventeen with all expenses paid by his millionaire parents. He attended Yale University and Princeton Seminary and inherited the estate of his father, who died while Bill was a freshman in college. Upon graduation he gave up the entire inheritance to Christian work and began to prepare for missions, depending only upon God.

Bill sailed first to Egypt to learn the language and religion of the Muslims, who he hoped to later work with in China. Immediately he organized a missionary effort in Cairo to evangelize the city. However, on March 21, 1913, he developed a severe headache. He was diagnosed with cerebral meningitis and died within two weeks.

After his death, a friend wrote, "This single-mindedness of his spiritual life was the secret of that fixity of purpose which took him straight along wherever he set out. What Bill started, he would finish."

Though Bill did not have a great number of years in his life, he did make much of the life he had in his years. Those who make a difference for God don't postpone or delay their response. Recognizing that Jesus gave all for them, they are willing to give all for Him. How foolish it is to be unwilling to live for the One who was willing to die for you. A life lived for God is always on purpose, never by coincidence. Bill's purpose of life allowed him to make the most of his very short life. Determine right now that whatever years you have left in this life will be lived to the fullest for God.

ACTION POINT: On a 3x5 card, write out Bill's famous quote and keep it before you for the next week as a good reminder: "No Reserve, No Retreat, No Regret."

—*Tom Palmer*

AUGUST 17
"GET OUT OF THE WOULDS"

Scripture Reading—1 Sam. 17:32
"And David said to Saul, Let no man's heart fail because of him;
thy servant will go and fight with this Philistine."

Have you ever heard someone say, "I would if I had more time"? Or "I would if I just had more money"? Or "I would if I was just more talented"? It seems to me that much more could be done for God if folks were not lost in the "woulds." Nothing will ever get done for God until you are willing to say, "I will." It's called dedication, and that is what we see David doing.

Dedication can be defined as a willingness to do whatever is necessary to get the job done for God. Somebody needed to deal with Goliath, but nobody would. Saul was not willing, and the men of Israel were not willing, so David said, "I will."

Here is a great statement for each person to consider:
I am one, and only one,
I cannot do everything, but I can do something,
What I can do, I ought to do,
And what I ought to do, by the grace of God,
I will do.

Imagine what it would be like if every Christian young person and adult took this statement as the mission statement in life. Not "I would and I could and I should," but, "I will." The work that needs to get done for God would get done. We would not need to beg and bribe to get workers to work and helpers to help. Instead there would always be enough people to do the jobs that need doing for God.

For me, the point of dedication came as a twelve-year-old boy at a Christian camp. Sitting under a tree with my counselor, I prayed a simple prayer and told God that I was willing to be what He wanted me to be. I have never regretted that decision. Serving God is the greatest privilege on the earth.

ACTION POINT: Pray this prayer of dedication for yourself: "Dear God, all that I am, and all that I have, it is Yours."

—*Tom Palmer*

AUGUST 18
ARE YOU A DOUBLE-MINDED PERSON?

Scripture Reading—James 1:8
"A double minded man is unstable in all his ways."

Every believer needs to hear the "voice of God." By this, we do not mean that you will actually hear a physical voice, but that you can and should hear God speaking to you through His Spirit and His Word, the Bible. We need God's guidance for our lives.

But, often we do not find that guidance because of what the Epistle of James describes as being "double minded." The first chapter talks about a man who lacks faith and wavers (James 1:6). The warning to him from God is, "For let not that man think that he shall receive any thing from the Lord" (James 1:7).

Then, the declaration comes, "A double-minded man is unstable in all his ways" (James 1:8). To be "unstable" is to refuse to be "at rest." A double-minded person is someone who cannot be happy or content with what they have or who they are.

How many church young people do you know who seem not to understand what they want in life? They seem to desire the friends and fun of this world along with the holiness of God at the same time (2 Kings 17:33; Hosea 10:2).

The double-minded person spiritually tries to be two people in two worlds. He or she is one thing at church, another at work or home. The double-minded person is one thing when talking, another when walking. Jesus warned, "No man can serve two masters: for either he will hate the one, and love the other; or else he will hold to the one, and despise the other. Ye cannot serve God and mammon" (Matt. 6:24).

A double-minded person, whether young or old, is a spiritual yo-yo. They are up one day, down the next. A double-minded person becomes an easy target for Satan to deceive (2 Pet. 2:14). It is best to surrender to God and His wisdom so you can be at rest and walk in peace.

PRAYER: Lord, I turn from being double-minded and trust your wisdom completely.

—*James Stallard*

AUGUST 19
NEVER FORGET THE BLESSINGS OF THE PAST

Scripture Reading—Num. 14:4
"Let us make a captain, and let us return into Egypt."

God had brought them so far and done so much for them. Yet, they did not want to go into the Promised Land because of the obstacles. They murmured and complained against Moses and Aaron (Num. 14:2). Standing on the threshold of victory, they headed toward defeat, desiring to go back to Egypt.

They had already forgotten what God had done for them. They had experienced the great deliverance out of Egypt. They had seen the people cross the Red Sea on dry ground and Pharaoh's army drowned there. They had seen with their own eyes the Cloud by day and Pillar of Fire by night that guided them through the wilderness, signifying the presence of God. They had already received the Law from God's hand at Mt. Sinai.

Yet, they forgot the blessings of the past. God does not forget, but we easily forget (Heb. 6:10). It would be a good exercise for each of us to make a list of how God has blessed us in the past. How were we saved? Who helped us to come to salvation? How have we been helped in ministry through the years? How has God answered our prayers?

Mickey Mantle, the great hall of fame baseball slugger for the New York Yankees, was asked what he enjoyed the most about playing baseball. He said he enjoyed hearing the crowd roar when he hit a homerun. But, he also added how quickly fans can turn on you. If he hit a homerun in his first at bat and then struck out three times, they always forgot the homerun. Yes, fans can be fickle. But, God's people can be also.

How strange it must be to God's ears to hear our complaining and murmuring when He has poured out blessing upon blessing upon us. We each deserve judgment, but Christ has paid our sin debt. What glory we share with Him (Rom 8:17, 18)! The promise of the future is even better! How grateful we should be for all of His past blessings.

QUOTE: "There will always be a better day ahead for the child of God."
—Source Unknown.

—James Stallard

AUGUST 20
THE CURSE OF EVIL SPEAKING

Scripture Reading—2 Sam. 15:6
"So Absalom stole the hearts of the men of Israel."

The men who came to see the king were not expecting what they saw. Outside the king's palace was one of the king's sons. The Bible says that Absalom, David's son, would stand and call out to anyone who came to the king for judgment. Here is what he did:

- He flattered the men of Israel with kind words (2 Sam. 15:3).
- He claimed to be on their side in any dispute (2 Sam. 15:3, 4).
- He pretended to be loyal to their cause (2 Sam. 15:5, 6).

In the end he stole their hearts with an evil tongue of gossip and slander. It is a sad thing to see a son use his tongue to try to take over his father's position. It is sadder still to see a whole nation hear the evil reports, believe them, and then act upon them.

One of the major dangers facing the home is the harm done by evil speaking. Words do hurt our families and us very deeply. Since "the tongue can no man tame" (James 3:8), God's help is very much needed if we are to have victory over our own speech.

There is no greater myth than that of the little saying, "Sticks and stones may break my bones, but words will never hurt me." Wrong words can destroy precious relationships and friendships. Every Christian should be alert to the damage his own words can cause to the lives of others.

It is tragic when someone in a family or a church gains a reputation of being an evil talker. When others see this and try to stay away from the one doing the evil speaking, the evil talker will often wonder why people want to stay away from him or her. Evil speaking will cause us to lose friends. So, let our words be few. The Bible warns that an evil speaker's "wickedness shall be shewed before the whole congregation" (Pro. 26:26).

ACTION POINT: Plan a time to read and study the Book of James together. Look for the following words or concepts: *busybody, boasting, babbling, beguilement, blaspheming,* and *backbiting.*

—*James Stallard*

AUGUST 21
SOMETHING FISHY ABOUT THIS PRAYER

Scripture Reading—Jonah 2:1
"Then Jonah prayed unto the LORD his God out of the fish's belly."

I love this thought, "When you come to the place where God is all you have, you will find that God is all you need." Have you ever been at a time when you felt that all you had left was God? That was what Jonah must have felt deep in the depths of the sea, trapped in the belly of a great fish. It didn't help that he was also dealing with the guilt of his sinful disobedience to God. Certainly for Jonah this was the "lowest point of his life," and his chances of getting back on top of things didn't look very hopeful.

At this point Jonah started to pray, "I cried by reason of mine affliction unto the LORD . . . out of the belly of hell cried I" (Jonah 2:2). Feeling disconnected and totally out of touch with God, Jonah quickly learned a great lesson about prayer—you cannot get so far from God that He will not hear you. In the same verse, he testified, "He heard me . . . thou heardest my voice." Thankfully God was listening.

Imprisoned by the ribcage of the fish, Jonah was no doubt gagging on seawater and pulling seaweed out of his hair, while his skin burned from the digestive juices in the stomach of the fish. However, his desperate situation caused him to recognize how desperately he needed God. When life is going well, many people take God for granted. Prayer is not a necessity when everything is OK. However, God is able to use experiences of loss, illness, or tragedy to bring people to Himself because they recognize that they really do need God.

As a result of this prayer, Jonah did experience deliverance and help from the Lord. It did not take long until he was on dry land headed to Nineveh to preach. His desperate situation got him "back on course" for God again.

ACTION POINT: Read Jonah 2:3–6, paying close attention to the description of where Jonah was when he prayed.

—Tom Palmer

AUGUST 22
MEMORIZING THE BIBLE

Scripture Reading—Ps. 119:11
"Thy Word have I hid in mine heart."

When I finished school I had no desire to take any more tests or memorize anything. It was hard work to commit facts to memory.

However, memorizing portions of God's Word is not an option for the believer. God requires it of us for our own benefit. Those that fail to do so miss some of God's richest blessings. If we realized the benefits and rewards of Bible memory, we would be diligent about it.

The Psalmist wrote that God's Word was "hid" in his heart (Ps. 119:11). The word "hid" means to cover something to hide it because of its value. The attitude the writer had toward God's Word was that it was a precious treasure. To him it was more than a mechanical duty of committing facts to rote memory. Rather, he did so because he cherished and loved God's Word.

Moses told parents that one of their primary duties was to keep God's Word in their hearts (Deut. 6:6). Of course, this requires memorization. Have you ever heard that memorizing Scripture is a key to being a good parent?

When we memorize God's Word, it gives us stability (Ps. 37:31), keeps us from sin (Ps. 119:11), gives knowledge of God's will (Ps. 40:8), brings joy (Jer. 15:16), and answered prayer (John 15:7). It is to "dwell in you richly" (Col. 3:16), and it gives strength to your inner man (1 John 2:14).

It has been my experience that I have memorized many verses simply by reading the Bible frequently. They find a lodging place in my heart. At other times I have memorized Scripture because of special needs in my life.

Years ago I felt in my heart a distance from the Lord, so I memorized Psalm 51, and it made my heart tender again. When I was going through a lot of stress, I memorized Psalm 37. I hope that you will start today to hide the Bible in your heart.

"This book will keep you from sin, or sin will keep you from this book," said D.L. Moody.

MEMORIZE: Psalm 23 or Psalm 4.

—Rick Johnson

AUGUST 23
The Wisdom of Being Quiet

Scripture Reading—Pro. 17:27
"He that hath knowledge spareth his words."

The Bible associates wisdom with being quiet (Pro. 17:27, 28). The principle in Scripture is that the less you say, the wiser you are. A closed mind and an open mouth are characteristics of a fool. One wag put it this way, "The narrower the mind, the wider the mouth."

The more a fool talks, the more he proves he is a fool. When a wise person talks, it is evident that he has understanding and insight. This is reason enough to be a good listener—to gain wisdom. We never learn anything while we are talking, but we learn plenty when we listen. This is how wise people "lay up knowledge" (Pro. 10:14). Someone wrote, "Folks who know the least often know it the loudest."

Being careful and limiting our words has great application to our family. It is crucial that parents especially be good listeners to their children and that spouses listen to each other. Our temptation is to want to explain ourselves and seek to be understood rather than listening to learn how the other person feels.

The Scripture speaks of "sparing our words," "holding our peace," and "shutting our lips" (Pro. 17:27,28). This is plain talk, but necessary if we are to grow in wisdom. The old adage is true, "Better to keep silent and be thought a fool than to open your mouth and to remove all doubt."

A godly man's words are precious, valuable, and worthwhile. A fool's words are a dime a dozen—cheap, inconsequential, and not worth your time (Pro. 10:20).

Just because a person talks a lot and with great emotion doesn't mean that they have much to contribute. I like the way Curtis Hutson expressed it, "You can't tell by the honk of the horn how much gas is in the tank!"

ACTION POINT: Today focus on how much you talk, and ask the Lord to help you to be a better listener so you might gain wisdom.

—Rick Johnson

AUGUST 24
THE OPPORTUNITY OF OBEDIENCE

Scripture Reading—John 14:21
"And I will love him, and will manifest myself to him."

In John 14:21 Jesus says, "He that hath my commandments, and keepeth them, he it is that loveth me: and he that loveth me shall be loved of my Father, and I will love him, and will manifest myself to him." Note that God "manifests" or "reveals" Himself to the child of God who has and keeps His commandments.

Many people, however, have the wrong notion that love is a warm, fuzzy feeling. That is not love. It is right for us to have a sense of devotional attachment to Jesus and to have our emotions focused on Him. We should *feel* our Christian faith. Who would want just a cold, academic faith? However, Jesus leaves us no option here because love involves more than feeling. It involves a choice—obedience and love must come together.

He is speaking of something beyond salvation. A child of God can draw near to God in such a way that God draws near to him (James 4:8). It is moments like these where fears dissolve and faith rises. To know that you are loved to the point that God is revealing Himself to you brings great security.

When I have visited the hospital rooms of hurting believers and have found them reading their Bibles seeking God, I have also discovered that the Lord has spoken to them and brought them great peace. Through God "manifesting Himself" to them, they have received comfort and encouragement in the most difficult circumstances.

Jesus promises with certainty that as we obey the Lord we will sense His love toward us. He will "manifest" Himself to the obedient child, and it is that manifestation of His presence that will help us not to be afraid in the midst of troubles. In such a case, His presence in our lives will cause us to be able to face any fear that the Devil can hurl at us.

Are you fretting today? Obey the Lord and look for Him to speak.

PRAYER: Lord, I surrender now to obey your Word and desire you to manifest your presence in my life as I am obedient to your commands.

—*James Stallard*

GOD SEES YOUR TEARS

Scripture Reading—2 Kings 20:5
"I have seen thy tears."

Sometimes we feel like God is far removed from us when we are hurting. Even a casual reading of the Psalms reveals this feeling (Ps. 42:2–4).

We must remember during these times that God is intimately acquainted with our burdens. The Lord Jesus was called "a man of sorrows." He was "acquainted with grief" and on The Cross has "borne our griefs, and carried our sorrows" (Isa. 53:3, 4).

Many things cause us to weep. There are tears of despair (Gen. 21:14-17); tears of sorrow (Gen. 23:2; John 11:31); tears of regret (Gen. 33:4; Matt. 26:75); tears of defeat (Deut. 1:44, 45); tears of discouragement (1 Sam. 1:10); tears of defeat (1 Sam. 30:4); tears of compassion (Jer. 9:1). Our Lord was often moved to tears from His heart of compassion (Luke 19:41; John 11:35).

There are tears of brokenness (Neh. 1:4); tears of pain (Job 16:20); tears of desperation (Mark 9:24); tears of ministry (Acts 20:19, 31); tears of separation (Acts 20:37); tears of prayer (Heb. 5:7); and tears of love (1 Sam. 15:35).

Yes, there are tears, but we have comfort in knowing that God knows about our tears and sees them. Everywhere we look people are hurting and weeping. The reason for all of this is sin, and we have a compassionate God who cares when we are hurting.

Two weeks before Christmas 2003, I stood by my brother at a bed in a small hospital room. His wife lay there having died unexpectedly from a heart attack at the age of 39. Their children were in school and didn't know what had happened. As we drove to get them, my brother said, "Rick, what do I tell them?"

There were lots of tears all day long and for a long time after that, but our great God was watching and caring for my brother. My friend, He sees your tears too, and He cares for you.

ACTION POINT: Look at the causes of tears listed above, and think of someone that is hurting from one of those categories. Pray for them, and let them know you are praying.

—*Rick Johnson*

AUGUST 26
GRATITUDE

Scripture Reading—Col. 3:15
"Be ye thankful."

I love being around people who have a positive attitude. There is one quality that every positive person has—a grateful spirit. We never say of a complaining, ungrateful person, "They have the best attitude." A grateful spirit and a positive attitude go hand in hand.

Being grateful to God and for His blessings is one of the key components in our walk with the Lord. Expressing thanks is to be part of our prayer life (Ps. 100:4; Dan. 6:10; Phil. 4:6). Gratitude is part of God's will for us (1 Thess. 5:18). It pleases the Lord when we are thankful every day for everything (Eph. 5:20).

D.L. Moody said, "God cannot use a discouraged Christian." I think it is also true that God cannot use a complaining, negative Christian.

I was riding with Clebe McClary, a war hero from Vietnam, years ago and quickly noted how grateful he was. He would notice a beautiful tree, a cloud in the sky, something that was common, and he would comment about it. I hadn't noticed them at all. When Clebe came home from the war, his left arm and left eye were missing after an explosion in a foxhole. He had dozens of surgeries for years afterward.

We stopped for coffee, and he used his mouth to take off the lid to put the creamer in the cup. He buttons his shirt with one hand, wears shoes with Velcro so he won't have to tie them, and he has other challenges that his handicap has given him. Yet, he is so positive and grateful. His consistent spirit of thankfulness convicted me.

I asked him, "Clebe, you are so grateful and notice small things most people take for granted. How do you cultivate that spirit?" He replied, "Rick, I only have one good eye, and there are microscopic pieces of shrapnel in it that if they move at all I will go blind in that eye, too. So, I don't take my vision for granted."

May we not take God's blessings for granted today.

ACTION POINT: Make a "Thank You" list of God's blessings.

—Rick Johnson

AUGUST 27
LISTENING INTENTLY

Scripture Reading—Pro. 5:1
"My son, attend unto my wisdom,
and bow thine ear to my understanding."

It is said that we think about four times faster than someone talks. This means we must be careful to focus and not allow our minds to wander when someone is speaking to us. It takes a lot of work to listen intently! It's important that we learn to catch those wandering thoughts and not drift off into daydreaming when we should be listening.

In this Proverb, Solomon is addressing his son and all young men regarding their need to be diligent in being given to truth and appreciative of those lessons taught by the experiences of others. In this particular passage, Solomon's appeal to listen intently involves the serious dangers of the wicked woman and the destruction that involvement with her brings.

While it is always important to listen to another person when he or she is speaking, it is more important that we learn to listen to the Lord as He speaks to us. Can you remember what your devotion was about yesterday? Do you recall what the preacher preached in the previous service? Do you remember the passage he used? It may seem harmless to allow our minds to wander or even nod off when reading the Bible or while the preacher is preaching, but it is actually a serious issue. Did you know that you will give an account to God of how you listen?

Once we understand that it is OUR responsibility to listen and apply what is being said, perhaps our thought process will change regarding the man of God and the Word of God. In Bible days, it wasn't uncommon for people to stand for hours while the Scriptures were simply read. Their willingness to listen reveals their attitude of reverence toward God's Word. We ought to teach our children early that when the man of God and the Word of God come together it IS a big deal.

ACTION POINT: Practice being a better listener. In fact, these Family Times with God are a great opportunity to practice sitting and listening intently to each other and God. Tomorrow, test your listening and see if you can recall what was discussed in this Family Time with God.

—Christy Ingram

AUGUST 28
ACCESSING GRACE

Scripture Reading—Rom. 5:2
"By whom also we have access by faith into this grace."

Grace is an often-used word, but not always an understood concept. So what is grace? The essence of grace is that it is a gift. You cannot buy grace. You cannot earn grace. You can only receive it. Now, of course, God is the Giver, and grace in the Bible is largely spiritual, not physical. Have you ever had "joy unspeakable"? How about "peace that passes understanding"? Have you ever experienced Christ's strength? All of these things are God's grace.

Years ago, a young man stood to his feet at a testimony service I was conducting and said, "Two days ago, I got saved. And if you're not saved, you need to get saved because getting saved is like having Christmas every day!" I think he understood the Christian life better than most Christians I know. You might be thinking, "My Christian life is not like Christmas every day." Well, that is not God's fault because every day He is giving you gifts (grace). Imagine if I came over to your house in July. I come into your house at your invitation and notice a stack of Christmas presents. I can tell they are Christmas presents because of the wrapping paper. With a little bit of consternation, I look at you and say, "What are those?"

"O, those are Christmas presents from last year, you say. "We'll get around to opening them sooner or later."

Would you find that to be strange? Unopened, those presents would be doing you no good. You could have a brand new computer in one of those wrapped boxes, but it is doing you no good there. In fact, it is probably now outdated!

I know the question you are asking: "How do we open grace?" Well, how did you open the first gift God gave you? "For by grace are ye saved through faith." You unwrap grace every time you believe God!

ACTION POINT: Ask your family members to describe times they have experienced God's grace!

—*Jim Van Geldren*

DO MIRRORS EVER LIE?
Scripture Reading—2 Cor. 10:18
"For not he that commendeth himself is approved,
but whom the Lord commendeth."

Have you ever looked into one of those wacky mirrors in a funhouse or at a carnival? They are warped, on purpose, to make you look both tall and super skinny or short and really wide! You laugh because you know that you're not getting the true picture of yourself. Did you know that some people only give you a skewed view of themselves just like those mirrors do?

Read 1 Kings 6:1, 11–14, 22, 37, 38. After reading this passage, you might conclude that Solomon was completely devoted to Jehovah. For seven years, he worked in building an elaborate house for God. He even overlaid the entire edifice with pure gold. That must have cost him a fortune!

"But Solomon was building his own house thirteen years." These opening words of Chapter 7 reveal that Solomon was not as single-minded as he looked at first. This anointed heir to the throne of Israel had a self-centered, sensual focus—his own confession in Ecclesiastes reveals the extent of it.

The lesson here is that apparent devotion to God does not necessarily reveal the true heart of a professed devotee. Sometimes the truth about an individual lies in the lesser-known obsessions of his private life. Since only God knows everything about a person, careful discernment of another's character must be developed by heeding godly counsel (Pro. 1:8; 11:14; 12:15; 15:22; 19:20, 21; 20:18) and by actively seeking God's discernment about a person (Jer. 17:9, 10; Pro. 21:2; James 1:5). Don't let yourself become romantically attached to a person before you truly seek God's direction and discernment in the matter. Ask your parents for counsel! Be careful about becoming close friends with anyone who may not really be all that he or she appears to be. Wrong companions derail you (Pro. 13:20; 1 Cor. 15:33); God's counsel will never fail you.

PONDER: Never judge a book by its cover, nor a person merely by what he says.

—Rich Tozour

"I'm Sorry" Isn't Enough

Scripture Reading—James 5:16
"Confess your faults one to another."

Even when the youngest children do wrong, they should be taught to deal with their wrongdoing. If not, as they become older, they will become very insensitive and complacent regarding their offenses. Situations that involve lying, cheating, stealing, and anger can evolve into areas of major sin if not addressed at the earliest of ages.

In addressing these situations, parents must be very thorough in training their children. Very often children are told to apologize by simply saying, "I'm sorry," which initially seems adequate, but it does not really go far enough in making things right. Basically, "I'm sorry," says, "I feel bad this happened," but really does little to clear things up and make them right again.

Genuine confession for the sake of clearing an offense should involve three basic elements. First there needs to be **remorse**. Remorse does say, "I'm sorry," but it also communicates sadness because another person was hurt by what took place. Secondly, there needs to be **responsibility**. When a person is willing to say, "I was wrong," they are not avoiding but, rather, accepting the fact that they are responsible for what took place. Thirdly, there must be **reconciliation**. In order to seek to be reconciled, a person must truly say, "Will you please forgive me." Requesting and receiving forgiveness allows the offender to ultimately be cleared of his offense. Only when these steps are applied can wrongdoing be made right and restoration of the relationship occur.

When dealing with young children, it may be necessary to guide them through these steps. You can do that with the use of questions such as, "Are you sorry? Were you wrong? Do you want to be forgiven?" This will allow the child to experience the fullest measure of clearing in the situation in which they were wrong. When this process is mastered early in life, it will eliminate the accumulation of "baggage" that must be dealt with much later in life.

ACTION POINT: Read Matt. 5:23, 24. Which would God rather have: a large gift in the offering or making things right with someone who has been wronged?

—Tom Palmer

AUGUST 31
EXPRESSIONS OF PRIDE

Scripture Reading—Pro. 16:18
"Pride goeth before destruction, and an haughty spirit before a fall."

All of our problems with God and people can be traced to pride. Most people that are proud don't even know it. It is at the root of our sin nature and grows so deep in our hearts that it cannot be easily discerned.

People react to our pride. Spouses have arguments with each other because of pride. Parents and children have conflicts because of pride. Until we deal with our pride, we are going to have ongoing conflicts with those whom we love most and with God. Knowing the symptoms of pride help us to be aware of its presence so that we might deal with it.

Two consistent expressions of pride are our countenance and our speech. The countenance is an external expression of an internal attitude. The Bible speaks of "a proud look" (Pro. 6:17), a "high look" (Pro. 21:4), and the "pride of his countenance" (Ps. 10:4). Our pride is communicated to others, and they read it on our faces. This is no small matter, or God would not have addressed it.

Pride is also expressed by our speech. Our choice of words, tone of voice, and the focus of our conversation can communicate pride (Ps. 12:3, 1 Sam. 2:3).

These symptoms point to the root problem—pride. Treating a symptom won't remove the cause, but it will let us know that the problem is there. If not confronted and dealt with, pride brings "shame" (Pro. 11:2), "destruction," "a fall" (Pro. 16:18), and brings us "low" (Pro. 29:23).

Unless we deal with our pride, these symptoms will always be there. They are the reason people react to us. As long as I tolerate them, the quality of my relationships will suffer, and, even worse, I will offend a holy God before Whom I have no right to be proud.

ACTION POINT: Ask several close friends or family members if your countenance or words convey pride.

—Rick Johnson

SEPTEMBER 1
HIDE AND SEEK

Scripture Reading—Pro. 28:13
"He that covereth his sins shall not prosper:
but whoso confesseth and forsaketh them shall have mercy."

One of my favorite games as a kid was hide and seek! These days I love to play hide and seek with my grandchildren, who are ages six and three. The three year old will hide in plain sight and giggle when I come into the room as I pretend not to be able to find her. Of course, she is always easy to find and then she helps me look for the six year old who is a much better hider.

It's cute to play hide and seek with a three year old who hides in plain sight, but it's not cute to play hide and seek with God. How foolish! In Jeremiah 23:24 we read, "Can any hide himself in secret places that I shall not see him? saith the LORD. Do not I fill heaven and earth? saith the LORD."

The Bible tells us that Adam and Eve "hid themselves from the presence of the LORD God" (Gen. 3:8). God had given them a beautiful garden and all they needed for a wonderful life together, and yet they chose to disobey His word and sin against Him. Then they hid! Why? Guilt and fear!

God came to Jonah and said to him, "Arise, go to Nineveh, that great city, and cry against it; for their wickedness is come up before me. But Jonah rose up to flee unto Tarshish from the presence of the LORD, and went down to Joppa" (Jonah 1:1–3). Jonah tried to hide from God by running away. Why? He made a choice to disobey the Lord!

Proverbs 15:3 says, "The eyes of the LORD are in every place, beholding the evil and the good." It is foolish to hide from the presence of our God who knows all, sees all, and is everywhere. Our verse today makes it clear that if we want to prosper in the Lord we must be willing to confess and forsake our sin! It is foolish (and can be dangerous) to play hide and seek with God!

PONDER: Are you trying to hide something from God? Do you have any secrets that need to be confessed and forsaken?

—Sammy Frye

SEPTEMBER 2
THE ASSURANCE OF SALVATION

Scripture Reading—John 14:6
"I am the way, the truth, and the life:
no man cometh unto the Father, but by me."

Christians have often been criticized for teaching that Jesus is the only way to be saved. Other religions are not the true way; only Christ is the true way. It is understandable that Christians believe this because Christ taught this when He said, "I am the way, the truth, and the life: no man cometh unto the Father, but by me" (John 14:6).

Mohammed spent his life inventing his own way. On his deathbed Buddha was reported to have said, "I still seek truth." Confucius taught his own principles for living life. But, all these men have one thing in common—they are all dead and their bones are still in the ground! But Jesus is alive, and the way of assurance can only be found in Him.

The Bible declares in 1 John 5:12, "He that hath the Son hath life; and he that hath not the Son of God hath not life." If you have Jesus, you have eternal life. Religion, psychology, and education will never bring the satisfaction of assurance to a troubled heart. Only Jesus can do that (Acts 4:12).

When we know for certain that we have Jesus in our hearts and lives, we have a powerful assurance. A professing Christian without assurance of salvation is like a man in a sinking ship. Every crisis will be magnified with fear, and a fretful spirit will overwhelm him. But a man with an assurance of his relationship with the Lord is in a position to conquer his fears.

He knows beyond the shadow of a doubt, regardless what happens in this life, that he will awake in the presence of the Lord. The Apostle Paul declared, "For I reckon that the sufferings of this present time are not worthy to be compared with the glory which shall be revealed in us" (Rom. 8:18).

This can only be true for a man who has assurance (Rom. 8:16). And this man has the potential to face any fear he has because he knows that he belongs to God and that he will never be forsaken.

SONG: Sing "Blessed Assurance" together.

—*James Stallard*

SEPTEMBER 3
THE PRISON OF BITTERNESS

Scripture Reading—Heb. 12:15
"Looking diligently lest any man fail of the grace of God; lest any root of bitterness springing up trouble you, and thereby many be defiled."

If anyone doubts that this world is a bitter place, they need only look at how many lawsuits are filed every year. While this bitter spirit should not be surprising when we look at the non-Christian world, it is surprising to find God's people filled with this same spirit of bitterness.

The Bible clearly warns believers not to allow bitter feelings to enter their hearts bringing trouble and defiling those around them (Heb. 12:15). We often feel that it is okay to be bitter and hold a grudge against someone who has wronged us. But according to the Bible *bitterness is a sin*.

Paul commanded believers, "Let all bitterness, and wrath, and anger, and clamour, and evil speaking, be put away from you, with all malice: And be ye kind one to another, tenderhearted, forgiving one another, even as God for Christ's sake hath forgiven you" (Eph. 4:31, 32). The sin of bitterness puts us in a prison with invisible bars. By refusing to forgive and blaming others, we bind ourselves into slavery and blind ourselves with deception. Jesus warned us to forgive others or we would not sense the forgiveness of God in our own lives (Matt. 6:14, 15).

Rather than be bitter we should long to forgive others. Peter asked the Lord, "How oft shall my brother sin against me, and I forgive him? Till seven times?" (Matt. 18:21). How quickly Peter wanted to put limits on the forgiveness. Jesus responded with "seventy times seven." He was telling Peter that it was to be complete and total forgiveness.

Who do you harbor ill feelings toward? Has someone done something to you that you cannot forgive? Have you made it right with them? Why not give up this very day that grudge you have held for so long? It can be a day of new beginnings for you and an encouragement to the one you forgive.

QUOTE: "Both the inner attitude and the outward act (of bitterness, etc.) are to disappear entirely. The Holy Spirit gives quarter to no evil feeling whatsoever." —Ruth Paxson, Missionary to China

—*James Stallard*

SEPTEMBER 4
PRIDE AND OBSCURITY

Scripture Reading—Pro. 27:2
"Let another man praise thee, and not thine own mouth;
a stranger, and not thine own lips."

Our sin nature is prone to pride. Someone said, "No man having caught a large fish goes through the back alley." We want to be recognized and boast about what we have done.

Humility is just the opposite. It motivates us to deflect praise when we are recognized. While we are to be grateful for kind words that honor us, we should see it as an opportunity to give honor to the Lord and other people that have helped you.

Bill Gothard said, "Pride is believing that I have achieved what God and others have done for me." Also, he states that humility is "recognizing that it is actually God and others who are responsible for the achievements in my life." The former leads to God's judgment, but the latter brings His blessings.

Pride and boasting will always go together. Humility and gratitude, likewise, go together. Both are rooted deeply in the heart and produce totally different kinds of fruits.

Gothard says, "Gratitude is communicating to others in precise ways how they have benefited my life and looking for ways to honor them." A proud, boasting person refuses to do this because it takes the focus off of him or her.

One way God conquers pride is by placing us in an obscure place where we don't receive recognition. In that place there is no one to brag on you. It is futile to exult perceived self-importance; no one is listening.

One wisecrack said, "Pride is the only disease known to man that makes everyone sick except the person who has it."

When we begin to become content with simply knowing that God is aware of what we have done, we are on the road to humility. Today, if recognition comes, deflect it to God and those that have helped you. Be faithful to your tasks and honor the Lord and those that have helped you along the way.

PONDER: Why did Joseph and Moses need obscurity? How did it help them?

—Rick Johnson

SEPTEMBER 5
PRAYING AND FASTING FOR THE IMPOSSIBLE

Scripture Reading—Matt. 17:21
"This kind goeth not out but by prayer and fasting."

God can do the impossible, but He asks us to do our part. This involves prayer and sometimes fasting. Every time fasting is used in the Bible, it is in association with prayer; they both go together.

Fasting is more than disciplining the flesh. Its power is in taking your focus from physical appetites and drives in order that you might focus on God in a more concentrated way. Paul fasted frequently (2 Cor. 11:27), and this is one of the reasons God did great things through him and for him.

Impossible situations demand prayer and fasting. There are different types of fasting, and each of them relates to God-given drives. We fast from food (Matt. 4:2) or sleep (Dan. 6:18). These are opportunities to focus on God and seek His face.

For daily provision we need only pray (Matt. 6:11), but impossible situations demand more. "This kind" of situation (Matt. 17:21) in our lives requires fasting and prayer.

I will fast for a prescribed amount of time, but in very serious matters I fast until the burden leaves. When my grandmother had a serious surgery for cancer, I fasted during my lunch hour at college and took that time to pray and seek the Lord for His mercy and help. I have fasted for my health, for people to be saved, and when my heart was cold and I needed personal revival. For me, the issue over which I have fasted most often has been for my children.

Rather than complaining, fretting, and doubting the Lord—pray and fast for His intervention. While fasting certainly shows God the sincerity of our hearts in a matter, the real value is that we are focusing on God's promises and Person.

Is there a burden you carry that is so heavy that you have stopped praying? Perhaps you need to fast and seek His face anew.

ACTION POINT: Research the topic of fasting (fast, fasted, fasting, fastings) in a Bible concordance and practice it as God leads you in times of prayer.

—Rick Johnson

SEPTEMBER 6
THE TRAGIC SIN OF NEGLECT

Scripture Reading—Heb. 2:3
"How shall we escape, if we neglect so great salvation."

Our verse today has a very important word to consider. That word is *neglect*. The Bible is telling us not to "neglect so great salvation" (Heb. 2:3). If we look up the word "neglect" in a dictionary or thesaurus, we will find it means not to give respect to, to disregard, to be careless, to omit, to default, to be slack, to procrastinate, or to have a nonchalant attitude. For example, people can neglect to pay their bills or taxes, to go to the doctor when they have pains, to go to church, or to eat and live right.

The problem is not that people are paying too much attention, but that people are neglecting the most important things that pertain to life and death. This is a tragedy not only for its consequences, but because it is so unnecessary. The Lord tells us to listen to Him when He tells us not to neglect what we hear, see, need, or feel (Heb. 2:1–4).

Many marriages fall apart because of neglect. Many families struggle under the weight of a father or mother who neglects their responsibilities toward the children. Many young people struggle because they neglect spiritual truth that their parents have taught them through the years. Neglect is a tragedy and will only lead to more tragedy.

Jesus told the Church at Sardis to "be watchful, and strengthen the things which remain" (Rev. 3:2). Then He went on to say, "If, therefore, thou shalt not watch, I will come on thee as a thief" (Rev. 3:3). The city of Sardis had a history of being a city that could not be conquered. Situated high above a cliff, it was almost unapproachable. Yet, in its history it had fallen to foreign armies because the guards neglected to keep their posts.

Whatever we face, we must not neglect those things that will keep us strong to follow the Lord. Only then can we help others not neglect the salvation God desires to give to them.

PRAYER: Lord, help me not to neglect the things you have taught in your Word that I need to follow.

—James Stallard

SEPTEMBER 7
GRIEVING GOD

Scripture Reading—Eph. 4:30
"And grieve not the holy Spirit of God, whereby ye are sealed unto the day of redemption."

Emotions are such powerful things. The Bible tells us that a merry heart is good medicine for the soul (Pro. 17:22). All of us enjoy a good laugh. As a child, I knew well the emotion of fear. Oh, how I wish that my parents would have taught me Psalm 56:3, "What time I am afraid, I will trust in thee." Fear is something that we all experience.

In Ephesians 4:30, Paul mentions an emotion of sadness—grieving. We grieve when a family member passes away or a favorite pet is lost. We grieve when disappointments come into our lives and trials come. It is understood that human beings can be grieved, but did you know that the Holy Spirit can be grieved also?

The Holy Spirit is grieved when sin is in the life of the Christian. In Ephesians 4:31, Paul mentioned sins like bitterness, anger, and evil speaking and how they need to be put away. According to Hebrews 11:25, human beings experience pleasure in sin for a season. But do not forget that God is always grieved by our transgressions. Psalm 5:4 tells us, "For thou art not a God that hath pleasure in wickedness: neither shall evil dwell with thee."

Why is it that we often grieve the people that love us the most? Children hurt parents with their disobedience. Parents hurt children with unfulfilled promises and misplaced priorities. Our Heavenly Father has never forsaken us or let us down, yet we make the choice to grieve Him with sin in our lives.

There were several occasions in my childhood when I watched my mother weep over my disobedience. When I saw my mother's face, my heart was broken, and the tears began to fill up my eyes too. It is time for God's children to look and see the look upon His face when we sin against Him. Now is the time to stop grieving God.

DISCUSS: What do people do when they are grieved? Describe bitterness, anger, and evil speaking. How does the Holy Spirit convict us when we grieve Him?

—*Alton Beal*

SEPTEMBER 8
GOD CAN DO THE IMPOSSIBLE

Scripture Reading—Jer. 32:17
"There is nothing too hard for thee."

At some point in your life, you are going to face an impossible situation. When you come to that place, if you fail to trust the Lord, you will experience a downward and negative cycle.

First there is discouragement. It has a negative impact upon your spirit and mood. If that isn't dealt with, you become pessimistic and cynical. It has a negative impact on those around you. And finally, if you continue in doubt and self-pity, you will give up and quit. Now it has a lasting impact upon yourself and others.

There is good news for those that know Christ—things that are impossible for us are possible with God. In fact, He delights to do impossible things. The Bible says He does "great things and unsearchable; marvellous things without number" (Job 5:9).

Part of the privilege of being a child of God is having the power to face and overcome difficult, even impossible, situations. Knowing He is able to do the impossible brings encouragement and strength to your soul.

God allows us to come up against impossible situations to show us His strong arm. Jeremiah confesses God's mighty power in creation to remind him of His omnipotence (Jer. 32:17). God created the universe merely by His spoken word without any existing material (Heb. 11:3; Ps. 33:6).

One of the ways the Lord encourages those that are weary is by pointing to His creative power (Isa. 40:28). This is why part of our worship is related to His work as our Creator (Rev. 4:11). Creation brings awe and wonder to our hearts and reminds us of God's wisdom and power.

Are you facing a situation that is beyond all of your resources—financial, emotional, physical? You will either be discouraged as you ponder your lack, or you will be encouraged to know that you have a living God that specializes in doing the impossible.

Remember, God is looking for people in whom He can show forth His power through their lives (2 Chron. 16:9). Would you be one of them?

ACTION POINT: Look at God's handiwork in nature and ponder His power to do the impossible.

—Rick Johnson

KNOW DON'T KNUCKLE

Scripture Reading—James 1:3
"Knowing this, that the trying of your faith worketh patience."

There is something God wants us to know so we will not knuckle under when times get tough. We can know the "trying (or testing) of our faith" is for a purpose. God's purpose is to increase and grow our patience. Romans 5:3 teaches us that "tribulation worketh patience." Patience can be defined as the ability to bear up under difficult trials. We must know and believe there is a purpose in our pain.

A pastor who had gone through a deep and tragic trial in his church family shared with me some insights he had learned through his difficulties:

- "God never uses anyone greatly without first wounding him deeply."
- "Nothing of consequence, in terms of progress or development, ever happens apart from trials and problems."
- "The crucible for growth is here on earth—there is no shortcut."
- "It is not so important what happens to you but how you respond to what happens to you."
- "You are what you are under pressure. You don't squeeze an orange and get Dr Pepper."
- "The real growth is the kind you can't measure—growth in character, deepening of faith and trust."

This pastor was able to minister to his church family and share the Gospel with a worldwide audience as a result of what he went through.

In the book of Genesis, we read about Joseph and the tears and trouble he went through. He had some real problems with his brothers. Conversely, his brothers were the ones with the problem! They rejected and mistreated him with hearts full of selfish, sinful envy because of their father's favoritism and because of Joseph's godly character. Yet, God had a purpose in Joseph's pain. He used Joseph to save not only a nation but also the very family members who had hurt him so deeply.

We can know that God has a purpose in our trials, and He desires that patience be developed to a greater degree in the lives of His children.

ACTION POINT: Is patience a part of your character? Why not pause and pray right now and ask God for grace to help you grow in this area.

—Sammy Frye

SEPTEMBER 10
Passing on Your Testimony

Scripture Reading—Judg. 2:10
"There arose another generation after them, which knew not the LORD, nor yet the works which he had done for Israel."

One of my treasured possessions is my father's Bible that he read and used. It is well-marked and worn. I have seven children and use seven different Bibles in my study and preaching so that I might pass them on to them one day. There is something else I want to pass on to them and that is testimonies of how God has worked in my life.

This means that I have to be attentive to God's work in my life and record it somewhere for them to be able to read one day. We are commanded to teach our children how God has worked in our own lives in the past (Ps. 78:1–8). Sometimes we fail to do this simply because we have forgotten God's kindnesses and power expressed to us. God often warns us about our tendency to forget (Deut. 4:9, 23; 6:10–12).

One solution to this problem is to keep a written record of God's faithful working in your life. It can take the form of a very detailed journal or just writing stories of specific events and people and how God worked in your life through them. It will not only bless you, but will also be a source that will jolt your memory so you can teach your children and grandchildren. This will be a precious treasure passed down after you are gone!

This means that you will have to turn off the TV and computer and discipline yourself to write down what God is doing. If we fail to write these things down, we will forget much of what God has done. We are only one generation away from our family walking away from God, even to the point of doing evil (Judg. 2:7–11).

ACTION POINT: Do you have a place to record the working of God in your life? If not, go out and buy a notebook and begin today. Parents, share your personal testimony of salvation in detail to your children or grandchildren this week.

—Rick Johnson

STRANGERS IN A STRANGE WORLD

Scripture Reading—1 Pet. 4:4
"Wherein they think it strange that ye run not
with them to the same excess."

Christian people look strange to this world. Our verse tells us "they think it *strange* that ye run not with the same excess of riot, speaking evil of you." The word *strange* refers to something viewed as unusual, different, foreign, alien, or weird. The world continually seems surprised at Christians who do not follow the wild living it practices.

Questions often come up like the following, "Why do you not drink alcohol? Why do you have to dress that way? What's wrong with the way we dress? Why can't you enjoy that office party with all its wild fun? Why do you believe it's wrong to gamble?"

The world looks at the dedicated, separated believer as some strange animal that crawled out of the woods. Unbelievers just smile and shake their heads at some of the convictions Christians live by.

Years ago a college girl was in the student union on her campus. An unsaved young man who wanted her to go out on a date with him approached her. She was a Christian and kindly explained that her father had to approve of the fellows in her life and that she could not be involved in a dating relationship with a non-Christian. She quoted the Bible verse which says, "Be not unequally yoked together with unbelievers: for what fellowship hath righteousness with unrighteousness? and what communion hath light with darkness?" (2 Cor. 6:14).

The unsaved young man was stunned and badgered her as if she was some kind of idiot. But, she stood her ground, being faithful to her God, to her parents, and to herself. The young man simply walked away thinking *that is some strange girl*.

In fact, the Bible tells believers, "Beloved, think it not *strange* concerning the fiery trial which is to try you, as though some *strange* thing happened unto you" (1 Pet. 4:12). Another way to say it would be this: don't think it strange if they think you are strange! Remember that and trust God with your life.

DISCUSS: Discuss how your family has experienced being viewed as strange by unsaved people that you know.

—James Stallard

Pray Don't Panic

Scripture Reading—James 1:6
"But let him ask in faith, nothing wavering."

What do you do when you are facing a difficult circumstance or a difficult person? Someone wrote: "When in trouble, when in doubt, run in circles, scream, and shout." God has a better idea. Pray don't panic!

Hezekiah became the king of Judah when he was 25 years old. The Bible says of him that he did right in the sight of the Lord, trusted and loved the Lord, and kept his commandments. As a result, the Lord was with him and prospered him. Yet, there came a day when Hezekiah faced a powerful enemy—Sennacherib, the king of Assyria who planned to overthrow Jerusalem. Rabshakeh, Sennacherib's messenger came with hateful words and a threatening letter that was full of insults against Hezekiah and the Lord. This was a day of trouble.

What did Hezekiah do? We read in 2 Kings 19:14, 15 that "Hezekiah went up into the house of the LORD, and spread it (the letter) before the LORD. And Hezekiah prayed before the LORD." The king humbled himself before the Lord in prayer and honored the Lord as the true and living God, who is the Creator of heaven and earth. In verse 17 we read, "Of a truth, LORD, the kings of Assyria have destroyed the nations and their lands." Hezekiah then cried out for help as he prayed in verse 19, "O LORD our God, I beseech thee, save thou us out of his hand, that all the kingdoms of the earth may know that thou art the LORD God, even thou only."

Hezekiah humbly honored the Lord as he honestly prayed and cried out for help. He was concerned that the Lord be known and glorified. That very night an angel of the Lord killed 185,000 Assyrian soldiers, and as a result, Sennacherib departed. Victory!

Hezekiah chose to pray and not panic when he humbled himself before the Lord, honored the Lord, was honest with the Lord, and cried out for help from the Lord!

DISCUSS: Talk about problems with relationships that you may be facing with a family member, a co-worker, or maybe someone in your school. Is it time to pray, not panic, and follow the example of Hezekiah?

—Sammy Frye

SEPTEMBER 13
THREE "IFS" AND A "THEN"

Scripture Reading—Pro. 2:1–5

"My son, if thou wilt receive my words, and hide my commandments with thee; So that thou incline thine ear unto wisdom, and apply thine heart to understanding; Yea, if thou criest after knowledge, and liftest up thy voice for understanding; If thou seekest her as silver, and searchest for her as for hid treasures; Then shalt thou understand the fear of the Lord, and find the knowledge of God."

"If" is one of the smallest words in our Bible, but as Jesus said, "One jot or one tittle shall in no wise pass from the law." We know that every word is vital in the Word. Here we find the word "if" three times in five verses. The word "if" is the hinge on which the door of God's promises swings. Verse 1 says, "If thou wilt receive my words, and hide my commandments with thee." We can look at, touch, and smell a delicious meal without ever tasting or eating it. Likewise, we can read the Word without receiving it. James tells us, "But be ye doers of the word, and not hearers only, deceiving your own selves" (1:22).

Verse 3 says, "If thou criest after knowledge." God is telling us to cry after (or pray with urgency and fervency) knowledge and understanding. We live in a complicated world and in a day when God's knowledge is a must to live according to His Word. Paul told the Colossian believers that he did not cease "to pray for you, and to desire that ye might be filled with the knowledge of his will in all wisdom and spiritual understanding" (Col. 1:9). We must ask before receiving.

Our third "if" has to do with seeking and searching. The value of God's Word is much greater than diamonds and rubies. Like hidden treasure, It should cause us to dig and search. The example of the Bereans was to search the Scriptures daily.

In verse 5, we see the word "then." This is the result of all the "ifs!"—the Holy Spirit will deliver the promise of the "fear of the Lord" and "understanding from God." But all is predicated on "if" we receive, hide, pray for, seek, and search. "If" is a little word with big promises.

ACTION POINT: Search the Scriptures to find other promises that are granted because of the word "if."

—*Wayne King*

SEPTEMBER 14
THE TRIUMPH OF AFFLICTION

Scripture Reading—Ps. 119:71
"It is good for me that I have been afflicted;
that I might learn thy statutes."

The above verse does not sound quite right. What could possibly be good about being afflicted? Whatever "affliction" means, it does not sound like a good thing. Yet, the Bible says it has a good and useful purpose in our lives. Whatever bad things may come into our lives, God wants to use them to bring us to Himself.

What is the good the Psalmist speaks of? The latter part of the verse gives the answer, "That I might learn thy statutes." There are several words used in Psalm 119 for the Word of God—law, word, ordinances, commandments, precepts, testimonies, statutes, and judgments. Affliction, or trouble, should drive us to God's Word to find help in time of trouble. There we find help for:

- Feelings of loneliness—He cares for us (1 Pet. 5:7).
- Understanding God's will—He guides us (Eph. 5:15–17).
- Crying out in distress—He answers prayer (John 16:23, 24).
- Financial help—He provides for our needs (Matt. 6:7, 8).

There are multitudes of helps to be found in the Bible for the believer who faces any kind of affliction. By going to God's Word, we not only find answers for our troubles, but we draw closer to God (James 4:8). In this we find the greatest purpose for our affliction.

No one could have been more afflicted than Joni Eareckson Tada. She became paralyzed from the neck down in a diving accident and faced the horror of living her life as a paraplegic. Through all the struggles she was driven to the Bible for help in her plight. She found a close relationship with God and became a vibrant Christian with a powerful testimony around the world. Her ministry Joni and Friends has helped millions of people face their trials and afflictions.

Perhaps her testimony should be that of each of us. Whatever afflictions we face should drive us to God's Word where we find the help of the Lord. Then we can help others as they face their times of affliction (2 Cor. 1:3, 4). All of this is a good thing.

SONG: Sing "Tis So Sweet to Trust in Jesus."

—*James Stallard*

SEPTEMBER 15
TRUSTING GOD FOR THE IMPOSSIBLE

Scripture Reading—2 Cor. 5:7
"We walk by faith, not by sight."

We relate to God on the basis of faith, rather than our senses. When we trust our senses, we miss His best for our lives. He is "able to do exceeding abundantly above all that we ask or think" (Eph. 3:20).

Sight says, "I can't do that." Faith says, "God is able." Sight says, "I'll believe it when I see it." Faith says, "Believe it, and you will see it."

It was impossible for Abraham and Sara to have a child, but they trusted God's promise instead of human limitations (Rom. 4:21). The nation of Israel lived below its privileges (Ps. 78:41) and settled for second best (Ps. 81:10–16).

The world is watching to see if we serve a living God. They ask, "Is thy God, whom thou servest continually, able to deliver thee . . .?" (Dan. 6:20). We reflect poorly on our mighty God when we live mediocre lives. Our mediocrity is a result of our lack of faith.

Our church had some severe financial challenges, and I was in a meeting with our deacons to prepare the budget for the coming year. I was very discouraged and tired from the struggle and pressure of living on thin margins, both personally and in our ministry.

I wanted a manageable budget with mild increases that I felt we could handle. One of our godly men had been challenged through a summer Bible study on living by faith (that I had led!) and stated, "Guys, let's establish a faith budget this year. It needs to be something that we know that when we reach it that only God could have done it."

We discussed it, and everyone agreed. However, I was hesitant about it. In my spirit I knew my friend was correct about trusting God and acting on that faith, but my mind doubted if we should do it.

The faith budget was implemented, and it was met. Through the years we did the same, and God has provided. God is glorified when we trust Him.

ACTION POINT: Confess your lack of faith and replace it with "God is able."

—Rick Johnson

SEPTEMBER 16
STUCK ON THE ROCKS

Scripture Reading—Luke 19:13
"And he called his ten servants, and delivered them ten pounds,
and said unto them, Occupy till I come."

A few years ago a man was enjoying the sights along the Capon River in West Virginia. As he walked alongside the beautiful river, he found a gentleman canoeing, stuck on the rocks in the low running current. After several minutes of conversation, the gentleman revealed he had been sitting there for several hours. Others who were canoeing with him continued on, assuming he would catch up.

The small rapids and the fear of tipping the canoe into the cold water had paralyzed his progress. In Luke 19 our Lord portrays Himself as a nobleman who entrusts his servants with an investment to be used wisely while he is away. At his return he found some were faithful with the opportunity he had given them and had grown the investment. Others partially invested, and some unfortunately had not invested the nobleman's interest at all. The reward and judgment was in accordance to their opportunity. Luke 19:20, 21, "And another came, saying, Lord, behold, here is thy pound, which I have kept laid up in a napkin: For I feared thee, because thou art an austere man." While others were rewarded, one servant lost all because he feared to put what he was entrusted with to work.

The gentleman on the river eventually flipped the canoe. He never finished the trip. He started well, but fear stopped him midstream! To sit by and not use the opportunities of time and the resources given us reminds me of that man in the river. Fear of the unknown and fear of failure will impede our progress. Soon, if we are not watchful, we end up just sitting and waiting for something to happen. That servant knew his Lord's will, but he would not act. Jesus said, occupy till I come. Do business with those things that I have entrusted to your care for My glory.

PONDER: The river of time is packed with opportunity. Don't get stuck on the rocks of fear.

—*Steve Rebert*

WHAT IS A CONSCIENCE?

Scripture Reading—Rom. 2:15

"Their conscience also bearing witness, and their thoughts the mean while accusing or else excusing one another."

God created every human being with a variety of unique human faculties, which make up the complete person. For example, the mind is the thought-producing faculty. The memory is the thought-retaining faculty. The spirit is the thought-analyzing faculty. The soul is the thought-appreciating faculty. The will is the thought-energizing faculty. Then finally we note that the conscience is the thought-convicting faculty.

The conscience is the part of our being that has been given by God to help us know the difference between right and wrong. When a person is confronted with moral choices, the conscience enables him to make the right choice regarding his own conduct. Our verse for today uses the words "accusing" and "excusing" to enable us to see how the conscience functions. By accusing it lets us know when we are guilty of wrongdoing, and by excusing it lets us know when we are innocent of wrongdoing. The conscience allows a man to be morally conscious of God's law, which is the ultimate standard of good and evil.

Someone asked a little boy to define the conscience, and he said, "It is something that makes you tell your mother what you did before your sister does." It also can be well said that the conscience is like a policeman who pulls you over to let you know that you have broken the law. I also like the thought that the conscience is like a watchdog that loudly barks when the safety and wellbeing of his owner is threatened.

When the little sister has nothing to tell or when the policeman doesn't need his siren or when the watchdog doesn't need to bark, it is a sign that we are living right. In this way, the conscience enables us to stay on course morally in a way that pleases the Lord.

ACTION POINT: Discuss this question as a family: "Why would a policeman want a reckless driver to know that he was breaking the law?"

—*Tom Palmer*

SEPTEMBER 18
A PRAYER FOR FORGIVENESS

Scripture Reading—Matt. 6:12
"And forgive us our debts, as we forgive our debtors."

There are very few words in the English language that are more significant than the word "forgiveness." It is through forgiveness that a sinner can be made right with God. It is also through forgiveness that a sinful person can be made right with another person against whom he or she has done sinful things. In other words, forgiveness is the key to establishing and maintaining relationships with both God and man.

As Jesus was teaching on prayer, He emphasized the need to deal with sin against God. This process begins with conviction, which occurs when we feel bad about our sin. Then there is confession, which involves agreeing with God about our sin. Finally, there is cleansing, which means being cleared of our sin. 1 John 1:9 says that God is "faithful and just to forgive us our sins," but that can only take place when we "confess," and He "cleanses." It is through the prayer of confession that forgiveness and cleansing become reality.

Jesus also addressed the need to forgive others who sin against us just as God forgives us. Unfortunately, wounds, hurts, and offenses do often occur in relationships between people, particularly people who are close to one another, as in a family. Again it is essential for forgiveness to be sought by the one who is the offender, and the one who has been offended must grant forgiveness. Through forgiveness, wounded relationships can be healed and restored. It was Jesus Himself who beautifully portrayed this spirit of forgiveness as He spoke to His Father from The Cross (Luke 23:34; Eph. 4:32).

There is no need to live life with an accumulation of unconfessed sin and unresolved conflicts. Both can be removed when a person is willing to work through the process of forgiveness. Going to God in prayer involves clearing anything that hinders prayer. Forgiveness is a significant part of that clearing process in both spiritual and human relationships.

ACTION POINT: Discuss why it can be so hard to seek forgiveness. Discuss why it can be so hard to grant forgiveness.

—Tom Palmer

SEPTEMBER 19
GOD CAN GIVE CHILDREN

Scripture Reading—Luke 1:37
"For with God nothing shall be impossible."

Children are a blessing, not a curse (Ps. 127:3–5; 128:3). We live in a culture that views children as hindrances to making money and being able to climb the ladder of worldly success.

I wonder if some believers speak out strongly against abortion (which we should), but at the same time do not love children. They tolerate the children of others and do love the children they have, but they are aggravated by the inevitable challenges and problems that having children brings.

More than once I have had conversations with couples that, with tears rolling down their cheeks, lament that they are unable to have children. They would love to have children, but physically they cannot. Of course, adoption might be God's will in this instance.

These words are addressed to those that want to have children but cannot for some reason: conception and birth are both miracles of God (Eccl. 11:5; Ps. 139:14–16). In the final analysis it is God that chooses to give us children or not.

One of the great Scriptures on God's power to do the impossible is at the top of this page. Isolated from its context it is still true, but the verse applies to God giving Mary a supernatural birth, as she would carry and deliver Jesus Christ (Luke 1:35–37). The same passage also alludes to John the Baptist being a miracle child. Another Scripture of God doing the impossible in reference to having a child is Genesis 18:14, where He tells Abraham and Sara of their son.

My wife and I wanted a child and could not. We prayed, and I asked someone to pray for us that we might be able to be parents. God heard and answered us. It wasn't the prayers or those praying, but our faith in God to give us a child to train for Him. Along with seven miscarriages, we also have seven children on earth. If it is His will, He can give you a child.

ACTION POINT: Pray for and help couples that are raising their children to serve the Lord.

—Rick Johnson

SEPTEMBER 20
THE OWNER'S MANUAL

Scripture Reading—Psalm 119:105
"Thy word is a lamp unto my feet, and a light unto my path."

Our family lives in a tour bus as we travel in fulltime evangelism. The bus is very large and contains many of the same things that are found in a house, like beds, a kitchen, a bathroom, and a shower.

But knowing how to operate the many parts of the bus can be challenging. For this reason, the bus contains a total of six owner's manuals that teach us how to maintain our "house on wheels." It's a lot of work, but we find that if we follow the owner's manuals, things go pretty smoothly for us. We also find that we are more confident in how to live in this environment. This confidence comes from knowing and doing what is contained in the owner's manuals.

Now imagine for a moment that our bus had no owner's manual. Imagine that the manufacturer of the bus never provided one. "That's crazy!" you might say, and you would be right. Such a vehicle, built by intelligent people, should always have an owner's manual. As a matter of fact, it would seem irresponsible for the bus maker not to provide one. So why is it that most people in this world live as if there is no owner's manual for life? Unfortunately, their lives negatively reflect this reality.

An intelligent Creator made you. And being the responsible God He is, He left you with an "Owner's Manual" for life. It's called the Bible. It contains all the information and wisdom you need to manage your life properly.

According to Psalm 119:105, the Bible is a light and a guide in a dark world that contains many obstacles, traps, and ditches that will cause you to fall if you fail to apply the Bible to your life. Satan is a constant foe who is trying to make our lives dark with sin. We need the light of God's word every day to drive the dark away. Are you reading the "Owner's Manual" every day? If not, why not?

ACTION POINT: Determine to read the Bible every day from this day forward.

—Paul Miller

SEPTEMBER 21
PAYING FOR WHAT I REALLY OWE

Scripture Reading—Heb. 13:18
"Pray for us: for we trust we have a good conscience,
in all things willing to live honestly."

Standing at the counter, I watched as the waitress totaled my bill for the sub sandwiches I had ordered. I knew she was about to give me a bargain, but I also knew that the amount she had figured was incorrect. As she handed me my sandwiches and told me the price, I informed her that the amount was well below what I really owed. With a perplexed look on her face, she immediately said, "Man, you sure are honest!" I quickly responded by saying, "Well, it's easier to go ahead and give you the money now, than having to come back later to pay you so I can clear my conscience."

Another very important part of maintaining a clear conscience involves making restitution. Restitution involves being honest enough to correct an error, even if the error was not our own fault. What should a person do when the clerk gives back more change than you should receive? It is easy to want to take the money and consider it to be your gain. What should a student do when the teacher overlooks a wrong answer or gives a grade that is higher than is deserved? Again it would seem easier to take the grade and keep it for your own advantage. What should a person do when they are accidently given more pieces or an additional part than what was ordered? Once again it would seem easy to grab and go with an unexpected bonus.

This is where honesty helps keep the conscience clear. Knowing what really is right, it is best to correct the error, and to make things right. In so doing, the Lord is certainly pleased, but we also give a great testimony about honesty. Honesty creates a reputation of integrity, which is always respected and appreciated. A clear conscience is always more valuable than an extra sandwich!

ACTION POINT: In 2 Corinthians 8:21, what challenge is given regarding the matter of honesty? Consider some examples of when this would apply to your family.

—*Tom Palmer*

SEPTEMBER 22
MOVING THE BOUNDARIES

Scripture Reading—Job 24:2
"Some remove the landmarks."

In Bible times, thieves were very careful how they moved landmarks. Usually they moved them under the cover of darkness. They would not move them every night because then it would be obvious. If done in very small increments, it wouldn't be noticeable over time.

Incremental change has affected our churches and Bible colleges. Satan patiently moves to achieve his goal. He will do the same in our personal lives and families.

While growth necessitates change, don't mistake change alone for progress. All improvement requires change, but all change is not improvement. We must have discernment as to the difference.

When we are children our parents seem to do no wrong. As teens we sometimes questioned their sanity. As adults we finally realize that their boundaries were there for a purpose. When you do not understand a boundary, it is vital that you discover why the fence was put up in the first place before you tear it down.

Children move boundaries of parents through justification. God established clear boundaries for Adam and Eve. Eve began to question them, and this led to disobedience, which brought severe consequences. We can justify anything in our own minds. But justifying wrong behavior will not ease a guilty conscience.

Children move boundaries through rebellion. Some have their heart set on moving the landmark no matter what God says and no matter the cost. The Old Testament term for this is "transgression," a willful violation of an established boundary.

Children move boundaries through compromise. Rather than God's Word being the umpire on our landmarks, we determine them by our feelings and opinions. We are fearful of what others might say, and we begin to make concessions in small areas. Soon, we have changed what God has placed firmly as a boundary in His Word.

ACTION POINT: Respond to this statement by John Phillips: "Being reared in a godly home only accelerates your accountability before God." Make a list of things that used to be considered wrong but that people consider acceptable today.

—Rick Johnson

SEPTEMBER 23
HOW TO RESPOND TO A CRISIS AS A BELIEVER

Scripture Reading—Job 1:22
"In all this Job sinned not, nor charged God foolishly."

The book of Job becomes a great proving ground for all believers when we find ourselves going through deep waters. Can any of us even imagine four messengers coming one right after the other announcing crisis upon crisis as in Job 1? Loss of wealth, loss of livelihood, encounters with emboldened enemies, and most of all, loss of family! Everything that you worked for and loved is now in ashes, even though you've tried to live a life that pleases the Lord.

We will become discouraged if we do not understand Satan's freedom in this world to bring trials upon mankind. Even so, he is like a dog on a chain and can only go where God has given permission. Job brings encouragement when we realize that God desires to show off His workmanship in the hearts of men, Job 1:8. Satan believes that our worship of God has no real merit and that God does not mean enough to us for us to continue to give Him our worship when we go through great trial. Satan's position was that Job would not love, obey, or worship God when he received evil things in this life for which there seemed to be no explanation.

We must realize how vital our response is in time of crisis. Is what Satan thinks true? Do we quit, blame God, or mold our lifestyle like the world because of crisis? God desires to show the work of Christ in our hearts to others. Can God "entrust" you with His testimony. Job refused to blame God or tarnish His name with accusations (Job 1:22; 2:10). Bringing evil upon man with the desire to hurt is not within the purposes of God nor in His nature. God has a purpose and will not waste one precious life given to Him.

THOUGHT: A few things that seemed to help Job:
- He was spiritually strong when the trial came.
- He understood God has goals for his life, but so does Satan.
- He did not blame God.
- He knew that he would face good and evil in this life.
- He allowed people to help.

—*Steve Rebert*

SEPTEMBER 24
PRAYING WHEN IT'S DIFFICULT

Scripture Reading—James 5:13
"Is any among you afflicted? let him pray."

My first response in adversity isn't to pray, but to solve the problem myself. One reason why God permits overwhelming trouble is to force us to pray.

This happened to King Manasseh (2 Chron. 33:11-13). It wasn't until he was in pain that he began to seek the Lord. Jonah prayed and got to know God as he never had before in a time of trouble (Jonah 2:1, 2). Rather than complaining Paul and Silas prayed when it all seemed hopeless (Acts 16:24, 25).

Our most effective praying is when it isn't easy. Prayer is like a wrestling in your spirit that brings fatigue (Luke 22:44; Col. 4:12; Gal. 4:19). Jesus prayed and wept with a broken heart (Heb. 5:7). Are we exempt from praying like this in our trials?

God delights to hear and deliver you during your time of trouble (Ps. 18:6; 50:15; 118:5; 130:1, 2; 143:6, 7). Often these are turning points in our lives when we are alone and pouring our hearts out to God. This was true of Jacob, and it was the defining moment in his life (Gen. 32:24).

It is no wonder that more significant things do not happen in our lives. We do not pay the price in prayer. It is in times of trouble when our richest times of prayer and blessing often come.

A man asked D.L. Moody if he might pray with him, and the time was agreed upon to meet. The gentleman said they went into a room and both knelt to pray. It was quiet for a while, and finally the guest began to pray. He finished and then waited for Moody to pray. Nothing was said for a long while. Moody never said a word. The guest only heard groans and sounds of grief. Finally a knock at the door and a man entered with a suit of clothes for Moody. He was soaked in sweat. They had been there for two hours, and the guest said he had never sensed the presence of God like he had during that time.

ACTION POINT: Rather than griping about your problem, bring it to the Lord.

—*Rick Johnson*

SEPTEMBER 25
Teaching that Transforms

Scripture Reading—Deut. 6:7

"And thou shalt teach them diligently unto thy children, and shalt talk of them when thou sittest in thine house, and when thou walkest by the way, and when thou liest down, and when thou risest up."

To influence our children for God, we must teach them what He has done for us. This is to be done diligently. The word "diligently" (Deut. 6:7) means "to sharpen a cutting instrument by using a whetting stone." It implies teaching that leaves a mark and is remembered. Effective teaching is not only intentional, but also given with diligence.

When something is of value to us, we are very intentional about it and give it our best efforts. Since God has given parents a mandate to be the primary teachers in the lives of their children, they should be the most diligent, intentional, and well-prepared teachers.

Effective teaching is not seasonal, but consistent. The Bible teaches that parents particularly are to speak of it "when thou sittest in thine house, and when thou walkest by the way, and when thou liest down, and when thou risest up" (6:7; 11:19).

Note that there are four times mentioned when we ought to speak about biblical truths ("sittest in thine house . . . walkest by the way . . . liest down . . . risest up). Three of these four incidences are inside the home. While we are to be intentional and formal in some of our instruction, this carries the idea of incidental and informal teaching too.

Some years ago there was a debate about what was most important in training our children—quality time or quantity time. I believe both are important. In fact, quality moments usually occur unexpectedly and are the byproduct of spending a lot of time together.

A mom or dad can never tell when a seed will be sown in the heart of a son or daughter that will grow and stay with them for the rest of their lives and that they will one day teach to their children!

ACTION POINT: What biblical truths can you remember that your parents or others implanted in your heart when you were young?

—*Rick Johnson*

SEPTEMBER 26
DRESSED FOR BATTLE

Scripture Reading—Eph. 6:11
"Put on the whole armour of God."

What to wear? It seems that it is a difficult matter to figure out how to dress for certain events. Should we dress casually, formally, or semi-casually—or is that semi-formal? It would be great if we spent as much time finding out what to wear spiritually as we do physically. What is amazing is that many believers are not even aware of the wardrobe God has provided for us.

It seems that many Christians come to the battle in casual dress rather than warfare dress. What kind of wardrobe does God provide for us? It is clear from Ephesians 6 that we can have the battle uniform we need to face the wiles, or methodical attacks, of the enemy (Eph. 6:11). Note the pieces of the armor that we can have if we allow the Lord to provide them for us. Also, look up and read the other verses to help understand the meaning:

1. Belt of truth (Eph. 6:14; John 8:30–32).
2. Breastplate of righteousness (Eph. 6:14; James 1:20).
3. Shoes of the Gospel (Eph. 6:15; Rom. 5:1–5).
4. Shield of faith (Eph. 6:16; Heb. 11:1–6).
5. Helmet of salvation (Eph. 6:17; 2 Pet. 1:5–11).
6. Sword of the Spirit (Eph. 6:17; Heb. 4:12).

What is this major event of spiritual warfare that we must attend and dress up for? It is the ministry of prayer. "**Praying** always with all prayer and supplication in the Spirit, and watching thereunto with all perseverance and supplication for all saints" (Eph. 6:18).

The ministry of prayer is the way through which God works to do His will in our lives. It is the way we battle our adversary, Satan. We must have on all the pieces of the armor to engage in this battle. This is a picture to us that these things must be in our life to properly pray to God. Look carefully at Ephesians 6:18 again. It is an aggressive stance to attack the enemy in prayer. Only in this way does our praying for friends or family or the church become useful.

ACTION POINT: Examine your life based on the pieces of armor. Is anything missing that would hinder your prayer life?

—James Stallard

SEPTEMBER 27
THE ABCDE CHART

Scripture Reading—Ps. 118:24
*"This is the day which the LORD hath made;
we will rejoice and be glad in it."*

When our children were younger, we made a simple chart that listed five basic goals to follow when starting the day. The chart also had a Scripture verse to remind them of God as they started the day. The chart included these things:

- **Awake**—get up on time. "I myself will awake early. I will praise thee O Lord" (Ps. 57:8, 9).
- **Bed**—make your bed before leaving your room. "When I remember thee upon my bed, and meditate on thee in the night watches" (Ps. 63:6).
- **Clothes**—get dressed in your outfit for the day. "I will greatly rejoice in the LORD, my soul shall be joyful in my God, for he hath clothed me with the garments of salvation" (Isa. 61:10).
- **Devotions**—spend time in the Bible and in prayer. "Man doth not live by bread only, but by every word that proceedeth out of the mouth of the Lord doth man live" (Deut. 8:3).
- **Eat**—enjoy a nourishing breakfast. "Therefore, take no thought, saying, What shall we eat? Or, What shall we drink? or, Wherewithal shall we be clothed? . . . for your heavenly Father knoweth that ye have need of all these things" (Matt. 6:31, 32).

Typically children left to "do their own thing" have a difficult time creating any structure in their day. This simple chart will assist teenagers and children in beginning their day with some organization and discipline. In the same way, parents need to follow some order in starting their day. Their example will show their children the importance of getting a good start to the day. When things get started well, they typically finish up so much better. This simple plan will build structure and responsibility into the lives of children. It will also help things run smoothly at your house in the morning.

ACTION POINT: Make a copy of this chart for each family member. It can be done nicely on the computer. Younger children may even enjoy drawing and writing it out on construction paper with crayons or colored pencils. Post a copy in each person's bedroom.

—Tom Palmer

SEPTEMBER 28
HAVING FAITH AS WE GROW OLDER

Scripture Reading—2 Sam. 21:17
"Thou shalt go no more out with us to battle."

While God never changes, we often do. As time goes by, we learn that the faith that won great battles for the Lord in the past will not be sufficient for today's battles. In other words, we cannot live in the past.

We all know the story of David and Goliath. As a young boy David's courage and faith were strong as he slew the giant with his slingshot (1 Sam. 17:45–51). But, later in his life David would face the Philistines again (2 Sam. 21:15–22). Perhaps these were the four brothers of Goliath who would have been felled by the other four smooth stones David had collected for his sling.

The Bible tells us at that later battle "David waxed faint" (2 Sam. 21:15). He needed help from some of his men or else he would have been killed in battle. So, his men encouraged David not to go out to battle again (v. 17).

As David grew older, his faith would be called upon to lay aside his pride and let others help in the battle. Is this not a good lesson for us to learn as we grow older? Whether it be fixing our cars or computers in the physical realm or making things right with family or friends that we have wronged in the spiritual realm—we tend to think we don't need anybody's help.

It is too easy to feel that we don't really need help because we were able to do this once before. In our younger days we were able to drive long distances in one day or play our favorite sport constantly. As we have grown older, those things aren't quite so easy.

When it comes to our lives spiritually, we cannot depend on last year's time spent in the Word of God to help us today. Praying and fasting in the past may make no difference in the present. We need help for today. We need God's presence upon our lives now. Remember, yesterday's glow will not shine on today's problems.

PRAYER: Lord, help me to allow others to help as I trust you today.

—James Stallard

SEPTEMBER 29
HELP IN THE NICK OF TIME

Scripture Reading—Heb. 4:16
"Come boldly unto the throne of grace . . . and
find grace to help in time of need."

Everyone will face a time when they need help. You cannot live on planet earth without experiencing trouble (Job 14:1). Multiple trials and adversities can come our way like waves that continually pound the shore. Often we get in over our head, and desperation comes to our heart and our lips.

Our verse challenges us "to come boldly unto the throne of grace." God wants to help us, and His throne is not one of judgment for the believer, but one of grace—or unmerited favor. He delights to pour grace upon our lives whenever we face trouble.

In fact, the grace we can get comes "in time of need," which is another way of saying that it comes at the right time. Or we might even say it comes "in the nick of time." When all seems lost, when our backs are against the wall, when there is no answer in sight—we can seek the Lord, and He will bring help, even if it is "in the nick of time."

During the Revolutionary War, General George Washington had led his troops to fight the British around New York City. The American troops occupied Long Island, and through miscalculation Washington was defeated. They had to make a treacherous retreat across the East River with winds against them and very little time.

With his soldiers on the verge of quitting the army, it became clear to the Washington that many of his troops would be left on Long Island for the British to capture come morning. When the overcast sky of morning finally arrived, a dense fog came out of nowhere and gave the troops cover to escape. The fog arrived by the Providence of God, and certainly came "in the nick of time."

Do you have a financial debt you cannot pay? Boldly come to God with your trouble. Are you having struggles in your family relationships? Boldly cry out to God for relief. He is a God who will be there for you in your time of need.

DISCUSS: Read and discuss Hebrews 4:14–16.

—James Stallard

SEPTEMBER 30
THE BORROWING BLUNDER

Scripture Reading—2 Kings 6:5
"And he cried, and said, Alas, master! for it was borrowed."

Where is the prophet when you need him? The sons of the prophets were men studying for the ministry under Elijah and Elisha. Their number had grown to the point that they needed a new place to stay.

With Elisha's approval they began to build a seminary, or a school where they could stay as prophets (2 Kings 6:1, 2). They began to cut timber to build the place near the Jordan River. The Bible gives us an interesting account of what happened to one of the sons of the prophets. "But as one was felling a beam, the axe head fell into the water: and he cried, and said, Alas, master! for it was borrowed" (2 Kings 6:5).

He was concerned that he had lost what had been borrowed. He could not give it back or make up for it. Fortunately for him, the prophet Elisha was close by, and a great miracle took place. The Bible says, "And the man of God said, Where fell it? And he showed him the place. And he cut down a stick, and cast it in thither; and the iron did swim. Therefore said he, Take it up to thee. And he put out his hand, and took it" (2 Kings 6:6, 7).

Are we sometimes like this son of a prophet when it comes to borrowing? We borrow items and lose them or do not return them. Or worse, we borrow money and find ourselves unable to pay it back. Wouldn't it be great to have Elisha around so he could bail us out of our borrowing blunders? There is no guarantee that even God will bail us out of financial decisions we have made that are contrary to His Word.

While living debt free is certainly the superior way to go, in today's world it is not always easy. Debts can pile up with unexpected hospital bills or a job loss that puts us in a bad situation. God understands the pressures we face and wants to help us through them. Trust Him to guide you back.

PRAYER: Help me, Lord, to make good decisions with my life.

—James Stallard

OCTOBER 1
PRAYING WITH A SURRENDERED HEART

Scripture Reading—John 5:30
"I seek not mine own will, but the will
of the Father which hath sent me."

When we pray we ought to come with two pieces of paper—one with a list of our concerns and another that is blank. The blank sheet of paper is where we record the things that God speaks to us that He would have us to do as we commune with Him.

This assumes that we already have an attitude of submission to the will of God. This was our Lord's heart before His Father—"Not as I will, but as thou wilt" (Matt. 26:39). In the same prayer in Gethsemane, He said, "Thy will be done" (Matt. 26:42).

There is a contrast in this prayer between the will of Jesus ("I will") and the will of His Father ("thy will"). This is a pull all of us feel when we are struggling with making decisions.

When Satan rebelled he said five times to God, "I will" (Isa. 14:13–14). When Jesus was praying in the garden, He said to His Father, "thy will" (Matt. 26:42). What a contrast! Which attitude is reflected in your prayers to God?

How did the Lord Jesus make this incredible surrender to the Father's will? It wasn't a one-time decision. He had lived a life of surrender on earth (John 5:30; 6:38). His prayer time was more than a formality, but the reflection of His constant heart of surrender to the Father's will.

Ron Dunn said, "Our greatest battles are not with Satan, but with God." I agree with him. Though God is not our adversary, but our gracious Master and Friend, His will requires a surrender with which we struggle.

"Prayer is not getting man's will done in Heaven, but getting God's will done on earth," Richard Trench said.

ACTION POINT: Next time you pray, take a piece of paper and a pen and listen to what the Lord has to say to you. Open with a declaration to God, "Thy will be done," and write down adjustments that need to be made as you pray.

—*Rick Johnson*

OCTOBER 2
THE MOST IMPORTANT TIME
IN YOUR HOME

Scripture Reading—James 1:19
"Wherefore, my beloved brethren, let every man be swift to hear,
slow to speak, slow to wrath."

There is an old-fashioned statement that says, "Children ought to be seen, and not heard." Now I understand that in that statement there is an element of truth, for children do need to learn how to be quiet, particularly in the presence of people who are older than they are. Yet on the other hand, we must realize that communication is the key to building solid relationships, particularly in the home.

Our verse for today places a great deal of emphasis on listening. Interestingly enough, God created us with two ears and one mouth, which might lead us to conclude that we ought to listen twice as much as we speak. God's Word is making it very clear that when someone is speaking, someone needs to be listening. For that reason, we draw the conclusion that the most important time in our home is when someone else is speaking.

On one occasion, I was talking to a young man who was getting ready to graduate from high school and go on to Christian college. I asked him what he thought was the best thing his dad, a high profile pastor, had ever done for him. He simply said, "My Dad was willing to let me talk, and he listened." When people are willing to listen to what someone is saying, they let the speaker know that they care about him as a person, and they are concerned about what he is concerned about.

Many times, relationships between family members have suffered greatly because of poor communication. Many times anger has been generated in the home because of poor communication. Mom and Dad, as well as all the kids, must commit themselves to speaking well, but each one must also determine to listen well. Good listeners make home a happy place where every member is important, and knows it.

ACTION POINT: Have a sharing time with your family, allowing each member to talk about some of his or her favorite things—like food, activities, or possessions. See how much you really know about each other.

—Tom Palmer

OCTOBER 3
LOVE WITH NO RETURN

Scripture Reading—Matt. 5:46
"For if ye love them which love you, what reward have ye?"

Everyone wants to be loved and appreciated. It is human nature. But the Bible focuses on loving others rather than our receiving love. Jesus asks, "If ye love them which love you, what reward have ye?" If all you do is love those who will love you back, then what kind of reward would you get from God?

The reward is based on our being like the Lord Jesus Christ. He gives the example of the publicans, or tax collectors, who were hated by the Jews. "Do not even the publicans the same?" If all we do is love those who love us, it makes us like the publicans, not like Jesus. Luke 6:32 tells us, "For if ye love them which love you, what thank have ye? for sinners also love those that love them."

We must love those who do not love us if we desire to be like Jesus. In fact, Jesus commanded us, "Love your enemies" (Luke 6:27). Our enemies don't usually love us, and so the command becomes a real challenge.

Paul serves as an example in this area. He faced a rebellious church at Corinth and declares to them, "And I will gladly spend and be spent for you; though the more abundantly I love you, the less I be loved" (2 Cor. 12:15). For Paul, love unreturned did not stop him from loving or ministering to God's people.

Love is not just a mere emotion. Love is a spiritual choice filled with activity, like prayer, doing good, and offering help on behalf of others. The one who loves initiates love toward its object. God Himself is the great example. "Herein is love, not that we loved God, but that he loved us" (1 John 4:10).

Think about those around you that you just don't care much about. It might be a relative, someone at work or school, or someone in the neighborhood. What would it take for you to show love to that person? Perhaps through the witness of the Gospel, the love of God could be demonstrated through you.

SONG: Sing the hymn "When I Survey the Wondrous Cross."

—James Stallard

OCTOBER 4
PRAYING WITH AN OPEN HEART

Scripture Reading—1 Sam. 1:15
"I . . . have poured out my soul before the LORD."

One of the reasons you want to be alone and quiet before the Lord is so that your heart can be open and transparent before Him. One of the warnings Jesus gave concerning our prayers had to do with "vain repetitions" (Matt. 6:7, 8).

The phrase means "to stutter" or to say the same things over and over. We often apply this to public prayer, but it is possible to do this in our private prayers. Even in our quiet time, we can repeat words from memory rather than pouring out our hearts before the Lord.

We are encouraged to come to God "boldly" (Heb. 4:16). The word means "to be frank, blunt, and plain in one's speech." Again, the emphasis is on honesty and openness in our prayer life. God loves to hear the prayers of a new convert unadorned with the terms that we sometimes use without meaning them from our hearts.

A friend of mine had come to know the Lord, and at our mid-week church service during prayer time, I motioned for him to come and pray with me. I knew he had never prayed out loud and thought he would be more comfortable with someone he knew.

As we chatted a few minutes before praying, I told him he didn't have to pray if he didn't want to, but if he did to just express whatever was in his heart to the Lord. I finished praying, and I was very surprised when my friend began to pray. Humbly and sincerely he stammered out his opening words, the first time he had ever prayed publicly, "Lord, I'm not very good at this."

I remember sitting there and sensing the presence of God in a special way as my friend simply talked to the Lord. It reminded me of the simplicity of prayer, a child of God speaking with his Heavenly Father (Matt. 6:9).

ACTION POINT: How long has it been since you opened your heart and poured out your innermost feelings to the Lord?

—*Rick Johnson*

OCTOBER 5
COMFORT IN THE HOME

Scripture Reading—1 Thess. 4:18
"Comfort one another."

When I was ten years old, I was at bat in a baseball game with the bases loaded. Our team was only one run down, and it was the last inning. All eyes were on me. To be truthful, I didn't want to be the one at the plate, but I had no choice. I struck out. The game was over, and it was my fault.

After we shook hands with the other team, our team gathered behind our dugout for a brief meeting. My dad came up behind me as the coach was talking to us and put his hand on my shoulder. As we walked away from the crowd and to the car, I began to weep because of my failure.

My father consoled me and told me there were plenty of other chances for us to win and that the loss wasn't all on me. Through my sniffles I listened to his reasoning, but best of all, as we walked he kept his hand on my shoulder. That was more than 40 years ago, and I still remember it.

We all remember being comforted in times of great distress and brokenness. When my father comforted me, I felt close to him, and I knew that he cared about me.

We all live in a fallen world where pain, suffering, and disappointment are inevitable. Our families should be places of comfort and encouragement. When they are, we look forward to coming home at the end of the day. Comforting each other also produces tender lifetime memories.

The word "comfort" (1 Thess. 4:18) means "to encourage or exhort." It carries the idea of being nearby to offer words of help. It's easy to become accustomed to the fast pace and stress of life and to become so focused on our own needs that we forget the hurts of others—even our family.

Today, take the time to come alongside someone in your family that needs comfort. They will never forget it.

ACTION POINT: Tell about a time when you received comfort and how much it meant to you.

—*Rick Johnson*

OCTOBER 6
LEAVING SOMETHING GOOD BEHIND

Scripture Reading—Pro. 22:1
"A good name is rather to be chosen than great riches,
and loving favour rather than silver and gold."

I grew up in a simple family. We rarely ate out. We lived in a very small home, and we had no idea that others had more than we did. When my father went to Heaven several years ago, he didn't leave behind a lot of money, though he was a very hard worker.

He left us something better, a good name. It is not unusual for me to go into a restaurant and have people come tell me a story about my father and how he helped them. Many opportunities that I have received in my life have been the result of the kindness of my Dad to other people.

As I grow older the more I value the legacy my father left us—and the legacy I am leaving my children and grandchildren. I suppose it is because I am more aware of the brevity and frailty of life and how precious it is. Because now time seems to move more swiftly, it is more valuable.

Many years ago I was attending the funeral of the father of one of our church members. Because of the lack of room, I was standing in the back by the door, and the family walked right past me as they went to their seats in the front. As I watched the line of family members—children and grandchildren of this dear man—proceed to the front, I thought, "I am watching the legacy of the man that is in the casket." It made me consider my own mortality and what I am leaving behind in the lives of my own children.

May we all take seriously the kind of legacy that we are leaving behind! You aren't going to live forever, so face the issue and be strategic about it. Remember, hope is not a strategy.

ACTION POINT: Share three or four qualities with your children that you think God wants you to pass down to them.

—Rick Johnson

OCTOBER 7
THE LOUDEST PEOPLE AREN'T ALWAYS RIGHT

Scripture Reading—Luke 23:23
"And they were instant with loud voices, requiring that he might be crucified. And the voices of them and of the chief priests prevailed."

Loud people enjoy getting their own way. Have you ever seen a child screaming at the top of his lungs in a grocery store aisle because he is not getting his way? His mother refused to buy his favorite cereal and potato chips, so he decided to scream loudly and let the whole store know that he was mad. More times than not, the parent usually gives in to the pleas of the spoiled brat and does what he wants.

Pontius Pilate experienced a similar thing in Luke 23. After examining Jesus, he knew that the Lord was innocent of any wrongdoing. However, he also knew that the priests and the rulers hated Jesus and wanted Him dead. In the hopes of striking a compromise, Pilate told the people that he would have Jesus beaten and let him go. Each time he suggested that, the people cried with loud voices, "Crucify Him!" Sadly, verse 23 ends with, "And the voices of the chief priests prevailed." The loudest people won, and an innocent man was crucified on The Cross of Calvary.

In the world we live in today, there are many loud voices that are crying out. Some are crying that the pleasure found in this life is the most important thing. Others are calling out that fame is the ultimate goal. The world and the Devil cry to us like a spoiled brat. To whom should we listen?

The answer is simple. Listen to the Word of God. God's voice is not always the loudest, but it is the truest. Learn from Pilate—don't listen to the loudest voices or you will make a big mistake.

PONDER:
- Am I the kind of person who raises my voice so I can get my own way?
- How can I hear the voice of the Lord today?
- Do I listen to my friends more than I listen to God?
- What things in my life try to drown out the voice of God?

—*Alton Beal*

OCTOBER 8
THE PRAYER OF SURRENDER

Scripture Reading—Matt. 26:39
"O my Father, if it be possible, let this cup pass from me:
nevertheless not as I will, but as thou wilt."

It would be impossible to study famous prayers of the New Testament without studying the prayer that Jesus prayed in the Garden of Gethsemane. In His Sermon on the Mount, Jesus taught about asking for the will of God to be known by us here on earth as it is known by the Father in Heaven (Matt. 6:10). However, in Matthew 26, Jesus was not just teaching about prayer, but showing how it was to be done.

There are two things that are evident in this prayer. Firstly, Jesus experienced the abandonment of His own will. Secondly, He also experienced the acceptance of the Father's will. True surrender is a combination of both. Jesus knew well that the cup before Him was the cup of sin and suffering, and He asked that it might be removed. Yet when He said, "Not as I will," He was abandoning His own will. When He said, "But as thou wilt," He was accepting the Father's will. This was demonstrated again in verse 42 after the realization that the cup was not going to be removed. His response is so clear: "Thy will be done."

Many folks wrongly assume that when we pray that we are endeavoring to convince God to give us what we want. For this reason many prayers are very selfish at best. However, though a prayer of surrender may initially focus on our will, it ultimately must become focused on God's will. Prayer is not overcoming God's reluctance to give us what we want, but rather is laying hold of His willingness to give us what we need. The prayer that Jesus prayed did not spare Him from going to The Cross, but rather it prepared Him for it. Surrender in prayer allows us to experience all that God's will has for our lives.

DISCUSS: Discuss what the ultimate results would have been had Jesus chosen not to accept the will of God regarding His life and His death.

—Tom Palmer

OCTOBER 9
GOD KEEPS YOUR TEARS

Scripture Reading—Ps. 56:8
"Put thou my tears into thy bottle."

We only keep those things that are very valuable to us. Tears aren't valuable to us, but they are to God.

It was a custom in Bible times during funerals to take a very small bottle and catch the tears of loved ones as they wept from grief. They would seal the bottle and keep it as a reminder of their love for the person that had died. They called them "tear bottles."

When we weep God catches our tears and keeps them in His tear bottle (Ps. 56:8). What a precious truth, that our Heavenly Father cares enough not only to be aware of our tears, but also to catch them. Tears are bitter to us, but very precious to God. They are so precious that He keeps them—every drop.

One night our phone rang, and I answered. It was my uncle asking to speak to my father. By the tone of his voice, I could tell something was wrong. After I called my dad to the phone, I stayed and sat on the bed while they talked. It wasn't a long conversation. Dad hung up and began to cry as we sat together. He told me his oldest brother, my uncle, had died. Though I sat by my father and tried to comfort him as a young teenager, God was there catching the tears of my father.

I'm grateful God has a tear bottle in Heaven for all of the times I have been hurting, but what about the times I should have wept and didn't. It is possible to have been hurt so deeply in the past that you vow to never again be hurt like that again. So you build a wall around your heart and keep people at a distance. The result is a hardened heart that isn't soft enough to feel and weep.

Rather than compassion there is apathy. Rather than feeling there is numbness. How blessed we are to have a God that knows when we hurt— and catches our tears.

DISCUSS: Discuss why people lose their tenderness and ability to weep.

—*Rick Johnson*

OCTOBER 10
THE THEME FOR YOUR TEAM

Scripture Reading—1 Cor. 10:31
"Whether therefore ye eat, or drink,
or whatsoever ye do, do all to the glory of God."

Having played soccer in high school and college, I was glad when the opportunity came to be a high school soccer coach. I loved the thrill of teaching my team to play a game that I loved so much. But there was a greater blessing in teaching them useful life principles. One life principle came from the verse that is our text.

Before every game, my teams had a routine that we followed to get ready for the game. After the team completed warm-ups, I would bring my team into a huddle on the sideline. I would give them my final words of instruction, and then we would recite together our verse for today. After a short prayer, we would then go out onto the field to "clean somebody's clock" you might say, or to "have our clocks cleaned" as the case may have been. Either way, win or lose, we were determined to glorify our God both on and off the field.

Glorifying God means making God look very good. He is a good God, but He desires that His children represent Him well wherever they go. Many athletes, from beginner to pro, have a tendency to focus on making themselves look good. They are consumed with gaining credit, compliments, and applause for what they have accomplished. A Christian athlete must make sure that all the praise goes to his or her God. Then, and only then, will God get the glory in "whatsoever we do" both in the game and in life. You will know that God has been glorified in your life and by your team when the fans leave the stands talking about your God. When glorifying God is the theme of the team, everyone will know that we are playing for a great God.

DISCUSS: Discuss what can be done to glorify God when our team wins. How about when we lose?

—*Tom Palmer*

OCTOBER 11
LIVING WITH AN OPEN HAND

Scripture Reading—Pro. 11:24
"There is that scattereth, and yet increaseth."

One of the best ways to cultivate wisdom in your life is to practice daily reading from the book of Proverbs. There God uses a picture of a farmer sowing seed, which results in a harvest. There is an irony in sowing; you start with much and scatter it until it is gone, but you receive more than you scattered.

The word "scattereth" conveys the idea of dispersing all around. We sow seed in expectation of a future harvest. In the present I give what I have in order that I might have more in the future. We can also sow bad seed and reap a painful harvest (Pro. 6:14, 19; 16:28; 22:8; Gal. 6:8).

The harvest is always certain, but the nature of the harvest is dependent upon what we sow. The law of sowing and reaping is a universal law God has imprinted on the universe (Gal. 6:7). If you break it, it will break you. If you honor it, it will bless you. Failing to sow means that you will live off what you have in the present, but you will have a sparse future.

The word "withholdeth" (Pro. 11:24) means "to hold back and to keep." It has the idea of keeping a reserve. Being generous goes cross grain to our natural thinking (Isa. 55:8, 9). You have to choose to listen to your thoughts or God's thoughts.

The way to receiving and living a blessed life is through generous giving (Eccl. 11:1, 6; Luke 6:38; 2 Cor. 9:6, 8). Those that live with a closed hand do so to their detriment. Ultimately, you control the quality of your future. It all depends upon whether you have an open hand or a closed hand.

I can testify from my life, my family, and our ministry that God has been faithful to provide as I have lived open-handedly. He is true to His promise and will be to you.

ACTION POINT: As you go through your day, be aware of what kind of life you are living—open-handed and sowing or close-handed and stingy.

—Rick Johnson

OCTOBER 12
FIRST THINGS FIRST

Scripture Reading—Ps. 27:8
"When thou saidst, Seek ye my face; my heart said unto thee,
Thy face, LORD, will I seek."

During the 1840s, William Booth, the founder of the Salvation Army, was a young man working in a pawnshop. As a dedicated Christian, Booth desired to prepare himself for a life of service to Christ. On a scrap of paper he wrote the following resolutions:

"I do promise God that I will rise early every morning to have a few minutes—not less than five—in private prayer. I will endeavor to conduct myself as a humble, meek, and zealous follower of Jesus, and by serious witness and warning I will try to lead others to think of the needs of their immortal souls. I hereby vow to read no less than four chapters of God's Word every day. I will cultivate a spirit of self-denial and will yield myself a prisoner of love to the Redeemer of the world."

It was this kind of dedication to the Lord that made William Booth the great soldier of Jesus Christ that he was.

Those who will be faithful to the Lord must dedicate themselves to godly priorities. First things must come first! The main thing must be the main thing! Unfortunately most Christians are inclined to excuse themselves from godly priorities because they claim to be too busy. I have learned this in life—I will always have time for what is important in my life. Time with God must be a matter of priority. In the home, the early morning hours can be quite hectic as everyone is getting up and each one is going his or her way to school or work. However each family member needs some time to meet with the Lord. Putting Him first in the day, assures that the day will have the touch of God upon it.

ACTION POINT: Make a chart for the next seven days. Allow each family member to check off the days when they had time with the Lord in the morning. Assist younger children as needed. Set a goal for each family member to go "7 Straight."

—Tom Palmer

OCTOBER 13
GROW UP AND FEEL BAD!

Scripture Reading—Heb. 5:14

"But strong meat belongeth to them that are of full age, even those who by reason of use have their senses exercised to discern both good and evil."

You won't believe what my eight-month-old grandson did the other night. He was sitting on the kitchen counter in his infant seat, watching the preparations for supper. Sitting nearby on the counter was a large glass bowl that was going to be used to prepare an item for the meal. When no one was looking, Carter reached over with his little hand and pushed the glass bowl off the counter, shattering it in hundreds of pieces on the kitchen floor.

Do you think he felt bad about what had just happened? Not a chance! He just sat there with that "So what?" look on his face like most little kids do when they demolish something. He didn't cry! He didn't apologize! He didn't offer to help clean up the broken glass! He just sat there.

I suppose his response or lack thereof was to be expected. After all, little kids like Carter don't care that they did something wrong because they don't know that they did something wrong. It is not until they are old enough to understand the difference between right and wrong that they can be accountable for the things they do. When a person becomes sensitive to right and wrong, it is a sign that they are growing up. Maturity is evident when a person feels bad because they did wrong.

This is the point in our verse for today. When a person cannot discern between "good and evil," as the verse says, they have a lot of growing up to do. Carter did what he did without even knowing it was a problem, but as he gets older he will come to understand that it is a problem if you make it a habit to break glass bowls on the kitchen floor.

ACTION POINT: Let each person tell a story about a time when they did something wrong without knowing it was wrong. Have some good laughs, but then apply the lesson from Scripture and learn from it.

—Tom Palmer

OCTOBER 14
THE BURDEN OF WRONG CHOICES

Scripture Reading—Ps. 38:4
"For mine iniquities are gone over mine head:
as an heavy burden they are too heavy for me."

Burdens sometimes are the result of our own foolish choices. We experience grief and pain, and it is no one's fault but our own. Even after being forgiven by God, regret over wasted time and hurt done to others can cause discouragement. In this fallen world our family and friends don't always make wise choices, and they carry a heavy burden from that. This type of burden is all around us, and in us.

Sin is it's own punishment (Ps. 31:10; 40:12). Nothing we do can deal with the stain of guilt on our souls. Only the blood of Jesus Christ can cleanse, forgive, and remove this guilt.

When someone repents and comes back to the Lord, they need our encouragement and help. Even after they have been forgiven, Satan will accuse them that the sun will never shine again for them. Fellow believers need to minister to people carrying the burden of sinful choices.

This is not optional. We are to "restore" them (Gal. 6:1). This is a part of bearing their burden. We are to help them with their despair and the feeling that they can never be used of God again. Our goal in restoration isn't to a specific responsibility in the church, but to their walk with the Lord and their ability to be used by God in some way.

The burden from making wrong choices is heavy to the one that has committed them. Satan wants to destroy them, and we must help them carry this burden. While only God can restore a person (Ps. 23:3), He has given us the privilege of being involved in that process. So, it is our joy to point them to Jesus and love them as He does.

Who in your world is discouraged because of making wrong choices? Will you step up and help them carry this burden after they have repented and been broken over their sin? Be gracious, kind, and careful. One day it might be you who is in need of someone to help in the same situation.

DISCUSS: Discuss some people in the Bible that God restored and the people He used in their life to do so.

—Rick Johnson

OCTOBER 15
GOD GIVES SECOND CHANCES
Scripture Reading—Pro. 24:16
"For a just man falleth seven times, and riseth up again."

One failure does not mean that all opportunity for success is lost. Some fail more spectacularly than others, but failure is something everyone experiences. Satan would have you think that everything is over when you sin, but that isn't true.

Years ago I was counseling a very gifted friend that had made some foolish decisions that required him to leave the pastorate. As we talked he said, "I'm thirty years old, and the best years of my life are over." My heart hurt for him. He had more than half of his life to live yet but felt hopeless. He had done wrong, but God wasn't finished with him yet.

God is committed to seeing His purposes fulfilled in our lives, even when we are broken. Our Lord specializes in giving second chances. He delights in it. This truth is all throughout the Bible.

Peter sinned, denied the Lord, and felt that his ministry was over. He quit the ministry and went back to his business career as a fisherman. The Lord Jesus gave him another chance (John 21:15–17), and he was restored to fellowship. Peter became one of the leaders in the early church and wrote two books in the New Testament. He failed, but his usefulness was not over.

Jonah failed to obey the Lord when He first called him, but in His mercy, God gave him a second opportunity (Jonah 3:1). He was used greatly as an entire city came to repentance and salvation.

Fast forward to today. Most believers didn't get saved the first time they heard the gospel, even many that are reading these words. God gives us a second chance, though He is not obligated to do so. Most people don't surrender fully to God's will the first time God deals with them. God is patient with them.

May we not allow the enemy to keep us down when we have failed, and may we encourage others that have failed to go on with God!

ACTION POINT: Identify others in the Bible that failed and God used them.

—*Rick Johnson*

OCTOBER 16
NO FRUIT, NO ROOT

Scripture Reading—Luke 8:13
"They hear, receive the word with joy; and these have no root."

Some people make decisions for Christ that last "for a while," but then they eventually "fall away" (Luke 8:13). They have "no fruit to perfection" (Luke 8:14). Over time their enthusiasm for spiritual things dulls.

God speaks of one that bears "fruit with patience" (Luke 8:15). This person is characterized by a consistent, Christ-honoring life.

The problem with some people is not that they are backslidden, but they are not born again. The evidence of all genuine Christians is that they bear fruit to some degree. Many professing believers make promises they cannot keep (Hosea 6:4). One quality of genuine conversion is endurance, especially in God's Word (John 8:31).

Some have never understood God's grace and the Gospel. They believe in Christ, but add works to their faith. Ultimately, their problem is that they have "no root" (Luke 8:13) of Christ's presence. Fruit is the byproduct of the nature of its root. We reproduce after our nature, not our intentions.

Some have believed "in vain" (1 Cor. 15:2). This means they gave mental assent to the facts of the Gospel as an historical event, but did not believe it from the heart and solely rely upon Christ to save. Do you know the plan of salvation, but not know the "Man" of salvation, Christ Jesus?

My wife grew up in good, Bible-believing churches where salvation was plainly taught and preached. When she was nine years old, she prayed alone in her room that she wouldn't go to hell. Soon after that, she was baptized and joined the church she attended.

After we were married she would occasionally be troubled about her salvation, and we would talk late in the night about it. Just before her thirtieth birthday, she came to the realization that she was religious but had never been born again. Being a pastor's wife had nothing to do with her salvation.

In her words, "I didn't have a relationship with the Lord and wasn't growing." It is impossible to have growth where there is no life. Once she rested in God's grace alone for salvation, spiritual growth followed.

ACTION POINT: Discuss and memorize Romans 4:5.

—Rick Johnson

OCTOBER 17
WHAT STATE DO YOU LIVE IN?

Scripture Reading—Phil. 4:11
"I have learned, in whatsoever state I am, therewith to be content."

I live in the state of Pennsylvania. I have travelled in 47 states in the United States. However, I don't think Paul was referring to geographical locations in our verse for the day. Paul was actually speaking of the state of being in his life that involved the conditions in which he was living and writing.

It is important to understand that when Paul wrote these words, he was not on vacation or on a trip to a speaking engagement, but he was writing from a prison cell. Philippians is one of the prison letters written by Paul late in his life while he was awaiting execution. Knowing that background makes this statement even more significant. It would appear that things were not going well for Paul but were, in fact, going very poorly.

So what was it that allowed Paul to maintain such a great attitude in such horrible circumstances? I think it comes down to the fact that Paul recognized God had placed him where he was and would take good care of him while he was there. Vance Havner said, "A mark of deep spiritual maturity is to be able to enjoy the journey when God puts you on a detour." Though Paul had not planned on being on death row, he recognized that even there he had God.

In verse 12 he talks about abounding and being abased, about being full and being hungry, and about abounding and suffering need.

In other words, Paul understood that, in the best of times and the worst of times, he still had his God and that God was good enough for him. Paul was content with having less. No doubt his prison cell was filled with an atmosphere of praise to God for Who He was and for what He was to Paul the prisoner.

ACTION POINT: As a family, discuss one of the toughest times you have ever experienced. What did it mean to you to have God with you at that time?

—*Tom Palmer*

OCTOBER 18
PREFERRING OTHERS

Scripture Reading—Rom. 12:10
"In honour preferring one another."

The culprit of problems in the family is our sin nature. The dominant expression of this corrupt nature is selfishness. D.L. Moody said, "If I kicked the person that gave me the most trouble, I wouldn't be able to sit down for a week!"

Each conflict in a home can be traced to two root causes: pride and selfishness. These prevent us from enjoying close relationships. If one continually takes in a relationship, he will soon make the other weary. God desires that we learn how to give and serve, especially in our family.

The "one another" commands in the Bible help us to build intimacy in our homes. One of the simplest, but most powerful, "one another" commands is "in honour preferring one another" (Rom. 12:10).

The word "preferring" means to lead the way in showing deference, insisting that others be put first. This is not natural, as we prefer people to serve us. It has the idea of taking initiative in serving and being the first to meet a need without being asked to do so. This is something that every family member can practice every day.

When we prefer that others be served ahead of us, it brings us great joy, and the person we serve feels loved and cared for. My mother has a fireplace and a wood box just inside the door to hold the firewood. One night when I was visiting her, she said, "Whenever Jake [her grandson] comes in the house, he always checks the wood box and makes sure it has wood in it."

Jake is taking initiative to meet the needs of his grandmother. It makes her feel loved and brings him joy to do so. Why don't we do this more often? The selfishness of the old nature is not attracted to serving, and we are blind to the needs around us. Preferring others is a supernatural life. Only the Spirit of God can enable you to be a willing servant.

ACTION POINT: Look for ways to put others first today, and take action on what you see.

—*Rick Johnson*

OCTOBER 19
THE HOPE OF HEAVEN

Scripture Reading—John 14:2
"In my Father's house are many mansions."

There can be no doubt that we are living in fearful times. All around us are cares and burdens that bring anxious moments. God's people are not immune to these things. We will not find the answer to our fears from the world. It will take more than a smiley face sticker that says, "Don't worry, be happy" on it.

Thankfully, the Lord not only tells us that we don't have to be afraid, but He also tells us why. The night before He was crucified, Jesus comforted His disciples with these words: "Let not your heart be troubled: ye believe in God, believe also in me" (John 14:1). Then He added these words: "In my father's house are many mansions: if it were not so, I would have told you. I go to prepare a place for you."

This place is called Heaven, and it is the sure hope of every child of God. Heaven is not a figment of the imagination, nor is it a fairy tale. Heaven is not a myth, nor is it a state of mind. It is not a crutch for weak people to stand on, but a reality that all believers can depend upon.

For the Christian, it is the ultimate destination, which ends his journey through life. Jesus said, "I go to prepare a *place* for you." That means that there is a place being prepared for all those who have trusted Jesus as their Lord and Savior. J.C. Ryle, an English minister of the 1800s describes it this way:

"That Heaven is a 'prepared place for a prepared people' is a very cheering and animating thought. When we arrive there, we shall not be in a strange land. We shall find we were known and thought of before we appeared."

Have you ever thought about this place and your part in it? Have you ever dreamed about this place and thought about its reality? Have you ever imagined going to this place called heaven? How comforting to know Jesus is preparing such a special place with each of us in mind.

PRAYER: Thank You for saving me and preparing a place for me in Heaven.

—James Stallard

OCTOBER 20
How to Get Rid of the Uglies

Scripture Reading—Pro. 31:30
"Favor is deceitful, and beauty is vain."

Every year when he went to the doctor's office, a man would read *People Magazine's* annual issue of the "50 Most Beautiful People in the World." He discovered that for thirty years in a row his name or picture was nowhere to be found!

This fascination with beautiful people has plagued the human race throughout its history. But because we live in the age of images and pictures, this fascination has increased and intensified as never before. Men and women continue to long for beauty, while all the time criticizing the beautiful people they wish they were.

The Bible warns us "beauty is vain" (Pro. 31:30). Many people fancy themselves as beautiful in every respect, but they are spiritually ugly without realizing it. The Old Testament tells us that Vashti, Esther, Rachel, and Bathsheba as well as King Saul, David, and Absalom were "beautiful" outwardly. So, God is not against beautiful things or beautiful people. But, we should never be obsessed with the outward while ignoring the inward. This is the road to ugliness.

Isaiah says of Jesus, "There is no beauty that we should desire him" (Isa. 53:2). Jesus was not a handsome man. If He walked into any church today in bodily form, He would look average. What drew people to Him was spiritual.

Outward beauty can be deceiving "for man looketh on the outward appearance, but the LORD looketh on the heart" (1 Sam. 16:7). The Bible speaks of the beauty of a "meek and quiet spirit" (1 Pet. 3:1–5) and the beauty of a "modest spirit" (1 Tim. 2:9, 10). It tells us to worship Him in the "beauty of holiness" (Ps. 29:2) and that God will "beautify the meek with salvation" (Ps. 149:4).

How many people have lost their spiritual beauty because they went after physical beauty instead? All they ended up with was the "uglies"—a life of bitterness and hurt. How tragic when the beauty of the Lord is just one step away. The spiritual mirror of God's Word will always be more important than the physical mirrors we look into every morning.

SONG: Sing together "Something Beautiful" from the hymnbook.

—James Stallard

OCTOBER 21
WHY DO WE DO WHAT WE DO?

Scripture Reading—1 Sam. 17:46
"This day will the LORD deliver thee into mine hand . . . that all the earth may know that there is a God in Israel."

Passion can be defined as an inward desire and drive that results in action. When David marched out into the valley to challenge Goliath, he took something much greater than just his sling and the five smooth stones he had gathered. David had a passion.

It is interesting to note that when David first arrived in the Israelite camp, he had asked what would be done for the one who slew Goliath. The explanation was given: "That the man who killeth him, the king will enrich him with great riches, and will give him his daughter, and make his father's house free in Israel" (1 Sam. 17:25). Initially it may seem that David was motivated by a self-centered desire to get all he could get for himself, but as you look more closely, you find that David really wanted to give all he could give for his God.

Ministry that is motivated by a paycheck, popularity, or praise is going to be profitable only for the one who is attempting to serve. David had a very different motivation. David had a passion to let the whole world know that his God was the true God. In other words, he was determined to make sure that if God worked through his efforts, God would also get all the credit for it. There is a great thought that says, "There is no limit to what God can and will do as long as He gets all the glory."

So, when it comes to living for God and serving Him, why do you do what you do? What motivates you? Those who make a difference for God have a high standard of motivation. David did gain much fame for defeating Goliath, but he did not seek to make himself famous. Instead he made God look great, which is just the way God desires it to be.

ACTION POINT: Look up and read Psalm 115:1 and discuss what is said about the glory of God.

—*Tom Palmer*

OCTOBER 22
GOD CAN PROVIDE FINANCIAL RESOURCES

Scripture Reading—Matt. 7:11
*"Your Father which is in heaven [shall] give
good things to them that ask him."*

The Bible is filled with God's promises concerning provision for His children (Matt. 7:7–11). Provision for your needs is not based on your bank account, but is according to God's wealth (Phil. 4:19; Ps. 50:10–12).

What are your needs today? Have you brought them before the Lord and asked Him to help you? Though God is not obligated to rescue you out of a mess, He is a God of mercy and is true to His promises. Our source of provision is not the company for which we work, our family, or the government. Our source is the living, Almighty God.

"He that spared not his own Son, but delivered him up for us all, how shall he not with him also freely give us all things?" (Rom. 8:32). If He gave His own Son for you, will He not provide for your grocery or utility bill?

When I graduated from high school, I knew that God had called me into ministry and had directed me to a specific school for training. My family financially was in the lower middle class, and paying tuition for college was out of the question.

With less than two weeks before school started, I still needed money to attend. Then I heard a message about God's promise to provide for us. That night by faith I brought my need to the Lord. The next week an unexpected check came to my Mom, and we paid my first month of school. In fact, during the four years I attended that school, I always paid my bill on a monthly basis. It was the way God chose to provide for me.

God's power of provision is not limited by your circumstances or your need. The old chorus states, "Why worry when you can pray?" Some would sing it differently, "Why pray when you can worry?"

Present your needs to your Heavenly Father. He will hear you and care for you (Matt. 6:25–34).

ACTION POINT: Create a detailed and specific prayer list.

—Rick Johnson

OCTOBER 23
PRAYING WITHOUT WORDS

Scripture Reading—Rom. 8:26
"The Spirit itself maketh intercession for us
with groanings which cannot be uttered."

Sometimes our burden is so heavy that our prayers do not give birth to words. There have been times when I have only been able to say, "Oh, God!" and other times when there were no words at all. At night while others are sleeping, I lie in bed and weep and struggle to frame the feeling in my heart with words.

There have been times when it was because of confusion and other times when my heart was so broken I just looked to the face of my Father in Heaven. God hears these cries from my heart (Rom. 8:15).

When your heart is heavy, don't worry if the issue isn't clearly defined in your mind. The Spirit of God knows your burden and expresses it to the Heavenly Father (Rom. 8:26, 27). John Bunyan said, "Sometimes the best prayers don't have words, but groans."

This inability to articulate how we feel is because of a broken heart, pain that is too deep to match any words to the hurt. There is just numbness and sorrow. This happened to Hannah and God heard her plea even though it was without words (1 Sam. 1:13–18).

The most important time to pray is when you don't want to pray and you don't know how to pray. Don't walk away from the throne room of mercy and grace, but go there anyway even when your energy and desire is gone. Your Heavenly Father is listening and understanding though you seem to be making no progress.

Spurgeon said, "Groanings which cannot be uttered are often prayers which cannot be refused."

Pray when you don't feel well or don't sense God's presence. He is listening. If you don't pray you'll never find the will of God, and if you stop praying you'll never finish the will of God (Luke 18:1).

God is bigger than your vocabulary. Pray on anyway.

ACTION POINT: If you are hurting, keep on praying even though it seems futile. If you know people that are discouraged, let them know that you are praying for them.

—*Rick Johnson*

OCTOBER 24
HOW TO LOVE YOUR ENEMIES

Scripture Reading—Matt. 5:44
"But I say unto you, Love your enemies."

Payback! It is the natural response of most of us. It is what our society teaches us. When someone hurts you, you hurt him or her back. Harder, better. Payback! This is the way of the world.

When Jesus walked this earth, He established a different idea. He commanded us, "Love your enemies, bless them that curse you, do good to them that hate you, and pray for them which despitefully use you, and persecute you" (Matt. 5:44).

The disciples who first heard these instructions must have been stunned. They had grown up hating the Romans, the tax collectors, Samaritans, and Herod. They had been trained for payback. "Love our enemies? That's not our way!"

Two thousand years later, it is still not our way. Payback usually is still our first response. Love often does not get considered. Yet, the words of Christ ring true, and they hold the key to moving on after suffering pain and rejection at the hands of others. In fact, the key to having a great testimony for the Gospel is to "love our enemies." How do we obey this command?

The rest of the verse tells us how. First of all, we must "bless them that curse you." Instead of cursing back when someone speaks badly of us, we speak well of them. Jesus was our example when He prayed concerning those who had nailed Him to The Cross, "Father, forgive them; for they know not what they do" (Luke 23:34).

Second, we must "do good to them that hate you." We are to return evil with good. Suppose someone shows disgust for you, what do you do? Find a way to do good for them. Perhaps we could be alert to a genuine need that person has and quickly try to meet it.

Finally, pray for them. This means we should pray for blessing to come upon our enemy even though he has despitefully used us. Bless—do good—pray for our enemies. In order to love, this is what we must do. When we do, our testimony will shine greatly for the Lord. We might be surprised what God will do!

PONDER: He prays best who loves best.

—James Stallard

LOSING YOUR COOL

Scripture Reading—Num. 12:3
"Now the man Moses was very meek,
above all the men which were upon the face of the earth."

The Bible says that Moses, apart from the Lord Jesus Christ, was the greatest man of meekness ever to live. A meek person is one who does not claim his rights and does not strike back easily. We see this throughout the life of Moses.

• When Miriam rebelled against Moses' leadership and was smitten by God with leprosy, Moses pled for her healing (Num. 12:13).

• When the ten spies gave an evil report about the Promised Land and led the people to go against the will of God, the Lord was going to smite the people with pestilence and disinherit Israel, but Moses interceded for the people (Num. 14:11–19).

• After Korah's rebellion God was going to destroy Israel, but Moses prayed for the Lord not to wipe out His inheritance so the nations of the earth would not mock the God of Israel (Num. 16:1–22).

Though Moses faced the brunt of many rebellions against his leadership, he rarely ever retaliated, and his spirit usually remained meek. However, once, while in the wilderness, Moses "lost his cool." He smote the rock twice out of an angry spirit toward Israel and disobeyed the clear command of God (Num. 20:10, 11). Personal retaliation did not find a useful purpose in the life of Moses—in fact, he was judged for it. Neither will it be useful in our lives.

Ask yourself some questions. Do you easily retaliate or strike back at someone who you think has hurt you? Do you hold a grudge against any of your friends or family members? Do you view people who oppose you as enemies? Do you get mad when you do not get your way?

A meek person is not a weak person. God views a person of meekness as strong (Matt. 5:5) and as someone who is like Christ (Matt. 11:28–30). This kind of testimony causes others to think well of us. Ask yourself—how do others think of you—as someone who is meek or as someone who easily loses his or her cool?

DISCUSS: Discuss what causes each one in the family to "lose their cool."

—James Stallard

OCTOBER 26
70 X 7 = TRUE FORGIVENESS

Scripture Reading—Matt. 18:21, 22
"Then came Peter to him, and said, Lord, how oft shall my brother sin against me, and I forgive him? till seven times? Jesus saith unto him, I say not unto thee, Until seven times: but, Until seventy times seven."

Have you ever had someone do something to you that hurt you? Maybe it was something they said or did that hurt your feelings. Or maybe that person has done it over and over and over again. How many times do we have to forgive?

Peter came to Jesus and asked the question: "How many times do I have to forgive one who sins against me?" In Jesus' time, seven was a special number that meant complete or perfect. Peter probably thought that he was being really generous by offering forgiveness seven times. But what did Jesus say to Peter's question?

Jesus answered and said, "Not just seven times. But seventy times seven." When you do the math that comes to 490 times of forgiving someone. That is a lot of times! Jesus was trying to show Peter that we must forgive and forgive and forgive.

Have you figured out yet that your brother or sister or mom or dad or friend will sin against you—not just once, but LOTS of times? We get tired of granting forgiveness and loving people through their selfishness and sin, and sometimes we're ready to throw in the towel. Having relationships with people is hard work. We have to remember though that we're sinners, and sinners sin. If you live with a sinner (which we all do), then it's just a matter of time before they sin against you. The question is: Will you forgive?

But let's take it a step further. How often does God have to forgive you? Do you sin just a little or a lot? God will never cease to grant us forgiveness because He is faithful and just to forgive us and cleanse us from all unrighteousness. Have you gotten tired of loving and forgiving someone, maybe even someone who hasn't asked for forgiveness? Let's act like Jesus and forgive again.

ACTION POINT: Is there someone that you struggle to forgive? Do you have a hurt that you've kept in your heart towards someone? Ask God to help you forgive them.

—*Aaron Coffey*

OCTOBER 27
A DEFENSIVE SPIRIT

Scripture Reading—Gen. 3:12
"And the man said, The woman whom thou gavest to be with me, she gave me of the tree, and I did eat."

No one likes to admit to being wrong. A proud man absolutely refuses to do so. The three most difficult words for a proud person to say are, "I was wrong." When a person says these words and means them, he is on the road to humility. Also, it's a lot easier to say, "I'm sorry" than it is to say, "I was wrong."

When we are slow to admit to wrong, there is one alternative: to blame others. And when we blame others we become defensive. We want to protect our ego and make ourselves look better than we really are.

Remember when Adam and Eve sinned? Rather than confessing and admitting their wrongdoing to God, they began to shift blame away from themselves (Gen. 3:12, 13). *One of the first manifestations of sin in the universe was a defensive (vs. transparent) spirit and a refusal to admit to personal sin.* This gene to blame-shifting is in all of us.

Years ago a survey was taken among teenagers. They were asked the primary complaint they had against their father. The number one response was overwhelming: "My father will not admit when he is wrong."

When I first heard that, it hit me hard. At the time I didn't even have children, but *I knew it was true because it was difficult for me to admit that I was wrong.* I didn't want my children to have to say the same of me one day.

Someone once wrote, "When a person is always right, there is something wrong." When was the last time that you apologized to your family? This is an indicator that speaks to your pride or your humility.

"There are nine words that will transform your family, 'I am sorry; I was wrong; please forgive me.'" —Harold Vaughan

"Temper is what gets us into trouble; pride is what keeps us there." —Source Unknown

ACTION POINT: Today humble yourself and say, "I was wrong" when you are corrected, rather than defending yourself.

—Rick Johnson

EVERYTHING BUT GOD

Scripture Reading—Luke 18:23
"And when he heard this, he was very sorrowful: for he was very rich."

He was a man who came to the right Person with the right question. But he left with nothing but sadness. This man was a young man who seemed to have everything in his life. He had riches, he had power, and he had youth. He had it all. *He had everything but God!*

He asked the best question he could have asked when he asked Jesus, "Good Master, what shall I do to inherit eternal life?" (Luke 18:18). He seemed like a ready-made candidate for salvation, but the response of Jesus shocks us because He tells him to keep the law (v. 20).

But the Bible makes it plain that we are not saved by keeping the law, but by trusting in Jesus Christ. Paul declares, "Therefore we conclude that a man is justified by faith without the deeds of the law" (Rom. 3:28). Then why did Jesus answer this rich young ruler this way?

Jesus knew the man's heart. First, he did not understand that Jesus was the Messiah (v. 18). Second, he was deceived into thinking he had kept the law through his young life for he declared, "All these have I have kept from my youth up" (v. 21). He did not understand that he was a sinner who needed to be saved.

Do you know who Jesus really is? Have you come to the place where you have admitted that you are a sinner who deserves judgment and needs to be saved? Whenever we think we are good enough to be saved, the Lord will challenge us as he did the rich young ruler. Jesus told him to sell all that he had and follow Him, but he left sad "for he was very rich" (v. 23).

What area of your life do you think makes you acceptable to God? Only what Christ did for you on The Cross and through the empty tomb can save you (1 Cor. 15:1–4). You must trust Him alone in order to be saved. Otherwise you could end up with everything but God!

PONDER: What are you trusting in to take you to Heaven?

—James Stallard

OCTOBER 29
GET OFF MY CASE!

Scripture Reading—Rom. 13:1, 2
"The powers that be are ordained of God.
Whosoever therefore resisteth the power,
resisteth the ordinance of God."

Mike had a dream for his life. He wanted to fly helicopters in the military just as his father had done in Vietnam. Mike was also one of the best players on my soccer team and my senior co-captain. But he had a problem—he didn't like to be told what to do. That made it difficult for him to respond to me as his coach, and it was going to be even tougher for him to handle the military if he didn't learn an important lesson.

On one occasion, I called out to Mike during a soccer game. Immediately Mike turned to me and blurted out, "Aw, get off my case!" I didn't say a word, and I allowed the game to finish.

The next day I called Mike to my office. I informed Mike that we had a serious problem because of his reaction to me the day before. He quickly apologized, and I quickly forgave him. I then informed Mike that he would have to sit out the first half of the next game. It was not going to help my team to keep him off the field, but it was going to help Mike to keep him off the field. It was time for him to learn the important lesson of obedience that would make him a better man for the rest of his life.

Before long, our season finished, Mike graduated from our Christian school, and he headed off to boot camp. I well remember the day later that summer when the phone rang, and it was Mike. He was calling to tell me that he had been promoted to platoon leader over sixty men. Instantly, I said to myself, "He got it!"

You see, every door of opportunity swings on the hinges of obedience, and Mike had learned that lesson on the soccer field, before he ever went to the battlefield. Years later his dream was fulfilled in part because of a lesson learned playing soccer. Lessons learned in athletics do last for a lifetime.

DISCUSS: Discuss the reasons why Mike was able to fulfill his dream.

—Tom Palmer

OCTOBER 30
BURDEN OF TRIALS

Scripture Reading—Num. 21:4
"The soul of the people was much discouraged
because of the way."

I heard of a song with the line, "Life can take the living out of you." That is true; life can be very hard. Romans 8:23 describes the difficulty we face when it says, "Even we ourselves groan within ourselves, waiting for the adoption, to wit, the redemption of our body." Not only does the longing for future glory make us "groan" but also trials make this life heavy.

Years ago a friend of mine was speaking at a church that was considering him as pastor, and he asked my advice about what to preach. I said, "I think you ought to encourage them. They need to know that you know how to encourage them as a pastor."

I was scheduled for a surgery that was supposed to relieve severe pain that I had been having for several months. The procedure had been postponed once and rescheduled. Then I received a call that it had been delayed again. I was overwhelmed with discouragement.

One evening at dusk, I walked out to our backyard and lay down on our trampoline. I prayed and cried out to God for His mercy and help. I felt alone in my suffering. I felt like no one understood, but I didn't want to be perceived as a whiner. I heard someone approaching as twigs on the ground cracked. It was my mother. She had come to encourage me and did so with some words of wisdom and Scriptures from God's Word.

I will never forget that gesture of kindness. I was burdened with a heavy trial that had left me discouraged, and my mother helped to lift my load that night. Encouragers are priceless!

ACTION POINT: Who is the best encourager in your family? Who are others that have been an encouragement to you? Take the time to write to them and let them know in specific ways how they have encouraged you.

—Rick Johnson

OCTOBER 31
STOP! DROP! AND CRAWL!

Scripture Reading—Pro. 4:10
"Hear, O my son, and receive my sayings;
and the years of thy life shall be many."

The young son of a missionary was playing happily along the edge of the yard that surrounded the house on the mission compound. Dense forest surrounded the compound, and branches from the trees of the jungle hung over the place where the child was playing.

Suddenly the boy heard the loud and stern voice of his father. "Son, stop what you are doing, get down on the ground, and crawl to me immediately!" Though the youngster wanted to continue playing, he promptly obeyed the instructions Dad had given and on his hands and knees made his way toward his father. As his father helped him to his feet, the boy immediately asked, "Dad, why did you make me stop playing when I was having so much fun?" The father never spoke, but with a hand on his son's shoulder, turned the boy around to face the area where he had been playing. As the boy's eyes followed the direction that his dad's finger was pointing, he breathed a huge sigh of relief. A large, deadly snake was dangling from the branch above where the boy had been playing just a moment before. His immediate response was to throw his arms around his father as he exclaimed, "Thanks Dad, you saved my life!"

Obeying does not always seem like the easiest thing to do, but it is always the best thing to do. Children and adults alike often want to question why they must obey. Sometimes there is even a desire to question God rather than doing what He has said. Unquestioning obedience is imperative even when we do not totally understand why we have been asked to obey. If the missionary's son had questioned or debated or argued with his father's command, he would have suffered serious consequences for his disobedience. Obedience truly was, and always is, the best way to respond.

DISCUSS: Discuss this question: "Do you ever get to be old enough that you no longer have to obey anybody?"

—*Tom Palmer*

NOVEMBER 1
THE KING'S FRIEND

Scripture Reading—1 Kings 4:5
"Zabud . . . was . . . the king's friend."

Those that befriend their leaders have a special ministry. King Solomon had such a friend named Zabud, an officer in his court. God thought it important enough for us to take note that he was "the king's friend." Our Lord characterized our relationship with Him as one of friendship (John 15:15). Paul had some close friends in ministry (Acts 20:36–38).

We all have common temptations (1 Cor. 10:13), but leaders have unique struggles. Satan targets them in a special way (Acts 19:15). They have pressures that most never know about (as do their families) and are criticized more frequently than others.

A leader needs a friend, but it is a challenge to find one. It is similar to being wealthy and wondering if someone is really a friend or is being nice because he or she wants something from you (Pro. 14:20; 19:4).

Wherever you are in the hierarchy of leadership, you need a friend. All friends are very precious, but a friend of a leader is a very special relationship. The Bible is careful to note that King David, too, had a friend named Hushai (2 Sam. 15:37; 16:16; 1 Chron. 27:33). God gave these leaders friends to help them as they led the nation of Israel. Those that befriend their leaders have a special ministry of encouragement and refreshing their souls.

Late one night someone knocked at our door, and when I opened it there stood one of our men from church. As a pastor it is not usually something good when someone comes by at this hour. I invited him in, and he declined and stood there nervously shifting his feet. He was a rugged man with a rough background.

Finally, I said, "Are you alright? How can I help you?" He replied, "I'm fine, preacher. I was driving around tonight praying for you and just wanted to tell you that I love you and your family." That was it. I thanked him, and he left, but I still remember his kind gesture of friendship. It meant a lot to me.

ACTION POINT: Thank the Lord for your friends and offer your friendship to those in authority over you as you have opportunity.

—*Rick Johnson*

NOVEMBER 2
PRAYING FOR YOUR ENEMIES

Scripture Reading—Matt. 5:44
"Pray for them which despitefully use you."

Do you have enemies? When I was younger I heard preachers talk about our enemies, and I couldn't relate to what they said. As far as I knew, I didn't have any enemies.

Something happened as I began to serve the Lord and work with people. I made some enemies. I didn't mean to, and sometimes I didn't even know I had made enemies. Some I made because of decisions that they didn't agree with. Others, I suppose, just didn't like me, and I found that some had heard and believed things about me that were not true.

The dictionary says an enemy is "a person who hates, opposes, or fosters harmful designs against another; a hostile opponent." I am guessing that many of you that are reading this would have people that would fit into this category.

One of God's appointed ways to deal with those that have deeply hurt, oppose, and hate you is to pray for them (Matt. 5:44). This is not a natural response, but supernatural. We can only do this through Christ as He lives in us.

David practiced this in his prayer time (Ps. 35:13, 14). Perhaps this was why he was called a "man after God's own heart." He behaved toward his enemies as Christ did. Jesus didn't criticize His enemies. He prayed for them and committed His situation to His Father (Luke 23:34; 1 Pet. 2:23).

When you pray for an enemy, something happens to your heart. Rather than hating them and desiring vengeance, you develop compassion and concern for them. The only place you are going to get the desire and power to do this is in your prayer closet. There your attitude of anger will melt into one of love and concern, and your bitterness will turn to joy.

Don't talk about your enemies to others. Talk to God about your enemies.

ACTION POINT: Who opposes you, dislikes, or even hates you? When you are tempted to think evil or speak against them, pray for God to bless them.

—*Rick Johnson*

MOPING AROUND IN MEDIOCRITY

Scripture Reading—John 10:10
"I am come that they might have life,
and that they might have it more abundantly."

The dictionary will define or describe **mediocrity** as that which is commonplace, indifferent, ordinary, unimportant, insignificant, petty, trivial, or inferior. When we examine John 10:10, it is clear that believers should not live mediocre lives, but live the abundant life promised by the Lord.

Unfortunately, the word mediocre describes the lives of many Christians in modern times. Our great God has offered us eternal life through faith in Jesus Christ (John 3:16–18). But, He also offers us "abundant life" through Christ. To settle for anything less indicates that professing believers are satisfied with a mediocre life.

Ask yourself some important questions. Where is your spiritual ambition? Where is the desire to live a holy life? Where is the desire to be used by God? Where is the desire to advance the cause of Christ in a pagan world? If Christians settle for a mediocre life by rejecting the abundant life promised by Jesus, what chance does this world have of seeing Christ in His Church?

Could you ever imagine a great athlete accomplishing any great sports feat by sitting around in mediocrity? Michael Jordan, perhaps the greatest basketball player ever to play professionally, did not become so great by sitting around complaining or settling for anything less than his best. He practiced and found the discipline and the desire to be the greatest.

The same is true for the spiritual realm. While the abundant life is for the believer to use to glorify God and not ourselves, still we should attempt to do wondrous things for the cause of Christ. Dwight L. Moody sat under a balcony hearing a preacher declare that the world had not yet seen what God could do with a man fully surrendered to God. Moody said, "By the grace of God, I will be that man." William Carey went to India as a missionary and declared, "Attempt great things for God, expect great things from God." We should all try to follow the example of Moody and Carey.

MEMORIZE: Daniel 11:32b, "But the people that do know their God shall be strong, and do exploits."

—James Stallard

NOVEMBER 4
DEFINING OBEDIENCE

Scripture Reading—Deut. 27:10
"Thou shalt therefore obey the voice of the LORD thy God, and do his commandments and his statutes, which I command thee this day."

As a young person I learned this definition of obedience: **Obedience is doing exactly what I am told, when I am told to do it, with a right heart attitude**. Early in life I needed to learn that when God spoke to me, or my parents, teacher, or coach, I needed to respond obediently.

First of all, I needed to learn to do "exactly what I was told." If I was told to mow the entire yard, but I only mowed the front yard, leaving the back yard uncut, I was disobedient. I was disobedient because I had only done part of what I was told to do.

Next, I needed to learn to do what I was told to do "when I was told to do it." If on a Monday I was asked to rake the leaves in the yard, but I waited until Tuesday to do the raking, I was disobedient. I was disobedient because I had delayed my job until a later time.

Finally, I needed to learn that my obedience also involved "a right heart attitude." Even if I washed all the dishes right after supper just as I was told, but did it with a lousy attitude, I was disobedient. I was disobedient because I was miserable about what I was doing.

In the home, obedience involves both action and attitude. Partial obedience, postponed obedience, and pouting obedience are all disobedience. When the actions and attitudes of children are proper, they bring pleasure to their parents and ultimately to the Lord. Proper obedience makes home a happy place where each member is willing to do his or her part.

While teaching children the third part of this definition, I have often said that "a right heart attitude" means with a smile on my face. Smiling faces and happy places are a blessing that all can enjoy together.

ACTION POINT: Assist each child in making a sign with the obedience definition on it. Put the sign in a visible place in the child's room.

—*Tom Palmer*

NOVEMBER 5
THE PEACE OF JESUS

Scripture Reading—John 14:27
"My peace I give unto you."

The implication of this declaration of Jesus is startling. He promises a special peace that comes only through Him. Jesus calls it "my peace." This makes it different from various kinds of peace that are offered by the world.

There is a *false peace* that comes from the world and that does not come from Christ. It can be a peace based on thrills, pleasure, philosophies, or religion. But this peace will always be temporary and comes with a delusion.

Years ago when I was in seminary, my wife and I rented an apartment. The landlord was a secular psychologist whom we really liked. One day we had the opportunity to share the Gospel of Christ with him and his wife. We shared the change Christ had made in our own lives and the peace that had come into our hearts.

His response surprised us. He said, "I'm glad that your faith has worked for you and that you have peace. But other things work for other people, and they have peace too." In other words, people do have a sense of peace from Buddhism, Hinduism, Islam, Humanism, and other beliefs. Some even get some sense of peace or satisfaction from part of a particular Christian denomination or church, thinking they are part of the "true" Church.

Jesus did not deny there were other sources of peace, and He did not promise a worldly peace. He promised "my peace," which speaks of a particular and peculiar kind of peace that only comes from the Living God. It would be a genuine peace that would help His disciples to face any fear. After His resurrection, He commanded His followers to bring His kind of peace into the world (John 20:21).

The Lord knows us better than we know ourselves, and He knows the end of all things. He would not have given us this exhortation to peace if it were not possible. If you struggle with fears, pray it through and meditate upon His Word. Face your fears squarely and honestly. He will see you through.

SONG: Sing the hymn "Wonderful Peace."

—*James Stallard*

NOVEMBER 6
STANDING ALL ALONE

Scripture Reading—Dan. 1:8
"But Daniel purposed in his heart that he would not defile himself."

Imagine being uprooted from your home and carried away captive. You may never see your homeland, your friends, or even your family ever again. What an incredible burden to be under!

This kind of burden had fallen upon Daniel as one of the Jews taken to Babylon in 606 B.C. One might think that a person's faith would be shaken and that his resistance to other beliefs and customs would be broken down. While this may have been true for many of the Jews, it was not so for Daniel. He remained faithful to the God of Israel. Though he had to stand alone, he was never alone!

Led by his knowledge of God's Word, Daniel tried desperately to keep God's ways. He maintained his convictions at the outset of his captivity. When confronted with an attempt to compromise his faith and adapt to new gods, Daniel refused. The Scripture tells us that "Daniel purposed in his heart not to defile himself with the portion of the king's meat, nor with the wine which he drank: therefore he requested of the prince of the eunuchs that he might not defile himself" (Dan. 1:8).

It would be a good idea for each of us to study the book of Daniel and see the blessings upon a man who was able to stand alone for the Lord. There are so many pressures in our day as the culture is getting farther away from God. More and more people reject the Gospel of Christ and mock the truths of the Bible. In an atmosphere like this, Daniel succeeded in staying true to God, and so can we!

Whatever pressures we face from those around us, we can still serve God faithfully with our lives. We can purpose not to defile ourselves just as Daniel purposed in his day. We can purpose to stand fast in our faith (1 Cor. 16:13), and the Lord will bless and keep us from falling (Jude 3, 24).

ACTION POINT: As a family, identify the various ways that the culture around you is trying to turn you against God's Word and His ways.

—James Stallard

NOVEMBER 7
WHO IS KING IN YOUR KINGDOM?

Scripture Reading—Matt. 6:10
"Thy kingdom come."

The Bible clearly teaches that someday Jesus will rule all the kingdoms of the earth. For example, the Bible says:
- "JESUS. He shall be great, and shall be called the Son of the Highest: and the Lord God shall give unto him the throne of his father David . . . and of his kingdom there shall be no end" (Luke 1:31–33).
- "The kingdoms of this world are become the kingdoms of our Lord, and of his Christ, and he shall reign for ever and ever" (Rev. 11:15).

Someday, Jesus the Son of God will reign supremely as Lord of all the kingdoms of earth, a position He rightfully deserves because He is God.

However, in anticipation of that day, each believer must first acknowledge His right to rule in the kingdom of our lives. When a person prays, "Thy kingdom come," he is expressing his desire for Jesus to be Lord of every part of his life. Charles Spurgeon said, "Oh, that thou mayest reign over all hearts and lands! Men have thrown off their allegiance to our Father, God; and we pray with all our might that He may, by His almighty grace, subdue them to loyal obedience. We long for the coming of King Jesus; but meanwhile we cry to our Father, 'Thy Kingdom come.'"

When we speak of the Lordship of Jesus Christ, we are speaking of His place as ruler of our lives. That means that His will is the priority of life. That means that in every decision, He has the final say. To live any other way is to live in rebellion against the King, the One who is to be Lord of the life. As you pray you must once again yield total control of your life to the Lord. In so doing He becomes Lord of your life. With that said, you must accept the fact that if Jesus is not Lord of all, He will not be Lord at all!

ACTION POINT: According to Romans 14:9, what is the often overlooked reason for the death and resurrection of Jesus?

—Tom Palmer

NOVEMBER 8
COMFORT FROM FORGIVENESS
Scripture Reading—2 Cor. 2:7
"Forgive him, and comfort him."

It is impossible to encourage a person whom you resent and have bitter feelings toward. Most likely, you don't want them to be comforted at all. You may even want them to hurt in the same way that they hurt you.

The Corinthian church had a member that was involved in immorality, and they had to exercise discipline upon him (1 Cor. 5). The man repented, and Paul wrote to the church later and encouraged them to forgive the man (2 Cor. 2). One of the tests of the genuineness of their forgiveness was their willingness to comfort him.

When a person knows that they have hurt and disappointed you, and you choose not to hold it against them but instead treat them as if they had never hurt you, they will be encouraged. However, if you fail to forgive a repentant person, they will be devoured by their grief and sorrow over their past actions.

The people that hurt you the most will likely be the people closest to you and the ones you spend the most time with—your family. I believe the most important quality in a close family is forgiveness. God has designed us in such a way that we know we have been forgiven when those that we have hurt encourage us with their words.

Who is it in your family (or at church, work, or school) that you have a difficult time encouraging? Take note, it is probably the person that has hurt you the most, and you are holding resentment towards. Until you forgive them fully, you will never be able to be an encouragement or comfort to them. An unwillingness to encourage is a warning flag that you are bitter and angry with them.

It is not Christlike to be forgiven; it is Christlike to forgive. Jesus never sinned and never had to be forgiven, but as sinners we both need to be forgiven and to forgive.

ACTION POINT: Who is it in your life that you need to forgive? Do so and comfort them with your kind words.

—*Rick Johnson*

NOVEMBER 9
BENEFITS OF SILENCE

Scripture Reading—Pro. 21:23
"Whoso keepeth his mouth and his tongue keepeth his soul from troubles."

Sometimes what we say isn't sinful, but it is foolish, unnecessary, and hurtful. The result is that we end up trying to get ourselves out of a sticky situation. The more we speak, the more we find ourselves in trouble. Untimely, unnecessary, and angry words provoke a person to push back verbally and even physically (Pro. 18:6, 7).

Someone wisely said, "One minute of keeping your mouth shut is worth one hour of explanation."

Many years ago I was going through a very difficult situation in which I had to make a leadership decision on a prickly issue. I was a young pastor and sought advice from one of my mentors, Dr. Lee Roberson. I presented the matter and my options. He counseled me not to get involved because of the potential problems that would arise that weren't worth the intervention.

During that conversation he said something simple that I never forgot, "Rick, if you say it, you will be quoted on it." I still remember those words and how wise they were. It was so simple, but powerful. And his advice was right on target.

Our family members aren't likely to quote our inappropriate or angry words to other people; but worse, they will quote them in their hearts over and over—sometimes for the rest of their lives.

The more a person says, the greater the tendency to say something that is hurtful and damaging. Of course, this happens especially with the people we spend the most time with, our family and friends.

Someone wrote, "No one has to explain something he hasn't said." There have been too many occasions when I have had to go to my wife or children and "explain" my comments. Most of the time what was needed wasn't an explanation, but a heartfelt apology. It would have been far better for all of us if I never spoke those things in the first place.

ACTION POINT: Begin to read the book of Proverbs and write down all the verses that deal with how we use our words.

—Rick Johnson

NOVEMBER 10
GRATITUDE AND THE SPIRIT OF GOD

Scripture Reading—Acts 16:25
"And at midnight Paul and Silas prayed, and sang praises unto God."

Gratitude in adverse circumstances is not natural; it is a supernatural response. The only way to be grateful every day for everything is through the Spirit of God controlling us. There is a three-fold evidence of a person being Spirit-filled: joy, gratitude, and submission (Eph. 5:18–21).

A Spirit-filled man is a grateful man. God not only gives me the desire to be grateful, but the ability to do so in trials (Rom. 5:3; 2 Cor. 12:10; James 1:2).

One of the ways God brings us to a place of brokenness and utter dependence upon Him is through suffering and pain. We press on as long as we can in our own energy and strength, and at some point we are emptied of our ability, even to the point of despair.

In these low hours we cry out to God in struggle and need. Finally, we surrender our will, plans, and future to Him. Once we are emptied of our own selves and egos, He can fill us with His Spirit. One of the ways we can tell this has happened is when we change from complaining about our trial to being grateful for it as God is working in and through it to make us more like Christ.

I have a debilitating illness that requires me to have frequent IVs. I distinctly remember a day when the home health care nurse was setting up my IV infusion bag on the pole, and I was so discouraged from my illness. As the treatment began I looked at that bag, which I had come to despise and began to talk to God about it.

"God, I am going to make this IV bag my friend. It is helping me to have a better life. Help me to be grateful for it." Gratitude changed my attitude. When I surrendered my will to God, His Spirit changed me.

D.L. Moody said, "The only way to keep a broken vessel filled is to keep it under the faucet."

ACTION POINT: Surrender your will and trial to God.

—Rick Johnson

NOVEMBER 11
GRACE UNDER PRESSURE

Scripture Reading—Job 1:21
"The LORD gave, and the LORD hath taken away;
blessed be the name of the LORD"

You can tell what a person is really like when he or she is under pressure. When you squeeze a lemon, what's inside will always come out. In the same way, pressure tends to reveal what a person is really like on the inside.

The Bible tells us that there was a man of great character named Job (Job 1:1). Satan was allowed by God to attack his riches, his family, and his health, but was not allowed to kill him. It would be significant to note that some things are worse than death. During his ordeal Job humbled himself in a heap of ashes (2:8), experienced a broken heart (2:13), desired to meditate on God's truth (Job 23:12), committed himself to have a pure heart (31:11), focused on meeting and being reconciled to God (9:2, 20, 32, 33), endured accusations of those closest to him (32:1–3), and finally prayed for the very friends who accused him falsely (42:10).

Think on these things carefully. Job practiced what Jesus would later preach in the Sermon on the Mount in what are called the Beatitudes (Matt. 5:1–12). No wonder God bragged on him to Satan! Satan thought Job would curse God and die. However, Job remains a remarkable testimony of godly character under pressure.

The New Testament remembers this testimony and encourages all of us— "Behold, we count them happy which endure. Ye have heard of the patience of Job, and have seen the end of the Lord; that the Lord is very pitiful, and of tender mercy" (James 5:11). To be happy is to be blessed by God. To have grace under pressure reveals what we have on the inside and will show others what kind of character we have.

PONDER: How do each of the members of your family deal with pressure? Could each one be described as showing "grace under pressure"? How did you handle the last incident of pressure in your life? How does your experience compare to the experience of Job?

—*James Stallard*

NOVEMBER 12
THE PROVISION PRINCIPLE

Scripture Reading—Matt. 2:11
"When they had opened their treasures, they presented unto him gifts; gold, and frankincense and myrrh."

Have you ever wondered what happened to the gifts that the wise men gave to Jesus? Shortly after, Joseph and Mary were fleeing Herod's wrath, traveling towards Egypt (Matt. 2:13). Perhaps they left the gifts behind in their haste to escape? Perhaps they took them with them?

The trip they took from Nazareth to Bethlehem (80 miles), where Jesus was born, would have paled in comparison with the trip to Egypt (350 miles). The expense for such a trip would have been enormous. How would they pay for it?

Is it possible the gifts paid for the journey? The Bible doesn't say specifically, but it does seem likely, considering their value. What we are left with is the intriguing idea that God, long before Herod was a threat to Jesus, was meeting a future need known only to Himself. God knew that Joseph and Mary would need those valuable gifts to finance their way to Egypt and preserve the life of Christ.

Here we see the wonderful mind of God at work. He is never surprised by any circumstance. He never has a problem. He plans things in advance so that when His servants obey Him and move at His bidding, they find their needs met along the way. It is our job to obey when He beckons. It is His job to meet the needs that will arise. Joseph and Mary did not know the wise men were coming their way with valuable gifts they would soon need. But God knew. And He knows your situation.

Hudson Taylor said, "God's work done in God's way will never lack God's supply." Philippians 4:19 says, "God shall supply all your need according to his riches in glory." God's riches are available to those who are committed to trust and follow Him.

Choose to follow God's way even if it doesn't seem to make sense and then watch Him meet your needs and strengthen your faith.

PONDER: Your God has your needs in mind before they are a need to you.

—Paul Miller

317

NOVEMBER 13
MAY THE WILL OF THE LORD BE DONE

Scripture Reading—Matt. 6:10
"Thy will be done in earth, as it is in heaven."

There are those who wrongly teach that prayer is a "name it and claim it" endeavor. They carelessly present the idea that you must simply "ask for it and you got it." This causes people to become rather foolish in their approach to God and in their requests that are offered in prayer.

In reality, Scripture does say, "Ask, and it shall be given you" (Matt. 7:7), and, "Let your requests be made known unto God" (Phil. 4:6). The key however is not just found in asking, but in having the correct attitude when we ask.

There is a sense in which, when we pray, we are asking for our own will to be done on earth. When we ask for a sick person to be healed or a problem to be solved or a need to be met, we are asking for our will to be done on earth. Our request must then be followed up by a request for God's will, as it is known by God in Heaven, to be done here on earth.

On several occasions I have prayed for the healing of family members or friends who were suffering with terminal illnesses like cancer. I truly asked God to remove the disease from the body of the person for whom I was praying. I then asked God for His will to be done in the life of the person that I was praying for. In several cases, God took the cancer away from the body of the one I prayed for. In other cases God chose to take the body of the person away from the cancer as He took them to Heaven. In either case the will of God was done, and it was fine with me. Through these experiences I also learned how to yield my will and to accept God's will, which is exactly what Jesus was teaching about prayer.

ACTION POINT: Ask God to teach your family that what He wants is always more important than what we want.

—*Tom Palmer*

NOVEMBER 14
HOW TO STUDY THE BIBLE

Scripture Reading—2 Tim. 2:15
"Study to show thyself approved unto God."

Some people like to study, and some people don't. Whenever there is a test to take in a high school or a college classroom, there will always be those who enjoy the preparation. They will enjoy taking the test, viewing it as a challenge to be conquered. The rest of the class does not view it as a challenge, but rather as a task to be endured.

When it comes to God's Word, we are commanded by God to study. In fact we are to be eager to tackle the task of trying to understand what the Bible teaches. Our text tells us, "Study to show thyself approved unto God, a workman that needeth not to be ashamed, rightly dividing the word of truth."

"Study" is a verb and refers to action. People must study for themselves and try to practice what they learn. The student of the Word is called a "workman" who studies in such a way that God is pleased with the result and gives His approval.

The student must also "rightly divide the word of truth," which means he or she must study in the right way. We must take the Bible as it is in its normal, plain sense, rather than twisting it to say what we wish it to say. Such a person will not be ashamed before God.

A pastor tried to help a man in his church who was struggling with some problems in his life. He gave him the task of memorizing Bible verses. The man came back a week later and made a confession. He said he was a 32nd degree Mason who had memorized all the false teachings of his group. But, he had trouble memorizing the simplest of Bible verses.

The truth is that most people have no trouble studying what they are interested in. People know their favorite sports team's stats, the latest news from the stock market, or the latest technology they possess. That's because they are interested in those things.

How interested are you when it comes to God's truth? People who study the Word do so because they really want to.

MEMORIZE: 2 Timothy 3:16, 17.

—James Stallard

NOVEMBER 15
LEAVE THE TWEETY BIRDS ALONE

Scripture Reading—Luke 8:17
"For nothing is secret, that shall not be made manifest;
neither any thing hid, that shall not be known and come abroad."

I suppose I was in about the fourth grade when my father allowed me to take a walk in the woods with a BB gun for the first time. I certainly was enjoying my hike when I came upon a small songbird sitting on a low branch not far in front of me. Just as I had been taught, I raised the BB gun, took careful aim, and squeezed the trigger. Much to my amazement the little bird turned upside down on the branch and then dropped to the ground below the tree branch. A short time later I was rehearsing the story to my father when he told me that there would be no more shooting at tweety birds—or any other good bird for that matter.

Several days later I was trooping through the woods, and this time I came upon woody woodpecker. Woody was on the side of a tree, banging away with his beak. He certainly did not know I was there as I again took aim and squeezed the trigger. Much to my amazement, just as the first time, the little bird tumbled down to the ground beside the tree. This time, however, things were different. My first reaction was to look around to see if anybody was watching. Then I ran to the tree, dropped to my knees, dug a hole in the dirt with my hands, and quickly buried Woody.

I never intended to tell anyone what had happened, and really had planned to keep it a secret. Fortunately for me, it didn't work that way. Several days later I had to go to my father and tell the whole story. Yes, I lost the BB gun for a while, but I also learned a good lesson about God. My father knew what happened because I told him, but God knew because He saw it happen. There are no secrets with God for He always sees and knows.

ACTION POINT: Make a sign with Proverbs 15:3 on it and display it in your home.

—Tom Palmer

NOVEMBER 16
Making Melody in the Morning

Scripture Reading—Ps. 57:7, 8
"I will sing and give praise . . . I myself will awake early."

What do you think of when you first wake up in the morning? Many times our minds are clouded and cluttered within the first moments of waking as we think of the events of the upcoming day. It is sad, but thinking about a spelling test, a dentist appointment, or a long drive to work can quickly depress us and throw a cloud over the day. That is where good and godly music can help.

In my life, I have found that the right kind of music can provide a real attitude adjustment. A song of praise can quickly change my outlook by simply reminding me of my God. In this way, music can become a morning blessing as it prepares attitudes for the day ahead.

If you are blessed with a Christian radio station that plays God-honoring music, why not have it playing as family members gather for breakfast. Another alternative is to have a good CD playing on the stereo in your bedroom or living room to help fill the atmosphere with praise to God. At times I have even kept a songbook with my devotional materials and have chosen a song to sing as part of my time with the Lord. A chorus sung by the family at the breakfast table can also be a refreshing blessing.

The human mind is an amazing creation of God. It has the unique ability to retain what is seen and heard for extended periods of time. Music is no exception. Many times I have heard a song that blessed my heart. Hours later the song was still being replayed in my mind and was still blessing my heart. Music is one of the ways that God keeps Himself foremost in our thought. Whether it is a chorus sung by a four-year-old or a worshipful anthem played by an orchestra, don't miss the blessing of making melody in the morning.

ACTION POINT: Pick a family "Song of the Week" and sing it this week as you come together as a family each morning.

—Tom Palmer

321

NOVEMBER 17
I DIDN'T DO IT

Scripture Reading—Jer. 16:17
*"For mine eyes are upon all their ways: they are not hid from my face,
neither is their iniquity hid from mine eyes."*

I still remember the *Curious George* books that I read as a child. George was the little monkey who belonged to the tall man in the yellow hat. George was described as "curious" because he was always getting into trouble for touching things that he wasn't supposed to or going places where he shouldn't. There is a real sense in which many children, beginning during toddler years, become like George. They often seem to be monkeying around just as George always did.

The one thing, however, that makes children different from animals is that you can ask them if they did wrong, and they can tell you, if they choose to do so. Unfortunately, kids often struggle to tell the truth. An item gets broken, a drink gets spilled, a tool is missing—and of course nobody seems to know how it happened. A toddler can be as guilty as guilty can be, but when asked if he or she is guilty, they can keep a straight face and proclaim, "Nope!" Sadly, that is humanity at its worst!

In the Garden of Eden, Adam and Eve chose to disobey, take of the forbidden fruit, and sin (Gen. 3:6). In the verses that follow, cover their sin (v. 7), hide their sin (v. 8), and blame others for their sin (v. 12, 13). Of course, none of their attempts worked because God knew exactly what had taken place. Eventually they, along with the rest of the human race, were forced to live with the consequences of sin even until this day (Rom. 5:12).

When we sin and God's Spirit confronts and convicts, it is best to simply agree with God. That's what confession is—an acknowledgment that God knows our sin and that we accept responsibility. It is foolish to act as if an all-knowing God doesn't really know.

ACTION POINT: What does 1 John 1:8, 10 say about the person who refuses to agree with God about his sin?

—*Tom Palmer*

NOVEMBER 18
CONSEQUENCES OF FAILING GRACE

Scripture Reading—Heb. 12:15
"Looking diligently lest any man fail of the grace of God; lest any root of bitterness springing up trouble you, and thereby many be defiled."

Bitterness comes anytime we respond to the wrongs of others or the difficulties of life with unbelief in God's ability or willingness to work them together for good. Have you ever said with clenched teeth, "That's terrible. Why did that person have to do that to me?" When we respond with a spirit of unbelief, we find no help from Heaven—no grace, if you will.

But that is only the beginning of the problem. After bitterness springs up, you will find yourself troubled. Bitter people are troubled people. You may mask it with humor, withdrawal, or some other defense mechanism, but in your heart, you know you are not happy. A few years ago, when I was involved in a counseling situation, an unsaved man burst out, "My life stinks!" That is the expression of someone who is troubled.

Next, bitterness will eventually defile others. I tell teens, "Bitter teens become angry parents. Angry parents produce bitter teens. Bitter teens become angry parents. Angry parents produce bitter teens." I think you get the idea.

Years ago a young lady told me after chapel, "Preacher, I'm adopted. My mother who adopted me has said to me on several occasions, 'I wish I had never adopted you.'" I was stunned with the unbelievable difficulty of that situation and with her cavalier demeanor, which I am sure was a defense mechanism. I remember telling her she had two options. She could get bitter and one day she would do the same things to her kids, or she could access the grace of God and stop the mess!

Someone has said, "Hurting people, hurt people!" How true that is. Bitterness causes people to be hypocrites. They are upset someone has wronged them, and they are wronging others. Their wrongs cause others to be tempted to get bitter as well. Bitterness defiles many. Only grace can free those who are provoked from becoming bitter as well.

ACTION POINT: Search your life for bitterness and confess it to the Lord.

—Jim Van Geldren

NOVEMBER 19
DOES JESUS BELIEVE IN YOU?
Scripture Reading—John 2:24
"But Jesus did not commit himself unto them, because he knew all men."

One question a Christian could ask a lost person could be, "Do you believe in Jesus?" It is a normal question that would seem appropriate to ask. However, the question might need to be different.

The Bible says that when Jesus was in Jerusalem at the Passover that many believed in Him because of the miracles they saw Him do (John 2:23). We would say, "Wonderful!" However, the following verse gives a warning. It says that "Jesus did not commit himself unto them, because he knew all men." The word "commit" means the same thing as "believe."

So, it could be said this way, "Many believed in him for the miracles that they saw him do, but Jesus did not believe in them for he knew all men." Maybe the question that ought to be asked is "Does Jesus believe in you?" It seems the reason why people come to Jesus is very important. We should each ask ourselves the question, "Why do we want Jesus in our lives?"

An honest answer to that question often will be one of the following: Jesus will resolve a problem for me; Jesus will heal me of my sickness; Jesus will give me food for my stomach; Jesus will pay all my bills.

Yes, Jesus often meets the needs of His followers, but why should a person come to Christ?

The motive of the heart needs to be sincere and not selfish. A person comes to God through Christ because he knows he is a sinner who deserves judgment (Rom. 3:23; 6:23). Christ, through His death on The Cross and being raised from the dead, provides salvation for those who will believe (Rom. 1:16).

Jesus understood that those who began to "believe in him" did so out of wrong motives because of seeing the miracles He performed. So, Jesus did not commit Himself to them, or we could say, "He would not believe in them" because He knew their heart. He knows your heart, too. Does Jesus believe in you?

PRAYER: Lord, help me to be sincere in my faith in You and to lead others to have a sincere faith.

—James Stallard

WHERE ISN'T GOD?

Scripture Reading—Ps. 139:7
"Whither shall I go from thy spirit?
Or whither shall I flee from thy presence?"

Omnipresence is a word that can only be used when speaking of God. It simply means to be everywhere at once. In contrast, a human being can only be in one place at a time. That is why we must ask the question, "Where isn't God?" Or in other words, is there any place where God is not?

Psalm 139 gives us a clear answer to that question. In verse 8 David speaks of going to the highest and the lowest points in the universe and finding that God is there. In verses 9 and 10, he speaks of dwelling "in the uttermost parts of the sea," and again God is there. In verses 11 and 12, he speaks of darkness not hiding anything from God because "the darkness and the light are both alike to thee." In summary David is making the point that the distances, the depths, and the darkness of this world have no limiting effect on where God is or what God knows.

It certainly is not hard to understand why David began this psalm with the words, "O LORD, thou hast searched me, and known me." In reality David understood that God knew more about him than he knew about himself. Typically human beings have things they would prefer to keep private and secret about the way they live. This is particularly true when it comes to areas of secret sin. On the other hand, when you understand omniscience, you will want to say like David, "Thou hast set our iniquities before thee, our secret sins in the light of thy countenance" (Ps. 90:8). As a result, the omniscience of God reminds us that we must never try to hide our sins from God.

ACTION POINT: Have each member of the family tell about the best hiding place they ever chose while playing "Hide and Seek." Let each one tell if they got "found." Then discuss the foolishness of playing "Hide and Seek" with God.

—Tom Palmer

NOVEMBER 21
DO YOU FEEL PARDONED?

Scripture Reading—1 John 5:13
*"These things have I written . . . that ye may
know that ye have eternal life."*

A prisoner sits alone in a stark, bare cell. He wrings his hands and stares through glazed eyes at the clock on the wall. It is only minutes now until the guards come for him. He has gone over and over in his mind what is about to happen. A slow, quiet walk down a silent hallway to the mournful farewells from his fellow prisoners, the rattle of the chains around his wrists and ankles, even the muffled tones of the chaplain trying to comfort him with some Scriptures. Then the awful electric chair!

Wait! What's that? He hears footsteps in the hallway approaching his cell. "Wait! It's not time! I have five more minutes!" A key is inserted into the lock and the door swings open. A piece of crisp, official-looking paper is thrust into his trembling hand. The combination of sweat and tears make it difficult to focus, but he begins reading. And then one word stands out from all the rest, "P-A-R-D-O-N-E-D," followed by the Governor's signature. Pardoned! He has received a pardon from the Governor. His life is spared!

Quickly now, ask him how he feels. He's numb with disbelief and still grappling with the reality of it all. Ask him if he feels pardoned. He shakes his head no. How do you know you're pardoned then? He slowly raises the paper and points to it. He has it in writing.

Many people often depend on their feelings. They pray if they feel like it. They read the Bible if it gives them some feeling. They look for emotions at church. They witness to the lost if it feels worthwhile. And too often they base their very salvation on feelings.

Feelings make the best servant, but the worst master. While God wants you to enjoy happiness, joy, peace, and a myriad of other good feelings, they are not the engine that drives the train. They should be the caboose.

The next time you wonder if you are truly saved because of fickle feelings, reach for the letter of pardon called the Bible. You can know you're saved because you have it in writing.

PRAYER: Thank You Lord for Your wonderful Word of pardon!

—*Jim Binney*

NOVEMBER 22
HOW TO BE ENCOURAGED

Scripture Reading—1 Sam. 30:6
"But David encouraged himself in the LORD his God."

In his wonderful book *Does God Still Guide?* J. Sidlow Baxter tells the story of the lone survivor of a shipwreck who washed up on a small uninhabited island. In his terrible situation, he cried out to God to save him and would look to the horizon each day to see any ship that might be passing by. He built a rough hut where he stored all his belongings salvaged from the wreck. One day while looking for food, he came back to find his hut engulfed in flames and smoke. This wasn't what he had in mind when he prayed to God. But early the next day a ship arrived on the island. When the shipwrecked man asked the captain of the ship what had caused him to come, he replied, "We saw your smoke signal!"

This man's horror had actually been his salvation. We often respond to immediate trials and burdens in a negative way. Sometimes it is hard to see how anything good could come out of them. Yet, we must remember that God's ways are not our ways (Isa. 55:8, 9).

David and his men had battled the Philistines only to come home to Ziklag to find the Amalekites had burned it to the ground and had taken captive their families. The men wept and then blamed David and were going to stone him. This evil was not David's fault, but he did what you and I should do whenever we come to a severe time of discouragement. He sought the Lord, no doubt, in prayer through the Word of God.

This is where we should turn whenever we are faced with strong discouragements. Through faith in the God who hears prayer, we receive peace (Phil. 4:6, 7), and through God's Word, we find that which will comfort us in our need (Ps. 119:71).

Whatever we face, we should be assured that the Lord will use the comfort and encouragement we receive as a way to teach others the same comfort and encouragement.

ACTION POINT: Divide the various Psalms among the family members and have each person take some time to find verses of comfort to share later.

—James Stallard

HOW TO HAVE A
HEART-TO-HEART TALK

Scripture Reading—Matt. 5:7
"Blessed are the merciful."

Four children are standing on a street corner when a dog walks up to them. It's a friendly dog, just wanting some love and attention, so three of the children reach out and start petting it. But the fourth—a little girl—backs away with a look of sheer terror on her face. "What's wrong with you?" they ask. To them her reaction is strange. Why wouldn't she want to pet the dog?

What they don't know is that two months earlier she had been bitten by a stray dog and now is fearful of dogs, and unless the three children make an effort to understand this fear, a gap will grow in their relationship. The little girl's fear is what is called a "perception." If the three children make an effort to understand their friend, they will show her what is called "mercy."

Mercy is crawling inside someone else's skin to feel what they feel (perception) and minister with understanding. This is what Jesus did when He was "made like unto His brethren," (Heb. 2:17) so He could minister to them. Jesus crawled inside human skin so he could feel what we feel, so that He could comfort us.

A "generation gap" has developed in many families today because the kids are so different from their parents, and they feel that their parents don't understand. At the same time the parents feel the children have no idea what they are feeling. The result is that conversations are limited to surface things and not true feelings.

Having a good talk with someone you love has more to do with their view than your own. What are they feeling, thinking, hearing while you are talking? The common goal of talking is to get a point across, but the biblical way of doing so is to understand the view of the listener and to reach out to him or her.

ACTION POINT: Try this experiment. Ask each other about your greatest joys, hardest experiences, biggest challenges, deepest needs, most memorable experiences, or best victories. Then ask why each person feels that way and make every effort to understand. That is mercy, and that is having a heart-to-heart talk.

—Jim Binney

NOVEMBER 24
THE BOUNDARY OF CHARACTER

Scripture Reading—2 Tim. 1:5
"When I call to remembrance the unfeigned faith that is in thee,
which dwelt first in thy grandmother Lois, and thy mother Eunice;
and I am persuaded that in thee also."

One of Paul's best protégé's was Timothy. He was an outstanding young leader. Paul spent more time with him and wrote to him more than any other of his young pastors. Paul had a profound influence in his life, but it wasn't the greatest—that belonged to Timothy's mother and grandmother (2 Tim. 1:5).

They established boundaries for Timothy's life by the way they lived. More important than the content of training is the character of the one doing the training. In a sense, the messenger is the message (2 Cor. 3:2).

Early in my life I learned that there were certain words and behaviors that were unacceptable in our home. I never saw my parents smoke, drink, or curse. I learned that the Bible was a very special book by seeing the respect Mom and Dad had for it. I learned that there were certain things that we would do no matter what others did. Sunday was a very special day set aside for God, and we went to church.

When I was growing up, television programming was black and white. One of the first shows to be in color was Disney's Wonderful World of Color. My grandparents had a color television, and I was excited about it. The problem was that it was on Sunday night during church.

I can remember trying to work up a tummy ache sometimes to stay home with my grandfather to watch the show. Mom and Dad saw through it though, and I went to church with them.

When I realized the landmark wasn't moving, I made peace with it and enjoyed life. The boundary was established not so much by what was said, but by what was modeled. There was an alignment in their words and actions.

ACTION POINT: Discuss what would have happened to Timothy if his mother and grandmother were not sincere and faithful believers, but talked one way and lived another?

—*Rick Johnson*

NOVEMBER 25
KEEPING UP WITH THE JONESES

Scripture Reading—Ps. 106:1
"Praise ye the LORD, O give thanks unto the LORD, for he is good"

There are very few things that lead to a spirit of discontentment more than when we compare ourselves to others. The simple truth is that most of us already have more than we need, and it is better than we will ever deserve. Unfortunately we have a tendency to forget that when we are looking over the fence or across the street at the things that someone else has that we don't have.

This is how it happens. Our family goes to spend an evening with the Jones family who attend our church. The Jones live in a new subdivision while our family lives on a side street in the old part of town. The Jones' house has 3,500 square feet of space while ours has only 2,100. The Jones have a paved driveway, but we only have a gravel driveway, which gets real muddy when it rains. The Jones get to sit and grill out on their deck, but we don't even have a deck on our house. The Jones have an inground pool with a sliding board, but the only sliding board we have is falling off the rusty old swing set. The list goes on and on, and the drive home after our visit gets more and more depressing the farther we go. Comparisons have caused us to forget what we really do have and have caused us to want more of what the Jones have.

Here is a great reminder for the family who has just made a visit to the Jones family. Whenever you think of someone who has much more than you do, you should remember that there are also ten people who have much less than you do. Contented people are always focused on what they do have—not what they do not have. Trying to keep up with the Joneses will only make you ungrateful, miserable, and discontent.

ACTION POINT: What are some of the things that your family has that many families do not have? Talk about God's goodness to you.

—*Tom Palmer*

NOVEMBER 26
BOASTING

Scripture Reading—2 Chron. 25:19
"Thine heart lifteth thee up to boast."

Pride is seen when we boast. Pride and boasting are associated with each other (Rom. 1:30; 2 Tim. 3:2). They are twins. Where you will find one, you will find the other.

In the sports world the phrase "bragging rights" is used when a team beats its rival and its fans boast of the accomplishment. It has degenerated into "trash talk" between people at work, school, and even at church. Now, I know it is supposedly all done in good fun, but that isn't the reality most of the time.

If we are honest we have all seen (and perhaps been drawn into) arguments over games, blown calls, and even been hurt by the constant flaunting of how "my" team is better than "your" team.

I'm not promoting passivity or the idea that everyone gets a trophy no matter how he or she finishes—not at all. We have lowered the bar so much that hard work is not attractive anymore because it is not honored, recognized, or compensated. I'm talking about wanting to be on the winning side to be able to crow about how we are better than others. At the root of all boasting is pride, and God hates pride.

We boast when we seek credit for accomplishments. We want people to know that we are responsible or had a large part in bringing the success to pass. We desire to be honored and receive glory for our input.

A synonym for boasting is "glory." To glory is to receive credit and be admired for what has been done. No one will be able to glory in what he or she has done to get to Heaven (Eph. 2:8, 9). That belongs solely to God.

Pride by its nature is competitive. We boast to tell how we are superior to others. This spirit of superiority begins in the heart, and God warns against it (1 Cor. 10:12). Boasting is the fruit; pride is the root. Seeking personal glory is the symptom; arrogance is the cause. Destroy the root, and the fruit will die.

DISCUSS: What is an area in which you are tempted to boast?

—*Rick Johnson*

NOVEMBER 27
THE HOLY SPIRIT AND GROWTH
Scripture Reading—Gal. 5:16
"Walk in the Spirit."

Many believers do not grow spiritually because they have not learned to walk in the Spirit. Walking in the Spirit is a moment-by-moment relationship with the Lord. It involves listening to Him and obeying Him. It is including God in everything you do.

Reducing your relationship with God to a list of regulations and conforming to a moral code will become a burden and is bereft of a relationship.

Part of walking in the Spirit is having a daily, meaningful time alone with God. Jesus had a daily appointment with His Father, and so should we (Matt. 14:23; Mark 1:35; 6:46; Luke 6:12; 22:39; John 6:15).

John Maxwell wrote, "The secret of success is found in your daily agenda." You will never see long-term life change until you make your time alone with the Lord a daily event. You know the old adage, "If you keep on doing what you have been doing, you're going to keep getting what you have been getting." Do you like the results of your spiritual life?

One reason we have so many spiritual casualties is that we place too much emphasis on commitment and not enough on surrender. At the root of being faithful to a spiritual commitment is being yielded to God (Rom. 12:1). Surrender precedes commitment.

When I began to read the Bible every day, it wasn't because of a commitment I made, though I don't have problems with making commitments in this area. It was when I surrendered my life fully to the Lord. Since that day Bible reading, memorization, and meditation have not been a problem for me.

The key to lasting change is in direct proportion to what you do with God's Word. It is the most important spiritual discipline in your life. Everything you do as a believer requires God's Word—meditation, prayer, worship, evangelism, discipleship, and your ministry philosophy require knowing the Bible.

Walking in the Spirit cannot be divorced from spending time in the Bible. Together they make us like Jesus (2 Cor. 3:18).

PONDER: Why is it difficult for some to have a daily time alone with the Lord?

—Rick Johnson

SATISFIED AND GLAD OF IT

Scripture Reading—Ps. 107:9
"For he satisfieth the longing soul,
and filleth the hungry soul with goodness.

Thanksgiving

My God, today I kneel to say, "I thank You."
For once my prayer holds no request, no names of friends for You to bless,
Because I think even You might like a prayer that's new—
Might like to hear somebody pray, who has no words but thanks to say,
Somebody satisfied and glad, for all the joys that he has had,
And so I say again, "I THANK YOU LORD."

This simple poem sums up what contentment is all about. Contentment will become reality when you learn to "want what you have." You see, if you cannot be content with what you have, you will never be content with what you want. Benjamin Franklin said, "Discontentment makes rich men poor, while contentment makes poor men rich." I have met people who seem to have so little financially and materially, but when you are with them, they seem to have so much. They don't murmur and complain. They are not envious or jealous. They are just happy with what God has done for them, and it shows. We should pity the man who seems to have it all—all except for happiness. He would do well to learn how to be satisfied with the goodness of God.

William Law said it so well: "Who is the greatest saint in the world? It is not the one who prays the most or fasts the most. It is the one who is always thankful to God, who receives everything as an expression of God's goodness, and has a heart ready to praise God for everything that he gets. That is a saint." Many people think of Thanksgiving Day as a holiday that occurs each November, but contented people celebrate a day of thanksgiving every day. They never get over the blessings of God's goodness, and they are thankful to Him.

SONG: If you and your family know the chorus "God Is So Good," sing it together. (Include the verse that says, "I'll praise His name" and "I love Him so").

—Tom Palmer

LENGTH OR STRENGTH?

Scripture Reading—Matt. 14:30
"But when he saw the wind boisterous, he was afraid;
and beginning to sink, he cried, saying, Lord, save me."

Peter was in a predicament. Now granted, he had done something that none of the other disciples had been willing to do. Unlike the others, Peter had been willing to get out of the boat and walk on the water during a serious storm. Though he initially had his focus on Jesus, it didn't take long until the wind and the waves had his attention, and he started to sink. At that point he prayed a prayer that may well be one of the shortest in the entire Bible—but it worked! Immediately Jesus responded to Peter's prayer and rescued him from sinking.

Notice first, if you will, the length of Peter's prayer. There certainly is a time for lengthy prayers, but this was not one of them. Anyone who has ever jumped into water knows that there is but a split second from when your feet hit the water until your head goes under. Had Peter gotten too eloquent in his prayer, he would have been under water. He needed to talk fast.

But then, notice if you will, the strength of Peter's prayer. Three things stand out. First, when he said, "Lord," it was clear that he knew Who he was praying to. Secondly, when he said, "Save," it was obvious that he knew what he was praying for. Finally, when he said, "Me," it was evident that he knew who he was praying for. His prayer reaction was extremely effective and resulted in a clear and decisive answer to prayer.

There certainly are those times in life when prayer must be a spontaneous reaction to the need at hand. It is also clear that the strength of the prayer matters even much more than the length of the prayer. Sometimes you may need to pray and fast. Sometimes you may just need to pray fast!

ACTION POINT: Read about another very short prayer in Matthew 15:21–28. Who was praying? What did she need?

—Tom Palmer

NOVEMBER 30
CRITICAL WORDS

Scripture Reading—Titus 3:2
"Speak evil of no man."

One of the easiest things to do is to criticize a person. One of the most difficult things to do is to keep your mouth shut when you want to criticize someone.

As a father I am to correct the behavior and attitudes of my children, but I must do it in a way that is affirming and encouraging. When I married my wife, it wasn't to criticize her. She is precious to me, not a project I am working on. Also, Paula wasn't attracted to me because I corrected her a lot.

Why do we criticize so readily? It is because of pride. A critical spirit and pride are always related. The Bible speaks of "the contempt of the proud" (Ps. 123:4). The word "contempt" means "to look down upon and to despise." We show this attitude in our spirit and our words. We become skilled at faultfinding and see things through a negative lens.

Criticism is different than discernment. God wants us to have discernment (Matt. 7:1–6). The difference is in the ability to make proper judgments without having a focus on finding fault with others.

We tend to judge others with our head and ourselves with our heart. Another way to express this idea is that we tend to judge others by their actions and ourselves by our intentions. If we reversed this approach, our words and spirit would be very different.

There are times when we all need constructive criticism. If we don't receive it, we will never reach our potential. However, have you ever been on the end of "constructive criticism" where you felt attacked and emotionally bruised, rather than built up and encouraged? The goal of correction should always be to leave the person feeling helped, not attacked.

Our challenge is that when we know someone well we are familiar with his or her flaws and soon tire of them. So, the bad becomes our focus, rather than what is good.

"Unsolicited advice is a form of criticism," said Curtis Hutson.

ACTION POINT: Make a list of the good qualities of those around you and focus on them.

—Rick Johnson

DECEMBER 1
TIME ALONE WITH GOD AND BUSYNESS

Scripture Reading—Luke 5:16
"And he withdrew himself into the wilderness, and prayed."

Here's an activity that will dramatically alter every part of your life if you faithfully give yourself to it. It is something that many do, but haphazardly. It usually gets the leftovers of our time, and we never enjoy the benefits it brings.

Most call it "devotions." Some call it "quiet time." I prefer "time alone with God," as it specifically describes the purpose and nature of the activity. It is easier to talk about than do. There are common hindrances that compete for this holy time with God.

One is the problem of busyness. Jesus' ministry was effective, and time alone was difficult to find (Luke 5:12–16). Your effectiveness can hinder your time with the Lord. The better you are, the greater in demand you are, and the more difficult it is to find time to withdraw to recharge your spiritual batteries. This happens especially to Christian leaders.

Never equate busyness with godliness. As busy as our Lord was, He did not allow busyness and expectations of others to supplant His appointment with His Father (Mark 1:29–35). We must not either.

God's first call to every Christian is to Himself and then to a task. Jesus said, "Follow me, and I will make you fishers of men" (Matt. 4:19). We are called to follow a Person, not a ministry activity.

This can lead to being misunderstood. As Jesus sought solitude some didn't have their needs met (Luke 5:15), and it appeared He was neglecting the primary for the secondary. Even His closest associates didn't understand the importance of spending time alone with the Father (Mark 1:35–37).

There will always be needs, but we cannot meet them all. It is arrogant to think we can. We must see time alone with Christ as a primary need in our lives.

"If you will take care of the depth of your life, God will take care of the breadth of your ministry." The depth of your life is cultivated in secret with the Lord.

MEMORIZE: Mark 1:35.

—Rick Johnson

DECEMBER 2
YOU AND YOURS PRAYING FOR
THEM AND THEIRS

Scripture Reading—Rom. 10:1
*"Brethren, my heart's desire and prayer to God for Israel is,
that they might be saved."*

Paul had a great burden upon his heart for his own people. According to Romans 10:2, the Jews had a "zeal of God, but not according to knowledge." He also knew that they were "ignorant of God's righteousness" and that in seeking to "establish their own righteousness" they had not "submitted themselves unto the righteousness of God" (v. 3).

Paul's burden weighed heavily upon him because he had family and friends who were of the Jewish nation, but they were lost. In Romans 9:2 Paul had stated that he had "great heaviness and continual sorrow" in his heart because of the spiritual condition of his brethren and kinsmen. Paul even went so far as to say that he would be willing to be "accursed from Christ" if it would mean their salvation. It seems hard to imagine someone being willing go to hell if that is what it took for his loved ones to get to go to Heaven! Yet that seems to be what Paul is saying. It was because of his desire to see Israel saved that he prayed much for the salvation of his own people.

Every family has an extended family. This may include brothers and sisters, aunts and uncles, grandparents and cousins, who are all a part of our "brethren and kinsmen." There is no greater prayer that you and yours can pray than for them and theirs that they might be saved. I fear that one of the saddest moments in Heaven will be the realization that there are loved ones and family members who are not there. For this reason, we must do all that is within our power to make sure that our family reunites, not just for reunions and holidays, but also in Heaven forever. This effort begins with a dedicated prayer effort, and must continue until our loved ones are saved.

ACTION POINT: Make a list of loved ones and family members who may not be saved. Begin praying through your list regularly as a family.

—*Tom Palmer*

DECEMBER 3
COMFORT OF YOUR PAIN

Scripture Reading—2 Cor. 1:6
"Whether we be comforted, it is for your consolation."

The degree of your encouragement is related to how God has encouraged you when you were hurting and broken—the deeper your hurt, the greater your capacity to comfort others. This means that God uses your valleys to bless and comfort others.

This truth is given to us in 2 Corinthians 1:3–7. The best comforters are often the people who have faced hard circumstances. God will use present pains for future ministry.

After Paul and Silas had been brutally beaten and put into prison, the Bible states that they "comforted" the believers in Philippi (Acts 16:40). Again, those that were the greatest encouragers had known the greatest pain.

One of our pastors had a severe motorcycle accident as a teenager and almost lost one of his legs. Being hospitalized for months, he missed much of his senior year in high school.

Decades later and hundreds of miles from where he had his accident, the brother of a young man in our church was involved in a terrible motorcycle wreck. This pastor quickly came to the hospital to minister to this young man. Out of all of the people that visited him, the person that brought the most comfort and hope was the person who had experienced the same hardship.

It was easy for my friend to help this young man, and he did an excellent job. But it came at the great cost of past pain. Dear friend, don't waste your pain and sorrows. God is going to take them and, if you will allow Him, make you a source of great comfort and encouragement to others.

Use your pain and disappointment as a bridge to speak into the hearts of others. You will not only bring the blessing of comfort, but you will also transform the environment you are in by your spirit of hope and faith.

PONDER: What hurts in your life can God use to make you a comforter?

—Rick Johnson

DECEMBER 4
CRYING OUT TO GOD IN AN EMERGENCY

Scripture Reading—Ps. 86:17
"Shew me a token for good; that they which hate me may see it, and be ashamed: because thou, LORD, hast holpen me, and comforted me."

Everyone needs to call on someone in an emergency. When an emergency strikes, we call 911 to get in touch with police, firefighters, or paramedics. While we should pray out of conviction most of the time, it is comforting to know that we can also pray in a crisis. Psalm 86 gives us a prescription for praying to God in trouble.

First, the Psalmist teaches that **it is proper to pray out of a heart of need**. David says "hear me: for I am poor and needy" (v. 1). We can come boldly to God in our time of need (Heb. 4:16).

Second, **it is proper to appeal to God's character**. He is a God of mercy (v. 5, 13, 15, 16). In a crisis, every believer needs God's mercy on his or her life. We also need His power or enabling to get us through the emergency. The Psalmist declares, "In the day of my trouble I will call upon thee: for thou wilt answer me" (v. 7).

Third, **it is proper to ask God for encouragement**. The token of Psalm 86:17 is a sign or ensign. The Psalmist wants a sign or a signal that the Lord is with him.

One day I had a sudden financial problem. Specifically, I needed $1,000 quickly. I cried out of a heart of need (1st point). Then I appealed to God's character of mercy to help (2nd point). Finally, I asked the Lord to meet this need to bring about a spirit of encouragement (3rd point).

After praying this way, within an hour, someone came to the door with a card of encouragement. Inside the card were twenty $50 bills or $1,000! God will not always answer so quickly. It may take time. But, He is there for us in every emergency if we are willing to cry out to Him.

QUOTE: "The God who bled on Calvary loves us too much to ever mock us or hurt us, and he never makes mistakes." —J. Sidlow Baxter.

—James Stallard

DECEMBER 5
DO YOU HAVE A GOOD NAME?

Scripture Reading—Pro. 22:1
"A good name is rather to be chosen than great riches,
and loving favour rather than silver and gold."

What's in a name? A name is a very important matter. The name we have identifies us to others and helps us to stand out in the world as special. When we hear the name Babe Ruth, what do we think of? Baseball! When we hear the name Michael Jordan, what do we think of? Basketball! When we hear the name Abraham Lincoln, what do we think of? The Presidency of the United States!

Our text above tells us it is important to have a **good name**. We choose a good name for ourselves by having a good reputation that makes that name stand out in a positive way. Sin diminishes the character of our name, so we must choose to live in such a way that God is honored and our name becomes cherished.

There are some names we would never give to our children. For example, most people would never want to name a girl Jezebel. Queen Jezebel was known for her evil and is no tribute to women. To name a baby girl Jezebel might taint her for life.

Likewise, today we never think to name a boy Judas. The name Judas has come to mean traitor, betrayer, liar, thief, and a host of other bad qualities. Before Judas betrayed Jesus, many baby boys were named Judas. It was a common name. But the one who betrayed Jesus destroyed a perfectly good name.

Our names come to say something to the world about us. The Bible is telling us that a good reputation is better than owning great riches. Having a good name brings "loving favour" to our lives from others (Pro. 22:1).

Also, our faithfulness to God can join our name to His. We become identified with Him. In fact, the name Christian means "a little Christ" or someone who is "like Christ." How about your name? Have you made for yourself a good name? What's in a name? Everything!

PRAYER: Lord, help me and every family member to uphold our family name with honor and holiness for God's glory. Amen.

—James Stallard

DECEMBER 6
WHEN PRAYER MEETING BECOMES AN ORGAN RECITAL

Scripture Reading—2 Cor. 12:7, 8
"There was given to me a thorn in the flesh . . . For this thing
I besought the Lord thrice, that it might depart from me."

If you have ever listened to prayer requests that are shared at prayer meeting, you know that many are related to physical concerns. There are a lot of doctor's appointments, medical tests, and surgeries that are related to hearts, stomachs, and lungs. Sometimes it seems like an organ recital because of the many physical needs.

Paul had a physical problem too. Though some have suggested it may have been related to his eyesight, no one is absolutely certain. Regardless of what it was, this physical problem had become a source of limitation and weakness to Paul. In response, Paul simply asked God on three occasions to remove his infirmity. There is nothing wrong with praying about medications, hospitalizations, and therapy, but we must learn from Paul's experience.

Paul prayed and God answered, but it was not the answer he thought would come. Rather than removing the infirmity, God gave grace to bear it (2 Cor. 12:9). It was through his weakness that Paul experienced God's strength. There are those who will say that prayer is a "name-it-claim-it" endeavor, but that was not the case for Paul. It may not be yours either. The key is learning to have the same attitude that Paul had. In verse 10 he said, "I take pleasures in infirmities" because he had learned that God can do things through infirmity that He would not have done without them.

The next time you hear a request for physical healing, go ahead and pray for it. However, make sure that you also ask God for His will to be done and that through the experience God's purpose would be accomplished. When that happens, the organ recital can quickly become a concert of praise to a God whose strength is made perfect in weakness.

ACTION POINT: Is there an area of limitation in your life because of physical need? Thank God for it, and ask Him to give His strength in place of your weakness.

—*Tom Palmer*

DECEMBER 7
DO YOU HAVE A HARD HEART?

Scripture Reading—Heb. 3:7, 8
"To day if ye will hear his voice, Harden not your hearts."

I remember my first physical exam as an adult. After the exam my Muslim doctor asked me some questions. His first question was, "Do you exercise much?" Before I could answer, he said, "I didn't think so!" With his glasses way down on his nose as he glared at me, he finally said, "You take time for your God, for your people in the church, and you take time for you! You get out there and exercise because if you don't, when you get to my age, you will be a big fat slob!"

My doctor was concerned about the "hardening of the arteries" and other problems that I could have in the future. However, in the spiritual realm there is a sickness that is much worse than any physical problem called the **Hardening of the Heart**. This condition comes when a person refuses to listen to God and has become "hardened through the deceitfulness of sin." Sin has a way of deceiving us. Just as the older we get problems can develop physically, so the older we get without dealing with sin in our lives, the easier it is to develop a hardened heart spiritually.

Whatever God is revealing to you, act on it NOW without delay! He says, "To day if ye will hear his voice" (Heb. 3:7). You must respond to God immediately. Confess your sin, make things right with your friend, leave your anxious care of unbelief with Him—do all these things now. Do not wait!

Have you become set in your ways, unwilling to change, or unable to respond to the truth? The spiritual disease of "hardening of the heart" may have set in. There are some people who may need simple spiritual help in an area of their lives, while others may need major surgery or a complete change of heart! God wants to speak to your heart—you must be willing to let Him. "To day if ye will hear his voice, harden not your hearts" (Heb. 3:7, 8).

PRAYER: Thank You, Lord, for speaking to me. I will do what You want me to do right away.

—*James Stallard*

DECEMBER 8
A BABY NAMED "ANSWER TO PRAYER"

Scripture Reading—1 Sam. 1:27
"For this child I prayed; and the LORD hath
given me my petition which I asked of him."

Hannah had a problem. It was a big problem. She had a desire as a woman to be a mother and have a baby of her own. However, she was barren and unable to bear children. To make matters worse, her own husband and family failed to understand and even mocked her because she was childless. As a result Hannah suffered greatly, being unable to eat, weeping much, and living in bitterness of soul. At times her agony probably seemed unbearable.

Realizing that there was nothing else she could do, she asked God to do what only He could do. At "the house of the Lord," she prayed and asked God to give her "a man child" (1 Sam. 1:10, 11). Her prayer was very sincere and very specific. Thankfully her prayer was soon answered with the birth of a baby boy. When choosing a name for her new baby, Hannah could only think of one name: "Samuel . . . Because I have asked him of the Lord" (1 Sam. 1:20). The name Samuel literally means "asked of God." Every time Hannah took her baby in her arms to feed him, bathe him, or rock him to sleep, she knew she was holding an answer to prayer. Several years later, Hannah brought Samuel to the tabernacle and presented him to the Lord as a testimony to answered prayer.

Sometimes our families have needs too, don't they? Some of these needs seem so big to us that we don't know what else to do. Thankfully, like Hannah we can pray, asking God to do what only He can do. When God answers prayer, He lets us know that He is real and that He cares about the things that we care about. Certainly Hannah's prayer is one of the great prayers of the Old Testament.

ACTION POINT: On a 3x5 card write down three special needs your family has right now. As a family, pray for them daily during the next week. See what God will do for you.

—*Tom Palmer*

DECEMBER 9
COMFORT OF YOUR PRESENCE

Scripture Reading—2 Cor. 7:6
"God . . . comforted us by the coming of Titus."

One of the best ways to comfort others in adversity is just to be there for them—no speeches or explanations, just your presence.

Paul was busy ministering and needed some encouragement. He had "no rest," was "troubled on every side," "without were fightings, within were fears," and he was "cast down" (2 Cor. 7:5, 6).

God encouraged him by the presence of his ministry colleague, Titus. I look forward to meeting this brother in Heaven one day! He must have been a special person.

All of us get discouraged at times. If it is not dealt with, it leads to depression and can ultimately result in despair. It is a downward cycle that must be halted. One way God helps us to come out of this whirlpool is by the presence of godly friends. Titus had the spirit of an encourager!

We have a sweet couple in our church that takes my wife and me out for dinner when things are tough in our ministry or our personal lives. They are like a breath of fresh air. We always feel strengthened after spending time with them.

One of the keys to being a good comforter is to be a good listener. Sometimes we dispense advice and don't understand the issue (Pro. 18:13). Active listening is difficult.

Job's friends were an example of this principle. They are commended for showing up, but it would have been better if they had not spoken to him. They were not encouragers, but "miserable comforters" to him (Job 16:2).

Job's family came to see him and didn't say anything, but brought him comfort (Job 42:10, 11). They "bemoaned him," which means "to nod and shake one's head in sympathy." They "comforted" him, which means "to sigh and breathe deeply." It wasn't their words but their presence and spirit that ministered to him.

Even when we cannot be with someone in person, we can show our concern with letters, calls, and emails.

PONDER: Who needs your presence today?

—*Rick Johnson*

DECEMBER 10
THE PRAYER OF THE LORD

Scripture Reading—John 17:9
"I pray for them: I pray not for the world,
but for them which thou hast given me; for they are thine."

Typically the Lord's Prayer is assumed to be the prayer that Jesus taught in the Sermon on the Mount in Matthew 6. There is, however, a very real sense in which the prayer found in John 17 could more accurately be titled the Lord's Prayer. In the prayer in Matthew 6, Jesus gives a model prayer that is basically a pattern for effective praying. In John 17 we have an actual prayer that Jesus prayed.

Herbert Lockyer calls this prayer the "Holy of Holies in the New Testament." It was prayed in the final hours before Jesus was betrayed and crucified. This prayer beautifully portrays Christ as the mighty Intercessor. In this prayer, He references Himself in the first eight verses. And in verses 20–26, He also prays for those in the world who would ultimately believe on Him. However, in verses 9–19, we find Him interceding on behalf of those referred to as His own—believers. This prayer is an encouragement for us as believers.

Jesus prays for their preservation in John 17:11. In this same verse He also prays for their unification. He prays for their satisfaction in verse 13, and in verse 15, He prays for their fortification. In verses 17 and 19, He prays for their sanctification, and He concludes this part of His prayer in verse 18 referring to their evangelization of the world.

As you read through the various parts of this prayer, it becomes evident that Jesus cared not only for His disciples but also for those in all generations who would be His followers. According to Hebrews 9:24, Jesus is now appearing in the presence of God for us. It is there that He makes intercession for us (Heb. 7:25). His prayer ministry, begun on earth, continues today in Heaven for us. The prayer of the Lord blesses us!

ACTION POINT: Take a Bible and look up each of the verses listed above and note the specific words that are a part of the requests Jesus made.

—*Tom Palmer*

DECEMBER 11
BEING STILL BEFORE GOD

Scripture Reading—Ps. 46:10
"Be still, and know that I am God."

Small children seem to have a difficult time sitting quietly in church. They squirm, make faces, gesture with their hands, and pull on their mom's dress to get her attention. Sometimes you wonder if the little ones will ever sit still.

But, one has to wonder why adults do the same thing with their lives. In church we might not be stirring around (but hopefully not because we're asleep!), but that does not mean that we are not squirming on the inside.

The Bible tells us, "Be still, and know that I am God" (Ps. 46:10). Yet, the Bible also explains how difficult that can be. Note the following:

- Moses had to say to the children of Israel, "Fear ye not, stand still, and see the salvation of the LORD" as they faced the Egyptians (Exod. 14:13).
- God told Jehoshaphat, "Set yourselves, stand ye still, and see the salvation of the Lord" as Israel faced the Moabites, Ammonites, and Edomites (2 Chron. 20:17).
- God told Isaiah that Israel did not need to make an alliance with Egypt to face her enemies, but Israel refused to be still. "In returning and rest shall ye be saved; in quietness and in confidence shall be your strength: and ye would not" (Isa. 30:15).

We have a tendency to fret about the circumstances in our lives. We refuse to be still and know that God is God in our situation. Today, all the trappings of our culture fight against a person being "still." We are always on the go in our fast-paced society. Our communication with cell phones, the Internet, and Facebook keep us moving at a fast pace. Because of these things we often get distracted and fail to pay attention to the Lord's voice. The reason—we simply are not still before Him!

Whenever this happens we need to spend time alone with the Lord and still our hearts. Through prayer and reading the Scriptures, we will be able to hear what He is saying to us. That "still" heart enables us to know what the Lord is doing in our lives.

SONG: Sing the Hymn "I Need Thee Every Hour."

—James Stallard

DECEMBER 12
ARE YOU LISTENING?

Scripture Reading—1 Sam. 3:13
"And he restrained them not."

It is vital that believers be good listeners. We need, especially, to be open to listen to the Lord and what He says to us through His Word and His Spirit. Yet, many struggle to listen, and others seem not to care what the Lord is saying to them.

This is the way it was after the days of the judges. God was beginning to raise up some prophets to speak for Him to the nation of Israel. He answered the prayer of a godly woman, Hannah, and gave her a son named Samuel. The Bible interestingly says, "And the child Samuel ministered unto the LORD before Eli [the priest]. And the word of the LORD was precious in those days; there was no open vision" (1 Sam. 3:1).

When Samuel had gone to sleep (1 Sam. 3:3), the Lord called to him, but he thought Eli had called him. Eli sent him back twice until he finally caught on—God was speaking to the little prophet boy! When the word came and Samuel responded, the Lord gave him a chilling message:

"And the LORD said to Samuel, Behold, I will do a thing in Israel, at which both the ears of every one that heareth it shall tingle. In that day I will perform against Eli all things which I have spoken concerning his house [home, family]: when I begin, I will also make an end. For I have told him that I will judge his house for ever for the iniquity which he knoweth; because his sons made themselves vile, and he restrained them not" (1 Sam. 3:11–13).

Why was God going to judge Eli? Why had God bypassed Eli to speak to a little boy studying for the ministry? *Because Eli would not listen!* He refused to let the Lord correct him. His lazy spirit and tolerance for evil immorality in his family resulted in the death of his sons and his own demise (1 Sam. 4:1–18). All because he would not listen!

DISCUSS: Are you listening to God? Who would you rather be: Samuel or Eli?

—James Stallard

DECEMBER 13
THE BLESSING OF A GOOD CONSCIENCE

Scripture Reading—Acts 23:1
*"And Paul, earnestly beholding the council, said, Men and brethren,
I have lived in all good conscience before God until this day."*

Paul knew the blessing of a good conscience. It was this testimony of a good conscience that he used as his defense while on trial before his enemies who sought to destroy him. Like all human beings, Paul understood that he was a sinner. He made that clear when he wrote, "There is none righteous, no, not one" (Rom. 3:10), and that "all have sinned, and come short of the glory of God" (Rom. 3:23). Paul even saw himself as the chief of sinners (1 Tim. 1:15) because of the way that he had persecuted the church (1 Cor. 15:9). In no way was Paul speaking about being without sin, but rather he was speaking about the way he had handled his sin.

Think for a moment about the typical dinner plate in your kitchen. Is it clean enough to put on the table the next time your family gathers for a meal? Hopefully it is, if it has been in a sink full of hot, soapy water or has been through a cycle in the dishwasher. This plate is clean, not because it was never dirty, but because, even though it was dirty, it has been made clean. The cleansing process has removed the spaghetti sauce, the melted cheese, and the gravy that would have disqualified it from use. Now that the plate is clean, it can again be used when a nice meal is being served.

Basically that is what Paul was saying in his testimony. Having been contaminated and corrupted by his sinful activity, he had been cleansed and cleared, and now God could use him. He was "squeaky-clean" before God and knew the blessing that this cleanliness brought. Paul experienced the blessing of what King David experienced when he said, "Blessed is he whose transgression is forgiven, whose sin is covered" (Ps. 32:1).

ACTION POINT: Read 1 Timothy 1:5 and 19 and discuss what Paul told Timothy about a good conscience.

—Tom Palmer

DECEMBER 14
TIME TO WAKE UP!

Scripture Reading—Rom. 13:11
"And that, knowing the time, that now it is high time
to awake out of sleep."

Anyone who likes sports knows what it means to see the end of a close game. You may be down to your last out in baseball, or the clock is running out in basketball or football. At the end of a close game, the tension can be quite unbearable.

In modern times, we are playing the most important "game" ever played. But in fact, it is not a game, but a serious matter of life and death. We are getting down to our last out, and the clock is ticking toward a final conclusion. This is one "game" where you do not want to be "left behind" to go into extra innings or face overtime.

The Bible tells us that we should be "knowing the time." Economic troubles, social struggles, rampant sin and rebellion, and international trouble between nations seem to be in the news every day. National leaders wring their hands for answers to solve their problems. It seems that everything has been tried—except the one thing that ought to be tried—the Word of God.

Unfortunately, many are asleep at the switch, following the culture around them. The Church cannot speak to this age if she has turned away from the God of the Ages. God's people have been lulled into a false sense of security, satisfied and content with the situation.

But God has told us "now it is high time to awake out of sleep" (Rom. 13:11). We can be like the sons of Issachar, "which were men who had understanding of the times, to know what Israel ought to do" (1 Chron. 12:32). Or, we can be like Jonah, who ran from God and fell asleep in the boat in the midst of the storm (Jonah 2:5).

Believers need to be awake to what is happening around them. The Bible is full of the cries of God's people to God to awake on their behalf. Doesn't it make sense that this same God has the right to call upon His people to wake up for Him?

QUOTE: "The times are desperate, but the saints are not." —Vance Havner

—James Stallard

DECEMBER 15
EXERCISE MEANS WORK

Scripture Reading—Acts 24:16
"And herein do I exercise myself, to have always a conscience
void of offence toward God, and toward men."

I well remember the youth meeting I was attending when I truly came to understand what it means to have a clear conscience. The speaker explained that a clear conscience was "the ability to say that there is no living person that I have wronged, hurt, or offended that I have not gone back and made it right." He then gave us a list of verses to help us understand that if we were not right with others, we could not be right with God. He concluded the meeting by asking us to make a list of those with whom we were not right.

Much to my amazement, within just a minute or two I had a list of twenty names. The speaker then asked us to talk to God and to make a promise to begin immediately to make things right with the people on our list. Looking back, it is even more amazing that by the time I went to bed that night I already had five names checked off my list. The first name I checked off was another teenager that I had mistreated when he attended our school. The next name was my mother who I had been disrespectful to that very day. The next three names were those of my younger brothers and sister to whom I had not been kind to in the past. In each case, I had been able to personally seek forgiveness for my wrongdoing.

It took a while, but I kept working at it, and eventually every name on my list was checked off. My conscience was clear because I did what I knew God wanted me to do. A clear conscience never comes as an accident or by coincidence. There must be determination to do the right thing, but also to stick to it until the job is done.

ACTION POINT: Ask God if there is anyone with whom you need to make things right. If so, do it right away. Make things right before you go to bed tonight.

—*Tom Palmer*

DECEMBER 16
WORDS OF COMFORT

Scripture Reading—Deut. 1:28
"Our brethren have discouraged our heart, saying . . ."

How do people experience comfort from us? One way is through the words we speak and the tone of voice we use. People that are known as discouragers use words that are not uplifting.

I heard about a man that would come to his pastor, put his arm around him, and say, "Preacher, I'm for you no matter what they say." The sad thing is that he walked away thinking he was a great blessing to his pastor.

A famous preacher, whose father had died when he was two years old, walked by a teacher's open classroom and overheard her say, "I like Charles." It changed his life. Today he is in his 80s, but he still remembers that word of affirmation. People remember our words of encouragement. We ought to use them often.

Our best words of comfort come from the Word of God. The Bible says to "comfort one another with these words" (1 Thess. 4:18). "These words" refer to God's promise of seeing our loved ones again after death.

Years ago I was visiting a lady who was in perpetual pain and had only a few days left to live. Before I left I read Revelation 21:1–5, which describes the condition of our heavenly home. As I came to the section where it states, "Neither shall there be any more pain," she listened and began to say quietly to herself, "No more pain, no more pain." Oh, there is great comfort from God's Word that comes from nowhere else!

We all feel and think encouraging thoughts about others. The problem is that they often go unsaid. If God prompts you to encourage someone, make sure to take the time to say it or write it to him or her in a note or email.

Our words are powerful either in bringing encouragement or discouragement to other people. When the spies returned from Canaan, their faithless words discouraged those that heard them (Num. 32:9; Deut. 1:28). May we not do the same today!

MEMORIZE: Proverbs 12:18.

—Rick Johnson

351

DECEMBER 17
THE MOST IMPORTANT FURNITURE IN YOUR HOME

Scripture Reading—Ps. 128:3
"Thy children like olive plants round about thy table."

We have often said that the family that prays together stays together. It could also be said that the family that plays together stays together. Now here is another thought regarding family togetherness. The family that eats together stays together. Sound like an old-fashioned concept? It is. Back in the good old days, meal time was a highlight of the day because the entire family came together and spent time around the table. It was a time for talking. It was a time for praying. It was time for laughing. It was a time when every member of the family was in his or her place. Family togetherness was at its peak around the dinner table as members of the entire family helped prepare the meal, cleaned up the meal, and of course, enjoyed eating the meal together.

Families in our generation have become very fragmented. Family life has deteriorated to a point where basically every member of the family is in his place, at his time, doing his thing. Sports leagues, music lessons, school activities, and for that matter, even church events clutter the calendar to such a proportion that family members are hard put to even see each other, let alone spend time doing something together. For many families, mealtime is a TV dinner, a microwave meal, or a fast food drive through as we eat on the run and keep running.

Do you need a dose of togetherness for your family? Consider planning a menu, setting a time, working together, and then, sitting down around the table and enjoying the best time together you have had in a long time. You may discover that you have been failing to use the most valuable piece of furniture in your home. Make mealtime a priority, and your family will love it!

ACTION POINT: OK Mom, let the kids plan a meal. Buy them or get them what they need and let them "lay it out" for you and your husband. It will be a great memory to talk about for a long time.

—Tom Palmer

DECEMBER 18
DEAL WITH YOUR HEART

Scripture Reading—Hosea 10:12
*"Break up your fallow ground: for it is time to seek the LORD,
till he come and rain righteousness upon you."*

God longs to meet with His people by showing them His presence and power! The Bible is filled with God's promise and desire to pour into the lives of His children His life and power!

The preaching of Hosea clarifies the responsibility that God sets before His people in order that they might experience His reviving presence. This verse has a two-fold responsibility for the believer before revival can occur: "Break up your fallow ground" and "seek the Lord."

Although, God wants to meet with us, He cannot until we seek Him. Christians, however, cannot seek the Lord, as they should, until a serious problem is resolved. The problem that hinders us from seeking the Lord as we should is a **bad heart**!

In this verse, Hosea is preaching to God's people concerning their heart problem (called "fallow ground") while offering hope through instruction for revival. The essence of revival is the return of God's children to what the Word of God describes as normal Christianity.

"Fallow ground" was understood as hard ground that had been ignored and left inactive, resulting in it becoming empty and barren. The picture that this ground represents is the heart of God's people, which had become cold, calloused, and hard. Hosea provided examples of the people's hard hearts through: their attitude of immovability (Hosea 4:16), impurity (7:4), indifference (7:8), and their lack of effectiveness for the Lord (7:16).

Have you grown insensitive to the Lord? Is there some sin that you have not dealt with? Have you refused to obey God in some particular area? Have you developed an "I don't care" attitude toward God's Word? Have you neglected to obey the Holy Spirit's convicting and prompting in any way? Has it been a while since you responded to a public invitation?

To this kind of heart, God is saying, "You, break it up!"

ACTION POINT: Ask God to show you anything in your life that displeases Him. Thoroughly deal with that sin or issue. Then, seek Him "till He comes" to you through the realness of His presence and fullness of His power.

—*Billy Ingram*

DECEMBER 19
BEARING BURDENS

Scripture Reading—Gal. 6:2
"Bear ye one another's burdens."

Most of life is mundane, routine, and unspectacular. Though we don't like it, nor would we choose it, the interruptions that crash in on us are what help us to know the Lord better and make us more qualified to be used of Him.

The one common denominator we all have is that we have burdens. Some of the most meaningful memories I have are when I was carrying a heavy burden and my family was there for me. Not every burden is equal. There are three levels, or types, of burdens.

The first are burdens I carry alone, personal responsibilities (Gal. 6:5). When people go hiking, each person is responsible to carry his or her own backpack. Though it is a burden, it is manageable. This also includes God's will for your life (Matt. 11:29, 30).

A second type of burden is one that I cannot carry alone without the help of a friend. This is the usage of the word in Galatians 6:2. This can be an overwhelming circumstance, a health problem, a relational conflict, or many other things. I need someone to come alongside of me to help me with it, as I cannot make it alone.

The third tier is burdens that no one but God can help me carry. This is the dark night of the soul when you are facing the most difficult time of your life, and you feel you cannot survive. No person has the capacity to understand or the wisdom to guide you out of it. These are God-sized burdens, and He instructs us to cast them upon Him (Ps. 55:22; 1 Pet. 5:7).

Satan takes our burdens and tries to destroy us with them, but God uses them to strengthen us. As believers our responsibility is to help people "bear" their burdens (Gal. 6:2). The Spirit of God will prompt you when you see someone with a problem to help. Be a burden-bearer for someone today!

DISCUSS: Discuss some examples of burdens people carry in each of the three levels.

—*Rick Johnson*

DECEMBER 20
COMMON BLESSINGS

Scripture Reading—Mark 6:4
*"A prophet is not without honour, but in his own country,
and among his own kin, and in his own house."*

The more common the blessing, the more we take it for granted. The closer we are to it, the less grateful we are. What are some blessings we become accustomed to and take for granted?

We tend to be ungrateful for our health. I was visiting in the hospital and passed a room where I saw a child lying in the bed listlessly, and the mother was rubbing his back. My heart was stirred as I thought about my children at home that were healthy, able to play sports, and living a normal life.

We tend to be ungrateful for our jobs. If you have an opportunity to earn a living, you ought to thank the Lord for it. Be grateful for a good boss.

We tend to be ungrateful for our family. When I was in college, one of the professors and his wife were in a terrible car accident, and she died instantly. Several months later he spoke in chapel and referenced the loss of his wife. He told us, "You never appreciate the water until the well runs dry."

We tend to be ungrateful for our friends. One of God's most precious gifts to us is our friends, and we fail to realize their value until they are gone. I have carried the casket of my best friend and know the pain of missing friends.

A man was selling his house, and his real estate agent wrote up a description of it to advertise it. He called the owner and read it to him, "A two-car garage, beautiful patio and landscaping, four bedrooms and two baths," and he read the entire ad he had written. Suddenly the owner said, "I don't want to sell this place; this is the house I have been wanting all of my life."

If we would consider what we already have, it would humble us at God's goodness, and we would be more grateful.

ACTION POINT: Be attentive to the common things with which God has blessed you.

—*Rick Johnson*

DECEMBER 21
ALMOST DROWNING

Scripture Reading—Titus 3:5
"Not by works of righteousness which we have done,
but according to his mercy he saved us."

As a boating instructor at a summer camp, I had to make sure that the boys could swim before allowing them to go into deep water. I did this by giving them a simple test; I stood on a diving platform a few yards from the boating dock with a ring buoy in my hand. I told the boys to jump into the water, swim to my platform, tread water, and then return to the boat dock.

All went well until Pete's turn. When he hesitated I called out, "Pete, are you sure that you know how to swim?"

"Sure," he replied with a slight tremor in his voice, and then leaped into the water. Immediately, I could see a problem! With arms thrashing wildly and eyes wide as saucers, he churned the water into froth! His head and shoulders were clear of the surface through the sheer force of his struggles, and yet he was going nowhere.

I threw the ring buoy to him. It landed directly in front of his face, but his hands were landing on each side of it without touching it! I quickly pulled it in and tried again. This time it fell behind him with the rope lying across his shoulder, but in his panic, he could not see it! I leaped into the water and pulled him to shore. Once on the beach I asked him, "Why didn't you tell me you couldn't swim?"

"If I had told you," he answered, "I couldn't have been in the boating class."

Because of his false confidence, Pete almost drowned. How like many who are drowning in their sin. They assert with false bravado that they can make it to Heaven if they try hard enough. But what is needed is to rest in the arms of our Lifeguard and let Him carry us to shore.

How about you? What are you trusting in? Remember, it's "not by works . . . which we have done, but according to his mercy he saved us."

ACTION POINT: Why not take a moment to remember how and when you trusted Christ for salvation and share it with someone?

—Jim Binney

DECEMBER 22
ATTITUDE DOES MATTER

Scripture Reading—Eph. 6:2
"Honour thy father and mother;
which is the first commandment with promise."

We have all been taught since the earliest age to obey our parents, but have we learned to *honor* them? According to Leviticus 19, God places one's responsibility of honoring their parents on the same level as observing the Sabbath. In Exodus 21, however, the Lord places the *dishonoring* of parents on the same level as murder and deserving of the same punishment.

The word, *obey*, in Ephesians 6:1, simply means to do what your parents say, while the word *honor* means to obey with the right attitude. To be content with obeying is never enough. God requires that children obey their parents with a right attitude that reverences and treats them with the respect they deserve as God's ordained authority in the child's life.

As a child, you can do what your parents tell you to do, but if, while obeying, you roll your eyes, sigh a sigh of disgust, or talk back, then you dishonor your parents. And that, according to God, is sin.

Parent, have you become lax in dealing with your children's disobedience and dishonoring? If so, begin today to change the way you allow them to respond. It may not seem like such a big deal right now, but you are teaching them a habit of responding incorrectly and that filtrates into how you will be treated as they get older and, more importantly, how they will respond to God.

This isn't just for little kids, but for all offspring, including moms and dads. Everyone that has a parent is responsible to honor them. Sure, adults are exempt from having to obey their parents, but even if you are a parent yourself, you must still honor the ones the Lord has given you, as you teach your children to honor you.

ACTION POINT: Look around at each other. How long do you have to love and respond properly to each other? If you haven't been honoring your parents, make today the day that you get right with them and with the Lord. The Lord said to obey and honor because it is right, and there you will find His blessing.

—Christy Ingram

DECEMBER 23
THE STAR OF BETHLEHEM

Scripture Reading—Matt. 2:2
"We have seen his star in the east, and are come to worship him."

It appeared out of nowhere. Rumors had circulated for centuries that a Jewish Messiah was coming to planet earth. The wise men, or magi, had searched the heavens as early astronomers for the sign spoken of in the Old Testament: "There shall come a Star out of Jacob, and a Sceptre shall rise out of Israel" (Num. 24:17).

What this star was the Bible does not tell us. The Word of God simply tells us that they saw "his star in the east." It also tells us that the star "went before them, till it came and stood over where the young child was" (Matt. 2:12).

Many have tried to figure out what this must have been. Some say it must have been an alignment of stars in the night sky, or the brightness of the planet Venus, or maybe a special supernova—an explosion of a star in the sky that brightened the night.

It is difficult to know what the star really was. Man is always trying to figure out those supernatural things that he does not understand. It could be that the star was simply a manifestation of the glory of God in the same way the pillar of fire led the Israelites in the night during Moses' day.

God's ways are not our ways. Whatever it was, the Star of Bethlehem signified that the presence of God had come into this world in a spectacular way. The place of this entry into the world was clearly prophesied in the Old Testament as the little village of Bethlehem. The prophet Micah told us hundreds of years before it happened: "But thou, Bethlehem Ephratah, though thou be little among the thousands of Judah, yet out of thee shall he come forth unto me that is to be ruler in Israel; whose goings forth have been from of old, from everlasting" (Micah 5:2).

So, every Christmas season men, women, boys, and girls read the Christmas story about the miracle of the Star of Bethlehem. Nothing could have been more fitting for the arrival of baby Jesus, the King.

SONG: Sing together "O Little Town of Bethlehem."

—James Stallard

DECEMBER 24
I GOT THE BIG ONE!

Scripture Reading—2 Cor. 9:15
"Thanks be unto God for his unspeakable gift."

Christmas was always a very big deal in our home. My wonderful Christian parents taught us the true meaning of Christ's birth. I loved to gaze at my mother's beautiful Nativity scene and dream of what it would be like to be a shepherd out in the field when the angels appeared, or what it would be like to be a silent watcher in the dark of the stable.

Of course, I can't deny that as each day passed, bringing us closer to Christmas Day, we also greatly anticipated the gifts we would receive. My sisters and I would return from school, running to see if anything new had been placed under the tree. Wrapped gifts of mysterious shapes and sizes arrived from our grandparents in distant states. My mother took great delight in building the excitement. She would wrap a few packages at a time and tuck them in among the others to see if we could spot them. Inevitably, there was always one package that stood out from the others, wedged way in the back—a present of looming largeness just beckoning to be unwrapped by eager fingers. We would gaze longingly and wonder, "Who gets the big one?"

Finally the great day would arrive. Our family always read the Christmas story from the Bible before going downstairs to where the tree and presents stood in all their glory. We would wait anxiously while Dad got his camera ready, and then we would tumble down the stairs at his signal.

Amid the flurry of dumped out stockings and flying tissue paper, there would eventually rise up a shout, "I got the big one!" The fortunate recipient of the biggest gift could at last enjoy the long-awaited treasure.

At Christmas and all year long, I feel showered upon by God's grace and blessings. But there will always be one gift that looms largest—the gift of salvation. Without the redeeming grace of God, all other gifts seem rather hollow. But when we can truly say, "I got the big one. I'm saved by grace!" our appreciation for the wonders of God's love will only grow.

ACTION POINT: Spend time sharing salvation testimonies today, telling each other about when you received "the big one."

—Abigail Miller

DECEMBER 25
SETTING TIME FOR GOD ON CHRISTMAS

Scripture Reading—Zech. 4:10
"For who hath despised the day of small things?"

It is our family tradition to read about the birth of Christ in Luke 2 on Christmas morning before we open presents. Everyone sits down, and the snacking of favorite foods stops while children take their place on the floor anxious for this special time. The Bible is passed from one to another as each person reads a verse. The bright-eyed children are excited to be included in what they know to be an important event.

The account of the greatest Gift ever given is then explained directly to the family, setting the tone for gift giving. The various lights on the Christmas tree remind us that Jesus is Light in this dark world. Christmas bells toll the good news of His Coming. What an appropriate time for parents to share their testimony of salvation. Giving the "where" and "when" of one's salvation might be information never shared with family members before!

Nestled in the hills of Southern Pennsylvania is a small farm owned by a set of godly grandparents. What made Christmas special to them was asking family members to share something about the Christmas season that they were thinking about or had experienced. One Christmas, the gravity of testimony from family members brought a 13-year-old boy to faith in Christ as he later testified. Zechariah 4:10 says, "for who hath despised the day of small things." Never think the time set aside for honoring the Lord will not have a lasting effect on our families.

We cannot allow the message of Christmas to be sounded outside our home and forget to make it clear inside our home. Here memories are forged with our loved ones and imbedded into our lives. Have you received that gift of salvation? Could you give a Bible reason for it? May the truth of Christmas be something that you share! Let it not be hidden in your heart like an unopened gift under the tree.

DISCUSS: What is the most valuable Christmas memory that you have? What is the most valuable Christmas memory that you wish to leave?

—*Steve Rebert*

DECEMBER 26
WITS' END

Scripture Reading—Ps. 107:28
"Then they cry unto the Lord in their trouble,
and he bringeth them out of their distresses."

In Psalm 107, we read about some folks who were in a storm. They were responsible, hard-working citizens who found themselves in serious trouble. Verse 26 tells us, "Their soul is melted because of trouble." Fear had replaced faith. Their hearts were like the melting snow. They were reeling and staggering in the storm. They had lost all hope!

Have you ever been there? I have! In a journal entry several years ago, I wrote these words: "Where's my faith? Where's my God? He is here. He is good. He loves me. My head knows but my heart wonders, and He is so silent right now, and I am so alone." My heart had melted. I was at my wits' end.

Don't make the mistake of assuming trouble comes to folks only because of their sin. (Remember, Job's trouble came because he was righteous.) But where do we turn when we are at our wits' end? Our answer is in verse 28: "Then they cry unto the LORD in their trouble, and he bringeth them out of their distresses." All too often prayer is a last resort when it should be our first response! It can be wise to seek counsel in times of difficulty. But sadly, some seek the counsel of man and neglect the greatest privilege we have as believers—prayer!

The Psalmist goes on to declare the wonderful power of God in verses 33–43. The truth is God cares, God hears, and God is able. Four times in Psalm 107 we read these words: "Then they cried unto the LORD in their trouble." And four times God heard, and He answered each time! Will you cry out to the Lord in your time of trouble? We may be overwhelmed at the circumstances we face, but our Lord is never overwhelmed! His grace is always sufficient, and He is always faithful!

ACTION POINT: If you are at your wits' end and facing difficult circumstances, will you take some time right now to pray? Will you pray for lost friends and family who need to come to the place where they cry out unto the Lord for salvation?

—*Sammy Frye*

DECEMBER 27
THE TRAGEDY OF FAILING GRACE

Scripture Reading—Heb. 12:15, 16

"Looking diligently, lest any man fail of the grace of God . . .
Lest there be any fornicator, or profane person, as Esau."

Grace is a wonderful thing. When we are wronged or face adversity in life, we can trust God. If we do He will grace us with grace, God's supernatural involvement in our lives. Someone has called grace "divine aid."

However, as wonderful as grace is, it is not automatic. Hebrews tells us we can fail grace. We can leave the gift of grace all wrapped up so that it is not experienced in life's difficulties. Have you ever muttered under your breath, "Why did that have to happen?" or "Why did my spouse say that?" Those are evidences of unbelief and, thus, no grace!

When there is no grace, man moves toward one of two tragic conditions. The first is toward moral impurity. One young lady testified that when she became bitter she began to search for filthy images. When she found deliverance from her bitterness, her thirst for filth was gone!

A man who spent his life in psychology told me he had dealt with numerous lesbians and homosexuals. He told me he had never met one who was not bitter! Bitterness opens the door for moral impurity.

Bitterness also opens the door for becoming a profane person. "Profane" has the idea of "common." When we treat the things of God like they are common, we are acting like a profane person. The text gives us an example: Esau. Esau traded something that was eternal, spiritual, and valuable for a bowl of soup! Years ago, I told a young lady who was in a tirade against a Scripture verse, "Do you know what your problem is? You hate God." I never forget as she looked back at me and said with steely eyes, "You're right." As I understand it there was much difficulty in her home. Bitterness had given way to her becoming a profane person.

DISCUSS: Discuss as a family each one's responses to wrongs and difficult circumstances. Do you believe God's in control, or do you doubt God?

—*Jim Van Geldren*

DECEMBER 28
BURDEN OF LEADERSHIP

Scripture Reading—Num. 11:11
"Thou layest the burden of all this people upon me."

Responsibilities naturally bring a burden with them, and leaders deal with multiple responsibilities. This is just as true in the family as it is in the business or church world. The greater the responsibility, the greater the burden.

When I coached little league baseball, I lugged the bags of equipment to and from the dugout. Sometimes people would help, but usually everyone scattered after the game. As a youth pastor, before and after activities there were a lot of things to do—setting up, tearing down, and cleaning up. Rare was the teenager that stayed around to help.

Even if you practice delegation, the burden of leadership is still on your shoulders. An army officer taught me, "You can delegate tasks, but you can't delegate your responsibility."

A great leader is not concerned with the benefits of position, but of meeting needs, even at great personal cost. Likewise, parenting brings a heavy weight of responsibility. Parents do not receive the same amount of love they give (2 Cor. 12:14, 15), but that is not why they do what they do.

One day I noticed that our bathtub needed to be cleaned. I began to think about my childhood. While we were assigned chores in our home, I don't remember ever cleaning the tub. My mother had done that many, many times. For the first time I realized how I had taken that burden on her for granted, especially since I was dirtier than anyone else in the family.

After football practice I would be covered with dirt, and not once did I help carry my load. In my immaturity and selfishness, I was causing my mother a heavier load than anyone in our home.

The more children a family has, the greater the burden to care for them. Laundry piles up exponentially it seems. Cleaned rooms are in disarray quicker than ever. That's not to speak of the burden of working to pay the bills and coming home tired.

Leaders are burden bearers and need help and our gratitude for their sacrifices.

ACTION POINT: Tell or write a note to your parents telling them how grateful you are for the burdens they bear for you.

—Rick Johnson

PRIDE AND THE SPIRITUAL LEADER

Scripture Reading—2 Tim. 2:24

"The servant of the Lord must not strive; but be gentle . . . patient."

At the root of divisions, anger, and arguments is pride (Pro. 13:10). Count on it—where there is arguing, there is pride. This is one of the reasons that God established the standard that spiritual leaders were not to be proud. Otherwise, their lives and ministries would not bless, but destroy.

Though parents are not pastors, they are spiritual leaders and have more influence over their children than a pastor. Spiritual leaders are not to be "soon angry" (Titus 1:7), but rather "gentle" and "patient" (2 Tim. 2:24).

An angry, argumentative leader is not only ineffective, but brings great harm to those under his leadership. Do you argue frequently? Is it important that you win on every point? Do your children hear you verbally war with your spouse?

A tranquil home that has little materially is to be preferred over one that has plenty but is filled with arguments (Pro. 17:1). Angry, disputing mothers that quarrel with their children make them want to run away (Pro. 21:19).

I know of a situation where a man argued frequently with his family and his friends. He died unexpectedly and peace came into that home. His spirit of pride brought conflict to all his relationships.

One day my children and wife will stand by my casket and look at my body. I don't want them to think, "Boy, Dad sure did like to argue. I won't miss his temper. He wouldn't back down when he was wrong."

None of us are perfect, but we can be real. We can learn to be quiet when we want to show that we were right. We can focus on looking for places where we agree and start there.

Someone wrote, "It's possible to continue a relationship without reaching a resolution. We don't have to be twins to be brothers."

ACTION POINT: Make a list of those whom you have argued with in the past and go to them and seek their forgiveness for your pride.

—Rick Johnson

DECEMBER 30
BE QUIET!

Scripture Reading—Zeph. 1:7
"Hold thy peace at the presence of the Lord GOD."

The great 19th century "Prince of Preachers," Charles Spurgeon, once said, "Sometimes, a still tongue proves a wise head." Learning when to keep silent is something that often comes with time and Christian maturity. Sometimes being quiet is part of a person's nature. For others, it's a real challenge. King Solomon touched on the benefit of holding one's tongue in Proverbs 17:28, when he said: "Even a fool, when he holdeth his peace, is counted wise: and he that shutteth his lips is esteemed a man of understanding." There is a time to speak and a time to keep quiet.

One of the most important lessons a Christian can learn early in his faith is the lesson of waiting in silent prayer before God. It can be a temptation to come to God with a huge list of wants and spend the entire prayer time rattling off the list, as if God is some type of divine "Santa Claus"—someone who exists in Heaven for no other reason than to give Christians everything they desire. Such a view of God will often leave Christians disappointed in Him, thinking that He isn't interested in meeting their needs.

The truth is that God wants to be seen as the One who meets our every need. But He also wants to be the One who reveals our true needs and then provides for them in His time and according to His will. Coming to this understanding requires quiet submission before God, while listening for His soft voice of direction. Hearing God's whisper is much more important than hearing our own ramblings.

As a father, I enjoy when my children bring their desires and requests to me. But then I also enjoy when they stop talking so I can give them guidance and wisdom. It's a two-way street.

Have you learned to hold your peace "at the presence of the Lord GOD"?

ACTION POINT: Determine today to make silent listening a part of your next prayer time with God.

—*Paul Miller*

DECEMBER 31
EVERY EXIT IS AN ENTRANCE

Scripture Reading—Phil 3:13, 14
"Reaching forth unto those things which are before, I press toward the mark for the prize of the high calling of God in Christ Jesus."

When you finish the first grade of school, you begin the second grade. Once you complete the second grade, you start the third grade. Every exit is an entrance into something new. When you finish primary school, you enter middle school. Then you exit middle school and enter high school. After high school, you enter college. Life is a series of exits that always lead to other entrances.

The past year is about over. We are leaving last year and entering a brand new year. Whenever you complete a project, it is always a good idea to **consider** what you have accomplished and **contemplate** what lies ahead.

Consider. Think about the blessings of the last twelve months—the challenges, the completions, the changes, and the circumstances your family has gone through. How have these things affected you? Rehearse and rejoice in every progress that has been achieved.

Contemplate. While it is good to recount our benefits, we must also have a forward look. David Livingstone said, "I will go anywhere as long as it is forward." A new year means new beginnings, new opportunities, new friends, new mercies, and new obstacles.

Sight is a function of the eyes, but vision is a function of the heart. You observe the physical world through eyesight. As you look back and look around you, *consider* the things you have seen and see now. By looking forward you *contemplate* the future. God says, "Eye hath not seen, nor ear heard, neither have entered into the heart of man, the things which God hath prepared for them that love him" (1 Cor. 2:9). God has prepared fantastic things for you in the coming year, not to mention in Heaven. Faith is spiritual eyesight to behold your future.

ACTION POINT: Rehearse the events of the past year. **Consider** the changes and growth your family has experienced. Take time to express your gratefulness to the Lord for all His benefits. Take a few moments to **contemplate** the new year. Ask each family member to name something they are looking forward to in the next twelve months.

—Harold Vaughan

TITLE INDEX

SCRIPTURE INDEX

Check Out These Other Helpful Resources

OUR FAMILY TIME WITH GOD
compiled by Harold Vaughan

Written with today's Christian family in mind, this devotional features 365 readings on a variety of topics, including prayer, holiness, God's will, witnessing, trials, worship, joy, the Ten Commandments, and much more.

REVIVAL IN OUR TIME
by Harold Vaughan

The purpose of this book is to lay before present-day Christians, not only the possibility, but the probability of revival in our day. The defeatism that has captured so many minds must be rejected and replaced with optimistic faith. The victorious life of the Lord Jesus is available and accessible. If we are to see Revival in Our Time, we must start thinking Outside the Box and get Inside the Book.

FORGIVENESS: HOW TO GET ALONG WITH EVERYBODY ALL THE TIME!
by Harold Vaughan and T.P. Johnston

"In a world filled with so much hatred and misunderstanding, few subjects are as timely as forgiveness. And yet, few works of biblical accuracy have been written on this important subject. Vaughan and Johnston's book is the best, purest, and most practical treatment of the subject I know. Everyone who has been forgiven should read this book to know how and why to forgive."
—Woodrow Kroll, *Back to the Bible*

STRENGTHEN THE INNER MAN PRAYER JOURNAL
by Duncan Campbell

Just as your outer man needs food and exercise in order to live and grow, so your inner man needs spiritual food and spiritual exercise. It is the ongoing contact with the presence of God coupled with the practice of personal devotion that gives us the needed strength to overcome sin, enjoy God for who He is, and grow in true holiness. This daily journal is a spiritual nutrition and exercise program designed to strengthen your inner man. Through a steady diet on the Word of God and the Spirit-filled practice of personal devotion, you'll discover what it means to "be strengthened with might by his Spirit in the inner man."

DEEP
Fire

Daily Challenges for a Burning Heart

Compiled by
Harold Vaughan

A collection of 365 devotionals—one for every day of the year—that will challenge and inspire you to seek spiritual renewal by meditation, prayer, and humble reliance on the Holy Spirit of God.

Each day explore a theme and see it expounded from God's Word with the quotes of wise teachers and faithful Christians both past and present. Then leave the place of devotion with a burning heart, eager to see the power of God at work in your life, the Church, and the world around you.

www.christlifemin.org

PRAYER
ADVANCE

For many years various ministries have sponsored prayer retreats for men, women, students, and couples. But prayer shouldn't be about retreating—it should be about advancing. Believers have retreated far too long. It's about time God's people started heading in the right direction!

The goal of the Prayer Advances is to provide a fresh encounter with the living God. The agenda of each Advance is red-hot preaching, fervent praying, heavenly singing, and fabulous fellowshipping.

Dynamic preaching at Men's Prayer Advance

For more information, please visit our website at **www.christlifemin.org**.